HOW TEAC
TAUGHₜ

Constancy and Change
in American Classrooms
1890–1990

SECOND EDITION

Research on Teaching Series

Teachers' Workplace:
The Social Organization of Schools
Susan J. Rosenholtz

How Teachers Taught:
Constancy and Change in American Classrooms, 2nd Edition
Larry Cuban

HOW TEACHERS TAUGHT

Constancy and Change in American Classrooms
1890–1990

SECOND EDITION

Larry Cuban

TEACHERS
COLLEGE
PRESS

Teachers College, Columbia University
New York and London

Published by Teachers College Press, 1234 Amsterdam Avenue
New York, NY 10027

Library of Congress Cataloging-in-Publication Data

Cuban, Larry.
    How teachers taught : constancy and change in American classrooms, 1890–1990 / Larry
Cuban.—2nd ed.
        p.   cm.—(Research on teaching series)
    Includes bibliographical references and index.
    ISBN 0-8077-3227-3 : $53.00.—ISBN 0-8077-3226-5 (pbk.) : $27.95
    1. Education—United States—History—19th century.   2. Education—United
States—History—20th century.   3. Teaching.   I. Title.
II. Series.
LA216.C82   1993
370'.973—dc20   92-31867

ISBN 0-8077-3227-3
ISBN 0-8077-3226-5 (pbk.)

Printed on acid-free paper

Manufactured in the United States of America

99 98 97 96 95 94 93   8 7 6 5 4 3 2 1

Contents

Part II: Open Classrooms and Alternative Schools: Progressivism Revisited, 1965–1975

Part III: Constancy and Change in the Classroom, 1890–1990

Foreword to the First Edition

Those who conduct research on teaching rarely consider historical investigations germane to their work. There is a sense in which history is treated as arcane, esoteric, and of little import to the concerns of policy and practice. In reading this book, I am convinced that precisely the opposite is true. Carefully conducted historical inquiry may well provide us with the most powerful guides available. Any study of teaching whose intent is to provide guidance for future practice or policy makes two assumptions. First, we must believe that the particular classrooms studied were representative of classrooms at large at the time the investigation was conducted. Second, we must further believe that the classrooms of interest to us, which exist in a time and place typically different from those investigated, bear sufficient resemblance to those studied to provide helpful insights.

Certainly it can be argued that the past prefigures the future, but the present never exactly mimics the past. Do we gain better advice from investigations plucked out of the temporal and cultural-ideological context in which they occurred, or are we better informed through studies that extend self-consciously through time, attempting explicitly to explain the phenomena described by connecting them meaningfully to other events occurring concurrently as well as to those that have preceded? In an unpublished essay, Lee Cronbach refers to educational research and evaluation as "quantitatively assisted history."

When we think of historical inquiry, we often imagine a scholar reading the letters, journals, newspaper accounts, and official documents of a given period and then aggregating those diverse forms of personal or collective impressions into the individual impression of the historian. As we read this monograph by Larry Cuban, we can begin to see how thin is the line that divides history from sociology or psychology, and hence educational history from the mainstream of empirical educational research. Cuban makes use of classroom observation records collected over many decades for diverse purposes: the evaluation activities of the Eight-Year Study; system-wide monitoring of curriculum and organizational changes in the public school systems of New York, Washington, Denver, and North Dakota, among many others; and hundreds of photographs of classrooms, which he uses inventively to infer how teaching was conducted during various periods. Never is any one source of data—photographs, personal diaries, classroom observations, district reports and evaluations, published articles, or even his own observations—taken as evidence by itself. Cuban is a careful historian who insists on carefully juxtaposing data sources, searching for both corroborative consistency and provocative contradiction among data sources, among different school sites during the same era, and among similar school settings during different decades.

Much of the richness communicated through this book is a consequence of the unique background brought to the enterprise by its author. Larry Cuban began as a classroom teacher, spending 14 years teaching secondary social studies in the school districts of Cleveland, Ohio, and Washington, D.C. He trained returned Peace Corps volunteers to teach in inner-city schools and subsequently directed staff development for a major program in the District of Columbia public schools. His interest in history as a subject area finally led him to Stanford University, where he studied educational history under David Tyack and wrote a masterful dissertation on the careers of three big-city superintendents. His *School Chiefs Under Fire* was based on that dissertation.

But Cuban was not content to study historically the administration of large school districts; he was committed to making that history as well. Upon completing his doctorate in educational history he was appointed superintendent of the Arlington County, Virginia, public schools, a position he held for seven years until he returned to Stanford in 1981 as a member of the School of Education faculty.

There are those who will read this volume as a pessimistic assessment of the failures of school reform. Despite the energy and rhetoric that have supported the reform of educational institutions in the direction of "progressive" ideals, especially the ideal of student-centered instruction in activity-based classrooms in which subject-area instruction is correlated and integrated, the general picture Cuban draws is of a rather stable, teacher-centered pedagogy sustaining itself from New York to Denver, from North Dakota to Michigan, from 1900 to 1980. But the picture drawn by Cuban is far more subtle than that. He finds that the portrait is not monolithic. Some reforms "take" better than others. Some settings (e.g., the elementary school) are more fertile ground for planned change than others. Even from the failures of reform he derives lessons for future planning and innovation. He asks not only why the reforms were not sustained, but what was right and adaptive about the traditional methods whose resilience he documents so vividly. From the very stability of certain instructional forms, he asserts, we may learn important principles regarding the fundamental character of school-based education—principles that can guide our future attempts to improve the quality of public education.

We thus confront the dual perspectives of historian and schoolman, the dispassionate "long view" of the disciplined scholar and the impassioned and practical concern of the front-line decisionmaker. This rare blend may occasionally offend the sensibilities of the historiographer who prefers his scholarship bland and distant. Yet this is scholarship of the highest, most meticulous order. Evidence for each assertion is carefully marshaled and contradictory findings are meticulously examined. Replications are sought in adjacent decades and/or in concurrent events in similar districts. Quantitative and qualitative indicators are used without fear of combining the incompatible. While undoubtedly a work of history, Cuban's study is also a masterful example of flexible inquiry that can be read with profit by all members of the research on teaching community. The highest praise I can give a piece of educational research is that it contributed substantially to my own education. *How Teachers Taught* did so for me, and, I trust, will do likewise for many others in the worlds of scholarship, policy, and practice.

Lee S. Shulman
Stanford, California

Foreword to the Second Edition

Larry Cuban's *How Teachers Taught* is one of those rare books that create a watershed in our understanding of education. By that I mean that its readers will never again see teaching in quite the same way.

David K. Cohen has observed that we have many historical studies about teachers but not about the heart of the educational process, instruction:

> Historians know more about nearly everything else concerning teaching—teachers' schooling, their working conditions and contracts, the curriculum they presumably taught, how teachers were exploited and discriminated against, even the buildings in which they worked—than about teachers' encounters with children over academic material. This central matter of teaching is a large area of historical darkness.

But, as Cohen notes, Cuban's *How Teachers Taught* is the striking exception.

In writing this book Cuban faced the challenges of an explorer in a new domain. He posed new research questions about the stability of traditional approaches to teaching, discovered new kinds of evidence, searched for plausible explanations of his findings, and interpreted what all of this meant to policymakers and practitioners. His was detective work of the first order. He ransacked libraries and school archives in Denver, New York City, and Washington, D.C., to find pictures of classrooms, surveys of practice, student newspapers, self-reports of teachers, and reminiscences of former pupils. He visited hundreds of classrooms and talked with teachers, students, and administrators in Arlington, Virginia, in Fargo, North Dakota, and in other districts across the country. He used different kinds of evidence, qualitative and quantitative, as a cross-check on the validity and reliability of his findings, candidly admitting when evidence was ambiguous. He proposed and criticized alternative interpretations of his findings. Furthermore, the book is a pleasure to read, punctuated by vivid metaphors, the human side of its topic revealed in sharply focused vignettes and carried along by lucid argument.

This revised edition enhances the excitement of that pioneering work, its sense of discovery, and strengthens it by responding to criticisms and by incorporating relevant scholarship of the past decade. Cuban now attends more to the broader socioeconomic context within which teaching takes place, for example, and devotes more attention to what is taught—the "it" of "I, thou, and it" relationship that David Hawkins sees as the heart of teaching.

In addition, he now deals directly with the policy issues that his study raises. As often happens to powerful books, some readers of the original edition skated over Cuban's careful qualifications of his findings to conclude that teachers have taught alike and still do, no matter what kinds of reforms are attempted—and that hence trying to change teaching is futile. While still arguing for a basic continuity in teacher-centered instruction, Cuban now stresses significant differences between elementary and high school teachers and discusses what he called "hybrids," or partial adoptions of student-centered instruction by many teachers. In his last chapter he directly addresses the policy implications of his work for policymakers, practitioners, and researchers.

There are no bumper-sticker solutions to educational problems here, no election-year gimmicks. Rather, this book presents the seasoned hopefulness and skeptical wisdom of a scholar-practitioner who gives us a better map of where we have been and a sense of where we might go.

David Tyack
Stanford, California

Preface to the Second Edition

When the chance to do a second edition materialized, I jumped at it. I had recently finished teaching juniors and seniors U.S. history for one semester in a nearby high school. After 16 years away from teaching teenagers (I had been teaching graduate students for a decade), strong feelings resurfaced about what I could and could not do in my class of 17 students who were labeled as low achievers lacking in academic skills. Those renewed feelings led me to reflect on what I had said in *How Teachers Taught* (*HTT*) about teacher- and student-centered instruction.

There were other reasons, of course. No other history of classroom pedagogy has appeared since *HTT* was published in 1984. Reviewers, for the most part, were kind and those who mixed generous words with insightful criticisms got me thinking about the shortcomings of the book. While *HTT* was frequently cited by scholars and practitioners, sometimes in ways that both puzzled and annoyed me, I became increasingly restive over the weaknesses in the monograph. I wanted a second chance. Jere Brophy steered me to Teachers College Press and I got that second chance.

In this edition, I have added recent studies to the research I completed almost a decade ago and have corrected errors that friends and reviewers have pointed out to me. Furthermore, I have reconsidered my earlier interpretations and conclusions in light of other studies that have appeared since 1982, when I completed the manuscript of the first edition.

For those readers familiar with the first edition and those who come to this study for the first time, I will summarize what I felt were the more compelling criticisms of the original study. First-time readers may have difficulty following the criticisms without knowing the text and may wish to read this part after completing the book.

- Some critics chided me for not taking a stand on whether teacher- and student-centered instruction was either effective for children or a form of teaching that I endorsed. Other critics scored me for not explicitly taking a stand in favor of student-centered instruction, since, in their opinion, my choice of language implicitly carried that message.

These critics touched a fundamental dilemma with which I had wrestled for many years (and continue to wrestle). They uncovered the conflict of values in my mind and heart, the ambivalence of a scholar-practitioner who, while working toward the ideal of producing objective knowledge, also seeks to improve teaching practices so that students benefit. Both values are important, and even as I try to finesse the inevitable tensions that exist between them I am uncertain whether readers will find my second tightrope walk between conflicting values any better. At the least in this edition I acknowledge openly the conflicting choices that a practice-oriented scholar faces.

- Only a few critics saw what I have come to see in the original study as an obvious limitation: In my framework for understanding why teachers teach as they do, I had no clear linkage between the practice of teaching and the economic, social, and political context of schooling (e.g., students' backgrounds, the neighborhood setting, the social class structure of the larger community). While readers will see that I am still not entirely persuaded that such factors definitely steered classroom pedagogy in one direction or the other, my earlier treatment of the economic, social, and political context of schooling minimized the influence that, I have come to see, such factors indeed do have upon classroom teaching.

- Some critics said the study focused too much on instruction and did not seriously treat curriculum. The official curriculum (what subject matter, skills, and values authorities expect teachers to teach) and the taught curriculum (what teachers believe about content and its presentation and what they actually do) are entangled. The intersection between the two needs to be elaborated and connected to what happens in classrooms.

I have found these criticisms both accurate and helpful. I have tried to include these points in this revision.

Incorporating the wise comments of critics also led me to make clear in this edition my stand on the meaning of constancy and change in classroom teaching. I have been surprised and sometimes shocked at the range of conclusions about the enduring character of classroom instruction that scholars, policymakers, and practitioners have extracted from *HTT*. Examples of exaggerated interpretations that go well beyond the evidence I offered or the findings that I presented are:

- Classroom teaching is the same now as it was a century ago.
- Teacher-centered instruction varies hardly at all in the nation's classrooms.
- Trying to alter what teachers do in their classrooms is futile.

In this revision, I explicitly state my conclusions about the durability of classroom instruction and the changes that have occurred.

This second edition, then, is a chance for me to revisit, in the light of praise and criticism of the first edition, new evidence that has emerged since. It is also my further reflection on two crucial questions fundamental to schooling and its improvement: How did teachers teach? Why did they teach as they did? Without convincing answers to these questions, policymakers, practitioners, and researchers will continue to grope for ways to understand and improve schooling, uninformed by past experiences of teachers and reformers.

Acknowledgments

I began this study as a school superintendent and completed it as a professor. The blend of practice and research at the university reaffirms my deeply held belief that worthwhile knowledge draws on both worlds. Indeed, the separation of practice from theory, of practitioners from scholars, is more often than not a divorce that is more symbolic than real. My quarter century of experience in public schools, of shuttling back and forth between teaching and administering, persuaded me not only that the daily realities of classrooms and schools produced valuable knowledge but also that I lacked deeper conceptual frameworks to improve my understanding of what those things I faced daily meant. The interplay between knowledge derived from classroom experience and the theories that researchers used helped me greatly in grasping the merging of political, social, organizational, and individual behavior in classrooms.

This study of classroom teaching over the last century is part of my ongoing efforts to understand the complexity of the process of change in schools. Because I had taught for many years and had served as a school superintendent for seven years, I needed to find answers to some long-standing questions I had accumulated about the process of teaching, both in schools where I had taught and those where I had served as an administrator. The questions I asked and the answers I found form the boundaries of this study.

Any investigation that takes 18 months to complete (and 9 months to revise) requires the help of many individuals willing to share their time and advice. For the first edition, historical research on teaching often meant time spent in libraries and school districts. In New York City, Pauline Pincus, who served in the school system's Professional Library, was especially helpful in tracking down sources I could not find elsewhere. Robert Morris of Teachers College took time to introduce me to their newly acquired archives from the New York City Public Schools. Professor Lillian Weber told me of her efforts in New York and her views of the informal education movement of the late 1960s and early 1970s. Her insights helped me to revise some of my assumptions.

Gordon York, then assistant superintendent of the Grand Forks, North Dakota, Public Schools, and Glenn Melvey, Fargo Assistant Superintendent of Instruction, arranged visits for me to each of the schools I had requested. I appreciated the patience of the principals and teachers who were patient with my note-taking and questions.

In Denver, Ellengail Buehtel, who directed the district's professional library, helped me locate a number of sources that I had given up on ever finding. John Rankin of the Public Information Department was especially gracious in arranging for me to use student yearbooks, clipping files, and photographs stored in the basement of the administration building.

Researching the Washington, D.C., schools of two time periods was made easier by the sources located in the District of Columbia Public Library's Washingtonia Room. In the school system, Erika Robinson and Maggie Howard of the Division of Research were especially helpful in locating sources and patient with my use of their space. Bill Webb of the Media Center showed me photographs of classrooms taken since the mid-1960s.

I also acknowledge the help of Charles Missar, then librarian for the National Institute of Education. He was especially gracious and patient with an ex-superintendent limbering rusty research muscles. And NIE itself (now long gone) deserves a brief acknowledgment for the original study, which they funded and from which this book derives. I feel awkward thanking an organization for betting that a school superintendent could carry off a complex historical investigation. Usually I thank individuals, but a large number of people were involved in making the initial decision to fund this research. I thank them for having confidence in this practitioner-researcher.

Reviewers of the first edition followed my instructions to give it a tough, close reading. I appreciated the prompt and full responses from Elisabeth Hansot, Carl Kaestle, Joseph Kett, Marvin Lazerson, Kim Marshall, and David Tyack. For the second edition, Ray McDermott gave the draft a thorough, demanding critique for which I am most grateful. My thanks also go to Brian Ellerbeck of Teachers College Press, who helped make a revised edition possible. All are absolved of responsibility for any errors in fact or judgment that exist in either edition.

Two reviewers deserve special mention. The editorial board of The Research on Training Monograph Series (Longman, Inc.) that published the first edition asked Lee Shulman to review the manuscript. His gentle and wise touch helped me eliminate some confusions I had created, and he urged me to pursue my arguments about teacher practices to their logical conclusion. David Tyack's generous advice on the first edition and astute prodding of me were most helpful. Of far greater importance was his abiding faith in the worth of researching classrooms as a crucial measure of policy implementation. By using this research and conducting his own on classroom teaching in the 1930s, he strengthened my confidence in the simple message to policymakers that no story of what happens in schools can be complete without addressing directly what teachers did in classrooms.

Finally, as in every writing venture I have undertaken, my wife Barbara has helped at every stage whether with the mechanics of editing and proofreading or with emotional support. For this second edition I was fortunate to secure as a copy editor my daughter Janice. As a former journalist, she helped me greatly in straightening out crooked syntax and being clear in what I wanted to say.

Over the last 30 years I have written a great deal about education. I cannot say what my writings have amounted to, but, of them all, this study has been the most satisfying. It scratched an itch that had been bothering me for a number of years.

Introduction

Over a 25-year period I worked as a high school social studies teacher and administrator in four school systems. Since 1981, I have been a university teacher and researcher. Over these years, basic questions on schooling rose that seemed unanswerable or had no convincing answer either in my experience or in the research literature. Here are a few of the questions that have puzzled me.

In the last two decades I have been in many classrooms. During the times I watched teachers in secondary schools, a wave of recognition swept over me. What I saw was almost exactly what I remembered from junior and senior high school classrooms that I had sat in as a student in the 1940s and as a beginning teacher in the mid-1950s. This acute sense of something familiar about how teachers were teaching occurred in many different schools. How, I asked myself, could teaching *seem* unchanged over a 40-year period?

During the decade I served as an administrator in two school districts, I had to deal with another question that troubled me: In institutions as apparently vulnerable to change as schools, why do so few instructional reforms get past the classroom door? Policymakers, foundation officials, and academics propose different ways of operating schools and teaching students; schools respond by embracing new reading programs, novel ways of organizing a school, and curricular innovations. School boards and administrators triumphantly display the new programs they have adopted and the innovations that keep them abreast of brand-new ideas in education. Yet many of those very same policymakers, officials, and academics scold teachers for their stubbornness in maintaining conventional styles of teaching inconsistent with the newly adopted policies, programs, and materials. The questions I ask, then, seem linked. The apparent uniformity in instruction irrespective of time and place appears connected to the apparent invulnerability of classrooms to change.

In an article I published in 1979, I sought answers to these questions through a study of curricular change and stability since the 1870s. In examining how various forces had shaped the curriculum and classroom instruction over the previous century, I used the metaphor of a hurricane to distinguish among curriculum theory, courses of study, materials, and classroom teaching. Hurricane winds sweep across the sea, tossing up 20-foot waves; a fathom below the surface turbulent waters swirl, while on an ocean floor there is unruffled calm.[1]

As tricky as metaphors can be, I compared that hurricane to any newly trumpeted curriculum theory and the policy talk that such theories generated. Professional journals, for example, echo arguments for and against a new theory. Letters to editors and sharp rebuttals add to the flurry. Books are written and reputations are made. Conferences host both skeptics and promoters. Professors of education teach the new wisdom to their students. Some school boards adopt policies and start an occasional program consistent with the novel concept. Yet most publishers continue producing texts barely touched by the new theory and most teachers use methods unmarked by either controversy or slogans. I used the metaphor to illustrate distinctions among theory, policy rhetoric, the content of programs, and, most importantly, the impact of all these factors upon teaching behavior.

In that article I wrote that curriculum theories did influence professional ideologies and policymakers' vocabularies, as well as courses of study and, to some extent, textbook content. But I did not find much evidence of significant change in teaching practices. However, I had not systematically or comprehensively examined primary sources in general or in particular school districts. I used, for the most part, secondary sources, and consulted a few primary documents that were available. Based upon this initial review, I found some evidence of a seemingly stubborn continuity in the character of instruction despite intense reform efforts to move classroom practices toward instruction that was more student-centered.

Deepening the paradox, the limited evidence suggested that teaching practices seemed uncommonly stable at all levels of schooling touching students of varied abilities in diverse settings over many decades, despite improvements in teacher education, state credentialing, and scholarly knowledge of teaching practices. In dealing with this paradox researchers have tied more knots than they have loosened. Some writers assert that student-centered instruction has been embraced by teachers, while others argue that such classroom changes have seldom been institutionalized. Common to all research is a dearth of evidence about what teachers have done in classrooms.[2]

The lack of evidence about whether or not instruction had evolved over time drove me to ask a basic question: How did teachers teach? If the answer I sought was to have weight and clarity, the fragmentary data about what teachers did in their classrooms needed to be brought together with reform efforts to alter practices. This study begins that task.

A framework for understanding different kinds of school and classroom reforms is a useful tool for trying to answer the question of how teachers taught and what classroom changes occurred over a century.

REFORMING SCHOOLS AND CLASSROOMS

To understand the deeper meanings of past and present efforts to improve teaching, and to connect broad policies of school improvement with classroom teachers' behaviors, I divide the reforms of the past century into *incremental* and *fundamental* changes.[3]

Incremental Reforms

Incremental reforms are those that aim to improve the efficiency and effectiveness of existing structures of schooling including classroom teaching. The premise behind incremental reforms is that the basic structures are sound but need improving. The car is old but if it gets fixed it will run well; it needs tires, brakes, a new battery, and a water pump—incremental changes. Illustrations of incremental changes within schools would include adding another curricular track to the three or four that already exist in a high school; introducing merit pay; decreasing class size from 30 to 28; adding two more counselors to a secondary school or an assistant principal to an elementary school; improving attendance procedures for the school; and changing parent conference times to accommodate single, working parents.

In the classroom, incremental changes would include new units for teaching civics or handwriting; in-service workshops to teach teachers to use a classroom computer to keep attendance and record grades; or introducing teachers to various techniques of maintaining classroom discipline.

Fundamental Reforms

Fundamental reforms are those that aim to transform—alter permanently—those very same structures. The premise behind fundamental reforms is that basic structures are flawed at their core and need a complete overhaul, not renovations. The old jalopy is beyond repair. We need to get a new car or consider different forms of transportation—fundamental changes.

If new courses, more staff, summer schools, higher standards for teachers, and increased salaries are examples of incremental enhancements to the structures of public schooling, then late-19th-century innovation of the progressives in the kindergarten and junior high school are instances of fundamental changes in the conduct of schooling. Other examples would be the broadening of the school's social role in the late 19th and early 20th centuries to intervene in the lives of children and their families (for example, in the areas of medical and social services) and giving parents the option of enrolling their children in private or public schools.

Applied to the classroom, fundamental changes would aim at transforming the teacher's role from that of a central source of power and knowledge to the role of a coach who guides students to their own decisions, who helps them find meaning in their experiences and what they learn from one another and from books. Teaching becomes structuring activities that enable students to learn from subject matter, one another, and the community. Teaching becomes less telling and more listening. Student learning becomes active and includes groupwork, play, independent work, and artistic expression. There is less seatwork and listening to the teacher explain. Such changes would represent fundamental alterations in the ways teachers think about the nature of knowledge, teaching, and learning, and about their actions in the classroom.

Some of these examples of incremental and fundamental innovations in teaching practices have stuck—that is, they have been institutionalized. Many, however, have not. The overall mortality rate for classroom reforms is high. Some reforms survive birth only to linger on for a few years and then pass away. Other reforms get incorporated into routine classroom activities. What accounts for the survival of some and not others?

Transforming Fundamental Changes into Incremental Ones

The kindergarten, junior high school, open-space architecture, and the use of computers are instances of actual and attempted fundamental changes in the school and classroom since the turn of this century that were adopted in many schools and yet, over time, either were marginalized into incremental ones or slipped away, leaving few traces of their presence. How did this occur?

Familiar examples of this unplanned process are the curricular reforms of the 1950s and 1960s, which were guided in large part by academic specialists and funded by the federal government. These reforms were aimed at revolutionizing teaching and learning in math, science, and social studies, and millions of dollars were spent on producing textbooks and classroom materials and on training teachers. Using the best instructional materials that scholars could produce, teachers would coach students to understand how scientists thought, to experience the pleasures of discovery in solving math problems, conducting laboratory experiments, and using primary sources to understand the past. Materials were published and placed in the hands of teachers who, for the most part, had had little time to understand what was demanded by the novel materials or, for that matter, to practice their use.

By the end of the 1970s, when researchers reported on what was now occurring in classrooms, they found the familiar teacher-centered instruction aimed at imparting knowledge from a text and little evidence of student involvement in critical thinking, problem solving, or experiencing how scientists worked. These federally funded efforts did, however, leave a distinct curricular residue in textbooks published in the 1970s. An attempt to revolutionize teaching and learning became, in time, new textbook content.[4]

A more complicated way in which fundamental reforms become incremental changes is what George and Louise Spindler call "substitute change." They studied a small school in a southern German village called Schonhausen for over a decade. Initially a rural area, the villages were undergoing changes in land ownership and wine production, that is, the creation of larger plots and introduction of machines to till and harvest grapes. Moreover, shifts in population were urbanizing the area.

For decades, the school curriculum had emphasized the land, the village community, and family values. The federal and provincial ministries of education, however, mandated a new curriculum and textbooks based upon life in cities, the importance of modernization, and high technology. The Spindlers studied the village and its school in 1968 and returned in 1977 after almost a decade of reform.

What surprised the Spindlers was that in spite of the clear attempt by ministry officials to make a village school more modern and more responsive to urban life, children, teachers, and parents continued to make tradition-based and village-oriented choices. In the school, trips that had once taken classes on day-long strolls in the countryside gave way to role-playing a petition to the village council. Much of the earlier content about the beauty of the land was lost but the cultural goals and values nourishing the traditions of the village were maintained. How?

The Spindlers found that the way teachers taught and how they maintained classroom order sustained village traditions in the face of curricular reforms. For a play about the village political process, a reading recommended in the new curriculum, the teachers substituted a romantic folktale from the previous curriculum. Thus, the focus of the classroom activity remained on the importance of life in the village. An effort to alter fundamentally the values of villages in that part of Germany so as to make them more responsive to urban life was transformed into an affirmation of village values.[5]

Another way of transforming fundamental reforms is to shunt them to the periphery of the regular school. For example, innovative programs that reduce class size, reconceptualize the student-teacher relationship, integrate subject matter from diverse disciplines, and structure activities that involve students in their learning often begin as experiments in regular classrooms but, over the years, migrate to out-of-the-way programs in the main building or faraway sites. The schools have, indeed, adopted and implemented programs fundamentally different from what mainstream students receive, yet it is the outsiders—students labeled as potential dropouts, vocational students, pregnant teenagers, those identified as gifted, at-risk students, and handicapped pupils—who participate in the innovative programs. Thus, some basic changes get encapsulated, like a grain of sand in an oyster; they exist within the system but are often separated from mainstream programs.[6]

These organizational processes that maintain continuity are seldom conspiratorial or even due to conscious acts on the part of school officials. Such transformations occur as a consequence of bureaucratic, political, and cultural processes deeply embedded in the different levels of schooling as they interact with the larger society. They occur as a result of deep-seated impulses within the organization to appear modern, to convince those who support the schools that what happens in schools is up-to-date and responsive to the wishes of their patrons. Thus, pervasive and potent processes within the institution of schooling preserve its independence to act even in the face of powerful outside forces intent upon altering what happens in schools and classrooms.[7]

How much of this framework for distinguishing between incremental and fundamental reforms and what happens to them over time applies directly to how teachers teach? It is easy to sketch out an argument that captures the broad outlines of how macro-policies get adapted after they are adopted. It is far more difficult to account for teachers' behaviors in varied classroom settings over an entire century.

To apply this framework to describing how teachers taught, I investigate teaching practices before, during, and after reform impulses in the 20th century aimed at fundamentally changing what teachers routinely do. In doing so I hope to give a clearer sense of what has persisted and what kinds of changes have occurred in classrooms.

But what are we to look for in classrooms marked by a bewildering variety of student and teacher behaviors? While no single study can do justice to the intricate complexity of classroom teaching, there is a useful tool for revealing a portion of that complicated terrain. The device of describing instruction as a continuum stretching from teacher-centered to student-centered instruction contains a limited but useful set of indicators describing important dimensions of what teachers do in their classrooms. While this continuum cannot capture the richness of the classroom environment or the intersection of curriculum and instruction, it nonetheless offers a glimpse behind the closed doors of classrooms that existed decades ago and allows us to map, in a preliminary fashion, their pedagogical topography.

Before proceeding further, I need to state plainly what I mean by teacher- and student-centered instruction. Teacher-centered instruction means that a teacher controls what is taught, when, and under what conditions within a classroom. Observable measures of teacher-centered instruction are:

- Teacher talk exceeds student talk during instruction.
- Instruction occurs frequently with the whole class; small-group or individual instruction occurs less often.
- Use of class time is largely determined by the teacher.
- The teachers rely heavily upon the textbook to guide curricular and instructional decision making.
- The classroom furniture is usually arranged into rows of desks or chairs facing a chalkboard with a teacher's desk nearby.

Student-centered instruction means that students exercise a substantial degree of responsibility for what is taught, how it is learned, and for movement within the classroom. Observable measures of student-centered instruction are:

- Student talk about learning tasks is at least equal to, if not greater than, teacher talk.
- Most instruction occurs individually, in small groups (2 to 6 students), or in moderate-sized groups (7 to 10) rather than being directed at the entire class.
- Students help choose and organize the content to be learned.
- Teachers permit students to determine, partially or wholly, rules of behavior, classroom rewards and penalties, and how they are to be enforced.
- Varied instructional materials (e.g., activity centers, learning stations, interest centers) are available in the classroom so that students can use them independently or in small groups.
- Use of these materials is scheduled, either by the teacher or in consultation with students, for at least half of the academic time available.
- The classroom is usually arranged in a manner that permits students to work together or separately, in small groups or in individual work spaces; no dominant pattern in arranging classroom furniture exists, and desks, tables, and chairs are realigned frequently.

I view these differences in teacher- and student-centered instruction as tools to help map what happened in classrooms. These instructional patterns have long histories.

For centuries, at least two traditions of how teachers should and do teach have fired debates and shaped practice. What I call teacher-centered instruction has been described as subject-centered, "tough-minded," "hard pedagogy," and "mimetic." What I call student-centered instruction has been labeled at different times as child-centered or "progressive," "tender-minded" or "soft" pedagogy, and as "transformative." While they are far from identical with these earlier notions, my definitions overlap with them sufficiently to be located in views of teaching that are millennia old.[8]

The two traditions of teaching are anchored in different views of knowledge and the relationship of both teacher and learner to that knowledge. In teacher-centered instruction, knowledge is often (but not always) "presented" to the learner, who—and the metaphors from different eras and places vary— is a "blank slate," a "vessel to fill," or "a duck to stuff." In student-centered instruction, knowledge is often (but not always) "discovered" by the learner, who is "rich clay in the hands of an artist" or "a garden in need of a masterful gardener."

Using these two historical traditions of teaching as tools for understanding constancy and change is limited because they lack precision. Much detail is missing about what happens when a teacher teaches within a tradition. Nevertheless, even with these shortcomings, these traditions can help sort out, however simply, various teaching patterns, especially if the patterns are arrayed on a continuum. Of even greater importance is to weigh these shortcomings against the fact that so few studies have captured what teachers have done in classrooms over time.

In using these constructs, I do not assume that actual changes in practice moved solely from teacher- to student-centered instruction; traffic flowed both ways, regardless of reformers' intentions. Individual teachers stopped at various places along the way. Nor do I assume that changes in teaching behavior were an all-or-nothing embrace of an entire approach. Quite often, as this study will show, teachers incorporated into their repertoires particular practices they found useful. Hybrids of familiar and new practices turn up repeatedly in classrooms over the last century. In 1929, for example, an elementary school teacher whose only classroom innovation in years was to divide her class into two groups for reading, teaching some students in front of the room while the rest worked at their desks on an assignment, nevertheless thereby added a new teaching tool to her repertoire. Likewise, a high school history teacher who in 1933 began using examples from contemporary political life to enliven his students' study of the French Revolution was modifying his routine practices.

While pedagogical progressives of those decades might have winced at my wording and labeled such changes as trivial, these teachers had selectively adopted child-centered practices. A continuum needs to have space for the hybrids of progressive teacher-centered instruction, just as it must have space for the various types of student-centered instruction more familiar to promoters of that approach.

The various adaptations of student-centered pedagogy that teachers over the last century have selectively incorporated into their practices are just as puzzling, if not as interesting, to policymakers and scholars, as those reforms teachers have ignored. Scholars also must unravel the mystery of what kinds of changes these hybrids are. Does an expanded arsenal of teaching approaches that meld student-centered techniques with a dominant teacher-centered approach mean that these are simply incremental changes, enhancements to the prevailing style of teaching? Or does it mean that these are incremental steps toward a fundamental shift in the emphasis of the individual teacher's approach? Although I take up these questions later, I raise them now to alert readers to the fact that many puzzles remain for scholars and policymakers to explore.

Despite these puzzles, observers can still categorize instructional patterns of individual teachers by careful attention to visible areas of classroom decision making over which teachers have direct influence. These classroom indicators are evidence of the dominant form of instruction, especially when they combine to create patterns. Such indicators include:

1. Arrangement of classroom furniture;
2. The ratio of teacher talk to student talk;
3. Whether most instruction occurs individually, in small groups, or with the entire class;
4. The presence or absence of learning or interest centers that are used by students as part of the normal school day;
5. The degree of physical movement students are allowed without asking the teacher; and
6. The degree of reliance upon texts and use of varied instructional materials.[9]

In describing classroom practices I had to narrow my scope. This study excludes descriptions of the emotional climate in classrooms and informal relationships between teachers and students. No judgments are made about the effectiveness of teacher- or student-centered instruction, nor are comparisons made among teaching practices. I assume that instances of effective teaching, however defined by scholars or practitioners, occur within both traditions. The central research issue for me is to determine how stable certain teaching behaviors were over the last century in the face of mighty efforts to move teaching toward student-centered instruction, not to determine the relative value of either approach in achieving desirable outcomes. But in trying to be objective about the two traditions of teaching, I cannot check my values and experiences at the door like a coat and hat. As a historian, I face dilemmas. A few words about these dilemmas may help the reader assess the worth of this study.

In seeking to be objective about the two traditions of instruction and their hybrids, I describe carefully my evidence and its sources and assess their strengths and limitations. I have met at least one condition of objectivity by telling readers at every step of the way how I carried out this study. In striving for impartiality, I have also tried to avoid describing teacher-centered instruction with such loaded phrases as "traditional teaching," "frontal teaching," or "conventional instruction," or student-centered instruction in terms such as "permissive" or "lacking academic standards."

While I work toward the ideal of objectivity in the methods I use and believe in the worth of that ideal, it is difficult to attain because I value certain kinds of teaching over others. I state my preferences for teaching approaches here so that readers can understand the value conflicts I face as a historian seeking to be fair in describing and analyzing reforms aimed at altering teacher-centered instruction and as a teacher and reformer eager to improve what happens in classrooms.

I began teaching in 1955. If an observer had entered my high school social studies class in Cleveland's Glenville High School a year later that person would have easily categorized my instruction as wholly teacher-centered. My students sat in rows of movable chairs with tablet arms; we carried on, more often than not, teacher-led discussions interspersed by my minilectures and occasional student reports, or a class debate or game to break the routine. Over 90% of instructional time was spent teaching the whole group.

By the early 1960s, I had begun to incorporate into my repertoire such techniques as student-led discussions, dividing the class into groups for varied tasks, creating instructional materials first to supplement and later to replace the textbook, and other approaches that could be loosely called "the new social studies."

In the early 1970s, one class of the five that I taught daily would spend the entire 50-minute period going from one teaching station to another. I used these stations at least once a week, sometimes more, depending on how much material I had developed. Most of the week, however, was spent on teacher-led discussions, supervised study periods, group meetings for particular projects, student reports, minilectures, and other non-traditional approaches. I had become much more informal in interactions with my students. They sat in a horseshoe arrangement of desks and chairs with the open end of the horseshoe facing my desk and chalkboard. Movement in the class and easy exchanges between me and students during small-group work and whole-group discussions spoke of a relaxed social organization in the classroom. I still decided, for the most part, what was to be studied, what methods were to be used, and how time and classroom space was to be allocated. At the same time, however, I was giving students a small but growing role in choosing topics within the larger framework I determined, in deciding how to use their time within the classroom when they had tasks to perform, and in making other instructional decisions.

Where along the continuum between teacher- and student-centered instruction did I fit? My dominant pattern remained teacher-centered but I had begun a journey in the mid-1950s and moved substantially toward the student-centered end of the continuum by the early 1970s. When I began teaching as a professor in 1981, the mixing of approaches began to be deliberate and explicit. When I returned to the high school classroom in 1988 for a semester to teach U.S. history to low-achieving students, the mixing of teaching approaches was even more evident. Over the years, then, I have come to see that I had developed a teaching hybrid that included features of student-centered instruction yet retained a dominant teacher-centered pattern.

Since the early 1960s I have also been deeply involved in improving the practice of social studies teaching, preparing new teachers for teaching in schools enrolling mostly poor, minority students, and making organizational reforms in one school district. Furthermore, I have written extensively about what policymakers, administrators, and teachers should do to improve schooling and teaching. So in my roles as high school teacher, administrator, and professor since 1955, I have mixed activism with reflection, practice with theory. That mixing has created many tensions within me; for example, even as I teach as a professor, I have come to value student-centered practices more and more over the years.

As my ideas of how knowledge is formed, learned, and used by both children and adults have changed over the years, so has my teaching. If students construct new knowledge out of their experiences, as I believe they do, then I, as a teacher, must grasp some portion of their experience and connect it to the knowledge I convey to them. How to connect what students already know to what they should know is the challenge facing every teacher. To secure that student understanding requires active student involvement in what is to be learned, different forms of representing that knowledge, and giving students many chances to practice and display what has been learned. This agenda, of course, tilts toward using student-centered practices in classrooms. Has this mixture of teaching practices that I have created over decades made me more effective in helping students learn? In other words, is it "good" teaching? The answer depends on one's definition of good teaching. Since I seek to make students think for themselves and put their fingerprints on any content that is learned in order to apply that content to their lives, I believe that my teaching is "good" teaching and that its effectiveness can be measured. Readers should note, however, that this study focuses on teaching, not on student learning. Any adequate definition of good teaching would require ample evidence of what students have learned as a consequence of the teaching approaches being evaluated.

This overview of my career as a teacher brings into focus a few of the dilemmas I face as a researcher committed to the ideal of objectivity in scholarship while practicing the art of teaching and also trying to introduce school and classroom reforms. I have tried to control for my biases in this study by using different forms of evidence, investigating different sites, and sampling from different periods. These devices are ways of reducing the effects of my preferences. The compromises that I have constructed to deal with the tensions of the competing, even conflicting values of a scholar, a practitioner, and a reformer may not please each reader, but I feel that readers should be aware of how I dealt with these inevitable quandaries.

Given the limits of this study, an obvious question arises: If this inquiry avoids defining what is "good" teaching or how some teachers succeed better than others at creating a classroom atmosphere where students want to learn, then what will be the practical uses of this research? This is a fair question because it raises the issues of the intersection between research and practice and the uses of historical investigation.

Because researchers, policymakers, practitioners, and reform-minded citizens know so little about which instructional practices have remained stable and which ones have changed over the last century, investigating certain classroom practices can illuminate both the potential for and the limits to altering how teachers teach. Exploring the terrain of the classroom since the 1890s should reveal what is durable and what is transient, what can be changed and what is invulnerable to reform. By learning more about the instructional quark that is the classroom, policymakers, practitioners, and scholars can come to have reasonable expectations about what teachers can and cannot do, what schools can be held accountable for and what is beyond their reach. Thus the outcomes of this study, however modest, should offer practical direction for the periodic surges of reform that sweep over public schools.

I also see an indirect, subtler use for this study of classroom practices. Powerful metaphors for schooling dominate the thinking of practitioners, scholars, and policymakers. J. M. Stephens writes that a common metaphor for schools is the factory. This image exalts rational decisionmaking, suggesting that schools are mechanical; each part of the machine is connected to the others by an assembly line and can be fixed or improved. Switch to the metaphor of farming, Stephens says, and schooling looks different. Through an ancient, stable process, farmers predict what the sun, the climate, seeds, plants, and insects are likely to do each year. By understanding the durability of the process and working within its limits, he argues, farmers can improve production. But, he continues, farmers cannot ignore these "older organic forces [they] have little control over." They have to work with and through them. The agricultural metaphor is a fundamentally different image of teaching and schooling that has direct consequences for what reform-minded policymakers believe can and cannot be done with and for classroom teachers.[10]

Many policymakers, scholars, and practitioners carry these or similar images in their heads. Such pictures shape their decisions. Historical maps of teaching practices over the last century have at least the potential for determining the accuracy of these metaphors and, in turn, suggesting directions for the periodic reforms undertaken by citizens and professionals alike. I will take up these points again in the last chapter.

Two specific questions guide this study:

- Did teacher-centered instruction persist in public schools during and after reform movements that had as one of their targets the installation of student-centered instruction?
- If the answer is yes, to what extent did it persist and why? If the answer is no, to what extent did instruction change and why?

In order to answer these questions I have drawn historical maps of teaching practices in three cities and many rural districts during the 1920s and 1930s; in two cities and one state for the decade between 1965 and 1975; and in one medium-sized school district in a metropolitan area between 1975 and 1981. The two periods of major reform efforts to shift classroom practices fundamentally from teacher- to student-centeredness were (a) the decades in the first quarter of the 20th century, when progressive education became the dominant ideology, and (b) the decade between the mid-1960s and the mid-1970s, when informal education, or "open classrooms," dominated the talk of policymakers, practitioners, and scholars.

To determine how teachers taught, I used a variety of sources:

- Photographs of teachers and students in class;
- Textbooks and texts used by teachers;
- Student recollections of their classroom experiences;
- Teacher reports on how they taught;
- Reports from journalists, administrators, parents, and others who visited classrooms;
- Student writings in school newspapers and yearbooks;
- Research studies of teaching practices; and
- Descriptions of classroom architecture, room size, desk design, building plans, and so forth.

Historians have to cope with the dilemmas of selectivity of evidence (i.e., what survives and is available may be atypical of the era being studied) and the inherent biases of sources (e.g., a photographer in 1900 posed students to illustrate the "New Education"). To minimize the effects of selectivity and bias I have sought multiple and divergent sources representing two periods of time and a number of different settings, from elementary to high school, from urban to rural.

From these sources I have gathered descriptions of over 1,200 class-rooms for the years 1890 to 1990. These descriptions are embedded within a larger set of data from each district and across the nation that indirectly reveal teaching practices in almost 7,000 other classrooms.

The patterns in teaching practice described in this study represent only a fraction of what teachers did in their classrooms. Anyone familiar with a class-room knows the kaleidoscopic whirl that it is—although its pace, intensity, and complexity are often obscured by student compliance with teacher-established routines. (To the casual observer, the classroom may, after 30 min-utes' observation, seem humdrum, even tedious.) How, then, can I capture only one slice of this whirl after it has disappeared?

The historian of classroom teaching is in the same bind as the paleontol-ogist who carefully and softly brushes away the dust from a jaw fragment of an apparent human ancestor. The bone is an infinitesimally tiny fragment of the skeleton, the skeleton an even tinier fraction of the population that the scientist wants to describe. The "bones" I have had to work with are class-room photographs, and written accounts by various participants.

Historian David Fischer suggests another image. Studying history is like trying to complete an unconventional puzzle. Take a Jackson Pollock painting and cut it into a puzzle with a thousand parts. Throw out the corner pieces, most of the edges, and half of the rest. The task of putting it all together comes close to describing what historians do.[11]

Trying to put the puzzle together also means trying to make sense of the Jackson Pollock painting. A study of constancy and change in American class-rooms over the last century must ask: Why did various teaching practices persist in spite of determined efforts to alter them and why did teachers invent new approaches and integrate them into their daily routines?

EXPLANATIONS FOR CONSTANCY AND CHANGE

There are a number of explanations for stability in teaching practices and instances of teacher-adopted changes. I mention these possible explanations briefly now to alert readers to both the range and character of the arguments. (I will use the words argument and explanation interchangeably in this con-text.) I will consider them at greater length after the descriptions of classroom practice unfold in the next seven chapters. The arguments are as follows:

1. *Cultural beliefs about the nature of knowledge, how teaching should occur, and how children should learn are so widespread and deeply rooted that they steer the thinking of policymakers, practitioners, parents, and citizens toward certain forms of instruction.*

Centuries ago, in European and American cultures, formal schooling was instituted in religious institutions with the aim of teaching students to spread the word of the particular gospel and to study its meaning. Books were rare and teaching and learning in church-related schools and colleges depended on those who were informed telling the uninformed what was important to know. Knowledge was a body of beliefs, facts, procedures, and opinions that largely went unquestioned.

For millennia, then, deeply embedded western beliefs about the nature of knowledge (a body of human wisdom accumulated and tempered over time that must be passed on from one generation to another), teaching (the communicating of that wisdom), and learning (the absorption of that wisdom) have marked efforts to school the young. These beliefs unfolded within the family when it acted as the first school for infants and toddlers. Strengthened by formal religions as they emerged over the centuries, these cultural beliefs shaped the character and direction of religious instruction before the introduction of tax-supported public schools. With the invention of public schools in Europe and later in the United States, teacher-centered instruction, stressing the teacher as the authority who passes on the required knowledge to students, who in turn are expected to take in and digest the knowledge, continued as the dominant form of instruction.

Occasional European and American philosophers and educators over the last 500 years objected to these ingrained cultural beliefs and maintained that education should focus on the child, rather than on a body of knowledge accumulated over centuries. Such reformers viewed the teacher's primary role as that of guiding the unfolding of the child's talents to their fullest and were eager to develop student-centered ways of educating the young. Twentieth-century reformers, for example, introduced the kindergarten, small-group learning approaches, the movable desk, and other child-centered practices into public schooling. These changes have come slowly and have often been diluted by the dominant cultural norms deeply ingrained in these schools.

Thus, it comes as no surprise that most descriptions of classrooms portray the persistence of teacher-centered classrooms consistent with the historical traditions that took shape when men and women lived guided by a deep reverence for the accumulated wisdom of their elders.

2. *The organization and practice of formal schooling function to socialize and sort students into varied socioeconomic niches.*

In the life of a growing child, the school is the only public institution that stands between the family and the workplace. Schools inculcate in children the dominant social norms, values, and behaviors that will prepare them for entry into the larger culture. Schools are organized into bureaucratic, age-graded settings where students are grouped, first by ability, in elementary schools and then by tracks in secondary schools. Schools and the adults who staff these institutions, then, unwittingly distribute dominant cultural knowledge (American history, grammar, math, and so on), inculcate mainstream values (punctuality, the work ethic, competitiveness, and so forth), and channel students into appropriate socioeconomic niches (the upper and middle classes into corporate, professional, and business careers, the lower classes into service and low-grade technical jobs).

Classrooms come to be dominated by particular teaching practices that concentrate on definite content and skills that have to be learned and by student attitudes toward conformity, productivity, and other traits required for minimal participation in social, bureaucratic, and industrial organizations. Mainstream beliefs and values have to be taught; children from other cultures who bring to classrooms languages, habits, and attitudes different from what is taught in school have to be transformed into American citizens. A standard English has to be mastered; classroom habits of turntaking and remaining quiet for long periods of time, for example, must be learned.

Students who have already learned the necessary etiquette at home meet teachers' expectations. Many are placed in advanced reading groups and, in the higher grades, on college preparatory tracks. For students who come from cultures or socioeconomic backgrounds where these school demands are unfamiliar, adjustment is difficult. Many, but not all, of these students are labeled by teachers and administrators as "slow" learners or misfits and are assigned to particular groups within a classroom or to separate programs.

Certain teaching practices are practical for both groups, but especially for children who come from different socioeconomic backgrounds: arranging desks into rows to secure uniform behavior; relying on textbooks to yield reams of homework for which credit is given or withheld; giving tests and quizzes to permit the teacher to sort students by their achievement or lack of it; and having students follow teacher-directed procedures for seatwork, recitation, and reports. These dominant teacher-centered practices endure because they produce student behaviors consistent with the requirements of the larger society.

3. *If educational policymakers had effectively implemented reforms aimed at changing what teachers routinely do, changes in instructional practices would have occurred.*

When attentive policymakers systematically and thoroughly put into practice policies aimed at fundamentally altering teaching behaviors, classroom practices changed. But where policy effort were ill-conceived and partially or haphazardly implemented, teachers remained largely insulated from reformers' designs for basic classroom changes.

Flawed implementation of student-centered instructional reforms accounts for a durable core of teacher-centered instructional approaches. Had deliberate and comprehensive efforts been undertaken to implement instructional changes, many more of the reforms begun in the early 1900s and in the 1960s would be apparent in the 1990s. Where implementation was carefully planned and executed, teaching practices changed substantially.

Student-centered approaches, then, infrequently penetrated classrooms because of the inattentiveness, unwillingness, or inability of school officials to convert a policy decision or formal approval of an instructional change into a systematic process that would gain teacher support for classroom adoption.

4. *The organizational structure of the district, school, and classroom shaped teachers' dominant instructional practices.*

The organizational structures of a district and school steered teachers into adopting certain instructional strategies that varied little over time. "Structures" refers to how school space is arranged; how content and students are organized into grade levels; how time is allotted to tasks; and how organizational rules govern the behavior and performance of both adults and students. These structures result from the basic imperative of public schooling: to manage large numbers of students who are forced to attend school and absorb certain knowledge in an orderly fashion. The age-graded school, self-contained classrooms, a curriculum divided into levels, 50-minute periods, and large classes are structures that have developed over time to meet this basic imperative.

The classroom organization nested within the larger school structure assigns to the teacher the task of managing 25 to 40 or more students of approximately the same age who involuntarily spend—depending upon their age—anywhere from one to five hours daily in one room. The teacher is expected to maintain control, teach certain subject matter, motivate students to learn, vary levels of instruction according to student differences, and display evidence that students have performed satisfactorily.

Within these overlapping school and classroom structures, teachers have rationed their energy and time. They have coped with multiple and conflicting demands by inventing certain teaching practices that have emerged as resilient, imaginative, and efficient strategies for dealing with a large number of students in a small space for extended periods of time.

Rows of movable desks and seating charts, for example, permit the teacher easy surveillance to maintain order. The teacher's desk, usually located in a visually prominent part of the room near a chalkboard, underscores quietly who determines the direction for what the class will do each day. Class routines that require students to raise their hands to answer questions, to speak only when recognized by the teacher, and to speak when no one else is talking establish a framework for whole-group instruction. Requiring students to ask for permission to leave the room bolsters a teacher's control over students and maintains classroom order.

Within these structures, teaching the entire class together is an efficient and convenient use of the teacher's time—a valuable and scarce resource—to cover the mandated content and to maintain control. Lecturing, recitation, seatwork, homework drawn from texts, and weekly tests are efficient, uncomplicated ways of transmitting knowledge to groups and determining whether students have learned the material.

Student-centered approaches where students work together, move freely around the room, and determine certain classroom tasks for themselves make a shambles of classroom routines geared to handling batches of students. These approaches are incompatible with existing school and classroom structures and would require a complete overhaul of basic modes of classroom operation. Few teachers are willing to upset their controlled, familiar world for the uncertain benefits of a student-centered classroom.

This argument stresses that the structures of the age-graded school produce regularities in instruction. Past teachers coped with the dilemmas imposed by these structures, over which they had little control, by inventing creative compromises in the shape of teacher-centered instructional practices.

5. *The cultures of teaching that have developed within the occupation tilt toward stability in classroom practices.*

The occupational ethos of teaching breeds conservatism, that is, a preference for stability and a cautious attitude toward change. This conservatism is anchored in the very practice of teaching, in the people who enter the profession, in how they are informally socialized, and in the school culture of which teaching itself is a primary ingredient.

The aim of teaching is to change children into youth viewed as desirable by parents and society. Yet teachers are wholly dependent on their students for producing successful results. Moreover, as yet there is no societal consensus about what are the desired outcomes of teaching. Understandably, teachers are often reluctant to take risks by modifying practices, particularly by embracing student-centered instructional reforms, which place even more reliance upon students for results.

Who enters teaching is another factor encouraging conservatism within the occupation. Often newcomers seek contact with children, appreciate the flexible work schedule, and, while acknowledging the limited financial rewards, still embrace the service mission built into the occupation. Of the young who enter teaching, women outnumber men. Men often move out of the classroom in search of greater social recognition, more organizational influence, and higher salaries. Attracted by work schedules that permit flexible arrangements with regard to family obligations and vacations, women and men who do remain teachers have few incentives to alter occupational conditions or seek major improvements.

Furthermore, recruits to the occupation lean toward continuity because of their prior school experiences. As public school students for 12 years, future teachers unwittingly served an apprenticeship as they watched their teachers teach.

Thus, classroom practices tend to be stable over time. After all, homework assignments, discussion, seatwork, tests, and an occasional film to interrupt the routine were all methods familiar to teachers in their own schooling and, more often than not, seemed to keep the class moving along. Instead of fundamental changes—such as teaching small groups, integrating varied content into units, planning lessons with students, and letting class members choose what to do—the basic conservatism of the occupation would favor tinkering with methods, polishing up techniques, and introducing variations of existing ones.

6. *Teachers' knowledge of subject matter and their professional and personal beliefs about the role of the school in society, about classroom authority, and about children's ethnic and socioeconomic status shape classroom practices.*

What teachers know about a subject gets converted into teachable language and activities for children. A social studies teacher, for example, not only has content knowledge of, say, United States history, but also knows how to convey, to 15-year-olds uninterested in academic subjects or in going to college, what the Bill of Rights means to teenagers today, through concrete examples drawn from actual court cases. The images a biology teacher uses to illustrate the concept of evolution to sophomores in a college preparatory class are not drawn from a textbook but from the experience the teacher has had with previous students' struggles to understand the concept.

If content knowledge counts, so do the teacher's professional and personal beliefs about how children learn. An elementary school teacher who believes that children working together in small groups can learn from editing one another's writing will organize classroom furniture differently than a teacher who views learning as having pupils memorize editing rules. The teacher who looks for connections between textbook content and daily events because he or she believes that students absorb knowledge more easily when it is related to their lives will depart from the text far more often than others to explore these connections.

Finally, those teachers whose social attitudes lead them to seek contacts with higher- rather than lower-status children, with children more similar to their own ethnic, racial, or religious background, will approach choosing content, managing the classroom, and structuring activities differently in teaching low-income black or Hispanic pupils than in teaching affluent white or Asian-American students.

The knowledge, beliefs, and attitudes that teachers have, then, shape what they choose to do in their classrooms and explain both the constancy and the change that have shaped the core of instructional practices that have endured over time.

Note how the six explanations for how teachers teach include the environment (cultural inheritance and social functions of schools), the organizational (implementation of policies and the structures of schooling), occupational socialization (the nature of teaching, who enters the occupation, and future teachers' long apprenticeship of observing their elders), and, finally, the individual whose knowledge and beliefs shape classroom behavior. Four of the arguments try to explain why teacher-centered instruction endured; two (occasional implementation of classroom reform policies and teachers' knowledge and beliefs) suggest reasons why classroom changes may have occurred. I will elaborate on these explanations in the next-to-last chapter.

The book is divided into three sections. Part I covers 1890–1940 and consists of five chapters. Chapter 1 begins with a description of teaching at the turn of the century, including the progressive education reforms of those years. This description is followed by chapters on New York City, Denver, Colorado, and Washington, D.C., during the 1920s and 1930s. Chapter 5 describes rural schools in those decades and ends with a national survey of teaching practices. In Part II, Chapter 6 treats informal education between 1965 and 1975 in North Dakota, New York City, and Washington, D.C. Chapter 7 offers an intensive look at classroom teaching in the 1970s in one school district and then turns to the national scene of teaching in the 1980s. In the concluding section, Part III, Chapter 8 examines the six arguments that try, in the light of the evidence presented earlier in the study, to explain why teachers taught as they did. From these explanations I fashion one that explains both constancy and change in teaching practices. The last chapter explores the implications of the findings of this study for policymakers, practitioners, and scholars.

Earlier I compared my task to that of fossil seekers. Let me shift disciplines to use the image of a 13th-century cartographer trying to map a new world on the basis of what knowledge seafarers brought back, what had been written in books, and informed guesses. The maps he produced contained numerous mistakes and lies, and yet sea captains who used them explored the world and returned with new information that reshaped subsequent maps. This study is in the tradition of 13th-century mapmaking.

PART I

Progressivism and Classroom Practice, 1890–1940

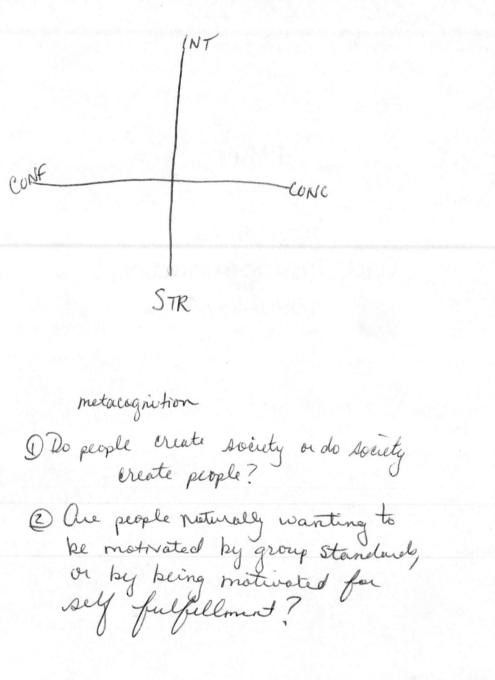

metacognition

① Do people create society or do society create people?

② Are people naturally wanting to be motivated by group standards, or by being motivated for self fulfillment?

CHAPTER 1

Teaching at the Turn of the Century: Tradition and Challenge

At P.S. 8 in New York City, William Chatfield taught the sixth grade. While he taught many subjects, he enjoyed the teaching of history enough to submit an article to *New York Teachers' Monographs,* a journal that printed contributions from city teachers. A glimpse of how Chatfield taught his sixth graders history in 1900 emerges from his description.

> The general method has been to first furnish the pupils with an outline of the work to be covered and to assign lessons from the text in conformity with this, and then to lead them by conversations to discover the reasons to think out the results.
>
> A part of the time each week is given to oral instruction and at the end of the week a written exercise is required of each pupil. In this he attempts to show what he has gathered from the oral work, his reading and the text book.
>
> Maps and pictures are freely used to illustrate the work, the former being drawn upon the blackboard and copied by the pupil. Upon these maps are indicated the movements of the opposing forces; and brief statements are made of the events which have made certain places and localities noted. The pictures are gathered from many sources and are distributed in the class.

Chatfield pointed out how he connected the climate and geography to what people did for a living. Finally, "to leave a lasting impression, the principal events are memorized in chronological order."[1]

I know little else about William Chatfield or his thousands of colleagues across the New York City schools. Few historians know what happened in those classrooms. Much is known about school—who went to school, how schools were operated, who was in charge, who taught, and what was taught—yet little is known of what teachers did in their classrooms. The few historians who have studied practice prior to the progressives' involvement with public schools have reconstructed a partial picture of classroom activities from teacher biographies, journalists' accounts, student recollections, popular textbooks on pedagogy, visitors' impressions, and the organizational context within which teachers worked (i.e., class size, room arrangement, age-graded schools, courses of study, and school board rules). Reconstructing what happened in classrooms at the turn of century requires a brief description of the schooling enterprise itself.[2]

ELEMENTARY SCHOOL CLASSROOMS

Public schools in 1890 were diverse. For example, in that year there were 224,526 school buildings housing almost 13 million pupils in elementary schools (including grades 7 and 8) and 222,000 students in high schools. Together these students constituted 69% of the population aged 5–17. Over 77% of the children attended school in rural areas, then defined as districts outside towns and cities of 4,000 or more people.[3]

By the 1890s over a half century had already passed since the common school movement had spread across a growing nation. Urban public schools had established policies and practices that would be familiar to observers a century later. Schools were age-graded. School was in session 9 months out of each year. Teachers were expected to have had some formal training beyond a grammar or high school education. Each teacher had a classroom to herself (by 1890, two out of every three elementary school teachers were female; 60% of high school staffs were also female). Rows of desks bolted to the floor faced a teacher's desk and blackboard (movable desks were introduced in the early 1900s but did not become commonplace until the mid-1930s). Courses of study set the boundaries and expectations for what had to be taught and when. Report cards and homework had already become standard features of urban classrooms in the 1890s. In brief, a terrain familiar to teachers and students today had been constructed a century earlier in urban schools.[4]

But rural schools differed. By 1890, rural school boards spent $13.23 per pupil while city boards spent $28.87. In particular, one-room school-houses received less of everything. They were housed in older, makeshift facilities with insufficient books, supplies, and equipment. In these ungraded schools, teachers with little formal education coped with 5-year-olds and young adults simultaneously. Students attended school fewer weeks a year than their urban cousins. These schools, soon to become the object of a vigorous campaign of consolidation, were the places where most Americans were taught. By 1910 rural schools still enrolled only two of every three children; per-pupil expenditure had increased to $26.13 but remained well below the $45.74 that city systems spent.[5]

What did teachers do in these urban and rural classrooms? Did teaching differ by setting? According to Barbara Finkelstein, who examined almost 1,000 contemporary descriptions of elementary school classrooms between 1820 and 1880, teachers talked a great deal. Students recited passages from textbooks, worked at their desks on assignments, or listened to the teacher and classmates during the time set aside for instruction. Teachers assigned work and expected uniformity from students both in behavior and in classwork. Teachers told students "when they should sit, when they should stand, when they should hang their coats, when they should turn their heads. . . ." Students often entered and exited the room, rose and sat, wrote and spoke—as one. "North and south, east and west, in rural schools as well as urban schools," Finkelstein writes,

> teachers assigned lessons, asked questions and created standards of achievement designed to compel students to assimilate knowledge and practice skills in a particular fashion. It was a fashion dictated by the textbooks usually—and often with dogmatic determination.[6]

Finkelstein found three patterns of teaching in these elementary schools. The "Intellectual Overseer" assigned work, punished errors, and made students memorize. The "Drillmaster" led students in unison through lessons requiring them to repeat content aloud. A third pattern, "Interpreters of Culture," she found only occasionally. Here the teacher would clarify ideas and explain content to children. Finkelstein found less than a half dozen descriptions of this type of teaching.[7]

Documenting these patterns, Finkelstein provides richly detailed accounts of monitorial schools established in cities by Joseph Lancaster and his followers in the 1820s, where group recitations and standardized behavior were routine, and rural one-room schools, where individual students sat before the teacher on a recitation bench and raced through their memorized text selections in the few minutes they had with the teacher. Consistently, Finkelstein stresses that the regularities in teaching she found crossed geographical and organizational boundaries. The settings, she concluded, had little to do with what the teachers did in their classrooms. Nor did she find much change over time. "One gets the impression," she writes, "that there was little linear change in the conduct of classrooms in the period from 1820 to 1880." Carl

Kaestle, however, notes that in those decades there was less corporal punishment, more uniformity in texts, some grouping by ability, and more grading of levels. Also, most of the city schools that had adopted Lancastrian methods in the 1820s and 1830s had dropped this form of school organization and teaching by the 1850s.[8]

Other primary sources confirm the existence of two of the patterns Finkelstein identified, the Overseer and the Drillmaster. Articles written by New York City grammar school teachers in 1900, for example, describe how they taught composition, science, geography, and arithmetic. These accounts reveal reliance upon whole-group instruction, drill, and recitation; uniformity in practice turns up repeatedly in these self-reports of classroom practice. A sizable number of teachers, however, seem to have embodied the Interpreter of Culture type. They tell how they used various materials in addition to the text, modified lessons to fit children's interests, and developed new topics for students to pursue. Note that these reports came two decades after the period Finkelstein studied.[9]

Photographs of elementary school classrooms were posed, since the camera technology of the period required subjects to remain immobile for 20 or more seconds while the film was exposed. Typically, these photographs show rows of children with hands folded atop their desks staring into the camera, with a teacher standing nearby. Occasionally activities are depicted. One Washington, D.C., photograph shows 27 children sitting at their desks, cheeks puffed up, ready for the teacher's command to blow on the pinwheel each child is holding in both hands. In the vast majority of these photos the teacher is the center of attention; sometimes a student under the watchful gaze of the teacher writes on the chalkboard, recites a passage, or reads to the class. Exceptions can be seen, however, in a series of posed black-and-white photographs taken in 1899 in Washington, D.C., classrooms to portray the "New Education."

Out of almost 300 prints of elementary school classrooms, nearly 30 show groups of students working with large relief maps in geography, preserved rabbits and squirrels being used for a lesson, students watching a teacher carve into a cow's heart to show the parts of the organ, and classes taking a trip to the zoo. The remaining 90% of the prints show students sitting in rows at their desks doing uniform tasks at the teacher's direction.[10]

Corroborating photos and teachers' descriptions are the pen portraits of elementary school classrooms drawn by Joseph Mayer Rice, the pediatrician-journalist who observed 1,200 teachers in 36 cities during a six-month period in 1892. Rice's articles in a popular magazine painted teaching in urban schools as grim, dreary, and mechanical (the latter being a favorite epithet of his). Instruction was married to drill and singsong recitations from children who lacked the faintest understanding of what they were saying, Rice said.[11]

PLATE 1.1 *Washington, D.C. elementary schools, Black, 1900*

As a self-proclaimed reformer, Rice described in minute detail the deadening drill and "busywork" students mindlessly pursued at the teacher's order. In Boston, Rice witnessed a teacher beginning the lesson with the question:

"With how many senses do we study geography?"
"With three senses: sight, hearing, and touch," answered the students. The children were now told to turn to the map of North America in their geographies, and to begin with the capes on the eastern coast. When the map had been found each pupil placed his forefinger upon "Cape Farewell" and when the teacher said "Start," the pupils said in concert, "Cape Farewell," and then ran their fingers down the map, calling out the names of each cape as it was touched. . . . After the pupils had named all the capes on the eastern coast of North America, beginning at the north and ending at the south, they were told to close their books. When the books had been closed, they ran their fingers down the cover and named from memory the capes in their order from north to south.
"How many senses are you using now?" the teacher asked.
"Two senses—touch and hearing," answered the children.[12]

PLATE 1.2 *Washington, D.C. elementary schools, White, 1900*

In New York City, Rice spoke with a principal about securing unquestioned obedience to a teacher's orders. When he asked her whether the children in a certain classroom were allowed to turn their heads, the principal responded, "Why should they look behind them when the teacher is in front of them?" [13]

In 6 months of school visits Rice found untrained teachers, unimaginative methods, and textbook-bound instruction in most classrooms except in a few cities that he extolled. I will return to these exceptions later in this chapter.

Other sources, such as surveys of school conditions conducted by the school experts of the day, also document the existence of the teaching types that Finkelstein found. For example, in the 1913 survey of the Portland, Oregon schools, directed by Ellwood P. Cubberley, the survey team visited 50 elementary school classes in nine schools. Except for teachers in the primary grades, the observers were highly critical of the instruction they saw. Some excerpts:

[Geography:] All the work observed . . . was abstract and bookish in the extreme. . . . The assignment for study and the questions, almost without exception, called for unreasoning memorization of the statements of the book.

[Arithmetic and grammar:] The teaching of these subjects seemed, on the whole, to be the best teaching observed. It is true that much of the technical grammar had little meaning for most of the children. . . .

[History:] There was not the slightest evidence of active interest in the subject; the one purpose seemed to be to acquire, by sheer force of memory, the statements of the assigned text. . . . [14]

Newton, Massachusetts, Superintendent Frank Spaulding drafted the report on elementary school instruction. "Passive, routine, clerical," he wrote, "are the terms that most fittingly describe the attitude of principals and grammar grade teachers toward their work." Except for one lesson "in all of my visits to grammar-grade rooms, I heard not a single question asked by a pupil, not a single remark or comment made to indicate that the pupil had any really vital interest in the subject matter." [15]

PLATE 1.3 *Washington, D.C. elementary schools, White, 1900; teacher dissecting heart with students gathered around*

While the survey report blamed a "mechanical system" of courses of study and quarterly examinations for suffocating imaginative teaching, the evidence contained in the report presents difficulties for a reader because it is impossible to gauge precisely whether conclusions apply to all, most, or merely some classrooms. Even more difficult for the reader is to disentangle these experts' desire for improvement from what they saw.

Additional data, however, do come from various articles and books by educators about teaching methods in these years. Take, for example, Vivian Thayer's *The Passing of the Recitation*. A professor who sought to make curriculum child-centered, Thayer traces the history of the recitation—a reform initially introduced to improve instruction by reducing lecturing and increasing student involvement—to its use in 1928, when the book was published.

Thayer points out how the child-centered ideas of Swiss reformer Johann Pestalozzi, as translated by his followers in Oswego Training School (New York) and elsewhere in the 1860s, were disseminated throughout the country. Yet within a few decades adherents of "object teaching" were being accused of "mechanizing instruction." Similarly, enthusiastic American followers of Johann Frederich Herbart took his description of how the child's mind worked and by the 1890s, according to Thayer, had transformed these ideas into a "method of instruction which requires that children, in the acquisition of new knowledge, move in lockstep fashion through five steps in learning." Detailed lesson plans included exact actions to be taken by the teacher, devices for holding the class's attention, and carefully crafted assignments. Thayer observes that in classrooms such techniques centered even more attention upon the teacher, which in turn tended to increase the teacher's influence.[16]

After summarizing the ideas of major 19th-century educational thinkers and their impact upon practice, particularly the recitation, Thayer concludes that by the 1920s,

> the developments since Lancaster [had] led to little more than pouring of new wine into old bottles. We teach different subjects and we have altered the content of old subjects. We have originated more economical devices for learning and we have profited from careful studies in the technique of acquiring skill and information. We classify and grade our pupils more skillfully. But withal we have not fundamentally reconstructed the recitation system which Lancaster devised a little more than a century ago.[17]

Although other evidence drawn from teachers' working conditions and their training only indirectly identifies classroom practices, it does suggest what teaching practices might be linked to common organizational features such as class size, textbooks, and the education of teachers.

Urban classrooms had between 40 and 48 desks per room, accommodating up to 60 students. Estimates of class size at the turn of the century are approximate but suggest that few desks were long empty, especially in rapidly growing cities of the Northeast and Midwest. To staff these crowded classrooms, teachers had to be found who could survive and stay. Yet teaching was an insecure job. School trustees decided each year whether or not a teacher would be rehired. Political and family ties played a disproportionate role in appointments. Moreover, the jobs demanded much from applicants who often lacked advanced education. Teachers expected to cover up to 10 subjects daily were often themselves not educated beyond the grammar or high school level.[18]

With a largely untrained corps of teachers expected to teach a variety of subjects and skills it comes as no surprise that textbooks flourished. By the 1880s textbooks had already become the teacher's primary tool and the student's main source of knowledge. Published courses of study also determined for teachers what had to be taught and when. These syllabi were often stuffed with page listings from textbooks for each subject.[19]

Exactly how powerful these workplace conditions were in shaping how teachers organized their classrooms for instruction is difficult to estimate. That class size, prescribed texts and curriculum, and limited education had some influence, however, is obvious from elementary school teachers' accounts of these conditions as factors affecting their work in classrooms.[20]

Were high school classrooms at the beginning of the 20th century similar to those in elementary schools?

HIGH SCHOOL CLASSROOMS

In 1890 just over 220,000 students attended 2,526 high schools for an average of 86 days a year, although attendance varied by region in the nation. A decade later, enrollments had increased sharply to 519,251 in just over 6,000 high schools. New schools were appearing at the average rate of one per day. Uncommon as it was for a 17-year-old to attend high school, it was even more unusual for that teenager to graduate. Of the 220,000 who went to high school in 1890, representing 3.5% of the total population of that age group, only 11% graduated. Of those who went to school and received diplomas, females outnumbered males two to one.[21]

High school teachers had more training and education than their grammar school colleagues. In New England, to cite one instance, 56% of the teachers were college graduates and 21% had done some work beyond high school. In Buffalo, New York, of the 182 high school teachers active in 1914, 72% had graduated either from college or from a formal teacher training school.[22]

Education beyond high school was often necessary for teachers since they were called upon to teach many subjects. Since half of the high schools enrolled less than 100 students, often one or two teachers taught the entire curriculum. For example, 23 of 59 Connecticut high schools had one or two instructors teaching the complete course of study. To cite a case, Henry King of Albany, Missouri, taught botany, zoology, Latin, history, English, etymology, and arithmetic. In city high schools, enrollments were larger and by the early 20th century faculties were organized into departments.[23]

The curriculum was geared to prepare students for college. In 1893, 44% of high school students took Latin; 56% studied algebra. In 1900, most students enrolled in English, U.S. and British history, algebra, geometry, Latin, earth science, and physiology. College entrance exams shaped the course of study and activities as much as did the rhythm of the school year.[24]

And teaching? If few historians studied elementary school classrooms at this time, none has yet examined those in secondary schools. Clues do appear: For example, photographs of classrooms show rows of bolted-down desks; in some newly built schools rooms were set aside for "recitation"; and master schedules typically allotted the major portion of time to teachers' asking questions of students. Beyond these clues, little is known about what happened in these classrooms. Although the major focus of this study is on the period after 1920, I offer a few vignettes that may suggest a partial picture of classroom practices.

Dayton, Ohio, had only one high school: Steele. In 1896, Steele High School was the subject of a detailed report by Malcolm Booth at the end of his first year as its principal. Submitted to the superintendent, Booth's report describes working conditions at Steele and what teachers reported they did in their classrooms.

Steele High School enrolled 846 students (60% of them female) in 1895–1896, an academic year lasting 36 weeks, a month less than the previous year. The 1896 graduating class had 92 students, of whom 71% were female. That year for the first time the high school was open continuously from 8:30 a.m. to 1:00 p.m. instead of having two separate sessions. The school day was divided into six periods of 41 minutes each running back-to-back except for a 15-minute recess between 11:18 and 11:33.[25]

The curriculum contained four courses of study (classical, scientific, English, and commercial) covering 4 years. The principal's report outlined the content of each subject, including the textbooks used, assignments, and what was expected of students. To teach over 25 required courses to over 800 students, there were 26 teachers, 38% of them female. They taught six periods daily (with about 30 students in each class). These six classes seldom meant teaching the same lesson six times. While Mr. Kincaid in the Classical Department, for example, taught only two subjects, Latin and Greek, he probably had five different lessons to teach daily: senior Latin, junior Latin, second-year Greek, first-year Latin, and junior Greek. Each class had different texts and requirements. Junior Greek, for example, included in the "Outline of Courses of Study" the notation "(5)," which meant that Mr. Kincaid was expected to hold five recitations per week.[26]

The teaching of botany, physiology, geometry, Latin, Greek, and advanced German demanded an education beyond grammar school. Of Steele's faculty, 54% had graduated from college, 15% had attended either normal school or college, and the remainder had finished high school.[27]

Some hints of what occurred during the 41-minute class periods surface in course descriptions that teachers submitted to the principal. English teacher Charles Loos, an 1869 graduate of Bethany College (West Virginia) and an eight-year veteran of Steele, was one of the three highest-paid staff, earning $1,500 per year. He described the methods English teachers used to teach mythology to juniors and seniors:

> The myths are to be studied at home and recited topically, none being omitted or left to careless reading. . . . The myths must be reproduced as exercises in narration, comparison, and description. . . . This study is to to be

PLATE 1.4 *Washington, D.C., Western High School, 1900; chemistry lesson*

PLATE 1.5 *Washington, D.C., 1899?; biology class*

accompanied by constant exercise in composition, both written and oral, with special emphasis upon good sentence structure and pronunciation.[28]

In teaching the novel, Loos and other English teachers planned the following:

> In recitation the class must be prepared to give an outline of the part studied and show its connection with what has preceded: to discuss the characters as they appear, [and] show how they affect other characters and the plot in general. . . . The recitation should cover oral and written reports, rapid questioning, informal discussion and the reading aloud of certain illustrative passages.[29]

Physics and botany teacher August Foerste, a Harvard Ph.D. (1890), who had been appointed to Steele in 1893, wrote to Booth that science instruction had improved with the Board of Education's recent purchase of equipment:

> With this apparatus it was possible for the teacher to perform, in the presence of the class, most of the experiments mentioned in the book. The pu-

pils were required to make notes during the experiment, and then to describe it at length in their note book.[30]

Foerste urged the purchase of more equipment so that students could work individually and create projects such as "an electric bell and burglar alarm, a telegraph sounder and relay, and a telephone" as "practical applications of physical laws." These ideas, he said, "are not wild." It is not essential for the "pupil to be a skilled mechanic in order to make them a success *educationally*" (original emphasis). This teacher's concern for practical application of knowledge and projects worked on by individual students was unique among reports submitted to the principal.[31]

Although Marie Durst, at Steele for eight years, included in her report on French and German a concern for daily usage of language, she said that "most of the classes in modern languages are too large. The teacher has no opportunity for giving any individual attention." Instruction, she said, is given in the language to be taught and "the pupils are led to express themselves in that language as soon as they have acquired a sufficient vocabulary." For grammar and translation, Durst used dictations frequently since "they train the ear to the strange sounds and require the strictest attention." Also, she added, students learn correct pronunciation and fluent speech by "memorizing and reciting selections of high literary merit." Such reports reveal teacher intentions and indirectly describe practice. No verification of what happened in Durst's classes, however, is available.[32]

A decade later, in another city, a professor did go into classes and reported what she saw and heard. Romiett Stevens visited an unspecified number of schools in and around New York City between 1907 and 1911 to study teacher use of questions. Using a stopwatch and a stenographer, she observed 100 English, history, math, foreign language, and science teachers whom principals had identified as superior. She recorded the number of questions that they asked. In a related study, she followed 10 classes through each period of the day to get a sense of the aggregate impact of teacher questioning on students.[33]

Stevens found that teachers asked an average of two to three questions per minute; the average number of questions that students faced daily totaled 395. The lowest number of questions per period that she found in the 100 classrooms was 25; the highest, 200. "The teacher," she commented, "who has acquired the habit of conducting recitations at the rate of from 100 to 200 questions and answers per classroom period of 45 minutes has truly assumed the pace that kills." Of the 100 teachers she visited, 28 asked questions at that tempo.[34]

With teacher questioning dominant, Stevens calculated exactly how much time during a lesson was devoted to teacher talk and how much to student talk. Using 20 stenographic reports, she found that teachers were talking 64% of the time. Of the 36% of utterances generated by students, many were brief, usually one-word responses or short sentences. There were exceptions, however. Of the 34 questions asked in one science class, 25 came from students. In a history lesson, the teacher let the students use the textbook while the class answered questions. General practice, according to Stevens, was for students to close the text once the teacher began asking questions.[35]

Stevens disliked rapid-fire teacher questioning where "pupils follow as a body, or drop by the wayside." To ask two to three questions a minute, "we commit ourselves as 'drivers' of youth instead of 'leaders,' " she wrote. With teachers assigning lessons as homework, students taking the book home to memorize the lesson, and teachers telling students the next day to close their books and recite answers, Stevens concluded that teachers were "drillmasters instead of educators."[36]

Three years after Stevens's study was published, the New York State Commissioner of Education's staff completed a survey of Buffalo, New York, schools. A portion of that report deals with high schools.

In 1914, Buffalo had four high schools with 182 teachers. "Inspectors," as members of the survey team were called, visited the classrooms of all teachers and reported their conclusions. Some excerpts suggest patterns although specific figures are missing in the report. For example, after visiting each of 25 English teachers three times for at least 15 minutes on each occasion, the inspectors assessed their teaching of grammar as follows:

> Instruction in grammar is usually much too detailed and formal. It is composed largely of such work as copying, composing, and correcting short illustrative sentences, selecting single types of constructions from sentences frequently too easy for the pupil, completing elliptical sentences, memorizing terms and definitions, diagramming and parsing in routine fashion.[37]

Of the 23 teachers of modern languages (Spanish, French, and German), the inspectors observed that "the usual method was to have one pupil read a paragraph, then to put a few simple questions to him about the part read, then to ask for forms and explanations of syntax." The survey team judged that assignments were often ambiguous and recitations poorly delivered, except in the case of four teachers whom they praised. "Usually the teacher sat uncomfortably behind her desk and let the pupils answer the questions."[38]

State Department officials observed 32 math teachers. Recitation, again, was the primary teaching method. Most math teachers, the report stated, "called on most of the pupils for some part of the recitation." Inspectors criticized math instruction in the four high schools for giving insufficient attention to preparing students for the new material to be covered the next day.[39]

Science teachers impressed the inspectors. Student time in the classes of the 15 teachers was divided between laboratory and recitations. In labs, students worked on completing exercises using equipment and facilities that the observers deemed adequate. "There was little evidence," they reported, "of slavish following of directions. . . ." For recitations, the "questioning was well calculated to test both the memory of a statement and ability to apply the definitions and principles." In two classes, the lesson consisted of student reports. "This appeared to be the habitual practice," the inspectors wrote. In other classes student responsibility was less defined, "with the result that the recitation became a lecture punctuated by occasional questions." In a number of classes teachers and students worked with "splendid enthusiasm."[40]

History instruction was also viewed favorably by the team of observers. Except for the minority of classes (no number was specified) in which teaching was "formal and mechanical" because it limited itself to the text and notebook work, the majority of "skillful" teachers used maps, discussions, debates, field trips, and other topics in the curriculum to make history "vivid and interesting."[41]

Such evidence of high school teaching drawn from surveys, reports, visitors' impressions, and photographs is piecemeal. It is suggestive but not comprehensive. Yet even from this broad outline certain teaching patterns emerge.

SIMILARITIES AND DIFFERENCES IN INSTRUCTION

When elementary and high school instruction are examined together, similarities appear. Generally, teachers taught the entire class at the same time. Teacher talk dominated verbal expression during class time. Classroom activities revolved around teacher questions and explanations, student recitations, and the class's working on textbook assignments. Except for laboratory work in science classrooms, teachers sought uniformity in behavior. The social organization of the turn-of-the-century classroom, then, was formal, with students sitting in rows of bolted-down desks facing the teacher's desk and chalkboard, rising to recite for the teacher, and moving about the room or leaving it only with the teacher's permission. The academic organization of the classroom hinged upon the whole class's moving as one through the course of study, text, recitations, and homework. Those who worked, succeeded; those who didn't, failed.

While similar in many ways, the two levels of instruction differed in some respects. Subject matter was stressed far more in the higher grades than in lower ones. Teaching was fragmented in high schools as students traveled from class to class to meet with five or more teachers in a given day, spending about an hour at a time with each. This was not the case at the elementary school, where the teacher would spend all day with the same students. Classes in high school were smaller than in elementary schools, and high school teachers had more formal education than their colleagues in the lower grades.

Considering the similarities and differences, the available evidence shows that teacher-centered instruction, as defined by the above categories, clearly dominated classroom instruction. Embedded within teacher-centered instruction were assumptions about the social and economic role of schools, knowledge, children, and learning consistent with the profound changes occurring at the turn of the century in the larger society. Schools were expected not only to build citizens but also to teach students the skills needed to work in an increasingly complex industrial society. Both corporate and school leaders prized notions of efficient bureaucracies and anything viewed as "scientific." School officials and teachers came to share many of these beliefs. The importance of certain subjects in Americanizing Southern and Eastern European immigrants, for example, gained vigorous support from teachers and administrators. Moreover, the infant science of educational psychology theorized that children learned best through repetition and memorization. These beliefs, reinforced by the scientific knowledge of the day about learning, anchored teacher-centered instruction deeply in the minds of teachers and administrators at the turn of the century.[42] And yet, as dominant as that tradition of teaching was, a competing form of social and academic classroom organization also existed at the turn of the century.

STUDENT-CENTERED INSTRUCTION

Two versions of student-centered instruction existed in public schools in the late 19th century. A commonsense, atheoretical, practical version had appeared in rural one-room schools, due in large part to the conditions existing in those settings. The lack of materials, isolation from inspection, and group spirit fostered by flexible teachers produced classrooms where students helped one another, moved easily around the classroom, received individual attention from the teacher, and learned content drawn from community life.

A more prominent and more theoretical version of student-centered instruction was embodied in innovations tried in small, mostly private schools. The origins of this version can be traced back to Socrates, Jesus of Nazareth, and Jean-Jacques Rousseau's *Emile*. The approach was elaborated further by educational reformers Friedrich Froebel and Johann Pestalozzi. In America the conversion of these reformers' ideas into a pedagogy that viewed the child, not the teacher or the subject, as central to instruction occurred through the work of Edward Sheldon, Francis Parker, John Dewey, and their earnest disciples, who spread interpretations of each man's work throughout the country. No one definition of student-centered instruction, the "New Education" that Joseph Mayer Rice promoted, or progressivism bound these men together other than the conviction that schools could transform children's lives and, ultimately, the larger society.

The point of reviewing, however briefly, the work of Sheldon, Parker, and Dewey is to establish that a defensible tradition of student-centered instruction existed and was practiced in schools operated by these educators and their followers throughout the late 19th and early 20th centuries.

Edward Sheldon

Edward Sheldon, teacher of orphans, organizer and secretary of a public school system, fervently embraced Pestalozzi's ideas and applied them to schools in the mid-19th century. "Object teaching," as the principles of the Swiss reformer came to be called by Sheldon and others, concentrated upon children's experience, perceptions, and language to develop in an orderly manner their powers of reasoning. A child's experience was supposed to replace books; how a child developed was to replace courses of study; and the teacher's careful direction of instruction was to replace recitation.[43]

Enthusiasm for "object teaching" penetrated magazines, books, conferences on teaching, reports, and elementary school courses of study, especially in arithmetic, geography, and science. In classrooms, however, object teaching became, in Thayer's phrase, "dismal formalism." Reprints of actual lessons reveal teachers asking questions about objects, adding little knowledge to students' understanding, and controlling the entire pace and structure of the lesson. Examples in lessons used at Oswego State Normal and Training School in New York in the 1860s contained specific points that teachers were expected to make in class and clear directions of how to lead students to correct observations. These directions resemble scripts.[44]

While object teaching was still evident by 1900, it was often indistinguishable from the dreary recitations that Rice and other critics condemned. Nonetheless, the ideas about children's development and expression underlying object teaching had had an impact. Perhaps that may explain the letter Sheldon received in 1886 from the principal of the Cook County Normal School, Francis Wayland Parker.

Francis Parker

"You," Parker wrote to Edward Sheldon, "touched every child in America." Strong praise, indeed, from the person John Dewey called the "Father of Progressivism." Parker had taught in country schools. During the Civil War he served in the Union Army, rising to the rank of colonel and suffering serious wounds to the throat. After returning to teaching, he soon became principal of a normal school in Ohio. His wife died shortly thereafter. Using a trust fund that a relative had left him, Parker went to Europe to study both philosophy and pedagogy. Coming back to America, he could not find a position until School Board President Charles Francis Adams, Jr., invited him in 1873 to Quincy, Massachusetts.[45]

In the years that he served Quincy as superintendent, a school system with 40 teachers and 1,600 students in seven schools including a high school, Parker changed the curriculum, methods of instruction, and materials. Within a few years, Quincy became a mecca for educators interested in the "New Education," as one admirer of Parker called it. Parker disclaimed any innovations, saying:

> I repeat that I am simply trying to apply well established principles, principles derived directly from the laws of the mind. The methods springing from them are found in the development of every child. They are used everywhere except in school. I have introduced no new method or detail. No experiments have been tried, and there is no peculiar "Quincy System."

Perhaps. But John Dewey, in a speech on Parker's work in Quincy, asked: "Did you ever hear of a man, who starting as superintendent of schools had reached a point in his career 25 years later where the anniversary of that beginning was an event to be marked by the educators of the nation?"[46]

Parker went on to serve as principal of the Cook County Normal School, which eventually became Chicago State University. He served as principal and director for almost two decades before his death in 1902. In the "practice school" Parker and his staff, many of whom were graduates of the Oswego Normal School, developed instructional and curricular techniques that brought to life "Parker's" oft-quoted sentence: "The child is the center of all education."[47]

In the 1880s the eight-grade school had a kindergarten, a library, a printing plant to provide classroom materials and publish teacher-written units, physical education equipment, manual training, and 20 acres of nearby land that became a center for nature study. Parker believed in integrating the various subjects ("correlation" was the word used then). Enabling children to see connections between science, art, math, and geography and express these connections became one of the school's achievements. Beyond linking subjects, teaching basic skills through integrated content, relying heavily upon expression through art, music, and drama, the school also taught cooking, sewing, pottery-making, weaving, gardening, and bookbinding.[48]

When a veteran school superintendent visited classrooms at the Normal School in 1892, he went away impressed by how easily and without any obvious coercion students did what practitioners in public schools called "busy-work." Superintendent J. W. Greenwood of Kansas City, Missouri, saw no fear of the teacher in children. No copying occurred. Work was done rapidly, without any apparent direction from the teacher. Each student "goes at it in a hurry and rushes 'his job' along. It is the kindergarten idea carried up through the grades." In the upper grades, Greenwood observed practices that were similar to laboratory work, "each [student] keeping a record of his own experiments." The grim, uniform recitation with which the Kansas City school chief was familiar appeared to be absent from Parker's school. Greenwood, like thousands of other visitors including school reformer Joseph Rice, went away quite taken with the Colonel's achievements.[49]

When Parker died, memorial services were held at the University of Chicago. John Dewey spoke:

> Twenty-five years ago, in Quincy, Massachusetts, the work he undertook was the object of derision. . . . To many he seemed a faddist, a fanatic. It was twenty-five years ago; and yet the things for which he then stood are taken today almost as a matter of course, without debate, in all the best schools of the country.[50]

Dewey knew Parker well. When Dewey moved his family to Chicago in 1894, he enrolled his son, Fred, in the first grade of the Practice School. The next year, Fred's sister Evelyn attended the school. When Dewey and his wife began an experimental school, they took their children out of Parker's school and entered them in their new Laboratory School at the University of Chicago.

John Dewey

Far more has been written about Dewey than about Sheldon and Parker. Rather than try to recapture the essence of Dewey's career as an influential theorist and practitioner, a task that others have done, I will mention briefly the years between 1896 and 1903 when he led the experimental school. In the Laboratory School he worked directly with children, teachers, and parents, turning his ideas of learning and child development into classroom practice.

In reading through teacher recollections, courses of study, teacher reports, and student memoirs it is easy to conclude that the Laboratory School, with its curriculum centered upon the work that people did rather than upon separate subjects, upon reading and writing learned through activities rather than through isolated tasks, and upon groupwork guided rather than directed by teachers, was just another progressive school. That would be a mistake. In the 1890s there were few schools in the country, public or private, that gambled on centering a curriculum around children's interests in adult work, family and community ties, group cooperation, and democratic practices geared toward larger social goals. As a private school of 140 children (in 1900) and 23 teachers (including Ella Flagg Young as supervisor of instruction, and later Chicago superintendent of schools), the Laboratory School was openly experimental, advancing ideas and trying innovations that would become familiar, if not clichéd, a generation later.

A snapshot of the first few months of the school year for Group III, the 6-year-olds, should convey a sense of the school, at least through former teachers' eyes. Daily the class would gather and review the previous day's work and plan for the day, "each child being encouraged to contribute." The day's work was decided upon and distributed by the pupils. At the end of the period, another group meeting summarized the results of the work and suggested new plans. An example of a project planned and executed by the children was a miniature farm, including a house, a barn, and cultivated land, made out of large blocks, twigs, and soil. The children discussed and drew up plans using rulers to make the model to scale. This group also cleaned up a 5-by-10-foot space in the school yard to plant winter wheat. As they proceeded through the school year, the class discussed plowing, what seeds to plant, how to plant, harvesting, and using the grain to make flour and then bread. "When they talked about grains in the classroom," a teacher wrote, "they cooked cereals in the kitchen." Measuring and other uses of numbers were easily incorporated into building the farm model and producing the winter wheat.[51]

During these first months of school an interest in reading also developed, according to the teachers, who wrote of the children:

> All the things they had found in their outdoor excursions were placed on a table. Sentences were written on the board, such as: 'Find a cocoon,' and the child who could read it was allowed to run and get the cocoon. After playing this game a few times, the same sentences were shown printed in large type, so that they could get the printed form simultaneously with the script. They seemed very eager to read and decided themselves to make a weekly record of their work.[52]

For older students, the same focus upon active involvement, adult occupations, group discussions, and decisionmaking with the teacher acting as a coach prevailed. Table 1.1 displays the typical program for 9- to 12-year-olds.

Opportunities to make decisions, use manual skills learned in classrooms, and work cooperatively presented themselves, for example, in a schoolwide project of building a clubhouse where students in the Camera and Dewey (debating and discussion) clubs could meet. Mayhew and Edwards wrote that this "enterprise was the most thoroughly considered one ever

TABLE 1.1 *Program for 9–12-year-olds in laboratory school*

Subject	Hours/day	Hours/week
History and geography	1	5
Techniques (reading, writing)	.5	2.5
Science or	1.5	2 or 2.5
Cooking or		1.5
Textile or shop		2
Art		1.5
Music	1 or .5	1.5
Gymnasium		2.5
Modern languages	.5	2.5
Total hours	4.5	21.5

undertaken by the school." Because it provided a home for clubs away from the main building, "it drew together many groups and ages and performed a distinctly ethical and cultural service."[53]

Writing in 1930, former student Josephine Crane recalled what she had learned at the Laboratory School:

> First as to the sciences, no matter how young we were—too young to understand very much—we were given a chance to use our eyes, to observe the facts of nature more closely. . . . Secondly, the activities—carpentry, cooking, weaving, sewing, art—all trained our hands and fingers to be useful. . . . People have often asked me where I learned to use my hands, and how it is I so easily learn to do new things with my hands. I tell them it is because I was trained to use my mind and hands and eyes together. I was trained to observe and given a chance to use what I observed in what I did. Third, the building of the clubhouse—the real and practical work—helped us to see what architecture really is. We got far more out of that than out of books.
>
> Fourth, I learned responsibility. When I was quite young, I was asked to teach art for two months to a younger class. . . . When I went into the room for the first time I had to realize that I must do something! I learned how to teach that way and this is responsibility finally realized.[54]

For teachers and students the Laboratory School was an exciting place. Grace Fulmer, a teacher at the school who left to direct a similar school in Los Angeles, recalled her two years (1900–1902) working under John Dewey:

> It was Mr. Dewey's idea that each child should be free to develop his own powers to some ultimate purpose through the guidance of one whose ex-

perience was richer. Such also was his own relation to the teachers in his school. I know there were things in my own work of which he did not approve and yet I always felt free to work on my own. . . .

The Dewey School, as it was so often called by teachers and friends, lost its namesake in 1904 when he accepted an appointment at Teachers College, Columbia University.[55]

Beyond the direct efforts of these men, there were public schools that partially or thoroughly implemented the "New Education," or "scientific pedagogy," as Rice and other enthusiasts labeled it. Writers who cite Rice's book for his descriptions of mindless instruction often ignore his passionate portraits of schools where the curriculum was "correlated" and where teachers introduced science work, encouraged children's expression in writing and art, and incorporated manual training into the elementary curriculum.[56]

Whether he was observing classes in St. Paul and Minneapolis in Minnesota or in Indianapolis and La Porte in Indiana, Rice quoted liberally from student work and described teacher activities that integrated varied subject matter. In La Porte, for example, he found instances of the "perfect lesson." It is "one that not only interests the child, but one that uses his energies to the best advantage."

> From the start the pupils are encouraged to be helpful to each other. Already in the first school year the children begin to work together in groups and to assist each other in making and recording observations of plants and animals, of the wind and the weather. . . . In the classrooms are found small square tables around which the pupils sit, particularly when doing busy work, performing tasks in which all the members of the group take part. . . .
>
> At the group tables things are made with which the rooms are decorated at the bi-monthly festivals which have become a custom in La Porte. Much of the number work is done at the group tables. . . .

Rice conceded that such school districts were a minority in 1892. He found only 4 school systems of the 36 he visited putting into practice the principles he fervently advocated.[57]

Two decades later John Dewey and his daughter Evelyn visited schools using progressive practices. In *Schools of Tomorrow*, the Deweys documented the spread of schools with "tendencies toward greater freedom and an identification of the child's school life with his environment and outlook, and even more important, the recognition of the role education must play in a democracy." While most of the schools they describe are private, the Deweys devoted much space to the Gary, Indiana, schools under William Wirt, a public school in Chicago, and two Indianapolis public schools, one of which served black students.[58] Concentrating on themes such as teachers' encouragement of student expression, groupwork, and a close tie between the content studied and the immediate surroundings, the Deweys concluded that "More and more schools are growing up all over the country that are trying to work out definite educational ideas."[59]

SUMMARY

Thus various versions of teacher-centered and student-centered instruction existed a century ago. The extent of each, their variations, and what impulses generated them cannot easily be determined. It would be reasonable to conclude, however, that by 1916, when the Deweys' book appeared, dominant teaching practices in most public schools continued to be teacher-centered insofar as furniture arrangement, grouping for instruction, classroom talk, student movement, and work activities. Variations of student-centered patterns appeared most often in small schools (having fewer than 300 students), private schools (although public schools using these approaches did exist), and elementary schools. Few, if any, high schools were described.

While teacher-centered practices continued to prevail in most classrooms, different conceptions of the school's role and teaching were slowly making their appearance. Challenges to the conventional wisdom of the day on what subject matter was best for students and how teachers should deal with children began to appear in Quincy, La Porte, Chicago, New York City, and Washington, D.C. These challenges to dominant beliefs and practices within teacher-centered classrooms grew in the decades that followed and produced classrooms where teachers tried to adhere to both mainstream and new ideas. Walking the tightrope of these tensions, teachers created mixtures of practices that mirrored broader conflicts between cultivating individual children's growth and preparing children to find a useful niche in the social order, between scientific efficiency and creative expression, and between education and socialization.

The decades after 1900 saw an increase in efforts to introduce student-centered teaching practices in public schools. By 1940, the vocabulary of pedagogical progressives had rapidly turned into the mainstream talk of both teachers and administrators. The next chapter examines whether mainstream ideas and language had become mainstream practice in urban and rural classrooms by the 1920s and 1930s.

CHAPTER 2

Behind the Classroom Door: New York, 1920–1940

The room was large and sunny, with ample windows letting in light to the rear and left. The windowsill held potted plants, some of which had begun to flower. Just above the sill, pasted to the window glass, were drawings made by the children. The classroom doors and the ledges above the blackboards held placards: "factors," "numerator," "denominator." Above the front blackboard in careful script was written: "SELF-CONTROL." On one door was posted the Declaration of Independence; on another was a certificate of membership in the American Junior Red Cross dated 1924.

This was Mrs. Spencer's fourth-grade class in a New York City elementary school. Forty-two children sat in rows, facing the teacher's desk and SELF-CONTROL, awaiting the teacher's direction. Fifteen bright children from 4A and 27 dull ones from 4B, according to Mrs. Spencer, made up her class. An arithmetic lesson was under way.

"Little helpers to the board," Mrs. Spencer directed. "George, Edith, Fred, Gertrude, each take two children who need helping." A dozen children arrayed themselves in groups of three around the room. "Begin at page 101 in your book and start with the first example. You others, in your seats, begin at page 115, example 4. Yes, you may talk to one another about your work." A quiet hum arose.

The teacher moved around the room helping individual students. After a while she looked at her watch and announced: "The coaching period is over. To your seats." As the children scurried back to their seats and settled back, Mrs. Spencer went to the board and wrote

$$37\frac{1}{2}$$
$$-25\frac{1}{2}$$

"Who can give me the least common denominator? Fanny? I called on you because you weren't paying attention. Well, then, Sam, you tell us. Ten, that's right. Now, then, Sam, what do we—oh, I hope you know it—what do we do next?" A long pause. A girl answered. "Oh, dear," said Mrs. Spencer, "there's a girl named Sam." A long pause. Finally, the teacher accepted an answer from another student.

"The arithmetic period is over," she announced. "Keep your papers in your books. Your homework is example 2 on page 114: divide 117,799 by 3,648." Stephen, the 9-year-old sitting directly in front of the teacher's desk for reasons that the entire class had come to know over the year, fidgeted in his seat. Mrs. Spencer asked him what was wrong.

"She keeps sticking her feet into my back," he said.

"Oh, dear, how dreadful! Such little tiny feet going right through a big thick bench right into your big strong back. I suppose you are too seriously hurt to go to Mr. Hazen's room and fetch me the map of Asia. You're not? Well, and you, David, go and get the map of Europe from Miss Flynn." As if launched by a slingshot, both boys were at the door. "Remember to say 'Please,'" Mrs. Spencer said and turned to the class. "Always be. . . ." She waited for the student to chorus back. "Polite," they said in unison.

"Yes, always be polite, it's worthwhile, you'll find."

Looking around the room and sensing a growing restlessness, she said: "Stretch up—deep, breathe out. That's better," as the students sitting at their desks raised their arms toward the ceiling, took a deep collective breath, and exhaled in unison.

"Take out your geographies and turn to the map of Asia. Page 185. Henry, what is Asia?"

"Asia—Asia—," Henry grasped for an answer.

"Class?"

"Asia is a continent," they said as one.

"Well, what is the meaning of 'continent,' Elsie?"

"A continent is the largest division of land."

"Right, when I talk about a continent, what do I mean? I mean land."

Stephen came back with the map of Asia in hand and placed it expertly atop the ledge above the blackboard. "Thank you, Stephen, it looks fine."

Question followed question, with children occasionally summoned from their desks to pick up the pointer used by the teacher and identify a place on the map. Recess interrupted the recitation.

After the students returned from the playground, Mrs. Spencer said: "Time for writing. Monitors, pass the papers. Everyone up and straight and tall and do your very best. Write your names. Don't forget to end with the upstroke. Two or three forgot about the upward stroke last time. It's just as bad as coming to school with your clothes unbuttoned or your necktie off. Write these words."

On the board she wrote: mountain, camp, August, glove, song, thumb, itself. "Do your very best. We have only a week or two before promotion day." Three girls sighed and covered their faces.

Pens scratched. Feet shuffled. Papers crumpled. Mrs. Spencer reviewed the words, asking certain students to spell the words without looking at their papers or the blackboard.

"Time for reading. And we are going to exchange readers with Miss Flynn's class. We shan't use our own readers today. But instead let's act out one of the stories. Let's do the Mad Tea Party. Who remembers it best?"

The teacher chose four children. They knew the lines by heart and acted out the parts as only enthusiastic 9-year-olds could. "Fine. You were all good," Mrs. Spencer said.

"Now we'll have a drill game on the word 'bring,' " Mrs. Spencer told the class. The game brought the morning to a close.[1]

The school in which Mrs. Spencer taught in 1924 had received city-wide notice and praise as a progressive school. Her principal had identified Spencer

PLATE 2.1 *Aerial classroom, Los Angeles Public Schools, 1927; geography lesson*

as an exemplar of progressive teaching in his building. Agnes DeLima, the journalist who observed this class, was a passionate advocate of child-centered schools similar to the private ones operated by Elizabeth Irwin, Felix Adler, and others. DeLima described this fourth-grade teacher sympathetically although she felt that Mrs. Spencer and other teachers like her conducted sincere but colorless imitations of the private experimental schools. She believed that progressive classes in experimental schools would die if placed within public schools. Large class size, administrative indifference or hostility, and a generally negative attitude toward child-centered classrooms would kill such efforts.

Who, then, were the progressives? Mrs. Spencer? Her building principal? Teachers in private experimental schools? The problem, of course, is in the word itself. The ideas nested in "progressivism" were diverse and ambiguous, appealing strongly to dissimilar reformers in the decades bracketing World War I.

Historians Lawrence Cremin, Michael Katz, and David Tyack distinguished among various educational streams within the larger political movement. Among the educational reformers, for example, Tyack described the administrative progressives (e.g., Teachers College's George Strayer, Stanford University's Ellwood Cubberley, and veteran superintendent Frank Spaulding), who used the latest concepts in scientific management to streamline the school district's organizational and instructional machinery. He distinguished these progressives from social reformers (e.g., George Counts, John Childs, and Willard Beatty), who advocated using the schools as an instrument for national regeneration, and from the pedagogical progressives (e.g., Francis Parker, Flora Cooke, and William H. Kilpatrick), who saw the child as being central to the school experience. Although substantial differences existed among the pedagogical reformers, they all drew deeply from the well of John Dewey's ideas.[2]

Because these chapters concentrate on classroom changes during the interwar decades, I pay particular attention to the efforts of pedagogical reformers. Administrative progressives, reconstructionists, and other reformers who are often mentioned in typical accounts of these years are absent from this description except to the extent that they tried to modify existing classroom instruction.

Diversity, not uniformity, marked these pedagogical reformers except for their common antipathy to "fixed grades in the schools, fixed rules for the children, and fixed furniture in the classroom." Among these child-centered school advocates deep and sharp differences surfaced over curriculum materials, instructional tactics, degrees of choice open to children, the role and extent of studying, and doing art and play in the classroom.[3]

Given their strongly negative views of the public schools and despite the diversity of doctrines implicit in the practices they advocated, there remained a core consensus on what constituted an appropriate school. For the most part pedagogical reformers wanted instruction and curriculum tailored to children's interests; they wanted instruction to occur, when at all possible, individually or in small groups; they wanted programs that permitted children more freedom and creativity than existed in schools; they wanted school experiences connected to activities outside the classroom; and they wanted children to help shape the direction of their learning. The tangible signs of these impulses that bound philosophers, curriculum theorists, psychologists, and practitioners together were classrooms with movable furniture, provisioned with abundant instructional materials, astir with children engaged in projects, and noticeably involved with the larger community. These commonalities leave untouched deep splits among reformers over the project method, how much freedom a child should have in school, the teacher's role in setting goals, and the proper amount of time to spend on basic skills. The commonalities, nonetheless, do suggest where in the classroom to look for changes in practice.[4]

Between the hundreds of thousands of students these professors taught and readers of their books, the thousands of newspaper and magazine articles written about the schools they or their followers directed, the hundreds of courses of study and textbooks that incorporated these ideas, and the scores of school systems that bought movable desks and chairs, their ideas seemed to touch schools across the nation. *Time* magazine pronounced it to be so in 1938. "No school," the anonymous writer declared, "escaped its influence."[5]

CLASSROOMS IN THE CITY

To what degree teachers embraced these ideas and practiced them in their classrooms can be determined in the following chapters on New York City, Denver, and Washington, D.C. In the 1920s and 1930s, city school systems were acknowledged as the frontier of innovation. If new ideas about schooling were to be implemented, city schools were the obvious place to observe what happened.[6]

All three districts had superintendents who built national reputations as strong leaders committed to improving schools. New York and Denver, at different times in the two decades, were recognized as leaders in initiating novel programs that put both pedagogical and administrative progressives' practices into classrooms. In New York City, the largest public school system in the world, the superintendent launched the Activity Program, the single largest experiment (about 75,000 students participated) ever to test new ideas in classrooms. Denver, a school district with over 45,000 students, became a national trendsetter by starting a unique program of improving curriculum through involving hundreds of teachers in writing progressive concepts into courses of study. Denver also furthered its reputation as a laboratory testing student-centered concepts with its participation in the Progressive Education Association's national experiment to improve the high school curriculum. All of Denver's junior and senior high schools joined the program, called the Eight-Year Study (1933–1941).

Although Washington, D.C., had a superintendent noted in professional circles as an administrative progressive and whose tenure spanned the entire period under scrutiny, the city's schools were inconspicuous on the national scene as instructional innovators. What makes the District of Columbia worth examining is how a racially segregated school system adopted a number of progressive policies resembling closely what New York City and Denver had done and determining what occurred in classrooms as a result.

A look at classroom teaching in these three districts during a two-decade period of strong interest in and acceptance of progressive ideas should provide a sense of what in teaching practice remained stable and what changed between the 1920s and the 1940s in districts renowned for their administrative and instructional reforms.

NEW YORK CITY SCHOOLS

The Setting

The numbers stagger the imagination; they intimidate. Imagining 683 schools, 36,000 teachers, and 1,000,000 children (in 1930) in one school district boggles the mind of anyone west of the Hudson River. Glossy annual reports of the system tried to capture the massiveness of the school operation with comparisons such as: The increase in children attending school between 1920 and 1921 equaled the number of students going to school in Nashville, Tennessee; or, If you lined up all the children in the district, arms apart, they would stretch from New York City to Toledo, Ohio; or, If the superintendent visited classrooms for 10 minutes each, 8 hours a day, 5 days a week, he would have done nothing else but observe each teacher once in 3 years.[7]

Size alone made New York's schools unique. Yet the school district's size cannot obscure the history of tensions and compromises over ethnic, religious, political, and class issues that mirrored what was happening in other cities across the nation in the first half of the 20th century. Because these issues in the school system's history have been described by a number of historians, I will not cover the same ground. My focus is on what teachers did in classrooms, a topic to which these researchers devoted little attention.[8]

Some narrative, however, is necessary to set the stage for what Sol Cohen called the "ultimate triumph" in 1934, when the Public Education Association (PEA), a reformist cadre dedicated to transforming schools into child welfare institutions, saw "its conception of progressivism in school principles and procedures capture New York City school officialdom."[9]

The Superintendents

Between 1898 and 1940, the largest public school system in the country had four superintendents to cope with social changes that schools could only adjust to, not alter: massive growth in school enrollment, sharply increased ethnic diversity, and, after 1930, cutbacks in salaries, positions, and programs resulting from the Depression and World War II.

William Maxwell.   Enrollment growth and diversity at the turn of the century taxed the ingenuity, skills, and stamina of William Maxwell, who served as the first superintendent of the consolidated five-borough district for 20 years. As a pragmatic school reformer who organized a bureaucracy while retaining interest in the "New Education," he had to cope with such basic needs as providing a seat for every student so that the schools could reach out, through the child, to improve the community. His tenacity, vigor, and persistence left a string of accomplishments recognized by his contemporaries: a uniform and broader curriculum; more schools to house students; expanded social services; after-school and summer programs; and key administrative initiatives (e.g., instituting the Board of Examiners) that would indelibly mark organizational routines for years to come. Combining the administrative progressives' passion for uniformity with concern for classroom practice, Maxwell cast a long shadow that few of his successors could escape, and none seemed inclined to do so.[10]

The three superintendents who followed Maxwell came up through the ranks as teacher, principal, district superintendent, and associate superintendent. In the latter position, each became a member of the Board of Superintendents, a body that advised the superintendent on which personnel and program recommendations to make to the Board of Education. Those who assumed the top post had sat in every key chair in the system as they rose through the ranks.

William Ettinger.   Superintendent Ettinger served for six years (1918–1924). He had been a teacher and principal for over a quarter century before being elevated to a district superintendency and worked for another decade in that position before joining fellow associate superintendents. Shortly after, at the age of 56, he was chosen by the Board of Education to succeed Maxwell—a hard act to follow. An advocate of more vocational education classes, Ettinger developed programs for the upper grades in elementary schools while consolidating and polishing initiatives that Maxwell had installed. He demonstrated his own interest in progressive practice by personally approving the use of a public school by the PEA for a school-within-a-school progressive experiment under the direction of Elizabeth Irwin in 1922.

Much of Ettinger's attention, however, concentrated on securing sufficient funds to decrease class size and provide adequate housing for old, overcrowded, and outmoded schools. Intense and prolonged quarrels with the Board of Estimate over adequate resources for the schools and constant bickering with the mayor over keeping top school posts free from partisan taint led to his contract's not being renewed in 1924.[11]

William O'Shea. Like Ettinger's, his successor's career began and ended in New York. William O'Shea taught for almost 20 years before being named principal in 1906. Gradually, he moved through the necessary offices on the trek to the superintendency. At the age of 60, he was selected from among the associates on the Board of Superintendents to follow Ettinger. The first 5 years of his tenure continued the pattern laid down by his predecessors: more buildings with larger capacities to house students, adequately trained teachers impartially selected, and a curriculum expanded and revised to cope with differences among children.

Using the vocabulary of reformers, O'Shea produced annual reports of the school system's achievements that reflected exactly the institutionalization of changes made over a quarter century earlier. "These schools," O'Shea wrote about the elementary schools, "are the front line trenches in the battle for health, for social wellbeing, and for moral advancement."[12]

District superintendents were required to submit reports with a section labeled "Progressive Steps." Occasionally these reports would include references to classroom activities or projects, flexible schedules, and new curriculum materials. More often, though, "Progressive Steps" for the districts listed new testing procedures, how children were grouped, and new services for children.[13]

If Ettinger left his mark on the system by expanding vocational education, O'Shea left his imprint on courses of study and new programs for students stressing the practice of thrift, citizenship training, and character development. He appeared less interested in bringing classroom practices recommended by the PEA into city classrooms, although he would often borrow reformers' language for his reports. The stormy relationship between the public schools and PEA over Elizabeth Irwin's experimental school at P.S. 41, for example, produced a demand for a formal program evaluation. O'Shea's lack of support was evident. The evaluation committee, made up of school staff and PEA appointees, recommended more formal and conventional instruction in basic skills. The PEA withdrew its financial support and eventually the experiment became a private school in Greenwich Village, "The Little Red School House." [14]

The launching of the only formal progressive experiment in the public schools occurred in the midst of the Depression, years that saw budget cuts shrinking gains made by previous school chiefs and boards of education. Class size increased. Fewer teachers were allocated to schools. After-school and summer programs were cut back. The last five years of O'Shea's tenure were marked by earnest efforts to preserve what had been done in earlier years. At the age of 70, O'Shea retired. The Board of Education again turned to the cabinet of associate superintendents for O'Shea's successor.

Harold Campbell. A graduate of the Maxwell Training School in 1902, Harold Campbell began his career as a teacher in both elementary and high schools, receiving his first appointment as a high school principal in 1920. Four years later he was promoted to associate superintendent for high schools. He served in that position and as deputy superintendent until the Board of Education named him their next school chief. After 32 years in the system, at the age of 50, Campbell succeeded O'Shea in 1934 in the midst of the worst depression ever to face the nation.

Characterized as a conservative educator by both newspaper and professional journals, Campbell followed his predecessors' policies, as funds permitted, in reducing overcrowded schools, expanding services to children, and differentiating programs for handicapped and gifted students. The template laid down by Maxwell persisted, except in one area. Campbell launched a "pedagogical revolution" that became a "key landmark in the triumph of progressivism," according to one historian. In 1934, just a few months after becoming superintendent, he approved the largest experiment ever aimed at determining whether progressive curricular and teaching practices could be installed in a big city school system: the Activity Program. A later section in this chapter describes this experiment. [15]

Aside from the endorsement of the PEA, there was little public reaction to the superintendent's decision. Few citizens or school professionals knew Campbell personally or anything substantial about the decision that he had made. After all, most New York City teachers seldom saw Campbell, O'Shea, Ettinger, or Maxwell other than in an occasional newspaper photo or as a small distant figure on a stage speaking to thousands of teachers. Few teachers could have recognized any of these men had they stepped into their classrooms. What teachers did know of their superintendents' presence came indirectly from headquarters' decisions establishing the working conditions within which they taught. These included the building itself, class size, double-session schools, revised courses of study, personnel transfers, and evaluation ratings—all of which influenced, to some degree, what happened in the classrooms.

ORGANIZATIONAL CONTEXT FOR CLASSROOM TEACHING

Within the classroom, what teachers do can be attributed to their decisions, the influence of the classroom as a workplace, district policies, and the nature of the students and the larger community in which the school is located. In trying to understand teaching practices, I chose those factors about which policy decisions are made by others far removed from the classroom. For example, in what neighborhoods schools are placed, the classroom design, how many students and which ones enter a class, required courses of study, district tests, report cards, and supervisory rules are concrete realities over which teachers are seldom consulted. Yet the consequences of others' decisions about such matters penetrate classrooms daily, in small and large ways influencing what teachers do.

The Physical Classroom

Consider classroom architecture. It should come as no surprise that the 19th-century uniformity so highly prized by the first generation of progressives, including Maxwell, became embedded in the design of classroom space. C. B. J. Snyder, architect for the New York City Board of Education between the 1890s and the 1920s, created the standard classroom plan that was used throughout the first half of the 20th century. Each classroom was built around the seats and desks of students and teacher: 48 desks bolted to the floor for grades 1 through 4, 45 desks for grades 5 and 6, and 40 for grades 7 and 8.[16]

Rows of desks bolted to the floor facing the blackboard made it easier for the teacher to scan the classroom for actual or potential disorder and monitor students' work. Yet reformers viewed movable furniture as essential to activity-centered classrooms, and second in importance only to light and heat. Few educators argued that it was impossible to implement progressive methods in rooms with rows of immovable desks, but such seating arrangements proved cumbersome, taxing the ingenuity of teachers in figuring out ways of circumventing this structural obstacle. Replacing stationary desks with movable ones, was, however, prohibitively costly.

The cost of desk replacement was never mentioned publicly. In the midst of the Depression, the capital investment in stationary desks for over 600 buildings was staggering. Yet the issue persisted because it was central to the reform of teaching practices. Compromises were struck. Beginning in 1935–

1936, a year after Campbell moved into his new office, the Board of Education approved the superintendent's recommendation that all new elementary school buildings have 35 fixed seats in rows with additional movable tables and chairs and one or more workbenches to supplement the fixed desks.[17]

The official position of the Board of Superintendents was stated in *The New York Times* in an article written by then Associate Superintendent Campbell in 1930 detailing all the progressive practices current in the school system.

> As for the movable furniture idea and the substitution of comfortable chairs for the traditional rows of seats. We adopted it long ago in kindergarten and special classes. In most classes, however, particularly when there are thirty to forty pupils, the scheme is not practical. The moving of furniture is creative of noise and confusion. One teacher might want the chairs arranged one way, another teacher another way. Ease is not always productive of attention and concentration.

The clincher argument he cited was the danger of fire. A building in which students were obedient to order and marched in straight lines could be emptied in 3 minutes.[18]

While classes of 50 or more students were common around World War I, class size had been dropping since that time. In 1930, the average class size in elementary schools hovered about 38 students. This figure, however, masked significant differences. For example, 17% of all elementary classes still had 45 or more students. Within a school, class sizes varied dramatically. Special classes for "dull" or handicapped students were kept around 25 while other classes in the same building might be well over 45. To a teacher in the 1890s facing 75 students daily, the prospect of having only 40 in a class would have been delightful. By the 1930s, however, there was a public commitment and philosophy that expected teachers to provide individual attention to each child.[19]

Given this tenet of progressive belief, how large was too large? Harold Campbell offered one answer in 1935. "It seems," he said, "almost inevitable that with more than 35 pupils of varying personality and capability a teacher can give but scant attention to the individual child." The ideal size for elementary classrooms of "normal children" where one teacher covers all subjects was, he wrote, about 30 children. When the Activity Program for elementary schools began in 1934, average class size was 38 students. A large class at that time was defined as having over 40 students; 41% of all elementary classrooms were large by that standard. By 1942, the Activity Program had been declared a success and had been extended to all schools. The average class size was 34 children, with 18% of all classes labeled large. In high schools the average class size was 35, although it ranged from 31 at Benjamin Franklin to 40 at Brooklyn Tech.[20]

The Curriculum

If physical space and numbers of children defined critical dimensions of the teacher's daily world, so did the course of study. The Board of Education expected teachers and their supervisor, the principal, to use in classrooms 10 syllabi initially printed in the 1896 bylaws of the Board of Education, thereby spelling out to teachers and principals the importance of particular content and its organization. By 1924, there were 26 curricular bulletins and syllabi directing teachers' attention to what should be taught and why.[21]

A districtwide survey of school operations by a group of outside evaluators in 1924 included a report by Massachusetts Commissioner of Education Payson Smith on elementary school curriculum. Smith's report blasted the curriculum for its inflexibility and lack of overall aims, its growth by "accretion," without concern for correlation of subjects. Too much time was spent on "obsolete and often trifling material"; no guidelines for principals and teachers existed to determine how much content should be taught at each grade level.[22]

The formal responses by district superintendents varied from passionate defenses of current courses of study to cautious agreement with Smith's conclusions. District Superintendent Taylor attacked Smith's assertions about the supposedly inflexible course of study shrinking a classroom teacher's freedom:

> . . . a school with fifty or a hundred teachers—many of them inexperienced—cannot afford to permit each teacher to interpret the course of study in a single school. The principal is there to organize, unify, and inspire the teachers in such a way as to realize the aims which she sets up for the school as a whole. . . .

Yet District Superintendent Stephen Bayne, who would later become associate superintendent for elementary schools, agreed, albeit guardedly, with Smith's assessment that the curriculum omitted important objectives, grew haphazardly, lacked coherence, and needed periodic revision.[23]

Even though the 1924 survey results and rebuttals from school employees were not published until 1929, Smith's critique triggered O'Shea's appointment of a Committee on the Revision of Courses of Study and Methodology. Copying to some extent what Denver, Colorado, had done earlier in the decade, the staff wrote, over a 5-year period (1925–1930), 19 new courses of study, complete with the rhetoric of progressive reformers on project methods, individual attention, and pursuing children's interests.[24]

Care, however, should be exercised in predicting classroom practice, as Bayne observed, "by the wording of a course of study," revised or not. Diversity in practice is assumed with almost 30,000 teachers. Once the classroom door closed, few principals and supervisors saw what happened or could determine how much teachers actually used syllabi. Did these revised syllabi produce changes in classrooms? Clues appear in the tests students were given, the report cards they received, the rating sheets used to judge teachers, and the character of supervision that teachers received.

Testing. In 1925 for the first time O'Shea ordered the annual testing of elementary and junior high students in composition, arithmetic, spelling, silent reading, and vocabulary. These achievement tests covered a great deal of factual knowledge and were linked closely to the revised courses of study. (In high schools the New York State Regents' academic examinations had been given since 1878.) By the 1930s, city educators' views conflicted over the classroom impact of these Regents' exams. At least half of the high school teachers and department chairmen saw these annual exams as freezing certain topics in courses of study, reinforcing drill, memorization, and cramming, and having a generally negative impact on what teachers did in their classrooms.[25]

While complaining that in his visits to classrooms he heard "entirely too frequent reference to these examinations," Associate Superintendent of High Schools John Tildsley stated bluntly in 1925 that these tests "seemed to be necessary as a means of checking upon the work of the schools. . . ." The exams took the place of the school inspections that, with "the force at the disposal of this Division, it [was] impossible to give."[26]

Report cards. Items on report cards also produce clues to instructional practice. Students received percentage and letter grades in subjects, as well as citizenship marks. The junior high report cards in the 1920s, for example, listed the required subjects of reading, grammar, spelling, composition, arithmetic, history and civics, and geography, with spaces set aside for the final grade, midterm, and final exam marks. Space was provided for grades on effort, conduct, and personal habits. On the high school report card, letter marks were given up to six times a year, or three a semester.[27]

A similar system of letter grades based upon the teacher's judgment of a student's proficiency prevailed in elementary schools until 1935, when the report card was revised to include a number of student behaviors and attitudes (whether the child works well with others, obeys courteously, is reliable, plays well with others, and so on). This innovation was consistent with revisions then underway in the elementary school program.

Rules and evaluation. In addition to tests and report cards measuring mastery of content and obedience to teacher directions, explicit and formal rules prescribed proper classroom behavior. During the interwar period principals and supervisors circulated to teachers rules for managing classes and executing lessons. While these rules did not describe what occurred in classrooms, they surely defined what supervisors believed to be "good" teaching practices.

For elementary and secondary school teachers in diverse subjects, these regulations beat the same drum. A sampling from New York City high schools:

- 1921—Evander Childs High School: For oral work insist on clear speaking. The student should stand erect, with head up, and speak with sufficient clearness to be heard in all parts of the room.
- 1926—For all elementary and secondary teachers in the Bronx: Size the children and assign seats. . . . Make a seating plan of the class. It helps discipline. . . . Drill on standing and sitting; on putting the benches and desks up and down noiselessly. . . . Place your daily plan, your time schedule on the desk where you can refer to them frequently. . . . Keep a strict account of tests, oral work, and other data that will aid in giving the child a just mark on the report card.
- 1930—Bushwick High School, Math Department: Plan for Geometry
    1. Assignment of new homework
    2. Presentation, development, and application of the new lesson
    3. Blackboard recitations on review of theorems. . . .
- 1932—John Adams High School, Latin Department: Recitation by pupils should be clear and easily heard in all parts of the room. Remember the placard posted in all rooms, "Stand straight! Face the Class! Speak Up!" Don't let pupils talk directly to you; get the audience situation.[28]

Supervision of teachers. One of the strongest signals to teachers on what they were to do in class was the evaluation rating and the way that supervisors practiced supervision. A new rating form was introduced in 1921 to eliminate the many complaints raised by both teachers and principals over the lack of uniformity in ratings and over abuses stemming from "secret reports" on teachers by principals that were used by the Board of Examiners in determining promotions.[29]

William O'Shea, then associate superintendent, chaired the task force that drafted the revised form. The letters A, B, C, and D to label performance were replaced with a two-point scale of "Satisfactory" and "Unsatisfactory" for the following areas: personality, control of class, self-control, discipline, and scholarship. Space was provided for the supervisor to describe instances of exceptional performance and weakness.

O'Shea wrote the handbook explanation for each of the areas to be rated; teachers received copies of the handbook explaining how evaluation would occur. O'Shea's language resonated with the "New Education." Project methods and pupil activity ran as themes throughout his discourse on appropriate instruction. "We learn to do by doing," O'Shea wrote. "The greatest possible participation of all the children is the real measure of success, and such success," he emphasized, "cannot be attained where the old type of individual question and answer recitation is used too largely."[30]

Among educators, supervision meant more than filling out a form. The essential goal of supervision, according to New York City officials, was to improve instruction. But supervisors were also inspectors required to judge a teacher's performance. The two expectations clashed, creating a dilemma each time a supervisor entered a classroom. Alfred Hartwell, Buffalo superintendent and one of the investigators hired to survey the schools in 1924, saw the dilemma clearly on his visits with principals and district superintendents as they supervised and rated teachers in 16 schools.[31]

Hartwell described one visit to a classroom where the district superintendent questioned the teacher in front of the class on her pupils' attendance and what professional courses she had taken. He asked her for the lesson plan book, which he examined and found in good order. She was then told to conduct the lesson for the visitors. The superintendent took notes and promised to discuss them with the teacher the next time he visited. While Hartwell found uniformity in the "recording of ratings," he saw much variation in styles and quantity of supervision. Too many principals and district superintendents practiced supervision, he concluded, in a manner that created fear among teachers at the very rumor of a supervisor's coming to the class. Moreover, too little time was available. District superintendents supervised about 1,000 teachers in 20 to 40 schools, depending upon the district. Hartwell mentions two officials who spent 20 minutes to a half hour in each class; they had made 400 to 600 visits during the previous school year. Principals told him they spent between 20% and 25% of their time in classrooms.[32]

In the mid-1930s a Brooklyn high school teacher wrote that his colleagues often feared a principal or supervisor as "someone to whom to cater so as to avoid his enmity." He chided principals for failing to reach the ideal: "the supervisor is superior, a sort of expert in the educational process and therefore can help teachers in the dilemmas that confront them." Citing instances of principals with particular instructional passions (e.g., good penmanship, following the time schedule to the minute, poetry and spelling, or using flashcards), he describes how these peculiar notions about teaching infect supervision and make teachers "timid, easily frightened, scared to have an opinion of their own." The accuracy of the teacher's description of particular cases is less important than his rendering of the beliefs that teachers held about supervisors.[33]

In describing classroom architecture, syllabi, class size, report cards, written rules, teacher ratings, and supervisory practices in the interwar years, I assume that working conditions, the tools available to teachers, and the explicit expectations of their supervisors describe an organizational context that affects what teachers do daily. Surely something can be learned about how people drive if we have some knowledge of traffic signals, driving conditions, and what good drivers are expected to do on the road. Similarly, organizational arrangements helped shape, and perhaps in some cases reinforced, patterns of instruction that had prevailed in classrooms across the city since the turn of the century. By the early 1930s, the New York school system had seen changes in syllabi that incorporated the progressives' vocabulary and suggested activities for teachers. But the connective tissue of instruction—classroom architecture, class size, report cards, rules, the evaluation process, and supervision—established the organizational framework for prevailing teaching practices. So did the make-up of the student body.[34]

SOCIAL CONTEXT FOR CLASSROOMS

Teaching children of diverse backgrounds whose vast numbers far exceeded available space in existing school buildings partially shaped how teach-

PLATE 2.2 *New York City Public Schools, 1938–1939; the test*

PLATE 2.3   *New York City Public Schools, 1938–1939; the answer*

ers taught. So did each teacher's own social class, race, and ethnic background.

The numbers of immigrant children entering the United States in the decades bracketing the turn of the century overwhelmed the schools. Going to school for only part of the day was common for those lucky enough to find a seat in the wards where families from Italy, Croatia, Serbia, Poland, and Russia found tenements in which to live. In 1897, at P.S. 75 on the Lower East Side, 500 children waiting on the sidewalks could not be admitted to school because the principal had already let 2,000 into a school that had capacity for 1,500. A near-riot ensued, according to the *New York Times*. Classes of 60 or more students were common in the lower grades, especially since non-English-speaking children were put in the first grade, regardless of age. To cope with the tide of immigrant children, Superintendent William Maxwell and his successors created new curricula, incorporating manual arts and vocational courses and the like, and special (called "vestibule" or "steamer") classes for teaching newcomers English before they were placed in a graded class. But, as one principal in 1905 complained to a newspaper reporter about new courses like drawing, sewing, music, and nature study,

> It might be possible to find good in the course of study mapped out for our use if there were classes of fifteen or twenty children. With classes numbering 35 to 70, the teacher is obliged to rush on without a single halt. She cannot turn back for a second to help a straggler. . . . [35]

If overcrowded schools and classrooms could make a difference in teaching, surely the cultural backgrounds of the students did also. The primary goal of public schools enrolling immigrant children was to transform them into Americans. Most often superintendents, principals, and teachers—reflecting the larger society's dominant attitudes toward Eastern and Southern European newcomers—saw their job as that of helping children discard their ethnic cultures in order to embrace what educators saw as American ideals and habits. In 1903 journalist Adele Shaw visited schools with large numbers of newcomers. She was surprised at the patience and skills of elementary school teachers facing 50 or more students from different countries and with a limited command of English. She marveled at the assimilation going on in front of her eyes: "I became so absorbed I overstayed my hour. It was here that Garcia, Mendelssohn, and Joshua sat in the same row and made well-proportioned pictures with yellow crayon and a nasturtium for a model." Other teachers were less patient: "Who told you to speak out?" Shaw recorded a teacher exclaiming to a student, "You are not still!" She heard one teacher say: "You dirty little Russian Jew, what are you doing?" [36]

Until 1912 a local superintendent in the city's system, eager to convert immigrants from Eastern Europe into English-speaking, proud Americans, forbade the use of Yiddish anywhere in the schools of her district. Julia Richman, herself from a German-Jewish family and of a higher social class than her students, was the first female district superintendent in New York City. A progressive school reformer, she initiated one of the earliest experiments to adjust the curriculum to the child by classifying students as "bright", "medium," and "poor" and then assigning the strongest teachers to the "poor" classes. She also believed that "the school must step in to wrest not only the child, but the whole family from traditions which enslave the mind and furnish some of the most stubborn obstacles to a proper assimilation of the alien." [37]

A generation later, the children of those Eastern and Southern European immigrants attended school, and concerns about preserving the cultural heritage of particular groups vied with the concern for bringing different cultures together into a harmonious whole. As a teacher and later principal of Benjamin Franklin High School in East Harlem, Leonard Covello worked to have Italian taught in the public schools. The Board approved the course in 1922 and by 1939 there were 15,000 students studying Italian. Jewish organizations advocated the teaching of Hebrew and in 1930 the superintendent authorized an experimental program at Thomas Jefferson and Abraham Lincoln

High Schools in Brooklyn. By 1939 there were 2,500 students enrolled in Hebrew classes.

Preserving the language of ethnic groups was one strategy for preserving their heritage. Another was the introduction of intercultural or multicultural curricula aimed at teaching the unique contributions of the many cultures that made up New York's population. Covello at Benjamin Franklin began the practice of multicultural assemblies in 1935. Such assemblies brought students from different ethnic groups together to watch artists perform and hear leaders from different cultures speak about their backgrounds. Homeroom periods in secondary schools were used for special lessons about the contributions and unique character of particular ethnic groups. Teachers also received in-service education about different cultures.

At the same time, impulses to Americanize immigrants and bring their children into cultural harmony were evident in these decades. At P.S. 114 in the Bronx, just after the United States entered World War II, the schoolday began as follows:

> First thing in the morning . . . is the salute to the flag and the singing of the Star Spangled Banner. This is no post–Pearl Harbor patriotism. It has always been the procedure from time immemorial. . . . An American flag hangs in every classroom and from the first day the children enter school they are taught to revere the flag and to love America. This was so when their fathers went to school and when their grandfathers went to school and it is still so. They begin to study American history from the moment they know how to read. The first stories are about America's heroes, Washington, Jefferson, Lincoln. . . . [38]

Large student bodies and varied cultural backgrounds influenced how administrators and teachers saw their social role, how they organized themselves for instruction, how they determined what to teach, and how they taught. However, while the organizational and social contexts of schooling provide the background needed for understanding the nature of school and classroom practices, the foreground has been shaped by policies of the board and superintendent. It is to these policies that I now turn.

IMPLEMENTING PROGRESSIVE PRACTICES

Elementary School: The Activity Program

In 1934 newly appointed Superintendent Harold Campbell authorized a six-year experiment that became the largest demonstration of progressive practices in the nation.

Called the Activity Program, the experiment was initially proposed by the Principal's Association to Stephen Bayne, who had just been appointed to head the Division of Elementary Schools. The experiment was approved at every step of the hierarchy. Assistant Superintendent John Loftus, a former elementary principal with a citywide reputation for installing innovative programs, was tapped to direct the program. Sixty-nine schools—10% of all elementary schools—were chosen to participate because they were typical of their district and viewed progressive practices positively. Over 75,000 students and 2,200 teachers in the 69 schools participated in the Activity Program for almost 6 years. Note, however, that not all classes in a school designated as experimental were involved; the total number of students and teachers in these 69 schools were 90,000 and 2,700, respectively.[39]

What was the Activity Program? While the definition shifted over the course of the experiment, the essence of the massive effort was distilled in a 1940 memo from Loftus and J. Wayne Wrightstone to J. Cayce Morrison, New York State assistant commissioner of education and head of the team that the Board of Education hired to evaluate the experiment. According to the memo, major concepts in the Activity Program were:

- Children and teachers participate in selecting subject matter and in planning activities.
- The program centers on the needs and interests of individuals and groups.
- Time schedules are flexible, except for certain activities . . . which may have fixed periods.
- Learning is largely experimental.
- The formal recitation is modified by conferences, excursions, research, dramatization, construction and sharing, interpreting and evaluating activities.
- Discipline is self-control rather than imposed control. . . .
- The teacher is encouraged to exercise initiative and to assume responsibility; the teacher enjoys considerable freedom in connection with the course of study, time schedules, and procedure.
- Emphasis is placed on instruction and creative expression in the arts and crafts.[40]

In a less sedate description, Loftus, speaking to teachers, called the Activity Program a "revolt against verbalism, so-called 'textbook mastery' and literal 'recitation.'" Teaching was tailored to each child. The "congenial group," or committee, was typical of activity methods, as was the "integrated curriculum" (what an earlier generation of reformers had called a correlated or unified curriculum).[41]

The six-year experiment stimulated staff development for teachers. In both regular and activity schools, teachers took courses offered by local universities, the Board of Education, and the Principals' Association. Elaborate directions, syllabi, classroom suggestions, and listings of community resources were compiled, published, and distributed to teachers who expressed interest in the Activity Program.

During the life of the experiment students, teachers, and administrators from both Activity Program and regular elementary schools took batteries of tests and completed questionnaires. Teams of trained observers using specially designed instruments visited regular and experimental classrooms to record student and teacher behaviors.

When the experiment was over in 1941, Loftus's office was inundated with final reports from Activity Schools. Scrapbooks, reports, and photographs spilled over tables and chairs, nearly filling his office. One school sent 46 illustrated reports of projects, each weighing about 10 pounds. Poetry, art, songs, weavings, vases, and hundreds of other examples of student work accompanied the reports.[42]

Few elementary school teachers put the Activity Program into practice for the entire school day. Teachers most committed to the informal curriculum (another phrase for the Activity Program) followed an activity schedule for at most three hours daily. Another compromise struck early in the experiment was spending an hour daily on "drills and skills" to accommodate students who were moving from one school to another.[43]

Beginning in the first year of the Activity Program, observers went to classrooms and described what they saw both in the experimental and regular classrooms. In a 1941 study of 24 classes in both types of schools, the investigators found that pupils in activity classrooms "spend somewhat less time on the conventional academic subjects and devote more time to arts, crafts, and certain other enterprises (show-and-tell, discussion, student dramatics, etc.)." Yet the researchers also noted that the amount of time spent on formal subjects such as arithmetic, reading, spelling, and social studies was "nearly the same in activity and control classes."[44]

The observers recorded whether students worked on tasks in small groups or together as an entire class. They found that the regular classes spent 93% of their time in the whole group working on tasks while the activity classes spend 84% in the same manner. A paragraph in the report tries to explain why the difference "is not as large as one might expect in view of the fact that the programs presumably are quite different."[45]

A related study funded by the Works Progress Administration (WPA) through Teachers College investigated, among other things, what happened in classrooms by observing almost 50 classes and over 2,000 children in 16 schools (8 activity and 8 regular) between 1937 and 1939. While the re-

PLATE 2.4 *Activity program in a New York City elementary school, 1935*

searchers expressed some dismay over the fact that their instruments failed to capture fully the sharp distinctions they saw between classrooms, they did find that the "average" activity class differed from the "average" control one in having:

- More outward appearance of pupil self-direction.
- More diversity and a larger range of tasks, especially during certain periods of the day.
- More projects of the sort that correlate various enterprises and skills as distinguished from the study of isolated subject matter.
- A considerably larger display of the pupils' handiwork.[46]

The major evaluation of the entire six years was commissioned in 1940 by the New York City Board of Education. National experts in testing, evaluation, and curriculum spent a year interviewing teachers, principals, and headquarter staff. They also tested children. The conclusions of the study were based upon an intensive investigation of 194 classrooms in 28 schools

PLATE 2.5 *New York City elementary school, fourth grade class, 1943*

(14 activity and 14 regular) of which 10 pairs (20 schools) had *not* been part of any previous evaluations.

In analyzing the degree of implementation in 100 activity classrooms, the staff found that:

- In 20% of the classrooms activity procedure was confused and ineffective.
- 38% of classrooms made substantial progress in developing an activity program but still required assistance.
- 42% of classrooms had a well-developed activity program.[47]

In 94 classrooms in regular schools,

> Many elements of the activity procedure are observable but poorly practiced due to lack of understanding of objectives or uncertainty as to means. Occasionally, some elements of the activity procedure may well be developed but be so intermingled with the regular procedure as to be disturbing or ineffective.[48]

The study confirmed top administrators' beliefs that New York teachers could implement the best of progressive practices, as defined by these evaluators.

Finally, the survey staff concluded that activity schools had been most successful in getting students to participate and cooperate in groups, encouraging student movement in classrooms, developing positive student attitudes toward school, teachers, and peers, and teaching "purposeful, orderly, courteous behavior." Teachers were less successful in developing flexible use of classroom furniture and of workbenches and tools, as well as in reporting regularly to parents.[49]

The study also revealed that elements of the Activity Program had spread to regular schools. "Our regular school," the final report observed, "had nearly as much of the activity program as two of the activity schools selected for intensive study. The evaluators found that 10% of regular classrooms had made "appreciable progress in translating the activity concepts into practice."[50]

The state team concluded that the Activity Program proved to be as effective as conventional methods of teaching in teaching knowledge and skills, creative work, attitudes, and behavior and superior to conventional methods in "educating children to think [and] improving pupils' attitudes and social behavior." Pronouncing the experiment a success, Morrison recommended that the Activity Program be extended throughout the school system gradually and on a voluntary basis.[51]

An experiment involving over 75,000 students from diverse settings was launched during a time of severe economic retrenchment. It received no additional funds for equipment, furniture, or instructional materials and experienced cutbacks in the number of special teachers even as class size increased. A high annual turnover of students, teachers, and supervisors occurred— principals, for example, changed in 45 of the 69 schools. Given these difficulties, school officials could be justifiably proud of having succeeded in making chicken salad out of chicken feathers. The extent of the experiment's impact became apparent when, on January 20, 1942, six weeks after the United States entered World War II, Harold Campbell approved the gradual extension of the Activity Program to all New York City elementary schools.

Determining the extent to which progressive practices, including the Activity Program, had been implemented in the entire district is difficult. Campbell had asked the question as early as 1930: "To what extent has the New York City school system made use of the so-called 'new' educational techniques and ideas of the progressive educationists as exemplified by the child-centered school?" His answer was: a great deal.

His evidence:

- Pupils managed clubs in many high schools.
- Students revised civics textbooks in 18 schools.

- Some elementary schools had miniature municipal governments and officials.
- Pupils were taking charge of many classes and conducting recitations.
- More and more project work was being done every year.
- 500 schools had savings banks.
- 100,000 children enrolled in homemaking classes, where they cooked meals and acquired housekeeping skills.[52]

Except for three items that dealt with instruction in the classroom, the changes were organizational and curricular ones engineered by central administration and implemented by principals, whose activities could be easily monitored through observation. This was not true of students' revising textbooks, leading class discussions, and working together on projects. Such activities could not be easily monitored or counted unless observers sat in classrooms. Few did. Those that said they were in classrooms seldom reported their findings.

A decade later, Joseph Loftus estimated that activity methods were used in 25% of all city elementary schools "in some degree." The estimate was no more than an informed guess since no one had visited all teachers to ascertain whether such methods were indeed practiced or to what extent. Furthermore, many concepts relating to child-centered classrooms and project methods, and even the word "progressive" itself, were interpreted differently by professionals and laymen. The teacher had a great deal of discretion in deciding which methods to implement (e.g., one teacher might let a class elect officers without changing any portion of her instructional repertoire, while another teacher might set aside the time between 2:30 and 3:00 each day for students to work on anything they pleased, and call that an activity program). Given these obstacles, one can only guess at the methods' broader impact over a two-decade period.[53]

Some schools, like islands in the midst of an enormous lake, remained untouched by the ideology of the progressive movement and the Activity Program. In 1942, for example, three Harlem schools with 6,000 pupils became the site for a project to improve both instruction and curriculum in the first grade. When the support team from central headquarters arrived, they found the pre-progressive curriculum and time schedules for each subject in every classroom for the entire day. Teaching practices were unmarked by any of the ferment occurring elsewhere in the city. First-grade teachers were familiar with progressive language but demonstrated no evidence of modified classroom practice.

Over a 2-year period, the Research Bureau's attention, modest resources, and staff development altered the traditional classroom, curriculum, use of time, and instructional practice sufficiently to make the target primary classrooms activity-oriented. How many of the other 700 elementary schools in the city were like these three in 1942, I cannot say. But exist they did.[54]

Furthermore, a sizable number of New York City teachers were opposed to the Activity Program for philosophical or other reasons (a common argument was that the program required extra work of teachers). The Morrison evaluation of activity and regular schools sampled teacher opinion after six years of the experiment. They found that 36% of teachers in the activity schools preferred the regular program; in regular schools an unsurprising 93% favored the conventional program. A considerable number of teachers, then, found the experiment lacking because they favored classroom activities that involved whole-group instruction, little student movement, and a question-and-answer format. Despite the supposed benefits of the Activity Program, these teachers remained convinced of the workability, if not effectiveness, of conventional instruction.[55]

Innovation in High Schools

The evidence from high schools is scant. Some schools initiated a highly touted innovation known as the Dalton Plan. As early as 1924, eleven high schools reported that a few teachers in each school were using individual contracts with students as a way of diversifying the course of study. Teachers submitted articles to *High Points,* the journal written by and for high school teachers in the system, on how they were modifying the Dalton Plan for their classrooms. But these references number less than a handful.[56]

In 1935, Teachers College professor Thomas Briggs sent a graduate student into 21 New York City suburban high schools to "observe the work of the best teachers of any subject." Principals selected the 104 teachers the observer would visit. Based upon these narratives, Briggs found 80% of the teachers "teaching from the textbook." The remainder had classrooms where pupil participation in discussions and panels occurred and substantial linkages between current events and subject matter were made. About 65% of the classes used the "conventional procedure of questions by the teacher on an assignment with answers by the pupils or of specific directions followed by board or seat work." The graduate student noted that 80% of the teachers engaged in the traditional recitation.[57]

Another example of high school instruction is an actual transcript of a demonstration lesson in an American history class at Washington Irving High School in 1940, witnessed by a teacher, a principal, and a department chairman representing three other high schools. The subject of the 40-minute lesson was the railways of the nation. The 35 students had been instructed to read two pages in the text and excerpts from the *American Observer,* a newspaper published for high school students.[58]

PLATE **2.6** *Springfield, Missouri, 1930s; high school English class*

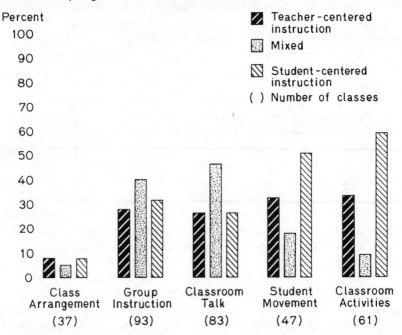

FIGURE **2.1** *Patterns of instruction in New York City elementary schools, 1920–1940*

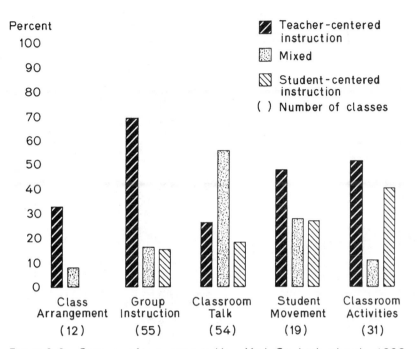

FIGURE 2.2 *Patterns of instruction in New York City high schools, 1920–1940*

The transcript carries 96 entries, 31 by the teacher and 65 by students. Of the 31 teacher entries, 26 were questions, many joined to long explanations. The 65 student responses were paragraph-length in the transcript, indicating that ample time for expression was permitted. The lesson included a whole-group discussion of a graph on railroad statistics, the class's responses to a question that one student copied on the chalkboard, and the teacher's writing other points on the board.[59]

The three observers agreed that the teaching was exemplary. They viewed it as an exceptional instance of classroom discourse dominated by student participation—what reformers called a "socialized recitation." The teacher channeled content into leading questions and periodic summaries, revealing the deft touch of a master teacher, according to the observers. They were impressed with the way students rose from their seats to answer questions, the extent of student talk, the fact that the teacher addressed students as "Miss" or "Mister" rather than using first names, and how comfortable students and teacher seemed with one another.[60]

Such individual descriptions of lessons are helpful but rare. In an effort to increase data on teacher practice, I located 152 descriptions and photo-

TABLE 2.1 Patterns of teaching: dimensions

Dimension	Pattern		
	Teacher-centered	Mixed pattern	Student-centered
Class arrangement	•Movable desks and chairs in rows facing teacher's desk and/or blackboard	•Movable desk and chairs in hollow–square, horseshoe, etc. •Up to half of class arranged at desks and chairs facing one another •No rows	•Students sit at tables or clusters of desks facing one another
Group instruction	•Whole class •Teacher works with individual while rest of class works at desks	•Teacher works with small groups •Teacher varies grouping: whole, small, and individual	•Class divided into groups •Students engaged in individual and small group activities
Classroom talk	•No one in class talking •Teacher talking •Teacher-led recitation/discussion	•Student reports, debates, panels, dramatizations •High frequency of both teacher and student instructional talk	•Student-led discussion or recitation •Students talking in groups or with individuals
Class activities	•Students working at desks •Teacher talking (lecture, explaining, giving directions, reading to class, etc.) •Teacher checking work •Students taking test, watching film, listening to radio, etc. •Teacher-led recitation, discussion	•High frequency of activities that indicate both teacher—and student—centered behaviors	•Class in small groups •Students work individually and in small groups •Students lead discussions/recitation •Students working on projects/centers
Student movement	•No movement at all •Student needs permission to leave seat	•Fewer than five students away from desks	•Six or more students away from desks at one time •Students move freely without teacher's permission

graphs of classrooms during the interwar period. The Appendix contains my rationale for looking at classrooms the way I do and describes the methods I used to categorize data. It also includes cautions on using these data. Table 2.1 describes the specific categories that were included for each teaching pattern. Figures 2.1 and 2.2 consolidate the data for patterns of instructional practice in New York City.

The data I collected from 152 classrooms support the survey results, evidence drawn from the organizational and social contexts, and evaluations of the Activity Program. No more than an estimated one of four elementary teachers, and an even smaller fraction of high school teachers, adopted progressive teaching practices, broadly defined, and used them to varying degrees in the classroom. The dominant mode of instruction remained a combination of teacher-centered and mixed patterns. Nonetheless, there is considerable evidence that many teachers incorporated student-centered practices into their repertoires, particularly in elementary classrooms.

Differences in the degree to which elementary and high school teachers adopted student-centered techniques were also evident in Denver and Washington, D.C., during the 1920s and 1930s. I turn first to Denver, a school district 2,000 miles from New York City, with a student population less than 5% the size of New York's.

CHAPTER 3

Behind the Classroom Door: Denver, 1920–1940

When Mira Scott Frank's children went to school and moved though the grades in the 1920s, she baked cookies, wrote letters, met with teachers and principals, and chaired parent meetings—in short, did what active PTA mothers do as they serve in local and district leadership posts. In 1939 Frank was elected to the Board of Education, on which she served for 12 years. Since the 1920s, she had worked with parents and school professionals. At the Valverde School dedication in the spring of 1951, she spoke passionately about a school system that had come under attack from groups outside Denver for its progressive practices.

> Over the years, because Denver's system had been recognized as an outstanding one, it has been chosen as one of the few cities to participate in national studies for the improvement of education. There has been much criticism of late leveled at so-called "progressive education." This has been a form of propaganda. Denver's educational system is its own. It has never been an importation from outside. True, in 1934, we participated in the Eight-Year Study, sponsored by the Progressive Education Association. . . . But everything done in that study was originated in Denver. What was good we retained; what was unsatisfactory was discarded some years ago.[1]

Board member Frank's defense of Denver's progressive practices was accurate: No school programs or directions were forcibly or even subtly grafted onto an unwilling or unaware school district. Even before Frank's tenure on the Board, Denver welcomed with gusto progressive practices introduced by former high school principal Jesse Newlon and the young educators he hired after he became Denver's superintendent in 1920.

In the years after Newlon moved into his offices at 14th and Tremont, Denver's newspapers, business community, and city officials took great pride in the school system's growing national reputation. A headline from a local newspaper, "Denver Leads Way in Progressive Education," would cause no historian to blink twice since such articles were common in the *Rocky MountainNews* and the *Denver Post*. But to see such an article in the *Taxpayers' Review*, complete with three photographs, was a surprise. Its appearance suggests that the ideas of Jesse Newlon and his successors found an enthusiastic response even among citizens normally vigilant about undertakings that might increase school expenditures. Progressive ideas introduced by Newlon were quickly adopted as a local product.[2]

Frank's memory of the Eight-Year Study was also accurate in linking the experiment in five Denver high schools to the cycle of curriculum revision that, again, Newlon had introduced in his first term as school chief. Frank did neglect to mention how fortunate Denver was in its continuity in educational leadership.

Between 1920 and 1940, four superintendents served the Denver schools: Jesse Newlon, A. L. Threlkeld, Alexander Stoddard, and Charles Greene. Except for Stoddard's tenure, which lasted less than 2 years, Newlon's influence extended over the entire period, since he hired Threlkeld as assistant superintendent in 1921 and Greene as the first director of research in 1923. Threlkeld succeeded Newlon and served a decade; after Stoddard's brief term, Greene, who had been Threlkeld's assistant superintendent since 1933 and had headed the Eight-Year Study in the Denver schools, assumed the superintendency in 1939, holding the post until 1947. The chronology underscores a continuity in leadership that the city schools enjoyed as it moved through two decades spanning a boom, a depression, and a world war.

Superintendent Jesse Newlon was an outsider. Born, reared, and educated in Indiana, Newlon taught high school and began his career as an administrator in 1905 when he became principal of the Charlestown, Indiana, high school. After moving through principalships in Illinois and Nebraska and taking time out to earn a master's degree from Teachers College (1914), he became superintendent of the Lincoln, Nebraska, schools in 1917. After 3 years there he was appointed to Denver's top post.

Threlkeld, who served as Newlon's assistant and deputy, worked as superintendent in three small Missouri towns for a decade before Newlon invited him to Denver. As assistant superintendent, Threlkeld also earned a master's degree at Teachers College (1923). After Newlon's departure to head Teachers College's Lincoln School, Threlkeld maintained the direction established by his colleague, elaborating and amplifying certain elements as the

Depression buffeted the Denver schools. His 10-year superintendency was the longest since Aaron Gove's 30-year stint spanning the turn of the century.

Both Newlon and Threlkeld believed in the progressive doctrines of social efficiency and scientific management. They blended administrative progressivism with clear pedagogical views on the pivotal role of the teacher in instructional and curricular decisionmaking and on the importance of flexible, activity-centered schools that linked daily life to what students learned. For two decades these two men built, both physically and organizationally, a school system that grew during those years from fewer than 33,000 students in 1920 to over 45,000 in 1937. More importantly, they helped make Denver a national pacesetter for city school systems in developing and revising curriculum and securing high rates of teacher involvement in these activities.

Their stature as school leaders who implemented efficient managerial practices, continuously revised curriculum, and advocated progressive teaching practices was noted by their peers when Newlon was elected National Education Association president in 1925 and when Threlkeld became president of the Department of Superintendence in 1936.[3]

Continuity in top leadership is one thing; what happened in classrooms as a result of decisions aimed at improving instruction and curriculum is another. Previous studies of the school system, usually a helpful resource for historians, are practically nonexistent for Denver. If New York City schools intimidate researchers with their size and complexity, at least they were surveyed and evaluated repeatedly. No so those of Denver, despite the fact that the city, with a population then of 250,000, is hardly a daunting object of study for historians. In 1916 Franklin Bobbitt, Charles Judd, Elwood Cubberley, and a flock of professors, graduate students, and practitioners studied the schools. A quarter century later, when the Eight-Year Study's results were released, all Denver secondary schools were included because they had joined the experiment as a group. In the two and a half intervening decades, no formal study of the schools occurred. This restricts the available external evidence about teacher practice.

In order to determine what occurred in classrooms. I will review the organizational context within which teachers worked, describe two major interlocking experiments that stretched over the entire interwar period, and analyze the data I collected from 133 Denver classrooms.

THE DISTRICT SETTING

Newlon came to Denver less than 2 years after the Armistice and 4 years after the 1916 survey. That survey revealed old, overcrowded schools with cramped, dimly lit classrooms. During the war, few expenditures for new buildings or renovations had been authorized. By 1922 a concerted campaign to pass a major bond referendum succeeded. With these funds and judicious use of money in the annual operating budget, 17 elementary, 5 junior high, and 3 senior high schools had been built by the time Newlon left for New York City. Before the full force of the Depression hit, Threlkeld saw 12 more elementary and 2 junior high buildings go up. So between 1920 and 1931 over half of Denver's elementary schools, 7 of 8 junior high schools, and 3 of 5 senior high schools were constructed. This massive construction of new buildings and expansion of the junior high program over a decade also brought movable furniture, lunchrooms, libraries, gymnasiums, and ample outdoor recreation space for both elementary and secondary schools.[4]

The new classrooms were built to hold 38 students, although by 1923 a definition of small (below 30 students), medium (30 to 40 students), and large (over 40 students) classes had emerged. By that year, 60% of all elementary classes had between 30 and 40 students; 13% had over 40, and, surprisingly, 27% of all elementary classes had fewer than 30 students. By 1934, however, the proportion of large classes had jumped from 13% to 33% and that of elementary classes below 30 students had shrunk from 27% to 3%. In all, 64% of all classes contained between 30 and 40 students. At the junior and senior high levels, district administrators tried to keep class size in the medium range. They succeeded and even saw one of every three high school classes with less than 30 students; 20% of the classes, mostly in nonacademic areas (e.g., music, art, physical education), had more than 40 students.[5]

That few administrators and teachers complained publicly about class size may have been because Denver had smaller classes at all levels than did systems of comparable size elsewhere. Class size, a perennial issue in New York City, failed to cause friction in Denver among school officials, parents, and teachers.[6]

Nor were courses of study a source of discontent. The ideas Jesse Newlon brought to Denver and translated into an ongoing program were simple, clear, and aimed at altering teacher behavior. In a 1916 paper he wrote while serving as a principal, he laid out concepts he executed 5 years later in Denver.

> When a group of teachers has worked upon this problem (making curriculum) during a period of two or three years, has carried on a series of investigations, has debated the issues pro and con in departmental meetings, in committee, and in faculty meetings, and has finally evolved and adopted a set of curriculums, and has determined upon the character of courses to be offered, that group of teachers will teach better and with more understanding and sympathy than they could ever otherwise teach.[7]

Teacher participation in making curriculum was uncommon. The practice in New York City and elsewhere was for district office administrators with some help from a few carefully chosen teachers to formulate goals and guidelines for selection of actual subject matter. After the curriculum had been completed, perhaps even reviewed by another group of teachers, the document was revised, printed, and delivered to each principal for use in the school. Supervisors might meet with principals to explain the new arithmetic or geography course; thereafter the principal was expected to see that teachers used the new documents. After a number of years, the syllabus would be reviewed and updated.

Newlon proceeded differently. He wanted widespread, active teacher involvement in determining what should be taught, because he believed that such participation produced better-trained teachers far more able and eager to conduct a classroom that is "more natural, more vital, and more meaningful to the students than it has ever been." He might have added; more progressive.[8]

The process that teachers went through, he believed, was just as important as, if not more important than, the course of study in its final version. Anyway, Denver administrators reasoned, if teachers and the specialists they hired designed an inadequate syllabus it would be quickly identified as such and would shortly be revised again, since both Newlon and Threlkeld directed that curriculum revision be a continuous, not a onetime, process. Apart from the novelty of letting teachers participate in developing the ideas they were expected to teach, the process owed its potential for success to a factor that neither top executive mentioned in their effort to upgrade teacher performance through curriculum revision: the high level of education among Denver teachers. By 1931, 54% of Denver elementary staff members had 4 or more years of college education; in cities of comparable size elsewhere only 22% had a similar level of schooling. Of Denver's senior high school teachers, 95% were college graduates; in New York City, 69% had earned their bachelor's degree.[9]

Between 1920 and 1930, Newlon and Threlkeld supervised the work of over 700 teachers and principals organized into 37 committees led by teachers. These committees revised 35 courses of study at all school levels. In Newlon's words, curriculum and instruction "must grow from the inside out."[10]

The numbers of teachers involved and their curriculum deliberations were unusual by standards of the time. In 1927–1928, for example, there were 1,400 Denver teachers, of whom 27% (376 teachers) served on curriculum committees. The membership of these committees included the following:

- 10% of elementary school teachers;
- 42% of junior high school teachers; and
- 48% of senior high school teachers.[11]

This process ensured that each school had at least one teacher on a committee. All secondary principals and one third of elementary principals belonged to these groups. Also, by 1927, five years after the entire effort had begun, 626 teachers had served on committees. Assuming that a number of teachers had retired, died, or left the system, I would guess that roughly between 30% and 40% of the entire instructional staff had participated in curriculum revision.

The mechanics of the process were as follows:

- Teachers chaired subject matter committees on which principals and central office administrators served.
- Teachers worked on curriculum during the day; substitutes were hired to replace them on the days they spent at the administration building.
- University curriculum specialists, over 30 scholars and practitioners forming the core of a national network of progressive reformers, came to Denver to work with teachers.
- Each committee prepared objectives, selected content, designed instructional methods (including questions to ask), and suggested varied projects and materials that their colleagues might wish to use.
- Committees revised syllabi after initial classroom trials, further comments from teachers, and extended use in classrooms.
- Committees reviewed curriculum test items that had been developed by the District's Department of Measurements for each course of study.[12]

In addition, a number of specific procedures involved teachers who were not on committees. Committee members were expected to report to their school's principal and staff on the revised course of study. Teachers were asked to complete an assessment form to critique the syllabus after they had used it. Committees used these replies to revise their course of study. After testing students, teachers submitted suggestions and concerns over specific items to the Department of Measurements.

Still, even as teachers revised courses of study in the large, airy rooms set aside for them in the new downtown administration building, more than miles still separated what they produced from the classrooms of fellow teachers. Top Denver officials gave an unusual amount of thought to implementation of teacher-designed syllabi. They were especially keen on developing organizational mechanisms that would turn curriculum revision into a tool for changing teacher practices.

Coordinating this complex process was the newly established (1925) Department of Curriculum Revision. While all of this sounds as cumbersome as changing clothes under water, the various procedures produced overlapping networks of staff members who exchanged information with one another, thereby increasing professional contacts and a sense of collegiality while greatly reducing the sense of isolation commonly felt by members of a large school system.

Finally, the superintendent ordered principals to install the new course of study. Each committee and its specialists briefed principals on the revised course and then principals held meetings with their faculties, gradually introducing the syllabus to the school. The message from headquarters was direct:

> In the installation of new courses the principal must be the leader in his school. . . . The principal must conduct a program of study and discussion of the new course before it is ready to go into the classrooms of his school. . . . It is assumed that if a principal takes an unusually long time to get a new course into classroom use he will be able to give good reasons for such delay.[13]

Seldom made explicit in the process was a formal commitment to progressive teaching practices. Content for courses of study was chosen, for example, on the basis of relevance to "life situations," an ambiguous phrase that produced many tortuous discussions among teachers. In home economics, for instance, the committee studied the activities girls did at home and chose content and teaching techniques linked to those activities. Similarly, in each of the academic areas, content was selected that teachers believed was both essential and connected to what students experienced or would experience. Latin, for example, at first glance a difficult subject to link to "life situations," made the leap in the 1929 Senior High School Courses of Study:

> It gives power in getting the meaning of new words; aids in spelling; and gives a clearer understanding of much in newspapers, magazines, and literature in general.[14]

Newlon, Threlkeld, and advocates of progressivism believed that if content was connected to current and future situations, and if students saw those links, their interest would be captured and channeled into productive, imaginative schoolwork. A later generation would call such links relevance.[15]

Another progressive approach implicitly embraced in curriculum-making was the project method. For content and method, this approach included secondary social science courses (so labeled as early as in 1919), many elementary school subjects, and the study of literature. I say "implicitly" because the charge given to the subject matter committees contained no explicit directions as to what goals or methods to pursue. But one did not have to be a weather forecaster to know which way the educational wind blew in those years.

By 1927, the Denver curriculum revision effort had gained national attention. Requests for the new courses of study poured in. Newlon and Threlkeld described the Denver experience to national groups of professionals. City after city, including New York and Washington, D.C., copied, in their own fashion, what Denver was doing. "A scientific masterpiece," A. E. Winship, editor of the *Journal of Education,* wrote of the new syllabi, comparing them to Horace Mann's Fifth Annual Report. Teachers College professor George Strayer, a nationally known expert constantly in demand to direct surveys of school systems (he was to study New York and Washington, D.C., in the 1940s) declared that "Denver has made one of the outstanding contributions to education in America through the development of its curriculum."[16]

Threlkeld succeeded Newlon in 1927 and pursued his predecessor's agenda, including curriculum revision. In 1932 the Progressive Education Association's (PEA) Commission on the Relation of School and College requested that Denver join their national experiment to reform curricula, subsequently called the Eight-Year Study. Denver's superintendent and Board readily agreed since participation dovetailed with their continuous revision effort. Instead of only one high school, Denver requested that all five high schools be included in the experiment. The Commission agreed.[17]

THE EIGHT-YEAR STUDY

What was the purpose of this experiment? The Commission established by the PEA sought to enliven high school instruction and subject matter and promote independence and imaginativeness by lifting the strictures that college requirements placed upon the existing curriculum. With the endorsement of most major universities, the Commission chose 30 public and private secondary schools in various cities, including Denver, Des Moines, and Tulsa. Participating schools were told to ignore college requirements, and instead reconstruct their curriculum and tap the imagination and ingenuity of their students and staff.

In September 1933 the Eight-Year Study began in each of Denver's five high schools with one class of 40 students who had volunteered to participate (parental consent was required), were average or above average in achievement, and, according to their junior high counselors, had the capacity to profit from such an experiment. In each succeeding year another class was added. Over the life of the experiment no school had over 30% of the student body enrolled in the program. A later generation would call such an innovation a school within a school.

To teach the experimental classes, principals chose two "core" teachers (one of English, the other of social studies), who also served as counselors for the group. Although the program differed from high school to high school, the members of the "progressive education" classes, as they were labeled, remained together for between one and three hours per day, depending on what year of the program they were in. For the rest of their daily schedule, students attended regular classes with their classmates elsewhere in the school.[18]

The schedule for the handful of experimental classes, usually located in a wing of each high school, provided time for key elements of the experiment. While no two high schools had identical programs, East High School's schedule for 1938 represented the general format and sequence of activities for sophomores enrolled in these classes. (See Table 3.1.)

The number of core teachers directly involved with the experiment remained a minority of the faculty. In 1939, for example, 12 out of 42 teachers (29%) at Manual Training were in the program; North High also had 12 participating teachers, but its staff was larger (80), which meant that only 15% participated. A number of these teachers had previously taken part in curriculum revision work.[20]

Because the 5 Denver high schools, and the 10 junior high schools that joined the experiment in 1938, received no central directives regarding what

TABLE 3.1 *East High School's schedule, 1938*[a]

Period	Monday	Tuesday	Wednesday	Thursday	Friday
			Day		
1			Classes in rest of school (all days)		
2			Classes in rest of school (all days)		
3			Classes in rest of school (all days)		
4					
5	Special interest	Free reading	Special interest groups	Group counseling	Special interest groups[a]
6			Core courses (all days)[b]		
7	Pupils dismissed; teachers' conference	Lab	Lab	Individual counseling	Lab[c]

[a]Based upon a student's interests in core content, he or she can pursue reading, music, crafts, art, current events, science, drama, writing.

[b]Initially, core courses were English and social studies, joined later by art, science, home economics, and industrial arts.

[c]Laboratories set up in each room offered individuals or small groups time to meet with the core teachers best qualified to help them. For example, a student working on a project could go to science, art, English, or social studies labs.[19]

to revise or what methods to use, the first 3 years saw small groups of students and teachers in each school stumble, catch themselves, and innovate. By 1936, the district's instructional staff began the task of coordinating goals shared by the high schools. A handbook circulated to staff in that year listed the operating principles and methods to be used by teachers:

- Core teachers were expected to teach the basic knowledge and skills of their fields "insofar as [they were] consistent with teacher-pupil goals."
- Core teachers were responsible for expanding student interests "and for helping them see relationships in all their work."
- Core teachers must replace the existing system of grades and punishment with "new drives for learning."
- In choosing subject matter, only content that "assist[ed] in the solving of problems and in the meeting of the needs of pupils" would be appropriate.
- Pupils and teachers together would plan the work.
- Usual subject matter lines "[might] be ignored."

Team planning, free time for students to pursue interests, study, and work in the community, no letter grades, and other operating principles in the handbook gave guidance to new and experienced teachers participating in the experiment.[21]

Courses taken by the experimental classes varied. Many, but not all, were jointly planned. Some "new" courses were merely old ones with trendy titles; most were genuinely innovative. After 8 years there was little doubt that substantial curriculum revision had occurred.

The core program at East High School offers one instance of change. Gone were the separate courses in English, American and world history, and so on. Instead the teachers chose to concentrate upon four areas: personal living, immediate personal-social relationships, social-civic relationships, and economic relationships. Teachers and students developed a series of units geared for use in grades 10 through 12, that included, among others, orientation to the school, understanding one's self, exploring vocational interests, studying Denver, understanding democracy and the American heritage, and exploring problems of living in the modern family.[22]

In 1940, the first evaluation report of the Eight-Year Study appeared. The experiment was declared a success. Students in these classes, the report stated, did as well in college as, and often better than, a control group of students who had completed a conventional program. As intended, curriculum had been revised; students had helped reshape courses and their interests were being used to explore nontraditional content closely linked to issues that they would face as adults. The educational hurricane had not only whipped up the surface but stirred the waters deeply. Did the turbulence touch the ocean floor?[23]

THE CLASSROOM

The data for Denver are limited. I located 133 classroom photographs and written descriptions of the period. For elementary schools there are descriptions of 34 classes, of which only certain ones provided information for the categories. Figure 3.1 shows the number of classes for each category. (To review these categories, see Table 2.1 on page 74.) Because Denver's curriculum revision and experimentation in the interwar period emphasized the secondary level, I will concentrate on what teachers did in high schools. Data on 83 high school classes (see Figure 3.2) will be supplemented by an examination of specific schools.

The dominant teaching pattern within high school was one where a teacher spent most of the class time instructing the whole group, and where his or her explanations, questions, and structured activities controlled most of

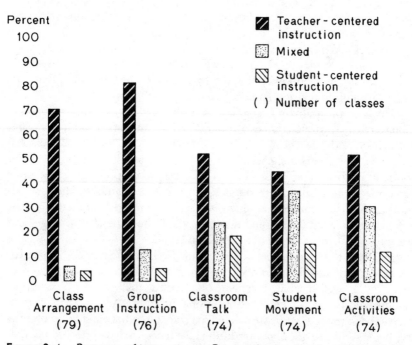

FIGURE 3.1   *Patterns of instruction in Denver high schools, 1920–1940*

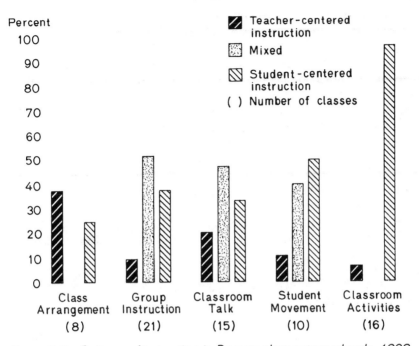

FIGURE 3.2 *Patterns of instruction in Denver elementary schools, 1920–1940*

the verbal exchanges with students. Even though classrooms contained portable desks and chairs, the furniture was often arranged in rows facing the teacher's desk and blackboard. Even so, some classes (less than 20% of the total) had extensive student involvement in groupwork, pupil choice of tasks and projects, and freedom of movement.

Compared to the portrait drawn of the classroom at the turn of the century, departures from the wholly teacher-centered approach are evident in a substantial percentage of classes where students worked cooperatively and moved freely about the room. The growth of a hybrid pattern of instruction revealed teachers to be using practices that involved students actively in classroom work. Note also that in all the categories high school classes show higher percentages of teacher-centered and lower percentages of student-centered behavior than do elementary classrooms—precisely the same pattern we saw in New York City during this period.

Examining particular high schools using the available classroom descriptions, student accounts, and teacher reports provides an outline of teaching behavior, although a complete picture remains elusive. Recall that in no Denver high school were more than one third of the staff involved in the Eight-Year Study. Hence, what "progressive education" teachers did in one wing of the building may or may not be what their peers did elsewhere in the high school. I located 20 written descriptions and photographs of experimental classes in the five schools between 1934 and 1939. Based upon counts taken from the annual yearbooks and master schedules of three high schools, I estimate that these 20 classes represent about a quarter of the teachers who taught experimental classes during these years. Fourteen teachers (70%) reported or were shown using panel discussions, debates, pupil-teacher planning, and other techniques associated with student-centered patterns of instruction. The rest of the classes disclose little movement away from the familiar teacher-centered configuration even though they were considered experimental classes.

Read, for example, what Ralph Putnam, Latin teacher at East High, wrote in an article for Denver teachers in the initial year of the experiment:

> I wish to emphasize . . . that nothing very radical is being or will be attempted. We are here to learn Latin and the mastery of Latin will always be our prime objective.

How, then, he asked, did work with 40 progressive education students differ from other Latin classes he taught? In reading Caesar's works on the Helvetian War, Putnam said, "the more rapid reading, possible in a special group, enables the pupils to follow more readily the thread of the story and thus to feel the vitality and vigor of the narrative." Moreover, far more attention could be given to the study of English derivatives and to extra reading because the class of 40 had "extra time," that is, larger blocks of class time. Putnam's goal of covering more material in depth seems not to have been shared by the majority of teachers.[24]

Another view of the progressive education program at East High comes from a 1938 report written by 10th graders during the first two semesters they spent in core classes, labs, special interest groups, and so on. Eight students planned and wrote a diary about the project. They described what it was like to be in a program with 235 students and six teachers for three periods a day. As they and their fellow students moved through the daily schedule, these eight described how they and their teachers planned units, and how class members chose activities, pursued their interests independently in core labs, worked in groups on projects, and went into the community on numerous field trips.

> We still consider our class very interesting, but we have discovered that it is also quite a bit of work. We must find our references by ourselves, outline

our own methods and means of study; use our own initiative throughout our work. . . . The sixth hour is our regular core period during which we have lectures, reports, motion pictures, or discussions of topics related to our community study. For example, during our study of crime and juvenile delinquency, two films were shown in our classroom. One was a cut from the picture *Big House,* and the other was a picture of gang life among boys. After the pictures, we had a class discussion on topics concerning the films. . . .

On Thursday the seventh hour is used as a laboratory period. Most of the work on our projects is now done in these periods. There are six of them, covering art, history, human relations, social studies, English, and science and statistics. . . . One girl selected a subject which required interpretation of long tables of statistics. She used several periods in getting help from the math laboratory on interpretation of these tables. [October 3rd, 1938, second semester of first year in core program]

Nine photos of students working at different classroom activities flesh out the student-written narrative. No teachers appear in the photographs.[25]

Other evidence on the teaching behavior of those participating in the Eight-Year Study comes from surveys completed in 1933 and 1940 in two high schools. In the survey from 1933, the first year of the experiment, 16% of the participating teachers chose the word "much" (as opposed to "not at all" or "some") to describe the degree of joint planning they did with students in selecting subject matter, class activities, individual projects, and evaluation. By 1940, 53% checked "much," a large increase for an activity considered crucial by pedagogical progressives (although it is likely that the teachers who completed the item seven years earlier were not the same ones who answered it in 1940).[26]

Finally, in early 1938, Wilford Aiken, director of the Eight-Year Study, visited each of the innovative programs in Denver's five high schools. He met teachers, students, and district administrators. His report concluded that "a real break with the traditional subject matter" had occurred. Substantial pupil-teacher planning took place. Life in the community had increasingly become a subject of investigation in core classrooms. Moreover, he wrote, "many of the old recitation techniques are disappearing from the classroom." The report did point out, however, that "in some classes discussion consists primarily of the pooling of misinformation." Generally complimentary toward the program, the report confirmed that curricular and teaching practices had indeed changed.[27]

These fragments of evidence suggest that many teachers involved in the Eight-Year Study taught in a manner consistent with the aims of the program. But not all could drop the baggage of teacher-centered practices, as we saw in the results of the formal evaluation of New York City's Activity Program.

THE IMPACT AND LEGACY OF REFORM

After the Eight-Year Study's final evaluation appeared in 1941, Superintendent Charles Greene, who had led the study as assistant superintendent, expanded the core program to all junior and senior high schools by mandating a 3-year course of study and 2 years of general education as a requirement for graduation. Using instructional units that had been developed and polished by high school teachers over the previous 8 years, high school sophomores spent one third of their time in general education classes. The amount of student time in these classes decreased to one period a day when they became seniors.[28]

By 1943, the graduation requirement was reduced to 1 year, with the five high schools given the option to design their own programs. North High School, for instance, had between 15 and 26 teachers out of a faculty of 80 assigned to general education classes between 1940 and 1943; by 1944, when local option was permitted, general education as a class assignment for teachers disappeared from the master schedule, replaced by such classes as diagnostic English, instructional communication, and social living. At East High School, general education became a 10th-grade course required of all students. The class dealt with counseling issues and vocational guidance. The general education teacher was also the counselor.[29]

Following the heated controversy over progressivism in the schools in the late 1940s and early 1950s (a furor that angered Mira Scott Frank, the Board of Education member whom I quoted at the beginning of this section), general education as a course was abandoned 3 years after Frank left the Board.[30]

The demise of Denver's general education courses in the 1950s was part of a national reaction to an intense barrage of criticism targeting public schools that had reputations for being progressive, as defined by these critics. The abolition of general education, however, should not obscure classroom changes in curriculum and instruction that had occurred since Jesse Newlon came to Denver in the summer of 1920. Courses of study, textbooks, and certain teaching approaches changed, although the degree of change varied between elementary and high school classrooms. Whereas in New York City such changes had occurred at a slow, very uneven pace, under Newlon and his successors there was a far more systematic and insistent drive to implement these reforms over the two decades in question.

One of the reasons for the speed and intensity of the organizational changes that touched a substantial number of Denver classrooms may have been the remarkable continuity in superintendent leadership, leadership that placed great faith both in progressive pedagogy and in the pivotal importance of the teacher, yet was tempered by the daily realities of schooling. These beliefs shaped the general direction taken by Newlon and his successors into the 1940s. Moreover, Denver's top school administrators gave much thought to the design and implementation of policies altering existing procedures. The curriculum revision program established a pattern of teacher involvement in systemwide policymaking for the classroom. Unusual for its time, the process emerged as an informal yet potent introduction of teachers to progressive pedagogy. Because the program was highly prized by the top leadership, incentives (e.g., released time from the classroom, recognition by the School Board, professional growth) were embedded in the effort. Since the venture lasted well over a decade, a substantial portion of teachers were sufficiently engaged to consider introducing these ideas into their classrooms.

Nonetheless, the evidence reveals that most teachers continued teacher-centered practices. Still, a considerable minority of teachers did adopt, in varying degrees, mixtures of existing and new practices. Thus, a top-down design of curricular and instructional change, endorsed and generously supported by the School Board and superintendents and wedded to a carefully crafted plan of teacher involvement, influenced classroom instruction— again, more in elementary than in high school settings.

Yet even in the high schools, the Eight-Year Study in Denver was unique among the nation's secondary schools. The teachers who were involved, a minority on each school's staff, used progressive techniques in dozens of classrooms although such practices seldom got past their colleagues' doors. Denver, then, qualifications aside, was a national pacesetter in implementing progressive education. Washington, D.C.'s schools and classrooms between the two world wars exhibit traits we have already seen in New York City and Denver, while revealing some peculiar to the nation's capital.

CHAPTER 4

Behind the Classroom Door:
Washington, D.C.,
1920–1940

When the present superintendent of schools took office on July 1, 1920, he knew that the administration of the school system involved many difficulties. Superintendents of other cities told him that it was considered by schoolmen one of the most difficult superintendencies in the United States. . . .

Educational progress in Washington is slow because under the present system of educational control and financial support the needs of the school system are allowed to become acute before consideration is given to improvement and relief then comes altogether too slowly. . . .

Failure on the part of the appropriation power to provide money for progressive educational activities makes an educational system unprogressive. . . . Failure to provide money for adequate salaries means mediocre teachers and ineffective education. Failure to build enough schoolhouses means overcrowded classes, portables and poorly adapted rented accommodations, and such conditions make impossible the best teaching. . . . [1]

These statements were made to the District of Columbia Board of Education by their new superintendent, Frank W. Ballou. Within 2 years of his appointment Ballou bluntly and concisely scored the divided authority of a Board of Education beholden both to judicially appointed District Commissioners and to two Houses of Congress that had produced the city's reputation as a graveyard for superintendents. Ballou went on to serve almost a quarter century (1920–1943), a longer tenure than that of any Washington superintendent before or since.

Born in 1879 and raised in rural upstate New York, Ballou graduated from a state teacher training school and taught in rural schools between 1897 and 1899. By 1904 he had completed a bachelor's degree from Teachers College and decided to move to Ohio, where he earned a master's degree at the University of Cincinnati. While there, he was appointed principal of the University's Technical School and directed it for 3 years. Switching to the college classroom, he became an assistant professor of education and taught for 3 years. Returning east, he enrolled at Harvard, where he earned a Ph.D. in 1914. For his dissertation, he studied how teachers were appointed in urban school systems.

The year he received his degree, the Boston school superintendent asked him to head the district's Department of Educational Investigation and Measurement, one of the few school districts in the nation with a research bureau. For 3 years his department administered, analyzed, and reported results from various batteries of intelligence and achievement tests. The frontiers of progressive practice in the use of tests for grouping students within classes and across curricula found Frank Ballou at the right place and time. In 1917 he was promoted to assistant superintendent of the Boston system, and for the next 3 years helped organize and develop the newest form of school organization—the junior high school. At the age of 41, he applied for the Washington, D.C., position and was named superintendent. Like his Denver colleague, Jesse Newlon, Ballou began his initial 3-year contract in the summer of 1920.[2]

Within the first decade of his tenure, Ballou had established himself locally as a determined, first-rate administrator unafraid to speak his mind and committed to scientific management as a tool in solving school problems. Nationally, his peers demonstrated their esteem for his talents by electing him president of the Department of Superintendence in 1925. That year he gave an address at the Indianapolis meeting of the NEA on the progress of a science of education since the turn of the century. In Washington he needed every bit of scientific knowledge and talent he possessed.

When Ballou railed at the city's maze-like governance, his voice joined a growing chorus of criticism against the Organic Act of 1906. This law, passed by Congress, created a nine-member Board of Education appointed to administer the largest segregated school system in the country. Unlike other big-city school boards, the District Board of Education split its authority (but not its responsibility) with three appointed district commissioners, who revised the Board's budget estimates, controlled all expenditures, allocated and audited funds, and purchased school equipment, supplies, and so on. In effect, the Board of Education had no independent authority to secure or spend funds, including the purchase of land and the construction of school buildings. Bad as this was from a superintendent's perspective, it became worse when Congress (which appropriated every penny going to the District), in

Ballou's words, "reviews, revises, and reduces" the school budget item by item, line by line initially in the House of Representatives, then in the Senate. If the totals between the two Houses differed, a conference committee settled the final amount that went to the schools.

The horror stories of delay, neglect, and confusion were legion to insiders familiar with the labyrinthine process of securing a budget in the District. In his 1921–1922 annual report, Ballou, using restrained language, detailed all the roadblocks he and the Board had to overcome to improve school conditions. To strengthen his case, Ballou drafted United States Commissioner of Education John J. Tigert to testify in behalf of the District schools in the final pages of his report: "The superintendent is so fettered up with overhead organizations that he is practically impotent, as I see it. I would not take the job at two or three times the salary." Ballou then turned to an "authoritative work on education," prepared by "leading American educators," to describe the organization of the District of Columbia schools. The *Cyclopedia of Education* minced no words:

> Educational conditions in Washington, from an administrative point of view, are among the worst to be found in any city in the Union, and the school system is behind that of cities elsewhere of equal size. . . . Until Congress can be made to realize that it is incompetent properly to administer such an undertaking and will give to the Board of Education the power and control which should belong to it there is little hope of a good, modern school system for the District of Columbia. The superintendency of the schools of Washington is generally regarded as one of the most difficult and most undesirable positions in the United States.[3]

To use a word much loved by superintendents, Washington schools were a "challenge." By 1940, when Ballou formally tallied up his administration's achievements over two decades, he was quite proud in listing changes that he had maneuvered through the labyrinth.

"School Achievements in Twenty Years," a document Ballou submitted to the Board of Education in 1941, listed his successes in securing administrative changes, new buildings, improvements in school organization, and improved supervision and instruction. Out of a 125-page report, 94 pages dealt with streamlined administration, new facilities, and improved teaching conditions (e.g., salaries and retirement guidelines). Twenty-five pages (20%) described improvements in instruction and supervision. Most of these pages were devoted to curriculum revision, expanded testing programs, and new grouping procedures—in that order. No mention of teaching methods, project activities, or any concerted effort to introduce progressive practices into classrooms appeared, although a major change had been announced in 1938 with the Child Development Program. The language of progressives, however, popped up in numerous places, including the formal statement of philosophy produced by curriculum revision between 1938 and 1940 (printed twice in the report) as well as a description of what a modern school should be like that sounded almost as if it had been lifted from a course description at Teachers College, Columbia University.[4]

The point of all this is to underscore Ballou's aims in administering the District schools. Defining the major issues as the need to secure more buildings, reorganize his administration, and navigate the shoals of Washington and congressional politics, Ballou concentrated upon guiding the system into the 20th century. A man who believed deeply in the science of education and in using that science to improve schooling, he was cut from the same cloth as those administrative progressives who had redesigned school systems in the first decades of the century. On instructional issues, his interests inclined more toward expansion of the junior high program, using tests to assign students into appropriate groups, and a tightly controlled version of curriculum revision. Closer in his thinking to New York City's Maxwell, Ettinger, and O'Shea than to Denver's Newlon and Threlkeld, Ballou left his mark on the organization. On instruction, his fingerprints were less apparent.

THE SOCIAL AND ORGANIZATIONAL SETTING FOR CLASSROOM INSTRUCTION

A central fact of schooling in the District of Columbia was racial segregation. In his 1911 report to the Board of Education, Superintendent Alexander Stuart described some of the effects of having two separate school systems segregated by law. With 32% of the students black and attending school separately from whites, costs, he pointed out, would inevitably be higher in a dual school system.

> It is obvious that were it not for the exactions of the race question, no city of the size of Washington would consider it necessary or wise to maintain two deputy superintendents, two normal schools, [and] two expensive manual training schools. . . . A study of the location of school buildings shows that to meet the needs of the white and colored children two smaller buildings have been erected in the same (attendance area) which, under other conditions, would have been merged into one larger building at greatly reduced cost. . . .
>
> Repeated examples are found throughout where a class of white children of a given grade is in one building and another small class of colored children of the same grade is in a nearby building. . . .
>
> The same causes explain in part the employment of a number of teachers in excess of most cities where white and colored children attend school together. . . . [5]

Stuart stressed the economic and organizational inefficiencies of segregation. White and black social attitudes also permeated curriculum and instruction in both obvious and subtle ways.

Because the District of Columbia was the nation's capital, since Reconstruction schools for the "colored population" had flourished there. It was generally agreed within the black community that their schools, while not as well funded as white schools, nonetheless offered educational opportunities that were greater than those most districts elsewhere in the nation could offer their black children. When the top black school official in the District, Assistant Superintendent Garnet Wilkinson, said that "the entire colored school system was the best in the United States," no black school official in the North or South challenged the statement.[6]

The caste system also created socially esteemed jobs for a small black, college-educated elite who prided themselves on educational achievements that, in some instances, outstripped those of white children. The first high school in the District of Columbia, for example, was founded by a group of blacks in 1870. It became the Dunbar High School, which schooled generation after generation of black students, many of whom entered college until 1955 when the District of Columbia schools were formally desegregated.[7]

The strategy of cultivating the talented minority of students who could benefit from advanced schooling helped to make Dunbar High School a place where rigorous academic studies were normal for black students, in some instances outdistancing Central, the premier white high school. Ivy League–educated black teachers demanded that their students memorize passages, write long essays, and carefully prepare homework assignments where every "i" was dotted and every "t" crossed. Furthermore, the growing availability of secondary schooling to members of the black community, particularly to those from working-class backgrounds and to recent migrants from the rural South (in the early 1900s many black children left school by the fourth grade) sharpened an awareness of social class among teachers and administrators. Howard University sociologist E. Franklin Frazier reported stories of children who heard teachers in class belittle the behavior of poor blacks on streetcars or in the auditorium.[8]

Educating a black elite was a goal deeply embedded in the thinking of those who operated schools for "colored" children. Top black educators, who were often also members of the social elite, believed that their primary obligation was to the ablest students, because these talented ones could use their education to make their way in a harsh, insensitive white world and ultimately help the race improve its standing. The linkages between this implicit philosophy and the sharply defined class differences between segments of the District's black community were evident.[9]

Strongly felt class differences, often woven around differences in skin

PLATE 4.1 *Washington, D.C. elementary classroom, 1942*

color within the black community, also shaped teacher and student attitudes about schooling. Frazier, who studied black youth in Washington, D.C., in the late 1930s, documented how concerns about shades of skin color and social class affected administrators, teachers, and students. After recounting teenagers' stories of how their teachers favored light-skinned peers over them, Frazier comments in a footnote:

> During an interview with a teacher who denied any preference was shown upper-class or lighter students, the interviewer observed that on three occasions when the teacher wanted a pupil to run errands or do something for her a light child was selected despite the fact that several dark chil-

dren eagerly sought the attention of the teacher when she asked for volunteers. . . . [10]

More obvious linkages between social attitudes and curriculum and instruction can be seen in the introduction in the 1920s of Negro History Week. (Historian Carter G. Woodson had founded the Association for The Study of Negro Life and History in Washington in 1915 and initiated Negro History Week through this organization.) The slow penetration of new subject matter into classrooms and the spreading interest, in these decades of race-conscious teaching, in the contributions of blacks are further evidence.

Organizational Context

Class size, classroom space and furniture, the schedule, and the official curriculum are organizational factors that help shape instruction.

Class size. How many students in a class inevitably influences a teacher's thinking about how much can be taught and in what ways. Class size numbers reported by the District administration were averages; averages conceal important differences in class size. In 1927–1928, for example, out of almost 1,200 elementary classes, 29% contained 40 or more students, about equally distributed between white and black schools. Classes with less than 30 students made up 18% of the total, with 85% of those classes containing white students. Thus, 53% of the elementary classes had between 31 and 39 students. Still, even these figures mask the differences in size between black and white classes. Such differences are apparent in Table 4.1, which shows figures for selected years in the decade 1922–1932. By 1948, when Professor George Strayer completed the first comprehensive survey of District schools, the gap had widened: The average number of students in white elementary classes was 32; for black classes the average was 39.

Class space and furniture. The buildings and rooms these students and teachers worked in daily between 8:30 and 2:30 changed substantially over

TABLE 4.1 *Differences in the average size of white and black classes in Washington, D.C., for selected years*

Year	Class Size	
	White	Black
1922	34.3	37.3
1927	34.9	37.9
1932	30.8	36.1

the years. Even after the major rebuilding campaign Ballou and the Board of Education maneuvered through Congress in 1925, overcrowded, antiquated classrooms remained in many buildings across the city, making, in George Strayer's words, "adequate instruction impossible." Over half of the elementary schools were built before 1925. Until the 1940s, classrooms contained long rows of stationary desks that together accommodated 40 pupils. "Today [1948], with a recommended maximum class enrollment of 30 in the elementary school," Strayer wrote, "many of these classrooms are still too small and a great many of them are crowded. . . ." He added, "The modern Child Development Program"—which the District had launched in 1938—"requires informal groupings of children, floor space for constructive activities, cupboards, [and] storage space for supplies. . . ." Even in the newer buildings existing space was inadequate, according to Strayer.[12]

As classroom space changed slowly, so did furniture. In 1920, almost two thirds of the desks bolted to floors had been in use since the turn of the century. Between 1920 and 1929 only 200 desks had been replaced. In 1930, the first year of a five-year program to replace stationary desks with portable ones, 7,000 were replaced. The Depression slowed down the conversion drastically. Nevertheless, when Strayer's team surveyed classrooms in 1948, all elementary schools had installed movable desks and chairs.[13]

Not so the secondary schools. Into those built since 1925 (13 of 19 junior high schools and 4 of 9 high schools), movable classroom furniture had been introduced throughout the 1930s. Meanwhile, in the Central and Dunbar high schools, constructed in 1916, bolted-down desks sat in rows, class after class, year after year.

The schedule. While the type of desks used was of some importance, what occurred in classrooms often depended upon how teachers allocated time for instruction. For years, teachers received copies of weekly schedules mandating the amount of time they had to spend on each subject. At the secondary level a schedule sliced the school day into equal segments of 40 to 50 minutes for each subject.

By 1927, elementary teachers, unlike their secondary colleagues, had to teach 11 subjects ranging from the usual reading, handwriting, and arithmetic through drawing, music, and physical education. A standard schedule determined the amount of time to be spent on each subject at each grade level. Arithmetic, for example, occupied 35 minutes daily in the first grade and 3.5 hours per day in third and fourth grades, falling to 2.5 hours daily in sixth grade. In 1936, the Board of Education adopted a new formal schedule that varied time allotments slightly. When the Strayer team visited schools in 1948, it found that the time schedule adopted 12 years earlier was still being followed, although the Child Development Program, initiated in 1938, called for specific amounts of time to be alloted to various clusters of subjects.[14]

When a school board approves a time schedule, teachers do not necessarily fall into step. In Washington, many teachers and principals, intent upon installing activity programs in their classrooms, departed from the schedule simply because it impeded the flexibility essential for informal classrooms. The teacher-printed daily schedule for a first-grade classroom in the 1940s read:

Our Big Plan Today

1. Look and see our trailer. The boys made it.
2. Let's go for a story ride.
3. Let's read our new story.
4. Let's play hot potato.
5. Have you done a reading card?
6. Let's be happy.[15]

While such primary classrooms used flexible schedules and departed from the approved one, such approaches were uncommon. Teachers indeed differed in how much time they spent on reading, arithmetic, and geography, but most diverged within a range that was implicitly recognized as reasonable. After all, the organizational signals to teachers and principals were plain. The Superintendent's words accompanying the time schedule available to each teacher left little to interpretation—"Every officer and teacher in the elementary school shall consider himself governed by this weekly schedule"—and principals were expected to inspect teachers' plans to "know that each teacher is observing the distribution of time. . . ." Furthermore, District teachers' instructional day was 30 minutes shorter than those in most districts of comparable size (5 hours compared to 5.5 hours), which may have generated pressure upon teachers to cover the crowded curriculum by following the prescribed time allotments.[16]

The point is that an outdated board-approved time schedule was ill fitted for a new program, especially one that was directed toward producing a flexible classroom where teachers and pupils jointly planned tasks. Such a mix-up suggests, at worst, a bureaucratic oversight, but more probably the existence of mixed feelings toward the new effort. Even were I generously to assume that most teachers followed the District's time schedule, many classroom teachers, less adventurous than colleagues who leaped upon the progressive bandwagon, probably thought twice before embarking upon a revised schedule, given the shorter day and the superintendent's directives, especially if their principal lacked enthusiasm for the new venture.

The official curriculum. Mixed signals also marked the curriculum revision efforts begun by Ballou in 1925 and continued fitfully into the 1930s. On the one hand, as a noted member of the NEA's Department of Superintendence, Ballou served on its curriculum commission and chaired the committee that revised the elementary science course of study written by Washington administrators and teachers. This course of study was published in the 1926 Yearbook of the Department of Superintendence and was approved by the Board of Education that year. In the same year, Ballou appointed committees to revise arithmetic, reading and literature, English, and geography courses.[17]

On the other hand, at least three major organizational differences separated Ballou's administrations from those of Denver's Newlon and Threlkeld. First, while teachers were assigned to committees, District administrators chaired these groups until the late 1930s, when an occasional teacher was chosen to direct a committee's work. Second, the committees began their work after 3:00 p.m., on the teachers' time. Third, no specialists were hired to help the committees, nor did committees receive any training on how to write objectives or a course of study.[18]

Similarities with Denver's curriculum development efforts existed, of course. Teachers did participate. Progressive vocabulary and references to activity methods studded the syllabi, and in-service education for teachers increased. Networks of like-minded professionals developed. All of this occurred in slow motion, unlike in Denver. Delays in the production of courses of study were common. Because the work was done after school hours, the process stretched out over years. Finally, teachers began to object to committee work between 3:00 and 5:00 p.m., noting that other cities provided substitutes to relieve participating staff from work. Nonetheless, by 1940, 7 elementary courses of study, (19 for junior high, 4 for vocational school, and 21 for senior high) had been published, and teachers were expected to use them. But did they?[19]

Other factors. This question refocuses attention on the classroom. How did District teachers teach? How extensive were teacher-centered and progressive practices in white and black classrooms from Anacostia to Georgetown? The organizational conditions described so far suggest the outlines of some possible answers.

As in New York, but less so than in Denver, classroom space and furniture presented more obstacles than opportunities for teachers to use progressive practices. Of course, the physical environment did not prevent use of small groups, pupil-teacher planning, activity units, and project work, but those teachers reluctant to experiment may have been further discouraged by lack of space, cumbersome furniture, and difficulties in securing supplies. Also, with over 35 students in a class, there were few incentives for teachers to work with students in small groups or individually, or to either prepare or beg for the necessary extra materials.

Another constraint was time. I have already mentioned the 5-hour instructional day in which up to 11 subjects were to be taught. Subtract opening exercises (Bible reading, collecting money, taking attendance) and recess, add teacher concern for covering the prescribed subjects, particularly in view of an unexpected principal visit, and the result is a reluctance to introduce new instructional practices.

Another line of reasoning is to ask what organizational mechanisms encouraged the spread of progressive teaching practices. Clearly, a curriculum revision process helped, especially as it was wired into a local and national network of similarly inclined professionals. While the District's organizational linkages were hardly as systematic or as carefully crafted as Denver's, one would expect that a number of teachers and principals would have been intrigued by the child-centered notions embedded in pedagogical progressivism or, already converted, would have gotten the green light from headquarters to move ahead on their own.

Teacher institutes, funded in part by private contributions from administrators and teachers, brought locally and nationally known professionals to lecture staff on varied topics, blacks meeting at Dunbar and whites at Central. During the 1920s teachers heard from W. W. Charters (the University of Chicago) on curriculum revision, Florence Bamberger (Johns Hopkins University) on classroom efficiency, Elbert Fretwell (Teachers College) on organizing social activities for junior and senior high schools, and Laura Zirbe (Lincoln School, Teachers College) on progressive reading programs. In addition, teachers met monthly, again in separate schools, to study current issues. These compulsory meetings were often organized in a lecture format with either a guest or the assistant superintendent delivering the talk. Topics included the activity method, adapting courses of study to projects, and the like.[20]

Another important mechanism supporting the spread of progressive ideas into classrooms was teachers' increasing level of education. The assumption was that the higher the level of teachers' formal schooling, the greater their awareness of modern trends in education, particularly if the schooling had been recently acquired. In 1931, 78% of high school teachers had at least a bachelor's degree, while 96% of elementary teachers had either between 2 and 3 years of normal school training or a bachelor's degree. By 1948, 78% of the entire staff were college graduates. Among elementary teachers, more blacks (74%) had bachelor's degrees than whites (61%), while the reverse was true of senior high teachers (85% of black teachers were college graduates; 93% of white teachers were). Teachers also reported to Strayer how recently they had received their last professional training. Within the previous 5 years (1943–1948), 55% of the teachers had taken courses; 29% had received their last training between 1933 and 1942; and 16% had not taken a course since they had been appointed.[21]

This review of organizational and social contexts that shape teaching practices offers hints but no direct evidence of how teachers taught.

Elementary Classrooms

That black and white teachers used progressive methods to varying degrees is undeniable. A group of black administrators appointed by Assistant Superintendent Garnet Wilkinson designed and implemented a 5-month experiment at Mott School and an unnamed "traditional" school in 1924. The aim of the experiment was to compare the effects of progressive education upon teachers and students. The new approaches used in the eight-grade school included the testing of students, new textbooks, additional materials, and movable furniture for grades 1 through 4. Teachers were encouraged to convert the formal course of study into projects. Mott teachers overwhelmingly approved the experiment, according to a survey: 74% said projects produced superior results with their students and 94% found that students showed more interest in projects than in regular schoolwork.[22]

Occasional articles in the *Journal of the Columbian Educational Association,* a publication written by and for black educators in District schools, displayed interest in progressive schooling. Mayme Lewis of Bruce School reported in a 1925 issue the details of her 2-day visit to the third and fourth grades of Horace Mann, a New York City progressive private school at Teachers College. At the Monroe Demonstration School, an adjunct to Miner Teachers College (the black teacher training institution in the District), a number of teachers, in concert with their student teachers, introduced and maintained innovations such as classroom centers, small-group work, and joint teacher-pupil planning. Finally, another piece of indirect evidence is the annual exhibit of elementary school activities where black teachers presented projects their classes had produced.[23]

Unfortunately, I have no way of assessing how widespread these classroom practices were in black schools (called Divisions 10–13 in the District of Columbia school system). In issues of the *Journal,* for each article describing an activity-centered classroom, three others laid out exemplary lesson plans revealing teacher direction and control at each step of the plan, without a hint of student involvement other than answering teacher questions.[24]

A similar problem surfaces in determining the extent of progressive practices in the white schools (Divisions 1–9). That schools and certain teachers introduced progressive methods in their classrooms goes without question. Articles in national professional journals (*Childhood Education* in 1932 and 1933, *Progressive Education* in 1936, and *Grade Teacher* in 1939) featured classes in Petworth and Ketcham schools constructing railroad stations, studying Mexican life, and painting. The *Washington Post* and other local papers carried articles on classroom projects. Julia Hahn, an elementary school supervisor who had been deeply involved in San Francisco schools' progressive efforts before coming to Washington, worked directly with teachers and wrote articles on the activity movement in District schools. Despite the various accounts of classroom practices, I found it difficult to assess how far these classroom practices had spread among the District's teachers.[25]

The only direct appraisal of the diffusion of progressive methods in the District schools took place in 1948 when George Strayer, at the Board of Education's request, brought his team to Washington to determine, among other things, how much of the Child Development Program had been implemented in classrooms.

The program was as ambitious as but far less systematically implemented than either New York City's Activity Program or Denver's Eight-Year Study. Ballou's formal effort at installing progressive education contained all the conventional language about a "child-centered activity program" spreading throughout District schools and pushing out the "traditional . . . subject-centered program." Classrooms were to become places where children shared in planning the work and actively studied the family, the neighborhood, the city, and the nation. Projects, centers, movable furniture, activity periods, and crafts—the often-cited repertoire that pedagogical progressives envisioned for public schools—were central to the Child Development Program.[26]

District supervisors and principals were charged to establish activity programs in the schools. Some schools, building on cadres of teachers who had experimented earlier with projects and centers, embraced the Superintendent's charge with great enthusiasm. Most schools, pinned to existing practice, apparently did not, or could not, institute the entire program.

Strayer's team had, as one of its objectives, the job of assessing to what degree the program, initiated in 1938, had been implemented a decade later. Strayer found "many" classrooms that met both the letter and the spirit of the Superintendent's mandate, in spite of numerous enervating obstacles, errors, and just plain poor judgments made by school officials that either frustrated or, worse, contradicted Ballou's efforts. Strayer observed that:

- Teachers were not given time or resources to produce new curricula for the new program. "This was a serious error."
- Only one new unit—math—was produced for teachers' use in 10 years.
- Rooms lacked space, cabinets, and equipment; teachers lacked textbooks and instructional materials.
- School days were short.
- Classes were large.
- Teachers were not prepared to institute changes.[27]

Too many teachers held fuzzy notions of what the program was intended for and what they specifically had to do (i.e., "What am I supposed to do Monday morning?"). Strayer divided District elementary teachers into two groups: those with "the child-development philosophy with its emphasis upon the whole child and upon purposive learning" and those with the "traditional" stress upon mastery of facts and skills. As with all such arbitrary categories within the survey, Strayer offered no specific numbers, only such vague words as "many." Hence, determining the spread of the program is difficult.[28]

The closest Strayer came to estimating the diffusion of the program was to describe how four staff members had visited all elementary schools and spoken with teachers, principals, and supervising directors. Based upon these discussions and observations, they rated the schools they saw as "superior," "good," "fair," and "poor." Unlike the Morrison survey (1940) of New York's Activity Program, where observers were trained, scales constructed and verified for validity and reliability, and data carefully sifted, Strayer's team judged a school "superior"

> if the program was designed to fit the needs of the children, the purposes of teachers and pupils were clear, there was a well organized program of child development activities, an effective instructional program dealing with fundamental knowledges [*sic*], understandings and skills, and a community program which secured the interests and cooperation of parents on the education of their children.[29]

These observers found 19% of all elementary schools to be superior, 35.7% good, 27% fair, and 18.2% poor. Only by a courageous inferential leap can one conclude that Child Development Programs existed in more than half of the District schools—that is, by adding up schools rated superior and good. Not only would such a leap be courageous, it would be precarious given the multiple and ambiguous criteria observers used, the probable differences among them in making judgments based on such loosely defined criteria, and the obvious fact that differences among teachers exist within a school as they do between schools (e.g., in the implementation of New York City's Activity Program).[30]

Strayer's observations about the organizational obstacles to the program's implementation and about how spottily the Child Development Program was executed draw a picture of unsystematic and uneven implementation in District elementary schools.

Further indications of the spread of progressive practices come from the 53 descriptions (20 of elementary classes) that I collected about Washington, D.C., classrooms. In Figure 4.1 student-centered teaching patterns appear in slightly more than one out of three elementary classrooms. The numbers,

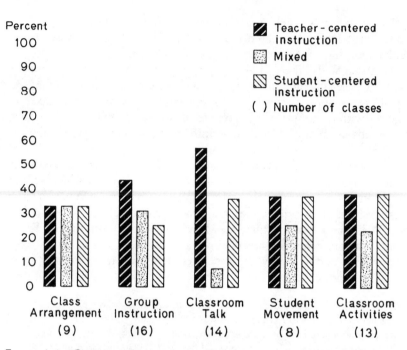

Figure 4.1 *Patterns of instruction in Washington, D.C. elementary classrooms, 1920–1940*

however, are small and hardly more reliable than Strayer's team's judgments on individual school quality. When combined, the data, individually flawed as they are, suggest that progressive teaching practices, as defined by the Child Development Program, penetrated a minority of the District's classrooms, although that minority may be as small as one quarter or as large as one third. We can also infer that certain progressive practices were incorporated by many District elementary teachers into hybrids of progressive and teacher-centered practices. This assumption would increase the estimated number of teachers who expanded their range of techniques.

High School Classrooms

Figure 4.2 shows patterns similar to New York City and Denver: For every category the occurence of teacher-centered practices at the high school level exceeds the occurrence of those practices in elementary classrooms. The graph draws a profile of a high school teacher teaching five or more classes

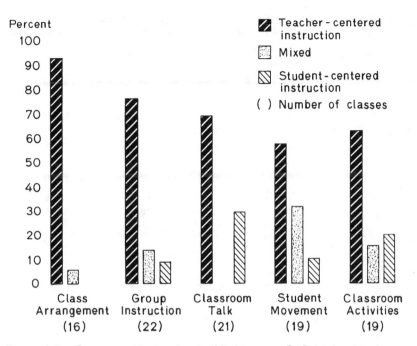

FIGURE 4.2 *Patterns of instruction in Washington, D.C. high school classrooms, 1920–1940*

daily, facing rows of students sitting at desks. In three out of four classrooms, the teachers instructed the entire group, talked most of the time, and permitted little student-initiated movement within the room. One way to corroborate that profile is to take a closer look at some District high schools, white and black.

Central High School. The school sits perched on a hill overlooking the Capitol, the Washington Monument, and downtown Washington, D.C. Its reputation for having a splendid view of the city began when it opened its brand-new doors to white students in 1916. A high school established in the closing decades of the 19th century, it claimed as graduates both J. Edgar Hoover, subsequently Director of the Federal Bureau of Investigation, and Helen Hayes, later to become a world-renowned actress. As Central students they probably read the student handbooks that described school rules, curricula, requirements for graduation, the daily schedule, extracurricular activities, and school cheers.

In the 1926 handbook, students were told to go to their section (homeroom) for opening exercises by 8:55 a.m. "In classrooms absolute quiet must prevail at this time," the handbook stated, because the students must have the "proper attitude" and "frame of mind necessary to start the day right." At 9:10 the bell rang to start the students' seven-period day—"six recitation periods" and lunch. Students had 4 minutes to move from one class to another. A rich array of activities was available at the end of the day, including the chance to write for *Brecky,* the senior yearbook, the *Journal,* a literary review begun in 1886, and the *Bulletin,* a weekly newspaper.[31]

In the *Bulletin,* from 1925 with the introduction of a section called "Class Notes" until 1938, when the column lapsed, students wrote items on what certain teachers did in their rooms. In these columns I identified 302 descriptions of teaching activities for 55 English, social studies, science, math, and foreign language teachers. Almost half of the teachers taught English, one quarter social studies, one fifth foreign languages, and the remainder science.

Student reporters noted unusual items about teachers' classrooms:

1. Student Participation in Class Recitation.
   November 24, 1925. In Florence Jayne's English class "various pupils, or monitors as they are called, record the attendance, test the rest of the class, read the questions from the true and false tests."
   April 2, 1930. In Alice Clark's Latin class "at each lesson some member of the class acts as teacher. . . . One of the pupils called on Miss Clark to answer one of the questions."
2. Non-Routine Classroom Activities (e.g., field trips, lantern slides, radio programs, outside speakers, panel discussions, acting out scenes from novels and plays)
   December 17, 1930. Bessie Whitford's sixth-period English class debated the merits of high school fraternities.
   October 20, 1932. Mr. DeShazo's third-period chemistry class "performed their first experiment by themselves. . . . They made oxygen and found its properties."
   January 19, 1933. Miss Gill's fourth-year French class held a bridge party with the players speaking only French.
   March 9, 1933. Alma Boyd's second-period English class presented *The Vicar of Wakefield* through a simulated radio broadcast.
3. Active Student Involvement in Class Activities (e.g., student-planned projects, groupwork)
   March 16, 1932. Students in Ruth Denham's second-period class made replicas of the Globe Theatre—"The theatre will be about large enough to place on a card table."
   February 15, 1934. "Freshman biology students in Miss E. C. Paul's class

are working on projects of practical application. Allowed to pick any topic in which they are interested, some students have chosen dish gardens, sprouting seeds, etc."

November 17, 1938. Florence Jayne's classes "voted for and attained certain changes in the teacher's system of marking."

In analyzing the 302 classroom activities of 55 teachers I found that 15 English and 4 history teachers were responsible for two-thirds of all activities that involved student participation, as reported by the student newspaper. This translates to about one fourth of the entire faculty in the mid-1930s. Of course, the sample of teachers is selective, reflecting classes that student reporters heard about or attended. The point is, however, that within this sample there were a variety of approaches among teachers using progressive practices.[32]

I found that fewer than 10% of all activities reported by students in these classes included joint student-teacher planning, a revised course content related to student needs, students leading discussions, or groupwork on proj-

PLATE 4.2 *Washington D.C., Woodrow Wilson High School, algebra lesson, white, 1943.*

ects—the teaching practices usually associated with pedagogical progressivism. Teacher-determined initiatives involving students stayed within a narrow range (e.g., 80% of these activities were student reports, debates, acting out scenes, and leading discussions)—and were linked to required content or textbooks. The evidence is that even among the minority of Central faculty who chose to use student participation to refresh existing content and instruction, the dominant mode of instruction was teacher-centered.

Instruction at Central, then, except for a small band of teachers described in a student newspaper, was seemingly tied to large-group instruction, use of texts, question-answer exchanges initiated and controlled by the teacher, and scant student movement and participation—all within classrooms arranged in rows of desks facing the blackboard and the teacher's desk.

Dunbar High School. By leaving Central High School and traveling down the hill along 13th Street toward the White House, then taking a left at O Street and going another dozen blocks, a visitor would have reached the steps of Dunbar, the black academic high school. In 1870, when it opened its doors to four black students in a church basement, Dunbar became the first black high school in the nation. It moved into a new building the same year (1916) Central did. Compared to Central's, Dunbar classes were larger, its books more frayed, its materials fewer, its furniture more scarred, and, in the words of a teacher who wrote lovingly of her school, even "the blackboards were cracked with confusing lines resembling a map." Yet this was the school that produced, as Thomas Sowell noted, the first black general (Benjamin O. Davis), the first black Cabinet member (Robert C. Weaver), the first black federal judge (William Hastie), the first black senator since Reconstruction (Edward W. Brooke), and the discoverer of blood plasma (Charles Drew).[33]

Dunbar's purpose was clear: to prepare students for college. Drawing from a pool of black students from across the city, the faculty, many of whom had earned advanced degrees from Northern and Eastern universities, set high standards for behavior and academics. They shared a belief in the "Talented Tenth," a cadre of educated blacks who would provide leadership to the race. The goal of equaling and even exceeding whites in knowledge, skills, and gentility was gospel among believers in this faith.[34]

In the 1924–1925 *Crimson and Black* (the student handbook), for example, rules for English students were explicit: "Write all lesson assignments in your notebooks. As you have at least three other lessons to prepare daily, do not attempt to trust your memory." For history classes students were warned: "To study history intelligently the student should follow the suggestions of the teacher as to the keeping of notebooks, map work, collateral reports and wider reading." Advice in the form of 12 rules for studying (with "nihil sine labore" as a subtitle) was proffered, prescribing the kind of light and space at home that would be adequate. Also included were "Hints for Dunbar Boys and Girls" (e.g., for girls, "Silks, chiffons, georgettes, [and] satins have no place in your wardrobe," and for boys, "Wear ties, socks, and shirts of quiet colors. Don't let them be conspicuous and showy. Keep your shoes cleaned and polished."). Rules for entering and leaving classrooms were clearly stated: "No talking or unnecessary moving about is to be allowed after the bell has sounded."[35]

The daily schedule of seven periods, with bells punctuating class changes, was the same as at Central, although how many courses teachers taught and class sizes ran higher at the black than at the white high school. The academic courses of study and texts were the same at both schools, as was the piece of required work in the senior year that drove students to parody it in their yearbooks and literary journals—Edmund Burke's "On Conciliation with America."[36]

What happened in Dunbar classrooms, with its clear and precise expectations of students regarding academic work and behavior, and its faculty with a high level of academic training, facing classes of 35 or more students five or six times daily in row after row of bolted-down desks, can only be inferred. Few descriptions of classrooms are available. What these scattered photographs, student newspaper items, yearbook vignettes, and official reports show are instances of project work and student participation in class-work (e.g., reports and debates) within a larger framework of teacher-centered patterns of instruction.

Harriet Riggs, head of the English and history departments at Armstrong and Dunbar high schools, reported in 1920 that in English "the socialized recitation was found valuable in teaching pupils how to think and how to study. . . . By this method of recitation each child contributed his part and learned to work for the welfare of the group." In all history classes, she continued, "emphasis was placed upon geography and map study. In many classes both teachers and pupils collected pictures and clippings bearing on the subjects studied. Constant effort was made to show the connection of the past and present." The senior English classes of Miss Howard and Mr. Hill did individual projects on 18th-century England, creating their versions of popular British magazines like the *Spectator,* models of villages, murals, and so on. The photographs of English and Spanish classes showed familiar patterns of teachers talking to the entire class; one photograph of a chemistry class shows the teacher conducting an experiment in front of the room and the students standing around him in a half-circle watching. Data are scarce for Dunbar. Only partial inferences are appropriate given the skimpiness of the evidence.[37]

Until an intensive recovery of more classroom descriptions of Dunbar teachers occurs, little more than informed impressions can be offered now.

These impressions and partial inferences link easily with the patterns revealed at Central High School and the set of other descriptions from high schools elsewhere in the city.

SUMMARY OF CLASSROOM PRACTICES IN THREE CITIES

In the District of Columbia, teacher-centered instruction prevailed in both elementary and high school classrooms. Some progressive practices were embraced by more elementary school teachers than those in the higher grades, but always in numbers that seldom exceeded one in three or four in lower grades and one in five high school teachers. This variation between levels of schooling resembles that in New York City and Denver.

The reasons for similar patterns in adopting progressive practices may differ for the three cities. Ballou's priorities, for example, were new buildings, reorganizing the bureaucracy, and the scientific uses of testing, to name a few. These were the abiding and passionate interests of an administrative progressive, not a pedagogical one like Newlon and Threlkeld in Denver. Ballou did initiate the District's Child Development Program and curriculum revision, but they represented no more than symbolic efforts, closer to copycat progressivism than to a comprehensively developed implementation of current ideas. Mild endorsements of progressive programs, enhanced by rhetoric but with little direct or tangible support for teachers, were simply insufficient stimuli for District of Columbia teachers to alter their daily routines with children.

Race and class influenced schooling. That racial attitudes counted in allocating funds, teachers, and buildings is evident from the District of Columbia data. That strategies of racial improvement as well as etiquette and class-based attitudes within the black community influenced curricula, instruction, and students in all-black schools is also evident from the data. I can only speculate, however, that race- and class-linked attitudes may have influenced the enthusiasm of teachers and principals of both races for progressive pedagogy—the belief that progressive practices were more suitable for white middle- and upper-class children than low-income blacks who had to exceed whites in knowledge, skill, and moxie in order to survive.

I can confidently state, however, that a pattern of mixed forms of teaching appears in data from the three cities. Mixtures of teacher- and student-centered instruction meant that a number of teachers constructed hybrids adapted to the classroom conditions they faced, the ideas they found congenial, and the demands of supervisors, whether urging them to introduce child-centered instruction or to continue traditional practices. Although they appear in a small minority of classrooms, these hybrids suggest that teachers, confronting conflicting expectations, invented unique compromises tailored to their settings.

The appearance of these hybrids also suggests a fundamental dilemma confronted by teachers and reformers who tried to transform public schools. For teachers, contradictions multiplied as they tried to resolve the tensions generated by partisans of progressive pedagogy and the daily realities they faced in their schools. After all, teachers knew that they were expected to concentrate on basic skills, maintain classroom order, and develop respect for authority; this was what the larger society expected of schools. Every teacher had to resolve individually this dilemma of wanting to embrace the values of progressive pedagogy (individual choice, self-expression, and independent thinking) while satisfying the social and organizational demands for children to obey authority, behave uniformly, and acquire a common body of knowledge.

Few reformers or school officials faced the tough choices some teachers had to make when they closed the classroom door. Of course, many, perhaps most, teachers saw no contradictions, felt no qualms, and did what they had always done in their rooms. But the appearance in these two decades of hybrids—what one might call a teacher-centered progressivism—suggests that many teachers began to see a fundamental dilemma in what they did and what roles they were expected to play.

These classroom dilemmas mirror larger conflicts between cultural values: individual concerns versus collective needs; the values placed on play and leisure time in an achievement-based society that often looks first to the bottom line of the profit-loss statement; and the tension between seeking efficiency—squeezing the last cent out of each dollar—and creative self-development. These conflicting values have grown up side by side in our culture and coexist uneasily in both public and private institutions.

By opening schools to the debate over what is best for the individual child and suggesting alternative pedagogies, a considerable number of teachers discovered their classrooms to be arenas where these conflicting values had to be finessed or, at best, maintained simultaneously in some practical manner.

Recall the New York City classroom where Mrs. Spencer taught 42 fourth-grade children in 1924, and which I described at the beginning of Chapter 2. Mrs. Spencer worked out compromises to solve these dilemmas. She used students as helpers; children coached each other; she permitted children to talk with one another during the arithmetic lesson; she moved around the room aiding individual students; complaints from the class were handled with humor; class activities included games, reading, play-acting, and whole-class recitation. The instructional climate of the room seemed both serious and tolerant of individual children. Here was evidence of a teacher's encouraging student expression and movement, giving students responsibility, helping individual children, and doing all of this with dispatch. Mrs. Spencer had changed some of her routine practices.

Yet in the same classroom, students sat in rows of bolted-down desks; the teacher decided what was to be studied and when, what was morally appropriate behavior, and what activities were to occur, in what order. The source of all authority was Mrs. Spencer. No pretense of student involvement existed except as monitors or helpers to do what the teacher had already planned to do. Teacher rewards and sanctions were clear to the class. Boundaries for individual expression were defined sharply by what the teacher felt was proper. Mrs. Spencer upheld basic patterns of authority and practice.

Thus, like teachers elsewhere, Mrs. Spencer, eager to try child-centered practices in her classroom, struck a compromise. The results were classrooms where contradictory behaviors appeared in an uneasy, often fragile configuration. This paradox of teacher-centered progressivism that grew in the interwar decades is one that has persisted since, creating classrooms where teachers are beset by conflicting impulses to be simultaneously efficient, scientific, child-centered, and authoritative.

CHAPTER 5

Rural and Urban Schools, 1920–1940

A Hillsdale County, Michigan, teacher in a one-room school wrote to her superintendent in 1939 of the changes she had initiated in her classroom since attending a summer session on a scholarship from the W. K. Kellogg Foundation. Leona Helmick reported what she had done at Grubby Knoll School:

School began one September morning. Enrollment was taken. Classes were called by a "tap" (children turn in their seats), "tap" (children rise from their seats), and "tap" (children pass to front of room where recitation occurred). This same call bell had called classes for fourteen years before this. Exact assignments were given in all subjects, an average of twenty-five classes were called [to recite to the teacher] and by much hurrying, school was dismissed at four o'clock. . . . We did art work once a week for enjoyment and training. . . .

Now the little bell is no longer used. The children come in large groups and sit with their teacher in a large circle at the front of the room. Here they read and talk as the need may be. Much of the studying is done here. Quick pupils assist slower ones near them. This eliminates walking around. When the group is finished another group comes. Arithmetic is privately worked out at their seats with some drill and blackboard work. Each one working according to his own ability and speed.

Instead of learning a lot of rules in grammar that many of them never understand and others soon forget, we study birds and write stories about them. We publish a bi-monthly paper. In this the children volunteer original poems, stories, and articles. . . .

We still follow the textbook in Geography although we enrich it with units on travel, transportation, special studies of products and places. Last year we did a good unit on Michigan.

I have learned to think of the needs of the pupils.[1]

At just about the same time Helmick wrote to her superintendent, *Time* magazine featured on its cover the portrait of Frederick L. Redefer, executive secretary of the Progressive Education Association (PEA). A related article reported that progressive education had "strongholds in the suburbs of greater New York, Chicago, and Los Angeles," and that the movement was now "predominantly a public school affair," even "transforming" major school systems such as those of Denver, San Francisco, Los Angeles, New York City, and Detroit.[2]

John Dewey, however, writing shortly before his death in 1952, viewed the changes in schools that had occurred as a result of the progressive movement quite differently than *Time:*

> The most widespread and marked success of the progressive movement has been in bringing about a significant change in the life conditions in the classroom. There is a greater awareness of the needs of the growing human being, and the personal relations between teachers and students have been humanized and democratized. But the success in these respects is as yet limited, it is largely atmospheric; it hasn't yet really penetrated and permeated the foundations of the educational instruction. The older gross manifestations of the method of education by fear and repression—physical, social and intellectual—which was the established norm for the educational system before the progressive movement began have, generally speaking, been eliminated. . . . The fundamental authoritarianism of the old education persists in various modified forms.
>
> There is a great deal of talk about education being a cooperative enterprise in which the teachers and students participate democratically, but there is far more talk about it than the doing of it. To be sure, many teachers, particularly in the kindergarten and the elementary schools, take the children into sharing with them to an extent impossible and inconceivable under the old system. . . .
>
> In the secondary schools, . . . however, there isn't much sharing on the part of teachers in the needs and concerns of those whom they teach. . . .[3]

The *Time* article, Leona Helmick's report, and Dewey's reflections show why it is difficult to determine the extent to which progessive ideas entered even one Hillsdale County classroom. To what extent these ideas turned up in rural and urban classrooms in the two decades between the world wars is one of a number of questions that this chapter will try to answer.

RURAL MICHIGAN CLASSROOMS

Hillsdale was one of seven rural Michigan counties that participated in a 3-year project aimed at improving rural life through transforming the schools. Between 1936 and 1939, the W. K. Kellogg Foundation provided funds to "give teachers and administrators a clearer understanding of the philosophy, psychology, and procedures involved in the newer concepts of education." From college extension courses, weekend gatherings at the foundation's camps, and special summer college courses teachers were expected to carry back to their one-room schoolhouses new skills and knowledge to improve rural education.[4]

In these seven counties there were over 1,300 teachers working in one-room schoolhouses. Their average level of schooling was 2 years beyond the high school diploma. In a remarkable document, 193 of these teachers who attended Kellogg Foundation–sponsored courses, workshops, or summer sessions wrote to Henry J. Otto, consultant to the Foundation, describing "the changes in classroom teaching . . . the administrative problems which had arisen in connection with these changes, and the procedures which were used to meet these problems."[5]

The accounts ranged from reports of sheer ecstasy over rejuvenated teaching to indications of an obvious, and almost embarrassing, absence of any change whatsoever. In order to assemble a coherent portrait of these rural teachers' class activities, I grouped the reported practices into categories extracted from progressive educational literature on "appropriate" classroom techniques and consolidated the information in Table 5.1.

Substantial numbers of teachers reported using activity methods, including projects to integrate different subjects and efforts to tie curriculum more closely to the lives of children. Fewer teachers reported other changes in how they grouped children, organized the daily schedule, evaluated students on report cards, increased pupil participation, and rearranged class space.

These figures summarize what individual teachers reported and therefore convey no sense of how many teachers employed one or more of these practices. Table 5.2 suggests the breadth of teachers' activities.

No criteria exist yet for determining what activities a teacher should employ, and how frequently, in order to be labeled "progressive." Aware of all the problems inherent in developing such criteria, I constructed two in order to analyze the data: (a) the number of progressive techniques teachers reported they used, and (b) any rearrangement of classroom space. Indicators of progressive practice generally included numerous teacher behaviors (grouping practices, student activities, pupil participation, arrangement of space, and so on). Also the tight linkage between a flexible use of classroom

TABLE 5.1 *Summary of reports from 190 teachers in one-room schools in Michigan who participated in Kellogg-funded activities*[a]

Category	Number of Teachers	Percentage
Physical changes in the room		
(1) Remove/modify student desks.	32	17
(2) Make room homelike (e.g. curtains, sofa, tables, etc.).	18	9
(3) Create centers for students to read, work, etc.	32	17
Did at least two of the above.	19	10
Grouping changes		
Teachers report combining classes, using small groups determined by ability, individualizing instruction, etc.	40	21
Schedule changes		
Teachers report any change in daily or weekly schedule aimed at introducing a new practice, different subject, or modified grouping.	37	19
Increased pupil participation		
Teachers report change in governance of class with students leading discussion, running clubs, electing officers.	43	23
Provisioning		
Teachers report seeking out books, supplies, equipment to satisfy changes made in instruction, curriculum, and other parts of the program.	43	23
Activity method		
Teachers report using method, describing projects, and integration of two or more subjects.	80	42
Extracurricular activities		
Teachers report initiating clubs (hot lunch, Mothers' Club, 4-H, etc.).	53	28
Changing report cards		
Teachers report using a card that focuses upon child's emotional development and basic subjects; does not use letters A–F.	25	13
Making curriculum relevant (excluding activity method)		
Teachers report use of field trips, current events, examples from daily life in instruction, etc.	77	40

[a]Because three of the teachers were listed as anonymous, I have used 190 reports in all of the analyses.

TABLE 5.2 *Summary of teacher activities*

Number of categories reported	Number of teachers	Percentage
0	11	6.0
1	58	30.0
2	36	19.0
3	34	18.0
4	27	14.0
5	9	5.0
6	9	5.0
7	3	1.5
8	1	.5
9	2	1.0
10	0	0.0
11	0	0.0
Totals	190	100.0

space and grouping practices or student activities was a commonly expressed and sought after fundamental in building a student-centered classroom.

Almost half of these rural Michigan teachers reported using only two "progressive" techniques; a quarter used four or more practices. Depending upon how much weight an observer gives to rearrangement of space as a sign of progressive approaches, particularly in these one-room schoolhouses where bolted-down desks were common, of the 51 teachers (27%) who used four or more new techniques, two out of three made some change in the room (e.g., created space for learning centers, unbolted desks and put them on skids, placed curtains on windows, or installed tables or a sofa). Of the 24 teachers who reported using five or more new practices, 87% had made some physical change in the room.

Such data have obvious limitations. The teachers are an atypical sample, only 15% of total staff in seven counties, and either were recruited to attend or themselves sought out foundation-supported courses. Moreover, self-reports are selective, are not independently verifiable, and may in some cases be efforts to please donors or supervisors rather than frank assessments of practice. Despite these drawbacks, the data yield a glimpse of (a) which progressive concepts were selected, and according to teachers, used, and (b) teachers' differing views regarding progressivism.[6]

Alice Dean in Calhoun County, for example, let students work individually one period a day in arithmetic problems, helping one another when necessary. She said, this was "the biggest change in teaching that [she had] undertaken" in the last 2 years. Leslie Engle, another Calhoun County teacher, reported as her sole innovation a system of recording each student's personal, family, and school information. Other teachers who had instituted such changes as a science center, adding tables to a room, or setting up a hot-lunch program in the face of a hostile parent community or indifferent superintendent considered such changes as personal triumphs and, in some instances, viewed themselves as progressive teachers.[7]

Finally, the data show that some rural teachers who were isolated from one another and received little support from superiors nonetheless introduced new practices into their classrooms. However, the majority found it difficult to install more than two progressive techniques over a 3-year period.

RURAL CLASSROOMS ACROSS THE NATION

Was southwestern Michigan a microcosm of rural schools across the country? Yes and no. The "yes" half of the answer comes from abundant evidence that progressive methods appeared in individual rural schools, both newly consolidated and one-room buildings, across the country. Highly publicized experimental rural schools garnered national attention in professional journals throughout the 1920s and early 1930s. Such efforts included Marie Turner Harvey's work at the Porter School in Kirksville, Missouri, Ellsworth Collins efforts to develop the project method in McDonald County, Missouri, and Fannie Dunn's work at the Quaker Grove School in Warren County, New Jersey.[8]

There were many less-publicized efforts to introduce progressive techniques into black and white rural schools. Some of these instances were collected in a survey conducted by the PEA's Committee on Experimental Schools in 1937. The Committee sent letters to over 300 schools and districts in 43 states. Of 78 replies, 44 came from public schools. In these 44 replies, rural teachers, supervisors, and superintendents in Connecticut, New York, North Carolina, Arizona, and California reported curriculum revision, integration of various content areas into schoolwide programs, activity programs, and other student-centered approaches.[9]

Even less known are the decisions individual teachers quietly made to try different methods at a cost to their pocketbooks and their precious leisure time. Consider this account by Mary Stapleton of Cuttingsville, Vermont:

> In the fall of 1932, I had an enrollment of about 20 pupils in all the grades. My superintendent told me about the Winnetka method (an approach that stresses individual instructional materials matched to differences in pupils) and suggested my reading some books. . . .

During the fall and winter of 1932–33, I did a great deal of research work, and in the spring I developed the technic [*sic*] in spelling. . . . I divided the words into units of 25 or 30 words each according to [students'] grade placement and ability. This method tests the children on words we want them to know before they study them and allows them to concentrate on the words they miss in the test, rather than wasting time studying words they already know. This plan in spelling proved so successful that I decided to try to develop arithmetic the next fall. . . . I collected all of my textbooks together with my state courses of study and divided the year's work of each grade into 8 units, each with 3 or 4 sub-units.

The next problem was the development of a set of diagnostic tests covering each detail. . . . I found it helpful to exchange tests with other teachers. For a small sum I obtained some tests from Winnetka. I cut out examples and problems from old books, pasted them on cardboard and placed them in my files. The last and perhaps the most important job was to supply the children with self-instructive practice material. Printed drill pads in arithmetic and English have been found helpful. . . . By the end of the year I had fewer failures than ever before. The children had begun to realize the objectives of this instruction and since there would be no repeating of grades, it was up to each to progress at his own rate of speed. . . . The activity side of the instruction can be worked out effectively in the social studies program. . . . For example, an activity dealing with Indian life is an opportunity for children from the first to the eighth grade, to make a contribution. . . . The question that confronted me as I worked out my units was: where can I get the materials to construct these activities? The question was answered by appealing to the children. . . . [10]

How many other Mary Stapletons labored hard to introduce new ideas into their classrooms and went unnoticed and unrewarded for their perseverance, I do not know.

The "no" half of the answer comes from numerous state and local studies of rural schooling since 1920. They confirm similarities with the rural Michigan data but also show that important differences existed.

Rural schools were diverse. One-room schools in West Virginia hollows, rickety shacks on a bare half-acre on a Mississippi plantation, and a newly plastered room in a recently built Iowa consolidated school are but a few examples of how varied rural schools could be. In 1920, almost half of all children enrolled in school attended rural schools, that is, ones located in the "open country" or in villages with less than 2,500 people. For the most part, I will use "rural" to refer to schools with one or two teachers, to village schools, and to schools consolidated through the closing of one-room buildings. [11]

More often than not these buildings were old, furnished with antiquated equipment, and isolated. Teachers had little education beyond high school. They were young (their median age was 21–23), had little experience, and were mostly female. Turnover was high and wages were low. Annual salaries in 1920, for example, ran between $300 and $800 at one-teacher schools, depending on the state, and were $500 to $700 more at village and town schools. Class size ranged from 20 to 60 students of various ages. Fifteen-year-olds sat in the back of the room, towering over the 7-year-olds, who sat in the front row of double-seat desks. The major difficulty was having many grades in one room—perhaps 30 pupils scattered across eight grades—with the teacher required to instruct in all subject areas for each grade.[12]

Few writers at this time sang the praises of the rural school. Administrative progressives' language and fervor located the one-room school somewhere between the flintlock rifle and the wooden plow. "Devoted reformers, philosophers, and educators," a U.S. Bureau of Education specialist in rural education wrote, "have been traveling the length and breadth of the land preaching the inefficiency of the little old red schoolhouse." Both preaching and consolidation cut the numbers of such schools. The number of one-teacher schools fell from an estimated 195,000 in 1917 to 153,000 enrolling 4,000,000 children a decade later. Still, some states had many one-teacher schools. In South Dakota, for example, four out of five teachers taught in one-room schools, as did half of the teachers in North Dakota and over 40% of the teachers in Iowa, Montana, Nebraska, and Vermont.[13]

What did teachers do all day in these isolated yet densely packed rooms? In the mid-1920s, a Teachers College graduate student surveyed 550 teachers in one-room schools in 24 states. Verne McGuffey found teachers reporting that they advised the school board on classroom needs (78%), visited parents (78%), provided drinking water (74%), oversaw school toilets (83%), and regulated heat and ventilation (88%). In terms of instruction:

- 82% kept several groups busy while one recited.
- 75% presented subject matter in short periods.
- 73% taught all subjects in eight grades.
- 66% planned and executed work with little or no supervision.[14]

In 18 Pennsylvania counties with mainly rural schools in 1920, 62% of teachers in one-room schools reported on who they were and what they did. The median age of teachers, of whom 76% were female, was 23. Most had begun teaching at age 19. Almost four out of five teachers lacked a high school diploma or any formal teacher training. Class size averaged 26 in the

PLATE 5.1 *Crossville, Tennessee, 1935*

18 counties, with about a quarter of the teachers reporting enrollments over 35 students.[15]

Teachers' reports of how many recitations they had—that is, how many times a day they questioned students in each grade within the class—would stagger today's teachers. One out of four teachers said they had conducted 30 or more recitations a day. The median was 26. Since the school day averaged 5.5 hours (330 minutes), apart from recess and lunch, teachers reporting 30 or more recitations met daily for at least 10 minutes with one or more students, dismissed them, met with another group, and so on. Even the State Department of Education's formal course of study recommended only 23 daily recitations. All of this suggests the hectic schedule a teacher in a one-room school followed, according to both expectations and self-reports.[16]

Shortly after the Pennsylvania study, Orville Brim, a professor at Ohio State University, led a survey team that evaluated Texas rural schools in 1922. Brim examined the published curriculum, surveyed county superintendents and teachers on how the curriculum was used, and, in a step unusual among researchers then and now, trained a set of observers to describe classrooms in 230 rural schools. These one-teacher schools, as elsewhere in the country, contained up to eight grades. Texas teachers, like their counterparts in other

PLATE 5.2 *White Plains, Georgia, 1941*

states, had limited education, received low wages, and faced classes of two dozen or so. The observers described what these rural teachers did in these short class periods of 2 to 10 minutes, 24 times a day.[17]

Brim and his colleagues summarized the percentage of time teachers spent on different classroom activities.

- Drill, 34%
- Formal textbook recitation, 27%
- Seeking meaning of text, 27%
- Enjoyment, 5%
- Construction work, 4%
- Discussion of vital questions, 4%

The textbook was the primary source of the lesson (88%), with little use of current events or children's experience (8%), according to Brim's team. The investigators found that virtually no special work or projects were given to students (this was done in only 3% of classes).[18]

Brim summarized what he and his team saw:

In practically all the work observed, the teacher is concerned in drilling the children upon some facts they are supposed to know or in asking questions that call for textbook answers. Occasions for thinking are few. Little, almost no, attempt is made to enrich a child's life with new interests. . . . Work does not grip the pupils. They add little to the facts of the lesson. . . . The teacher then arbitrarily assigns the next lesson in the text without any effort to develop interest or insight. The class is returned to its seat to memorize the text for the next recitation. Here they work blindly or half-heartedly or idly sit, with occasional admonitions from the teacher to study their lessons.

This, Brim concludes, is the picture in "70 to 85 percent of the schools in all parts of the state."[19]

In other states throughout the 1920s and 1930s the demands of teaching in a one-room school all elementary school subjects to students scattered over eight grades produced the rat-a-tat of recitations bracketed by opening exercises, lunch, and recess. Consider the following data, collected in 1928 for a master's thesis, about actual daily programs in one-room schools in North Dakota. At School Number Three, Norway District, Traill County, with 24 pupils, the teacher held 22 recitations, averaging about 15 minutes each, between 9:15 a.m. and 4:00 p.m., with two recesses and an hour for lunch. In the same county, School Number Three in the Belmont District had 13 students and 21 recitations, also averaging about 15 minutes, within a school day of the same length as in the Norway District. For a Cass County school where the new Rural Course of Study was being implemented, the teacher's daily program called for 22 recitations of about 15 minutes each for 19 students, although in this case the teacher had grouped students by primary, intermediate, and grammar levels rather than by grades.[20]

Julia Uggen summarized 11 studies identifying instructional problems encountered by over 3,200 rural teachers in over 20 states. All of the studies were based upon teacher reports of their problems. The similarity of the problems disclosed by these investigations with those described in previous paragraphs is striking. Heading the list was the category of inadequate time. Teachers complained that they lacked time to:

- prepare plans for every subject for all grades;
- help individual students; and
- allow for pupil activities.

"There is general agreement in these studies," Uggen concluded, "that the most frequent and most difficult problems of rural teachers are due to the one-room ungraded type of organization. . . ."[21]

Yet ingenuity and persistence surfaced in the face of these obstacles, suggesting that teachers, like most people, did the best they could with what they had. For example, Stella Lucien of Lewistown, Montana, described how she addressed the ever-present problem of insufficient materials for seatwork:

> I obtain one copy of Laidlaw's *Silent Reading Seat Work* for each grade. Many of these lessons direct the child to make some article such as a bird house, a bubble pipe, etc. I cut out such lessons and paste them on cardboard. We then have seat work which may be used over and over without additional cost. We keep them in boxes and use them year after year.[22]

Teacher Ruth Cederburg of Firth, Idaho, wrote how she got primary students to be neat:

> I tacked a strong string across the front of the room; on this I fastened a balloon in front of each row of desks. Each evening before dismissal, aisles and desks were examined. If every child in a row had tidy desks and clean aisles the balloon in front of that row remained up. But if a single child had an untidy aisle or desk the balloon was taken down and remained down the following day. It was not long before every balloon remained up.[23]

RURAL BLACK SCHOOLS

None of these studies specifically mentioned black rural schools. Plagued by working conditions similar to those described above, untrained, poorly paid teachers with little formal education, teaching with few books and materials, coped with an organizational context that affected how they taught: pupils of different ages spread over eight grades, mandates from school board and superintendent to cover all subjects, and insufficient time to do it all.

Fisk University sociologist Charles Johnson directed the 1924 survey of Louisiana black schools. In their visits to 132 one- and two-teacher schools representing 65% of all black schools in the state, his team found the dreary catalogue of problems familiar to informed observers of rural schools in other states. According to Johnson, a situation typical in these schools, occurred in the Shelton School in a parish in eastern Louisiana.

Approaching the church in which the school was housed, the researchers saw two small privies surrounded by thick Delta mud next to the front entrance. Inside the school 60 students spanning seven grades sat next to one another on long wooden benches, fidgeting while they listened to a teacher talk. Because of the chill in the morning air, there was much shifting around to allow students to get closer to warm areas near the small stove in the back of the room. No ventilation stirred the air in the room except for the draughts that came through the many cracks in the floors and walls. The walls, darkened by smoke, held kerosene lamps. One of the lamps hung from an equally dark ceiling. Just above the pulpit at the rear of the room stood a washstand with a cracked pitcher.

The visitors watched the teacher pass out two half sheets of paper to each pupil, saying, "It's got to do you all day, so be careful with it." She looked at one observer and said: "We don't have no pencils; we don't have no books; we don't have anything." She looked back at the class and began giving out assignments in history and spelling, grade by grade, to the restless but quiet students.

> Take pages 45 to 50, seventh grade. Sixth grade, take pages 20 to 30. Now read this and tell me what you read when I come back. . . .
>
> All right, fourth and fifth grade, spelling. The first word is *correspond.* It means to write people. Second, *instrument*—something you use. Do you know any *instrument* you'd like to play? Come on, talk up. Do you have a speller, Fred? No? Well, just sit and listen. You'll just have to do without. Third, *examination,* sometimes we have *yes* and *no*—that's *examination.* Fourth, *tennis*—that's a game. Fifth, *ninety,* counting from *one* to *ninety.* All right, that's your spelling. Use them in sentences.

The teacher, walking around the room with a switch in her hand, then moved to reading for the lower grades. She read a single line from a book and the children repeated the line. She completed the lesson in that manner.[24]

Johnson also offered a portrait of a one-teacher school that, in his judgment, "stands in sharp contrast to the mass of one-teacher schools in the state." The Brooks School, a tiny white-washed frame building on a cleared plot of ground in East Feliciana Parish, was visited the week before Christmas. On a table in the room was a class-built scene of the manger and the Christ child. The worktable in the rear and the bookshelves along the side of the room were covered in bright red and yellow oilcloth, while the shelves in the rear of the room contained water glasses individually labeled for the students. The room was spotless.

As one group of children sat in their seats making gifts for a party, another group stood at the work table making "favors" with scissors, paper, and paste. The teacher moved from group to group, quietly listening and giving advice when asked.

The class had just completed a unit on cotton. The teacher, who had worked on a farm, had shown pictures of the various stages of cotton production and of actual plants. The class had gone through the process from seed to clothes with all eight grades, using arithmetic and reading where appropriate. In the first grade the teacher used flash cards marked with COTTON or related words. In the second and third grades, pupils made sentences about the plant, and in the sixth and seventh grades they wrote short stories about it. On many occasions, the visitor was told, all of the children participated in discussion. Even with all of the grades and subjects to cover, the teacher moved the class through the subjects in an orderly manner, the teamworker reported.[25]

The Brooks School was an exception. Of 100 teachers in Louisiana, 75 had never done a unit that included a project or similar activity. The 25 teachers who reported that they had done projects listed as topics Indian life, gardening, products of Louisiana, health, sewing, cooking, and life at home.[26]

PHOTOS AND WRITTEN ACCOUNTS OF RURAL CLASSROOMS

This incomplete picture of black and white rural schools began with Hillsdale County teacher Leona Helmick and her colleagues in southwestern Michigan, who had received some formal exposure to progressive methods of teaching. I had asked whether these one-teacher schools were a microcosm of the rest of the country. Crisscrossing the country, a number of state and national studies suggested both "yes" and "no" answers. Numerous instances of progressive practices surfaced, but they seemed to be tiny islands in a vast ocean of teacher-centered instruction.

The final data that I offer are descriptions of 103 classrooms (excluding those of the 190 rural Michigan teachers) I collected from 32 states in every region of the country. (See Figures 5.1 and 5.2) Do these data converge with or contradict the results of the diverse studies already reviewed?

While the 103 photos and written accounts differ from the sources used in the studies of rural schools described above, they nonetheless echo that data. Teacher-centered patterns of instruction register strongly; student-centered practices scale no higher than 40%, and in most classrooms constitute 25% or less of activity. Very few of these 103 teachers tried projects or centers, which show up in fewer than 10% of the elementary school classrooms. Progressive practices, as defined in these categories, existed in rural classrooms nationally but were probably a very small minority.

One curious fact is the high percentage of group instruction and class activities in the mixed pattern of teaching. Half of the teachers used a blend of large- and small-group instruction accompanied by work with individual students; almost half of the classrooms had activities involving a mixture of student-centered and teacher-centered approaches. Compared to the other settings, these percentages are high and may stem from factors within the rural classroom unlike any faced by teachers in city schools. With students spread among several grades in one room, for example, teachers would generally call upon a few students to recite near the teacher's desk, leaving the rest of the class to work on various assigned tasks until they were called to the

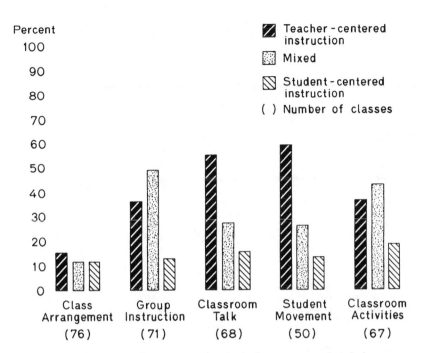

FIGURE 5.1 *Patterns of instruction in rural elementary school classrooms, 1920–1940*

recitation bench. The necessity of having students work in groups and help one another in one-room schools, then, may explain why practices in ungraded rural schools varied from those in graded urban schools.

The dominant patterns of instruction were teacher-centered and mixed—a configuration similar to, but not identical with, those that surfaced in the three cities examined here. A later generation of reformers interested in constructing student-centered classrooms would look to rural one-room schools and see embryonic child-centered settings. They ignored the drumbeat recitations, rote instruction, poorly trained teachers, inadequate school rooms, and poverty-level wages of the 1920s and 1930s.

Teachers in rural one-room schools used mixed forms of grouping because students spread across eight grades required varying amounts of attention. Latter-day reformers interpreted this as individual instruction. Children helped one another with assigned lessons while the teacher listened to students recite at her desk. The content of the curriculum drew from rural concerns and daily life, a linkage that subsequent school reformers would admire. The family-like atmosphere of the schoolhouse, where a school trustee was

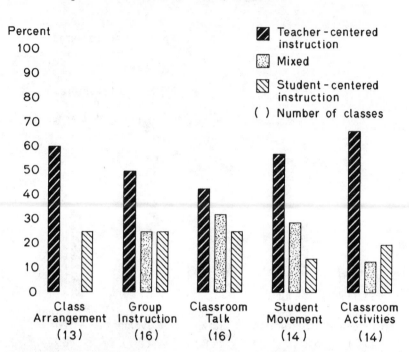

FIGURE 5.2 *Patterns of instruction in rural high school classrooms, 1920–1940*

someone's uncle or the teacher a cousin of a child in the class, was exactly the climate that reformers sought to create decades later for large, urban graded schools.

Overriding many of these natural practices in most one-room school-houses, however, were traditional parent attitudes that valued only a few months of schooling, instruction in the basic skills parents themselves had learned as children, and the methods by which they had been taught. More-over, untrained and inexperienced teachers used frequent and brief recitations drawn from inadequate textbooks and narrowed student responses to what could be recaptured by rote. All of which was often enforced by birch-sapling discipline. Few reformers recalled these realities and weighed them against their enthusiasm for selected aspects of the one-room school.

PREVALENT TEACHING PRACTICES IN RURAL AND URBAN SCHOOLS

So far I have tried to reconstruct teaching practices at the turn of the century and between World Wars I and II, in three cities and in rural schools.

Now I turn to teaching practices that prevailed nationally in the interwar period. After summarizing similarities and differences that I found among rural and urban schools during the 1920 and 1930s, I contrast them with teaching practices in 1900 to determine what changes, if any, had occurred in classrooms by World War II.

In examining evidence of what teachers did in their classrooms, I concentrate on those teaching activities that had become targets for change: formal recitation, whole-group instruction, and lack of student movement in the class. The data yielded by classroom descriptions about group instruction, classroom activities, and student movement in the four settings are summarized in Figures 5.3 through 5.6.

Recall that the teacher-centered pattern of group instruction involved teaching the entire class as a unit, while a student-centered pattern involved

PLATE 5.3   *Questa, New Mexico, 1943*

PLATE 5.4 *Big Rock School, Breathitt County, Kentucky, 1940*

dividing the class into small groups and letting individuals work independently. The mixed pattern described teachers who used varied grouping techniques ranging from teaching the whole class to letting students work independently. Elementary classrooms in Denver and New York City showed the highest levels of work in small groups and the least amount of whole-group teaching. In these two cities' high schools, teachers favored grouping the entire class, although percentages for rural classrooms were lower. Similarly, urban high school teachers infrequently divided their classes into groups, whereas the sample of rural teachers were slightly more likely than their urban cousins to use small-group instruction, although the number of teachers who did this is small.

Similar patterns surface under the heading of "Class Activities," meaning recitation, discussion, project work, seatwork, and the usual instructional tasks. More student-centered class activities and fewer teacher-centered ones turned up in elementary than in high school rooms. Otherwise, no systematic similarities or differences among city and rural classrooms emerge.

"Student Movement" yields the same relationship between elementary and high school teachers, except in rural classrooms. Students move about more in lower than upper grades, with Denver and New York classrooms

PLATE 5.5 *Williams County, North Dakota, 1937*

showing slightly higher percentages in both teacher- and student-centered patterns. Finally, the percentage of elementary classrooms that had project work was highest in Denver, New York City, and rural Michigan classrooms, although Denver's figure is inflated due to the sources used.

These graphs describe occurrences of specific teaching behaviors in almost 300 classrooms. They show general instructional patterns suggesting the extent to which student-centered practices surfaced in how teachers organized their classes for instruction, in the activities they structured, and in the degree of student mobility they permitted. What about specific teaching methods like using the recitation, textbooks, student projects, and cooperative planning between teacher and student? A small body of evidence offers some answers.

In the recitation, for example, the teacher asked questions and students recited answers from a textbook, a workbook, blackboard work, or previously memorized content. The familiar pattern of many teacher questions and short student answers had been lamented throughout the last quarter of the 19th century by journalists, professionals, and reformers. Romiett Stevens's transcription of lessons in 1908–1911 documented what others had observed. In

PLATE 5.6 *First grade, Gee's Bend, Alabama, 1939*

the decades that followed the publication of her study—I suggest no cause-effect relationship—the format of the recitation was relaxed somewhat.

The "socialized recitation" emerged as a technique that allowed the students, instead of the teacher, to cover the subject matter through student-led and panel discussions, reports, staging of scenes from novels or plays, and debates. This practice transformed the formal recitation. Verbal exchanges between teacher and students still pivoted on questions asked by the teacher and could either slip into a quasi-conversation or shift back toward the formal recitation. Students standing at their desks reciting, a familiar image in classrooms for decades, had become by the 1940s a custom outmoded in urban classrooms. It was replaced by the now-familiar image of arm-waving pupils vying for the teacher's attention.

Pedagogical reformers, divided as they were on what classrooms should be like, probably saw the relaxation of formalism as a plus. But they sought more. They wanted smaller groups working on topics that integrated different subjects, joint teacher-pupil planning, explicit links with life beyond the school, and active involvement of students in class tasks such as building models, painting murals, and dozens of other activities—all orchestrated by

PLATE 5.7 *One-room school, Grundy City, Iowa, 1939*

the teacher in a subtle, non-authoritarian way. Studies of teaching practice between the two wars, however, suggest that Vivian Thayer's title *The Passing of the Recitation* (1928) was premature and could instead have been "The Persistence of the Recitation."[27]

A few investigators in these years went into classrooms and observed teaching methods. Of the few who did, only a handful counted what they saw. Counting has no special virtue given the varied meanings observers attached to such words as "child-centered," "progressive," and "modern." Hence, in summarizing the results of seven studies of classroom instruction, I have restricted myself to those studies that I considered less judgmental, and reported events that seemed less vulnerable to interpretation—in short, examined behaviors that could be quantified: groups of students working together, students answering teacher questions, use of movable or stationary student desks, students giving reports or leading discussions, and so on.

I examined studies that investigated 1,625 elementary and high school classrooms in California, Illinois, Indiana, Minnesota, Texas, and Wisconsin in addition to national reports generated between 1922 and 1940 by urban and rural superintendents, supervisors, principals, and college professors. In

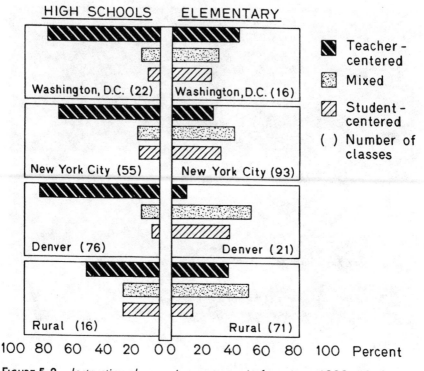

FIGURE 5.3 *Instructional grouping patterns in four sites, 1920–1940*

some investigations, trained observers used carefully designed instruments; in others, hastily written impressions and self-reports from teachers formed the basis of the study. Rather than analyze the details of these seven studies, I have included tables incorporating their data and narrative describing each one.

In 1922, Margaret Noonan, a New York University professor, went to Texas to direct the portion of a state-wide study that examined black and white city schools. An ardent advocate of progressivism, Noonan stated clearly the standards by which she would judge instruction in Texas city schools: the presence of group work, joint pupil-teacher planning, evidence of connections between classwork and life outside the school, and concern for "the whole child."

Trained observers used a list to check off what they saw in black & white teachers' rooms in nine Texas cities. Many statements on the list were open to broad interpretation by the observers (e.g., "students show enjoyment and appreciation of activity"). A few items did include specific references to furniture, pupils' work in groups, and topics of discussion and are shown in Table 5.3 (p. 139).

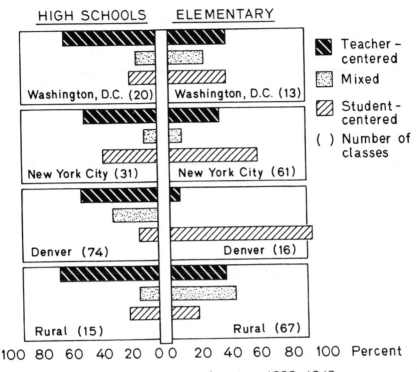

FIGURE 5.4 Class activity patterns in four sites, 1920–1940

On a larger scale than Noonan's work, Teachers College professor William Bagley conducted a national study of teaching methods in 1930 that summarized results from state, city, and rural surveys between 1900 and 1930. "One who studies such reports over a series of years," he wrote, "could scarcely escape the conclusion that the work of the typical American classroom, whether on the elementary or secondary level, has been and still is, characterized by a lifeless and perfunctory study and recitation of assigned textbook materials."

To verify the accuracy of the survey's conclusions, Bagley wrote to superintendents, principals, and local and state supervisors of instruction across the country asking them to use an observation instrument he had developed to evaluate teaching methods. He received over 500 completed forms from officials in over 30 states, unevenly distributed between rural (169) and urban (356) schools and between the elementary (342) and secondary (183) levels. Acknowledging that observers may have used varied perspectives in describing teachers, he cautioned readers that these observations "cannot be regarded as thoroughly typical of what is going on in classrooms. . . ." Al-

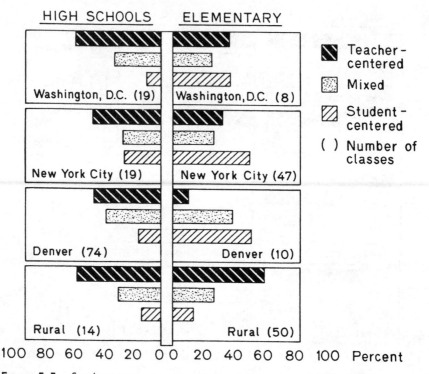

FIGURE 5.5 *Student movement patterns in four sites, 1920–1940*

though I combined some categories to provide clarity, the main results of his survey are shown in Table 5.4 (p. 140).

How did Bagley explain the differences between the results of formal surveys, which implied that textbooks dominated instruction, and results submitted by observers who sat in classrooms and found that student-centered practices had penetrated classrooms considerably both in the city and in the countryside? Were school officials, in responding to a professor, trying "to make as good a showing as possible" during the heyday of progressivism? Or did supervisors visiting classrooms for which they were responsible display a "natural tendency to interpret what they saw as conforming closely with generally accepted standards?"

Noting both explanations, Bagley dismissed them and concluded that "contemporary educational theory seems to be affecting elementary school practice in a fairly profound fashion, and it is apparently not without its influence upon the secondary school." Whether or not a range of 15%–25% individual work and groupwork observed in classrooms is considered "profound" influence, tendencies similar to ones I found appear in Bagley's survey. Differ-

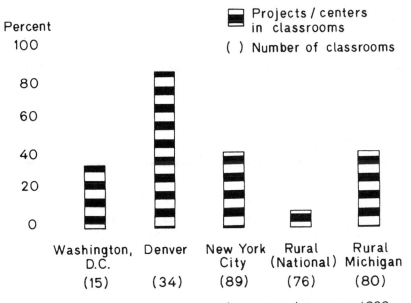

FIGURE **5.6**   *Use of projects/centers in elementary classrooms, 1920–1940*

TABLE **5.3**   *Selected items reported in a 1922 survey of 176 white and 40 black schools in nine Texas cities*

Category	Percentage in white schools (N=176)	Percentage in black schools (N=40)
Furniture fastened to floor	70	77
Activity suggested by pupil or class	2	0
Pupils at work on same activity	56	42
Pupils at work on group activity	14	22
Pupils at work on individual activity	3	2
Current events discussed	22	45
Pupils moving freely	24	20

ences between elementary and high school are evident in levels of recitation and student-centered activities. The incidence of individual work and group-work is comparable to percentages of student-centered instruction under the category "Class Activities."

In 1940, L. W. Krause, a public school teacher, completed a study in 10 Indiana cities of 217 fourth-, fifth-, and sixth-grade classrooms. Again many

TABLE 5.4   Percentage frequencies of type of recitations and project methods, 1929–1930 (N = Number of classrooms)

Method	Rural Elementary (N=108)	Rural High School (N=61)	City Elementary (N=234)	City High School (N=122)
Textbook/ Recitation	16.6	28.8	10.4	22.5
Individual and group work				
•Individual reports	7.3	10.0	7.7	5.5
•Group reports	5.0	1.1	5.2	3.1
•Projects	9.0	5.5	12.2	6.0

TABLE 5.5   Average percentage frequencies of selected items reported in a 1940 survey of 217 Indiana upper elementary school classrooms

Category	Percentage
Movable furniture	46
Several groups of pupils at work	2
Variety of materials present	16
Teacher has unit of work in progress	1
Students helping to plan work	4

of the criteria he used to identify progressive practices (e.g., the teacher conducted the class on democratic principles, children showed signs of self-discipline, the teacher encouraged clear thinking) required an observer's opinion. Some items, though, did call for describing the presence or absence of actual activities, reducing, but not eliminating, the margin for variations in interpretation. These tallies are shown in Table 5.5.

A number of studies of high schools between 1924 and 1930 concentrated on what teachers did and said in their classrooms. Covering all of the academic subjects in large and small, urban and rural schools, these investigators compiled data about almost 600 experienced teachers in Midwestern and California high schools. The results are remarkably similar to those of the earlier study by Romiett Stevens (1912) in revealing a high level of teacher control over the amount and direction of classroom talk, a narrow margin of time available to students to respond, and a lack of variety in the activities that occured in the typical 45-minute period.

Between 1924 and 1926, university researchers visited 346 classrooms in the Minneapolis, Minnesota, area and found that four activities (recitation, supervised study, assignments, and tests) accounted for 90% of each class period. Recitation consumed an average of 62% of class time. Two Northwestern University professors went into 116 Chicago social studies classrooms in 1929 and concluded that "teaching is still largely question and answer recitation." They found that 82% of the teachers asked questions, some as many as 150 in a 45-minute period. They were surprised at how few students (10%) raised questions during the recitation or offered any comment (8%). "The changes," they noted, "being advocated in our methods of teaching are not finding their way into the schools to any considerable extent." In the same year. A. S. Barr sat in 77 social studies classes by Wisconsin teachers designated as "good" or "poor" by their principals and superintendents. Within a 40-minute period, he found, the teachers asked 93 and 102 questions, respectively. Stenographic records verified that teachers monopolized air time during the class, talking during almost 60% of the recitation portion alone. He also found eight teachers who used the "problem-project organization or learning by doing." Finally, in 1930, a Stanford student observed 42 English and social science teachers in five San Francisco–area schools. Charles Bursch found that "class discussion" averaged 59% of each class period.[28]

From these seven studies of 1,625 classrooms, three points emerge: First, evidence collected by very different methods from large and small, rural and urban, elementary and high schools in different sections of the country shows notable convergence with the data I obtained independently for almost 300 urban and rural classrooms. Second, the pattern of using the entire class as the primary vehicle for instruction and relying on the question-answer format and the textbook that Rice, Stevens, and others observed decades earlier seemed to persist in the nation's classrooms in the years between the two wars. Third, more selected progressive practices entered elementary classrooms than appeared in high schools. Projects, joint student-teacher planning, and small-group work simply did not appear as often or in as many high schools as they did in the lower grades, at least based on the reports of observers who sat in classrooms, on descriptions written by teachers and others, and on photographs.

Yet evidence drawn from principals' and superintendents' reports shows far higher percentages of certain progressive methods in high school classrooms than suggested above. The congressionally mandated 3-year Survey of Secondary Education (1929–1932), for example, produced a massive body of information from 8,600 secondary schools (about one out of every three such schools in the country at that time). Regarding project methods, 27% of the schools reported that they used this form of instruction, although only 4% reported its use "with unusual success." Similarly, for the phrase "Individualized Instruction," 25% of the schools checked off the space indicating use. Here again, 4% of the schools said they used it "with unusual success."[29]

What makes precision impossible, of course, is that the terms may mean various things to the people reporting the practice. If a few social studies teachers out of a faculty of 100 in a school of 3,500 students produced class-room projects in the semester preceding the survey, the principal would re-port the school as employing this approach. Equally troublesome is the am-biguity of terms like project method. Quite often this and other phrases (e.g., Dalton method) were indistinguishable from one another in school officials' minds. Reforms did get implemented, but administrator reports unwittingly inflated the spread of new practices.

J. Wayne Wrightstone, New York City school system evaluator and a pro-fessor during the later surge of interest in activity programs, made this point in a study conducted for the General Education Board. He tried to separate the experimental practices that high schools had undertaken in the 1930s from other factors. Leaning heavily upon the National Survey cited above, the Eight-Year Study sponsored by PEA, and a network of contacts he had cultivated with high school experiments across the nation, Wrightstone con-cluded that major strides had been taken in introducing new subjects and content into the high school curriculum, especially the correlation of school subjects. But, he noted, the centers of gravity in classroom instruction re-mained the recitation, the textbook, and whole-group instruction.[30]

SUMMARY

Based on this study of urban and rural classrooms and an analysis of national studies of the years between the two world wars, I can make the following statements about the extent of the spread of progressive teaching practices.

1. *A core of progressive teaching practices did penetrate a considerable number of elementary schools.*

In the districts I examined and the studies I reviewed the number of classrooms so affected, however, never reached anywhere near a majority in a school district. This core of practices—increased levels of student participa-tion through small-group work; project activities; more student expression; increased use of varied classroom groupings; integration of two or more sub-ject areas; more contacts with the community through field trips; and more freedom for students to move around the classroom—was unevenly imple-mented within classrooms, and for only a portion of the school day. I estimate that such teaching practices seldom appeared in more than a quarter of the classrooms in any district that systematically tried to install these reforms. In districts that devoted little organizational energy to implementing these practices, the number of teachers adopting this core of practices probably hovered between one fifth and one tenth of elementary teachers. The percentage would be higher if certain practices were counted since teachers were quite selective in what they chose to incorporate into their classrooms. Less frequent in elementary classrooms were other practices such as students deciding what content to study and how to spend class time and choosing activities.[31]

2. *In high school academic subjects few progressive practices modified teacher-centered instruction in the interwar period.*

In a few isolated high school classrooms, an activity program, varied groupings, flexible space arrangements, and joint pupil-teacher planning did exist. Few progressive practices appeared in most high school classes, however. Course content changed, generally in English and social studies. Some loosening of the formalism connected with the recitation occurred, with more discussion, student reports, and debates. Traces of child-centered practices could be seen in increased student talk in the classroom, occasional trips in the community, and subject matter that touched upon student concerns or life outside the classroom. But the percentage of time allotted to specific subjects—except for those schools that adopted a core curriculum or general education for a part of the school day—remained the same. Even with movable furniture, classroom space often continued to be arranged with the teacher's desk at the front facing rows of tablet armchairs or portable desk-chairs.

3. *Hybrid forms of progressive teaching practices emerged in many classrooms.*

Mingling of teacher-centered practices and pedagogical progressivism appeared in many elementary and secondary school classrooms. Varying strains of teacher-centered progressivism existed in a considerable number of schools. A public-school version of a progressive classroom appeared that had adapted itself to rigorous climatic conditions: classes with 35 or more students; courses of study prescribing the skills and content to be covered; teachers untrained in progressive approaches; antiquated furniture, limited space, supplies; and unselected, often unmotivated masses of students.

Enough of the familiar rhetoric and symbolism of progressivism existed in these hybrids for school officials and teachers to point with pride at the minority of teachers who had incorporated these new practices into their daily instruction. Yet these tiny outward signs of the progressive dream to alter teaching practice drove reformers outside the public schools to condemn these very changes as mere replicas of the "real thing." Whichever perspective is taken, what is evident is that substantial numbers of teachers did, indeed, modify their classroom repertoires.

4. *District pressure and support seemed to make a difference in the limited spread of progressive teaching practices.*

These practices fared best in school districts where top administrators formally approved the effort, established organizational machinery to carry it out, and persisted in its implementation. Yet even in Denver and New York, these new teaching practices did not penetrate most classrooms. In rural districts where teachers were isolated, possessed limited schooling, and had insufficient books and materials, fewer progressive methods seemed to have spread, except for certain practices that were already indigenous to multigrade, one-room schools (e.g. grouping). Islands of progressive practice also appeared in those unique schools that grew out of the persistence and dedication of tireless individuals (e.g., Ellsworth Collins and Fanny Dunn, who established progressive rural programs).

The one effort to spread progressive approaches into rural schools that I reported offers a glimpse of another way to change practice. The Kellogg Foundation in the mid-1930s used a strategy, motivated by the dispersal of teachers in southwestern Michigan, that concentrated upon the individual teacher. Through extension courses and summers at colleges, some teachers did alter their classroom methods, according to their self-reports, but in a limited and erratic manner. Higher percentages of teachers reported using projects, for instance, than in other studies or in the classroom descriptions that I analyzed. Finding out what happened over the years in those teachers' rooms would add greatly to our knowledge of the durability of changes in teaching practices. Such evidence could determine whether the reported changes that occurred in one-teacher schools in Michigan were substantively different from those in classrooms where systematic districtwide implementation occurred, and whether such changes endured.

5. *The dominant pattern of instruction, allowing for the substantial spread of these hybrid progressive practices, remained teacher-centered.*

Elementary and secondary school teachers persisted in teaching from the front of the room and in deciding what was to be learned, in what manner, and under what conditions. The primary unit of grouping for instruction was the entire class. The major daily classroom activities involved a teacher lecturing to, explaining to, and questioning students while they listened, answered, read, and wrote. Seatwork or supervised study was an extension of these activities.

Restrictions on student movement within the classroom loosened somewhat. Teachers permitted more mobility within the class. Movable furniture provided an option for teachers to rearrange desks and chairs into groups, although most teachers continued lining them up in rows. Students less frequently had to rise from their seats to recite. In short, the classroom climate became informal enough for teachers and students to reach across the boundaries that had kept them at arm's length from one another.

CONCLUSION

Important incremental changes had occurred since 1900. Even though the teachers in 1940 were not the same as those who had taught in 1900, instruction still tilted toward teacher-centeredness. Yet substantial numbers of new and veteran teachers were modifying their methods in ways that had not been apparent in public schools at the turn of the century.

By 1940, alternatives to standard teaching methods were available, widely known, used by a minority of teachers, and considered respectable by professional norms. The narrow range of existing practice had stretched to include a larger repertoire, although the implementation of those practices remained limited. For every Leona Helmick in Hillsdale, Michigan, there were dozens of teachers who found such practices too time-consuming, too upsetting to existing routines, or too far removed from the conditions they had to face daily. For every Mary Stapleton in Cuttingsville, Vermont, who explored the Winnetka approach on her own time, there were scores of teachers who kept their classroom doors closed to such techniques. They closed their doors because of the high price in energy and time that innovations would have required. They closed their doors out of fear that by introducing changes they would isolate themselves from colleagues. They closed their doors because no explicit incentives to make such changes were available. Finally, they closed their doors because no one knew with confidence whether the promised outcomes would, indeed, benefit the children. How, then, to make sense of this constancy and change in teaching?

At midcentury, John Dewey, who had been an honorary president of the PEA decades earlier, observed that progressivism had altered the "life conditions in the classroom" and little else in elementary schools, with hardly any change appearing in high school classrooms. He noticed how much more talk there was about change than there were actual alterations in classroom teaching and learning. He also observed that the "fundamental authoritarianism of the old education persists in various modified forms."[32]

I found much evidence to support Dewey's observations about the extent and quality of the changes that had occurred since 1900. His comments on "fundamental authoritarianism," however, I have yet to explore. Such a remark directs attention to the instructional practices teachers introduced into their classrooms and why those practices were selected and not others.

Why, for example, did those elementary teachers who embraced some form of progressive pedagogy encourage more movement of students in classrooms, project activities for part of the day, and mixed forms of grouping over other methods such as student decisions on what topics should be studied? Why was it rare for a teacher to delegate to students the decision of how the daily schedule should be arranged? Teacher-centered progessivism incorporated some new techniques and not others. Perhaps these hybrid practices permitted those adventurous teachers who risked introducing some changes into their rooms to choose activities that did not threaten their classroom authority or schoolwide curriculum.

Dewey's comment is intriguing because it suggests that the hybrids themselves may have strengthened rather than weakened the foundations of a teacher's classroom authority. Examining a subsequent effort by reformers to introduce informal education, incorporating approaches similar to progressive pedagogy, in the late 1960s and early 1970s may clarify this uncertainty.

PART II

Open Classrooms
and Alternative Schools:
Progressivism Revisited,
1965–1975

CHAPTER 6

Informal Education, 1965–1975

In a North Dakota city of 35,000, a university researcher went to an elementary school of 180 children in 1972 and interviewed a second-grade teacher.

Interviewer: To begin with, would you describe for us a typical day in your classroom?

Teacher: The morning is spent with children doing the activities they schedule for themselves. We always gather together after lunch in a group and I read to them. At this time, the children also schedule and announce if they are going to put on a play or if they have something to show. We schedule a time for those kinds of activities to occur later in the afternoon. The other children choose whether or not they wish to attend. If they do, they include that in their schedule. . . .

Interviewer: Okay. Now I'd like you to describe the classroom. . . .

Teacher: As you come in the door, we have a high shelf area. That is our hospitality counter with our guest book, coffee, juice, and cookies for the visitors and kids. The math center is on the other side of these shelves. There's a bulletin board right there. We have a long combination blackboard–bulletin board at the other end. A typewriter and our creative writing area are in that particular part of the room. Then we have an old trunk. It is our drama trunk and is filled with a variety of hats, dresses, coats, and some props, like a cane. Then we have a table 6 feet in length that has a listening center with records, a View Master, [a] filmstrip previewer, and a reading machine. . . .

We have a large carpeted area that has a davenport, lots of pillows, and stuffed animals. Bookshelves are on the sides, kind of a reading center is what you'd call that. Going on, we have a game shelf, then the science center [and the] plant and animal center. Then you'd see the cooking area with recipes written on chart paper of all the things we've cooked over the year. . . .

Interviewer: On a typical day in the classroom, how many children would be involved in language arts and reading?

Teacher: The only time we would be working as a whole group would be during sustained silent reading. Reading, though, is a part of each child's daily schedule. During the day, when they come to that part of their schedule, they go into the reading center. They would read by themselves, to a buddy, to a tutor or other adult that might be in the room. . . . [1]

If a time machine could have swept fervent advocates of child-centered practices in the 1920s across decades and set them down in this second-grade North Dakota classroom in the early 1970s, they would have felt far closer in spirit to this primary teacher than to Mrs. Spencer in her 1924 New York City progressive classroom or to Leona Helmick's rural Michigan one-room school in 1938—even though both of those women had been trying student-centered approaches. The North Dakota classroom's use of space and furniture, its high level of student participation both in instruction and in rule-making, the reach of a curriculum that included both academic and lifelike situations, and the signs of student independence reported by the teacher suggest an informal, child-centered classroom. This North Dakota teacher was part of a national surge in lay and professional fervor for open classrooms and alternative schooling that an earlier generation might easily have labeled progressive education. This North Dakota teacher worked within a tradition of student-centered instruction stretching back centuries.

But student-centered instruction's line of descent from the 1930s to the 1970s is broken and meandering. Three decades separate an activity program classroom in New York City from the second grade in North Dakota that we just read, or a core classroom in Denver's East High School in 1936 from a school without walls in Washington, D.C., 30 years later. This educational progress, in the words of Philip Jackson, "could be more easily traced by a butterfly than by a bullet."[2]

THE SETTING FOR INFORMAL CLASSROOMS: THE 1960s

Rather than retrace the post–World War II history of public schools, I concentrate on those conditions that seemingly led to the brief enthusiasm over informal and alternative schools that peaked in the early 1970s. I also suggest comparisons with the earlier progressive movement.[3]

Parallels with Progressivism

In the midst of the media's fascination with informal and "free" schools in the late 1960s, Lawrence Cremin drew parallels between progressive education and the then-current ardor for these reforms. He saw two themes in the "new progressive movement" that echoed the earlier one: child-centeredness and social reform. Locating the rebirth of the focus on children in the publication in 1960 of A. S. Neill's *Summerhill,* a book that was selling over 200,000 copies annually a decade later, Cremin saw the writings of school critics John Holt, George Dennison, James Herndon, and Herbert Kohl as contributing to the momentum for seeking different kinds of teachers and schooling that would free children's imagination and creativity from deadening routines, tyrannical authority, and passive learning.[4]

At the same time, Cremin pointed out, in the aftermath of the civil rights movement, blacks and other ethnic groups were trying to shape schools to fit their aspirations for identity and a sense of community. "We have seen," he commented, "a fascinating interweaving of the child-centered and political reform themes in the literature of the movement, so that open education is viewed as a lever of child liberation on the one hand, and as a lever of radical social change, on the other." Noting differences between the two themes, he found the literature "notoriously atheoretical and ahistorical." Those who established new schools "have not read their Francis W. Parker or their Caroline Pratt . . . with the result that boundless energy has been spent in countless classrooms reinventing the pedagogical wheel." Yet he saw a fundamental similarity in both movements: The tool of reform remained the public school. Even Charles Silberman's *Crisis in the Classroom,* "surely the most learned and wide-range analysis to be associated with the present movement," proposed the open classroom as "the keystone in the arch of educational reform."[5]

Leaning heavily upon Cremin's work on the progressive movement, Vito Perrone, then Dean of the University of North Dakota's New School (subsequently renamed the Center for Teaching and Learning), and prominent in the national network of reformers committed to informal education, located the roots of open education in turn-of-the-century progressivism. Although he did not distinguish between the social reform and child-centered themes in the surge of interest in open classrooms, Perrone described both. He broadened his search for roots beyond progressivism, locating them in the civil rights movement, as did Cremin, but also in the growing public awareness of government policies—for instance, concerning the environment and the war in Vietnam—that were viewed as mindless, inhumane, and destructive. Moreover, he credited the English primary schools with giving "considerable stimulus," especially after the publication of the British government's report *Children and Their Primary Schools* (1967), to the practice of informal education in the United States.[6]

Roland Barth's search for the sources of open education took him back to 1961. In that year, William Hull, a Cambridge, Massachusetts, private school teacher, went to England to observe and report on the work of primary schools. His enthusiastic words led a growing number of American educators to travel to England to see firsthand the "Leicestershire plan," the "integrated day," and the "developmental classroom." The Education Development Center in Newton, Massachusetts, where Hull worked became a clearinghouse for information and materials about English primary schools. Barth traced the movement's growth in the United States from its early locus in an interlocking network of private schools, foundations, and federally funded curriculum developers, through a series of articles by Joseph Featherstone in *The New Republic* and the publication of Silberman's *Crisis in the Classroom,* to state departments of education, universities, public school administrators, and teachers. He pointed out the unsystematic, uneven, yet persistent spread of informal classrooms across the nation.[7]

Sources for the origin and spread of open classrooms varied, according to these writers. Yet none of the writers discussed the appearance (and disappearance) of curriculum reform. As part of the national wave of change before and after Sputnik, reformers in the 1950s and 1960s generated math, science, and social studies texts and materials in which students handled Cuisenaire rods and light bulbs, simulated situations, and in general behaved like scientists. While many of the enthusiastic proponents of and participants in the change effort ended up disappointed in what actually materialized in classrooms across the country, the focus upon children's interests and motivation and the tying of content to contemporary concerns echoed the work of earlier generations of reformers.

The themes of social reform, child-centered pedagogy, curriculum change, and self-liberation that had marked the progressive movement decades earlier reappeared in the late 1960s. Moreover, the concerns of the earlier generation of academics, writers, and professional reformers, who had seen public schools as constraining, ineffectual, and even harmful to children found a new voice in the critics of the later period, who viewed how schools were organized and the instruction they offered as mindless and destructive.

Contrasts with Progressivism

Beyond these similarities, however, substantial differences separated the two generations of school reformers. By 1940, for example, varied forms of progessivism had become accepted by most citizens and professionals as the modern form of public schooling. Administrative progressives rated the efficiency of facilities, business procedures, and new building construction on scientifically constructed scorecards. Pedagogical progressives had developed an architecture of teaching methodology. Social reformers wrote books that became bestsellers among informed educators.

Progressivism was mainstream. The movement found expression in formal organizations, annual conventions, informal networks of like-minded individuals, journals, teacher-education curricula, and graduate courses of study for training school administrators. The vocabulary of practitioners and policymakers mirrored the absorption of progressive ideas. To be part of the educational establishment and to be a progressive educator had become synonymous.

The nova of informal education contained few of these features. Its glistening streak across the sky was intense and brief compared to the decades that progressive beliefs took to become mainstream. Informal education never took a deep hold organizationally among the ranks of educators. The suddenness of its appearance may explain that. Or its partisans' reluctance to establish formal ties among themselves and with mainstream educators may account for the shallowness of the organizational root system nourishing open classroom enthusiasts. Occasional groups of advocates joined together in efforts to spread ideas and practices, but these casual networks were marginal to the educational establishment.

Compared to earlier reform efforts, the brevity of interest in informal schooling was astonishing. The movement is generally considered to have begun in the mid-1960s; by the mid-1970s, concerns for basic skills, test scores, traditional alternative schools, and minimum competencies had replaced open classrooms on the agendas of school boards, superintendents, principals, and teachers. A barometer of the sudden shift in interest is the number of articles about informal schooling referred to in *Education Index* and the *Current Index of Journals of Education*. Between 1969 and 1973, there was a burst of publications that stretched for pages in these indexes; by the years 1975–1979, references to the topic had shrunk to occupy a page or two. As brief as this interest in informal education was, no uniformity in definition or practice emerged even in the peak years of 1967 through 1973.

The media explosion included articles in newspapers, popular magazines, professional journals, and books, supplemented by television coverage and films. Print and nonprint sources documented the array of differences among schools broadly labeled informal: open classrooms, free schools, open education, alternative schools, schools-within-schools, personalized education, humanistic schools, minischools, and so on. While many critics shared a strong distaste (if not revulsion) for public schools, most professional and lay reformers believed that public school teaching could benefit from some version of informal education.

In my discussion of informal education, I will concentrate on those efforts to alter classroom teaching practices in public elementary and secondary schools. I use the terms "informal education" and "open classroom" synony-mously in describing change in elementary schools. At the secondary level, "alternative" will be the preferred term for the range of innovations that spanned the late 1960s and early 1970s. A number of elements common to both levels became targets for classroom reform.

OPEN CLASSROOMS: THE 1970s

After the initial fervor for informal schooling ran its course, advocates worried about school practitioners' headlong rush to freeze into orthodoxy something called an "open classroom." Assumptions about teaching, learn-ing, the nature of the child, and the process of developing an informal setting, they argued, were what mattered—not some product labeled open class-room. Roland Barth, Joseph Featherstone, Vito Perrone, Charles and Arlene Silberman, Lillian Weber, and others wrote and spoke often about the dan-gers of missing the fundamental issues in informal education by confusing means and ends, and of searching futilely for prescriptions to be administered to classrooms. "Tempering a Fad" was the headline of a *New Republic* article by Featherstone in 1971. "Although there are many prophets rising in the land," he wrote in another article that same month, "there is no educational Gospel." His warning went unheeded.[8]

Warnings seldom deflected the strong impulse to define what was an open classroom. Researchers, school administrators, and board members seized by the public and professional passion for informal schools in the early 1970s drew up lists of items that distinguished open classrooms from conven-tional ones. Some advocates reasoned that such listings risked making a com-plex process trivial, yet, they argued, that risk was offset by the need to offer specific directions for creating more informal classrooms. By 1971, checklists, diagrams, and ways of assessing a classroom's degree of openness began to appear. In 1973, Barth complained that American educators had copied Brit-ish primary classrooms mindlessly: "We have made a neat package of the vo-cabulary, the appearance, the materials, and sold it to the schools."[9]

Even with these concerns, writers agreed upon some common elements. The style of teaching in open classrooms was flexible both in use of space and methods. Students were involved in choosing activities, and the classroom had abundant materials that were handled directly by students. Curriculum was integrated—"correlated," to an earlier generation. Grouping for instruc-tion leaned toward using small groups and independent work, although the entire class would be taught as one when this was appropriate.[10]

Charles Silberman, sensitive to any dilution that might sap the vitality that teachers bought to open classrooms, warned advocates to be cautious.

He feared that unthinking true believers in open classrooms would do what drunks had done to alcohol: give it a bad name.

> By itself, dividing a classroom into interest areas [learning centers] does not constitute open education; creating large open spaces does not constitute open education; individualizing instruction does not constitute open education. . . . For the open classroom . . . is not a model or set of techniques; it is an approach to teaching and learning. . . .
>
> Thus, the artifacts of the open classroom—interest areas, concrete materials, wall displays—are not ends in themselves but rather means to other ends. . . . In addition, open classrooms are organized as to encourage
>
> - active learning rather than passive learning;
> - learning and expression in a variety of media, rather than just pencil and paper and the spoken word;
> - Self-directed, student-initiated learning more than teacher-directed learning. . . . [11]

Given these warnings and advice to policymakers and practitioners, to what degree did these approaches to teaching and learning enter classrooms? To answer this question I examine schooling in three locales—North Dakota, a state that tried to reform teaching practices through an ambitious statewide certification program; New York City; and Washington, D.C.—all centers of ferment in installing open classrooms between 1967 and 1975.

The signs of informal education that I seek out, unfortunately, are the very artifacts Silberman warned against. Clusters of desks with students facing one another, learning centers, unimpeded student movement within the classroom, small groups and individual instruction, and student choice of activities are all raw indicators of open classrooms. However, these outward signs of openness reveal nothing substantial about teachers' views of learning and children's development, or about their concern for improving student skills. My behavioral analysis of the classroom can be criticized for being narrow and incapable of capturing the holistic qualities inherent in informal education. To such criticisms, I can only say that teachers themselves saw these visible signs as evidence of moving toward informal classrooms and that, at the least, such artifacts point to a tangible effort on the part of the teacher to incorporate some aspects of the open classroom.

NORTH DAKOTA

Within an eleven-month period The *Saturday Review, Atlantic, Newsweek, Readers Digest, Life,* the *New York Times,* and the *Wall Street Journal* carried feature articles on the reforms sweeping one-room schools, villages, towns, and small cities on the high plains of North Dakota. By 1972, the Public Broadcasting System (PBS) and the Columbia Broadcasting System (CBS) had shown documentaries on the state's open classrooms. "Hinterland as avant garde" reform was too irresistible an angle for the media to ignore. The Carnegie Corporation–sponsored study that Charles Silberman had published as *Crisis in the Classroom* devoted a glowing chapter to the state's reforms. In all of these feature articles, professional journals, and books the University of North Dakota's New School of Behavioral Studies on Education (hereafter called the New School) played a primary role in providing ideas, funds, teacher training, and support for informal education.[12]

The fact that open classrooms took root in a rural, politically conservative state requires explanation. The general version of the story has been told elsewhere. A 1967 study documented that North Dakota was last among all states in preparing elementary teachers: two out of every five lacked a bachelor's degree and the range of school opportunities available to grade school children (e.g., kindergarten classes, special teachers, services for the handicapped) was limited. To upgrade the 40% of the teachers lacking college degrees, whose average age was 43, the staff of the study recommended that an experimental teacher education school be established with a program to match the circumstances many of those teachers came from: small schools with students scattered over several grades. In Featherstone's *New Republic* articles on British primary schools the staff saw a match between informal education and the needs of small, isolated schools in a rural state. The New School was established at the University of North Dakota not only to certify teachers but to introduce "radical" changes in how teachers taught, their use of the curriculum, and how classroom decisions were made.[13]

Vito Perrone was appointed as the new dean in the hope that his ingenuity and emotional electricity would power the infant venture. Perrone hired like-minded teachers, some of whom were knowledgeable about English primary schools or had worked at the Education Development Center in Newton, Massachusetts, where materials for open classrooms were developed and published. Perrone crisscrossed the state telling legislators, school officials, teachers, and parents of the virtues of open classrooms and New School interns (young men and women hired to replace teachers without degrees, who then went to the New School to get their degree and certification). Using imagery of rural schools that parents found familiar, especially many grades in one class and close ties to the surrounding community, Perrone and his colleagues promoted informal education as a variation of the familiar schooling that many North Dakotans received.[14]

Between 1968 and 1973, over 50 districts (about 20% of the state total) with 80 schools (enrolling about half of the state's elementary school children) joined the New School in its venture. The campaign of the New School and other state colleges to help teachers earn a degree sharply reduced the percentage of teachers without degrees, from 59% in 1968 to 13% in 1973.[15]

While cautious about freezing open classroom concepts into a gospel, Perrone and his colleagues needed to explain these different approaches to teaching and school life in terms parents would understand. The North Dakota version of informal education contained a core of approaches found in British primary schools, with local adaptations that the New School stressed, particularly student involvement in classroom decisions, evaluation of non-academic growth, and parent involvement.[16]

Interns introduced open classroom practices in Starkweather, Minto, Devil's Lake, Fort Yates, Fargo, Bismarck, Minot, and Grand Forks. City, town, village and one-teacher schools—all were touched directly or indirectly by New School interns or federally funded outreach programs in the first 5 years. After 1973, however, federal funding of New School programs across the state evaporated. Outreach activities dwindled to include only what motivated and energetic New School teachers did on their own time.[17]

Determining to what extent open classrooms spread in the state is complicated because no other state in the nation embraced a policy to introduce open classrooms. The uniqueness of North Dakota's effort prevents comparison with other states and should be considered in any assessment of the effort's effectiveness. That open classrooms spread swiftly throughout the state in the early 1970s is obvious. In Fargo, for example, at the request of the superintendent, the New School in 1969 established a center for interns at Madison Elementary School, which had a record of persistently low student academic performance. The two principals who served Madison between 1969 and 1977 were both affiliated with the New School.

Principal Vincent Dodge described the changes that had occurred by 1973. Classroom walls came down. Cross-grade teams were organized. Teachers established learning centers for math, science, social studies, creative writing, reading, and art, with individual stations for students, to enrich and motivate students and link the community to the school. In addition, students made tables, chairs, carrels, magazine racks, supply bins, games, and puzzles out of cardboard and other materials. Finally, no letter grades appeared on report cards. Checklists of specific academic skills, cooperative behaviors, and interpersonal skills were sent home twice a year, and two formal teacher-parent conferences were held. In short, here were all the artifacts of open classrooms as well as the spirit of teacher-pupil planning and decision-making, according to the principal. The *Fargo-Moorhead Forum* ran articles about the Madison, Clara Barton, Lewis and Clark, and Horace Mann schools describing centers, small-group activities, and freedom of student movement in classrooms. "Fargo Schools Lead Education Revolution," one headline proclaimed.[18]

Less than a hundred miles north of Fargo, Grand Forks, in the words of Superintendent Wayne Worner in 1969, had become a "mecca for innovation." He declared that there was not one school in the district "where you find 30 students in a box." The Washington elementary school established a formal relationship with the New School, itself located a few miles away. Larry Hoiberg, principal in 1970 of the school, which embraced kindergarten through sixth grade and had 220 students, described how Washington merged the "child's school world and his home world." Photographs and narrative captured small groups, learning centers, students' free movement, and the flexible space arrangements in which New School interns, parent volunteers, and aides worked.[19]

In another Grand Forks school, district administrator Jerry Abbott told how a federal grant to introduce aides into a newly built school had helped create an open classroom program at the Kelly School. Learning centers, small groups of students at clustered desks, individualized reading programs, abundant materials, and a dozen other signs pointed to the presence of an open classroom and altered teaching practices. "What happens to the traditional role of the teacher?" Abbott asked rhetorically and answered quickly: "She is no longer at the front of the room directing the same . . . lesson for all children. As the children work in teams she is free to move among them and to help those who need it."[20]

Elsewhere in the state, visitors and reporters noted the appearance of informal classrooms in unlikely places. Arlene Silberman followed students in classrooms in Starkweather (population 250), where the school of 200 children in grades 1–12 had four elementary teachers (all New School degree candidates) holding classes "more exciting and certainly more innovative than anything one can find in the Scarsdales, Winnetkas, Shaker Heightses, and Palo Altos of the United States." She visited schools in Edmore (pop. 405), Lakota (pop. 1,658), and Minot (pop. 33,477), staffed by New School graduates supplied with pegboards, cash registers, and Cuisenaire rods, that had classrooms divided into math, reading, science, and art areas. She saw small groups of students working together, some children by themselves, others at a table with the teacher, still others in corners or sprawled on a carpet.[21]

The Spread and Durability of Open Classrooms

Trying to document the extent to which open classrooms in various forms spread across the state and the persistence of these teaching practices over time is more difficult than simply counting instances of such classrooms. As in assessing the spread of progressivism, the problem is twofold: how to determine the degree of implementation among classrooms labeled "open," and how to assess the inevitable variations among classrooms in which informal practices (centers, small groups, etc.) have been used.

The first part of the problem involves using the global term "open classroom," with teacher reports and direct observations providing the data from which to draw conclusions. Such data are difficult to interpret because of the varied meanings that teachers and observers assign to the phrase "open classroom." As I have already suggested in analyzing progressivism, informal education or open classroom as an unidimensional construct is less useful than a construct composed of varied elements that teachers have selectively and unevenly put into practice.

The second part of the problem involves the sources of information themselves. Among researchers, awareness is growing that teacher and principal reports of progressive and open classroom practices tend to be inflated. The evidence I have collected on North Dakota is vulnerable on these points.[22]

One way to determine the extent of informal practices in the state is to find out how many New School interns and graduates worked in the schools. By 1973, over 500 New School teachers and interns had taken their ideas of open classrooms into 80 schools, or almost 15% of the schools in the state. Whether or not these New School–trained teachers continued their activities over the years is a question explored in a study completed by a New School researcher in 1975. Through questionnaires, he compared a sample of 56 New School interns' classrooms with a random sample of classes of 342 North Dakota teachers in a number of areas related to informal teaching: the extent to which teachers dealt with children individually; the degree to which the teacher centralized or dispersed classroom decisionmaking; different types of classroom activities and tasks; the integration of these experiences; and the extent to which all of the teacher's arrangements and classroom organization contributed to children's learning from one another.[23]

The researcher concluded that New School (by this time renamed the Center for Teaching and Learning, or CTL) interns "have classrooms significantly more open than those of teachers in general in North Dakota." While graduates of the New School maintained their commitment to informal education, there was "a tendency for their overall attitude toward open education to moderate."[24]

In another study, a University of North Dakota researcher asked teachers to describe the use of math materials such as fraction discs, Cuisenaire rods, and chips in their classrooms. These materials were common to informal classrooms since they lent themselves to individual and group use by children in centers. Thus, the extent of the use of these materials becomes a clue in determining the spread of informal techniques. Almost 1,000 teachers (or about one third of those in the state) from 116 schools replied to the questionnaire. Ninety percent of the teachers reported having two or more of these materials in their classrooms. Teacher use of these manipulatives, however, was low. Fewer than half of the teachers said they used them "a little" and only 7% said they used them "extensively." Also, the researcher found a strong relationship between the materials children handled and the presence of leaning centers—that is, teachers who reported frequent use of the materials were also teachers who reported they had centers. Of almost 1,000 teachers, 25% said that they had centers. The percentage of centers was the highest at the kindergarten level (40%) and fell thereafter, so that in the fifth and sixth grades 14% and 15% of teachers, respectively, reported having centers.[25]

The impact of the New School in disseminating ideas and practices about informal classrooms is evident. The Johnny Appleseeds of open classrooms from the New School sowed their seeds broadly. Between 1968 and 1975 a substantial minority of North Dakota teachers adopted, in varying degrees, different versions of the open classroom.

Open Classrooms a Decade Later

In 1981, I spent a week in Grand Forks and Fargo visiting six schools and observing 63 teachers (20% of the elementary school faculty in these two cities) to see what teachers were doing in their classrooms a decade after the introduction of open classrooms. Of the 63 teachers, 8 were New School graduates. I spent the week at Madison elementary school and other schools that had been sites for interns and university faculty. I expected that the influence of informal education would be high in these settings.

Each city had about a dozen elementary schools, with class sizes averaging 25 students. At least one out of every four elementary schools in each city contained open spaces created by movable partitions, 8-feet-high dividers, or homemade walls built from bookcases and portable blackboards. While open-space buildings are not the same as open classrooms, advocates for the latter often argued that providing open-space buildings would be a necessary condition for encouraging teachers to adopt informal education.[26]

In both cities, teachers told me that they were pleased that the central administration was about to act on their requests for the erection of walls so that each teacher would now have a separate room. This included Fargo's Madison elementary school, where walls had been knocked down a decade earlier to create spacious double rooms. The teachers I observed had training beyond the bachelor's degree. Rooms were copiously stocked with overhead projectors, sets of books, math and science materials, and equipment. Project activities were evident.

What patterns of instruction did I see in the classrooms of the six schools? Keep in mind that my observations lasted between 15 and 30 minutes per teacher, generally occurred in the morning (when elementary teachers concentrate upon teaching basic skills) and often involved more than one teacher, since in some buildings I could watch three to four teachers work with their classes simultaneously.

Table 6.1 shows that teachers taught the class as an entire group a majority of the time, talked most of the time, and structured classroom activities that concentrated upon students' listening to the teacher and working as a class on workbook assignments or seatwork. More than half of the teachers arranged furniture in ways that encouraged students to talk with one another. In two of every three classrooms I visited, students were allowed to move around the classroom without permission from the teacher. Small-group and individual instruction and student-centered class activities occurred infrequently.

Almost one third of the classrooms had at least one learning center. At Grand Forks' Benjamin Franklin school, four 5th- and 6th-grade teachers used a dozen centers for that part of the morning or afternoon when language arts and science were scheduled. They were the exception, however. When I asked teachers how and when they used the centers, invariably the response was: before and after scheduled activities such as reading, language arts,

TABLE 6.1 *Patterns of instruction in a 1981 survey of six elementary schools in Grand Forks and Fargo, North Dakota*

Indicators	% of teacher-centered Instruction	% Mixed pattern	% of student-centered instruction	Number of classes
Class arrangement	43	30	27	63
Group instruction	62	25	13	
Classroom talk	60	24	16	
Student movement	37	0	63	
Class activities	59	30	11	
Classes with one or more centers				32

lunch, or recess, and as enrichment, a reward for good behavior, or skills drill. Except for the four teachers at Benjamin Franklin, centers were supplementary to the existing program.

Of the eight New School graduates teaching in the schools that I visited—and I had no way of knowing how typical they were of New School alumni—two used centers extensively for portions of the school day. In the other six classrooms I saw no evidence of centers. Four of those six listed on the blackboard the tasks the class would do that day.

In short, while elements of open classrooms could be seen in many of these 63 teachers' rooms, the primary mode of instruction involved a variety of teacher-centered practices. This brief glimpse of classrooms in two North Dakota cities less than a decade after an intense effort to install open classrooms in the state suggests which elements of informal education had persisted and which were less durable.

A predominantly rural legislature endorsing fundamental classroom reforms in the late 1960s in order to upgrade the state's elementary schools is a very different setting from introducing open classrooms in the nation's largest school district. In New York City in the early 1970s, enthusiasm for informal education appeared suddenly and, like a meteor, fell from district headquarters in Brooklyn to schools in the five boroughs.

NEW YORK CITY

Compare the city's schools in 1940 and 1980. In 1980 the system still had about a million students in nearly a thousand buildings with 50,000 teachers. It still had a Board of Education and a superintendent, although the latter's title had been upgraded to chancellor. When I visited DeWitt Clinton High School, scarred, bolted-down desks still sat in rows in classroom after classroom.[27]

Beneath this surface, however, a number of profound alterations had occurred to the New York City schools in four decades. Consider the following:

- Since World War II, wave after wave of newcomers had changed a school system that in 1940 was predominantly white to one in which by 1960 black and Puerto Rican children were 75% of the elementary school population.
- Before World War II, 1 of 10 children attended private school; four decades later, 1 out of 8 attended private school.
- In 1940, New York City schools were viewed as national leaders in public education. The Activity Program, elite high schools, and high test scores produced intense competition for teaching and administra-

tive vacancies. By 1980, staffing classrooms with qualified teachers had become a major task. Test scores, reported annually school by school in newspapers, had been sliding downward for over a decade, though the beginnings of a turnaround were evident. Retrenchment measures resulting from the city's unprecedented fiscal emergency had driven class sizes into the mid-30s and low 40s, stripped schools of critical support services, and buried a number of novel efforts to improve schooling. The image of the school system was that of a troubled, chaotic organization unable to cope with the problems at hand.[28]

The changes of these four decades were reflected in the high turnover of superintendents at the system's headquarters at 110 Livingston Street in Brooklyn. While four school chiefs served the system in the first 40 years of the century, nine occupied the top post between 1960 and 1990. State laws had mandated the division of the school system into 31 school districts (K–8 schools), each run by a community school board empowered to hire and fire its own teachers and administrators. Protracted and divisive teacher strikes and parent boycotts closed schools down numerous times between 1960 and 1970.

More than anything, public attitudes had changed. Belief in the legitimacy of the school board and staff as guardians of children's intellectual and moral development had eroded. During the post–World War II years confidence diminished in the public schools' ability to fulfill their mandate. In those years, New Yorkers heard of school officials' corruption in constructing new schools. They saw school boards and superintendents paddling first on one side of the canoe, then on the other side, keeping a straight course but reluctant to deal frankly with the issue of desegregation. They watched the fumbling attempts of top administrators to wrestle with teacher union and parent activism. And New York parents with children in the schools experienced the results of squabbles between the Board and unions and parents groups in repeated strikes and boycotts that shut schools down for all children. This unrest reached a crescendo of raucous anarchy between 1968 and 1970 when confrontations between union members and community control advocates unleashed racial bigotry, saw parents and teacher activists arrested, and led to intervention by the State Commissioner of Education and the legislature. Substantial changes in the governance and organization of the entire school system ensued.[29]

While intense criticism of public schools was familiar to New Yorkers— recall the 1912 Hanus Report and the barrages of charges that Superintendent William Maxwell and his successors absorbed during their tenures—the recent period differed because criticism was accompanied by an erosion of public confidence in the schools' ability to educate children. Within the political context of the late 1960s and early 1970s, open classrooms and alternative schools popped up like mushrooms after a rain.

Adopting Open Classrooms: Rhetoric and Action

Here is a vignette of a 1967 school program getting under way one morning in Harlem's P.S. 123:

> At 9:30 a.m. teacher aides and student teachers begin to line the small, L-shaped section of the corridor with tables and chairs. Out of a storage room they bring out boxes full of materials and spread the contents on the tables. There are scales, Cuisenaire rods, water vessels, musical instruments, a dozen different kinds of match puzzles, counting devices, hexagons, trapezoids, animals, clay. . . . Singly, and in pairs, threes and fours, children filter into the corridor from five classrooms, the doors of which are open and inside which teachers are conducting lessons. . . .
>
> The corridor has become another kind of place. Some children move directly to activities, having learned the corridor's offerings. Others, sometimes with a friend in tow, shop around before settling down to one thing. . . . At one table a four-year-old girl is manipulating a game about people, identifying relationships. Behind, a six-year-old has spread herself on a piece of newsprint on the floor while a student teacher traces her form in crayon, which she will then measure in blocks and hang on the wall.
>
> Other children are pacing off distances, measuring with string. . . . A few feet away a group of four has been working steadily for an hour weighing shoes. . . .
>
> Children return to their classes, others come out, work continues in all the rooms. . . . Inside the room, run along formal lines, there is a striking absence of restlessness. Children are hard at work despite the sounds and movements from the corridor. In sharp contrast, a second-grade class next door operates informally in small clusters of children. . . . By 11 a.m. the corridor begins to clear. Materials, tables, and chairs have been returned to their storeroom. Left on the corridor walls are the paper cutouts of children figures.[30]

This description of the first Open Corridor program, instituted by City College of New York Professor Lillian Weber, illustrates another variation of informal education as adapted to American conditions. Weber had spent a year and a half visiting British primary schools and had written about them.[31]

In 1967, at P.S. 123, she found an opportunity to apply her ideas of informal schooling by placing student teachers there and in nearby schools. In subsequent years, Weber pursued her belief in the central importance of the teacher as decisionmaker, the importance of teachers' joining the program voluntarily, and informal classrooms uniting children with different abilities, while retaining a deep aversion to labels about openness. Her strategy as a professor and as director of a center for informal education outside the school system was to encourage a series of small, voluntary changes by teachers and schools. These small changes, she argued, would over time produce transformed teachers and schools. Never, she said, "was it our intention to convince the whole New York City school system that they should go this way." Instead, she wanted "to work in a small way to create an exemplar of what could be possible in the public schools. . . ."[32]

From five K–2 teachers at P.S. 123, a network of contacts spread outward in Manhattan until in 1971 10 schools and 80 classrooms were formally linked to Weber's City College Advisory Service to Open Corridors, which became the Workshop Center for Open Education. Four years later, an inventory of schools and teachers affiliated with the Open Corridors program listed 17 schools and 156 teachers, with almost 4,000 children in classes.[33]

By 1978, when Weber's friends and admirers, including Charles Silberman and Vito Perrone, gathered to celebrate a decade of her involvement in informal education, 26 elementary and 2 secondary schools had 200 teachers with almost 5,000 children in open classrooms tied directly to City College. In addition, over 1,000 teachers, aides, principals, and parents visited the Workshop Center annually.[34]

Elsewhere in the city, individual teachers and whole schools adopted versions of open classrooms on their own initiative or with the help of other privately and publicly funded groups working out of universities and storefronts. Other teachers, unaware of the innovations or determined to construct a form of open classroom tailored to their style and students, went ahead and did so. While Herb Kohl and Gloria Channon wrote books about their personal odysseys in opening up their classrooms, other teachers wrote, in master's theses, of similar journeys, some of them painfully unsuccessful.

Between 1970 and 1973, national interest in open classrooms surged. Locally, a similar welling up of enthusiasm among parents and teachers occurred amid the heavy emotional fallout from the 1968–1969 school year's three teacher strikes and creation of over 30 community school districts. The racial strife that erupted in the wake of the teacher strikes reverberated for the next decade among teachers, administrators, and community activists. It also occurred in the midst of a yearlong national search for someone to assume the newly created post of chancellor. After Sargent Shriver, Arthur Goldberg, Ramsey Clark, and Ralph Bunche—all national figures—had turned down the Board of Education, Harvey Scribner, Vermont's commissioner of education, accepted the post in 1970.[36]

The naming of Scribner as chancellor and the public position taken by United Federation of Teachers President Albert Shanker in favor of informal education coincided, raising hopes for the future of open classrooms in the city. Fifty-six-year-old Harvey Scribner, a former teacher in rural Maine who had been superintendent in Teaneck, New Jersey, prior to his stint in Vermont, rang all the bells that informal classroom enthusiasts wanted desperately to hear. His "Vermont Design for Education" (1968) laid out 17 objectives that captured the main tenets of informal education. He quoted John Holt in his speeches. He met with Gloria Channon, a fifth-grade teacher and author of a book on her conversion to open classrooms. He drew often upon his experience as a rural teacher who tried to get out of the way of students who wanted to learn, as he often said. "There is no one design of education that can serve the needs of all people," he told a reporter. "We must give children an opportunity to learn in their particular manner," he said, "to proceed at their own rate, to work at their own level. We must give them many alternatives." [37]

Pledging to make decentralization work and to reform schooling in order to produce more choices for students in classrooms and schools, Scribner visited schools, spoke frequently to teachers and administrators, and sought out like-minded people in the city in an effort to build coalitions for change. [38]

Working the other side of the street, Albert Shanker told a reporter: "We intend to get teachers to read Silberman [*Crisis in the Classroom*] and see him as a hero, a constructive critic." Endorsing the informal classroom as a vehicle for reforming schools, the teachers' union's president pledged to inform union leadership of the merits of open classrooms, sponsor community forums, and support systemwide efforts in that direction. At a later citywide meeting of teachers, Shanker urged that parents be permitted to "shop around" to find an open classroom. The new chancellor and a savvy union president publicly supporting informal education indeed made for a special moment. It lasted no longer than a sand castle in the incoming tide. [39]

Two and a half years into the job, Scribner announced he would leave the post when his contract ended in June 1973. He gave as his reason "a widening gap of confidence" between the Board of Education and himself. Trying to reform the New York City schools, Scribner discovered, was akin to trying to turn around an ocean liner in the East River. By 1973, even before Scribner left, Shanker's public statements about the joys of open classrooms diminished. By 1975, union-supported Teacher Centers largely ignored informal classrooms as appropriate targets for teacher change. Budget cuts, ballooning class sizes, staff firings, mass transfers of teachers, increased emphasis on improving test scores, and basic skills instruction replaced talk about reform and informal classrooms. [40]

The Spread of Open Classrooms

Despite the applause for open classrooms from teachers' union leaders and top officials at the system's headquarters, determining what most teachers did in their classrooms remains, as always, difficult to ascertain. Yes, there is evidence that hundreds of teachers began centers, rearranged furniture, equipped their rooms, taught small groups, and prized student participation. But there were over 600 elementary schools and over 25,000 teachers. To what extent did elements of open classrooms appear among them? The answer is similar to the one offered regarding progressive practices two generations earlier. Definitions of openness varied, teachers were selective in what they introduced, and the pattern of adoption was uneven both within and across schools.

What can be said with a modest degree of confidence is that the spread of open classrooms, however defined and implemented, did not exceed the generous 25% of teachers Joseph Loftus estimated to be using activity methods in their New York City classrooms shortly before World War II. Recall that he made his estimate after years of high interest in the methods and a 6-year formal experiment sanctioned and promoted by the superintendent and staff that involved over 75,000 children in nearly 70 schools.

Scribner served less than 3 years; he shaped no sustained set of policies and organizational procedures, nor did his ideas enjoy widespread support among central administration and middle-level managers. Words were simply insufficient to generate changes beyond 110 Livingston Street. Also, a general political instability entered the system with the birth of 30 community school districts in the aftermath of acrimonious teacher strikes. Lacking a formal institutional framework that encouraged open classrooms, teachers embraced informal practices on an ad hoc basis, finding occasional support from colleges, private groups, or cadres of like-minded individuals elsewhere in the system. How many schools and how many teachers eventually implemented open classroom practices is impossible to determine with any precision since no formal classroom survey was undertaken in the 1967–1975 period.

If a survey had been done and had showed that more than one teacher in four or five had maintained an open classroom, even broadly defined, I would have asked for a recount. Yet the basis for my estimate is also suspect. While City College, Fordham University, Queens College, Bank Street, and the Creative Teaching Workshop were active in spreading informal classroom techniques, data for the Open Corridors are available and provide some basis for an estimate. The 17 elementary schools where Open Corridors existed in 1975 had a total population of about 13,000 students and around 550 teachers. Of that population, over 3,000 students and 150 teachers were part of the program. By 1978, in 26 elementary schools linked with the workshop on Open Education, there were 3,900 children and 180 teachers involved in the program. These schools had an estimated 21,000 children and 800 teachers. This level of involvement existed in schools where one would expect diffusion to be contagious since non–open classroom teachers worked next to colleagues heavily involved in the program. No doubt some schools had heavy participation because they had long been associated with City College, whereas other schools may have joined recently.[41]

In other schools across the city, where teachers lacked outside support from a university or advisers, the level of involvement would have been lower. None of this is to suggest that the influence of the Workshop on Open Education and similar efforts was insubstantial. Teachers trained in Open Corridors took administrative posts throughout the system and worked elsewhere in school programs (e.g., Teacher Centers). Also, when funding was cut for Open Corridors advisers, community boards often found funds elsewhere in the budget to support the work of consultants.[42]

Teacher Reports and Direct Observation of Classrooms

Another basis for an estimate comes from the numerous reports I have read of New York City teachers in these years and how they coped with the daily issues of steering 30 or more students through a half dozen subjects in self-contained classrooms. Some of these teachers, intrigued by talk about informal classrooms, gingerly tried some techniques. Most, however, seemed too busy, too exhausted, too intimidated by superiors, too intent upon surviving, or else simply disagreed with the direction. They hesitated to try out new approaches that required preparation of new materials, more contact with children in and out of the classroom, and possibly extra time at home working on classroom tasks.

In the late 1960s, a number of teacher accounts described the conditions under which teachers taught and what they did in their classrooms. The school Gerald Levy wrote about in *Ghetto School* was located in a midtown slum and had 1,300 children and 70 teachers, half of whom were inexperienced and newly appointed. He records passionately and with much disgust how they stumbled through 1967–1968, a year marked by a wildcat teachers' strike, intense parent involvement, and administrative fecklessness. Order replaced learning as the primary goal. Except for the kindergarten teacher and one second grade teacher, instruction was a series of mindless routines designed, he wrote, to keep children quiet and busy at their desks. Reading like a topsy-turvy version of Joseph Rice's dreary chronicles of New York classrooms seven decades earlier, the book portrays children and teachers who display a strong distaste for schools.[43]

Gloria Channon's frank description of how she introduced 22 Harlem fifth graders to an open classroom in 1967–1968 contains unsparing observations drawn from a painful internal struggle to free herself of a mindset that a dozen years in New York schools had imprinted upon her. The following is from the January 31, 1968, issue of the *Staff Bulletin,* a district headquarters publication:

- During recitation lessons, pupils should raise hands to indicate desire to make a contribution; they should be encouraged to speak in full sentences. . . .
- Pupils must ask permission to go to the bathroom. . . .
- Gum chewing is forbidden anywhere in the school building. The teacher must set the example. . . .
- Pupils should empty their desks regularly under the routine supervision of the teacher and everything other than approved books and materials should be discarded on the spot or taken home at 3:00. . . . [44]

Channon observed that by the third grade the New York curriculum "gets whipped into shape."

> Children sit at their desks for hours. Notebooks and textbooks become the main focus of their activity. Lessons are formally organized into spelling, penmanship, reading, composition, and math. Silence and good behavior are at a premium, now as never before.[45]

In another Harlem school, one with 1,350 children, Donna DeGaetani chronicled her experiences in 1972—her third year as a teacher—in a building dominated by a principal she feared and where parents were pushing for open classrooms. Her frankness is disarming. DeGaetani described her reactions to a formal observation by her principal:

> Knowing that she was to observe you teaching resulted in such actions as adjusting shades to regulation height, picking up stray pieces of paper . . . dropped on the floor, bringing your bulletin boards up to date, and prepping the children on their behavior. . . . I admit I was a coward, cowed by an authority I did not believe in but had not the strength to challenge.[46]

After this principal retired, 4 teachers (of about 30) in grades 1 through 3 opened up their classrooms slowly through centers and activities chosen by students for an hour or so a day. Proud as DeGaetani was of her progress, the weight of the Metropolitan Achievement Tests bore down on the teacher. "Too often the cloud of achievement tests," she wrote, "pressures teachers into compromises. . . . I know I will teach my children how to take the Test, although I realize this is basically against what I believe in." Why did she succumb to the pressure? "I do not have the energy nor, at this point, the willingness to fight the system. I know the scores of open education classes in our school will be compared with those of traditional classes. The comparison is itself fallacious. I know that. . . . But most parents don't. Many administrators don't and the system doesn't."[47]

In a nearby school similar to DeGaetani's, Alicia Montalvo kept a diary of her third year as a primary teacher in 1971–1972. The six other first-grade teachers had classes "conducted in the traditional manner. Each child has an assigned seat and all tables face the front of the room." In order to start an open classroom, a "Bank Street" one, as she called it, "I had to get special permission from the principal." Because she often stayed after 3:00—the time when, according to their contract, teachers could leave school—to prepare materials and change centers, the principal called her in to say that she had to leave by 3:30 because no one could be responsible for her after that time. "I really don't know if this whole idea of mine is worth the effort," she wrote in her diary for that day, "I'm so disgusted." She got even angrier later in the year when she switched the children from their work with Cuisenaire rods to the conventional way of teaching addition and subtraction after the principal told her that "the children were going to be tested to see whether or not they were learning in the open classroom."[48]

At P.S. 198 in Manhattan, Dorothy Boroughs, a fourth-grade teacher of 30 students, differed from her colleagues described above in enjoying an easygoing relationship with her principal. In a unique series of almost a dozen articles for *The New York Times,* Joseph Lelyveld describes his periodic visits to Boroughs's class during an entire school year (1970–1971).[49]

Lelyveld described Boroughs as "a brisk, energetic, and strongly committed young teacher who is usually among the first at school to punch in," and as being dedicated to getting children to read at or above the fourth-grade level. He described her when she laughed, scolded, pleaded with children, and showered them with a mixture of touching praise and earnest demands. The children responded with openness and seriousness, if not outright affection for their teacher. Students sat at clustered desks facing one another, working individually, in small groups, or as an entire class on tasks that the teacher had assigned. Her high expectations for achievement and behavior mingled with a vibrant charm that few children could resist.[50]

Lelyveld also provides a glimpse of some organizational processes that affected what Boroughs did. Take, for example, the visit of her supervisor, Assistant Principal Edmund Fried, to evaluate her teaching of a social studies lesson. Sitting in the back of the room, Boroughs gave him the daily plan composed of the aims, procedures, and activities that she intended to follow as she taught the lesson. "Miss Boroughs," Lelyveld writes, "had been worrying about the lesson plan for a week but had not actually committed any thoughts to paper until the lunch hour that day. Normally she prepares lesson plans to satisfy the demands of her supervisor but never works from them."[51]

After teaching the lesson on explorers, Boroughs brought the period to a close with the question "Why are we studying the explorers?"

"Because he's here to watch," said Shaun Sheppard knowingly, nodding in the direction of Mr. Fried.

"Fooled you, Shaun," the assistant principal declared, "I know about them already."

On his way out, Mr. Fried noted that Pizarro was the only Spanish explorer mentioned in the text who had not been mentioned in the lesson. He told Miss Boroughs that later on he would go over with her the comments that filled two sheets on his clipboard.[52]

Or consider Boroughs's exposure to the open classroom. In the spring semester she had enrolled with some other P.S. 198 teachers in an after-school course on open classrooms offered by Hunter College. After hearing from her student teacher about three teachers at P.S. 42 on the Lower East Side who had opened up their classrooms without funds or outside help, Boroughs got permission from her principal to spend a morning in these teachers' rooms. The Hunter College class and these visits spurred Boroughs's thinking and even led her to rearrange furniture to create a math corner. When two P.S. 42 teachers were invited by the Hunter College professor to speak to the P.S. 198 class, Boroughs' principal announced on the public address system that the entire staff of 55 were invited to hear the teachers describe how they opened up their classes. Twelve teachers, most of whom were registered for the class, showed up at the meeting.[53]

Boroughs was interested in open classrooms. "But," Lelyveld wrote, "she seemed uncertain as to how far or fast she herself would move in that direction." By the end of the week, "debate over educational theory had faded. The supreme reality was Spring."[54]

Not far from P.S. 198, poet Philip Lopate worked at P.S. 90 in the early 1970s as a writer charged to help teachers and children to write creatively. Working in a bilingual, experimental school with open classrooms, Lopate received advice from a friendly veteran teacher:

> This school may look free and groovy on the surface but don't be fooled, there's a lot of conservative feeling. Nothing from the outside will take root at P.S. 90 unless it's introduced very cautiously and slowly.

After being in the school for a while, Lopate noticed that some classes were mostly white while others were predominantly black and Puerto Rican. Denise Loften, a colleague, explained why:

> Denise said the reason for this was that the parents were given a choice at the beginning of the year whether they wanted to place their children in "open" or "more formal" classrooms. The white, liberal parents of the Up-

per West Side tended to select open classrooms. The parents from ethnic minorities opted more for traditional classes, feeling that open education might be soft on basic skills. . . . [55]

These teacher and journalist accounts suggest that the idea of open classrooms spread here and there through personal contacts, and that where informal approaches took hold, they seldom dominated an entire school.

Supporting this observation are limited data drawn from over 30 elementary classroom descriptions from across the city. Figure 6.1 shows that student-centered practices in furniture arrangement and student movement occurred in over half of the classes, but that in no more than one fourth of the classrooms did these practices appear in grouping for instruction and classroom tasks. Note, however, two items: (a) the substantial percentages of a mixed pattern that appear under the headings of group instruction and classroom activities, and (b) the number of classrooms that contained learning centers. These figures again suggest that teachers were selective in what they chose to put into practice.

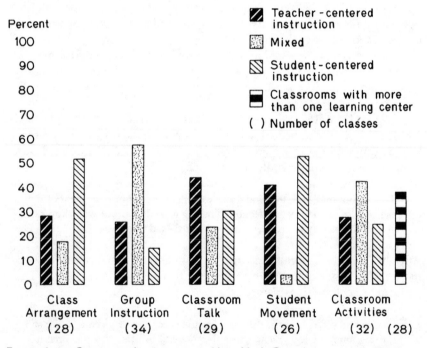

FIGURE 6.1   *Patterns of instruction in New York City elementary school classrooms, 1967–1975*

Given the limitations of the data I presented, it would still be fair to say that open classrooms, at varying stages of development, dotted the school map of the city in these years of peaking interest in informal classrooms. But these dots probably did not add up to more than one teacher in four or five. What about high schools?

REGULAR AND ALTERNATIVE HIGH SCHOOLS

Alternative High School Classrooms

Alternative schools were not simply the secondary counterpart to open classrooms, although there were similarities between the two types of organization. The roots of alternative high schools differed somewhat from those of informal education. These roots were located in student protest against university programs, in the Vietnam War and civil rights concerns, and in a melange of other issues that converged in the late 1960s. Protest filtered down to high schools. Growing disaffection with high school rules and behavior requirements, conventional instruction, a lack of participation in decisions, and a curriculum viewed as alien to current youth concerns found expression in student boycotts, underground newspapers, dropping out, and the establishment of new private and public alternative schools.[56]

The Murray Road school in Newton, Massachusetts, and New York's Harlem Prep opened their doors in 1967. Wilson Open Campus School in Mankato, Minnesota, was established in 1968, and a year later Philadelphia's Parkway program, a "school without walls," sent students into the city itself to learn. By the height of the movement in 1972 hundreds of secondary alternative schools had been created. The mortality rate ran high. Still, by 1975, public alternative secondary schools were a fact of life that most school systems accepted and, in a number of instances, nurtured.[57]

"Schools without walls" (where the city is the classroom), storefront schools, minischools within larger conventional high schools, theme or magnet schools (e.g., specializing in science or the arts)—all fall under the heading of alternative high schools. I exclude vocational, continuation, and other schools targeted toward certain groups of students, most of which were established prior to 1965.

No easy generalization, then, can capture the diversity of these schools. A number of commonalities, however, existed, including:

- School as a community;
- The teacher serves as an advisor;
- Active rather than passive learning;
- Student participation in major decisionmaking; and

- Incorporation of the needs and experiences of students into curriculum and instruction.[58]

Individual alternative schools varied greatly, stressing some features more than others. Nevertheless, all alternatives differed from regular high schools in size, school climate, teachers' relationships with students, the process of curricular decisionmaking—particularly constructing elective courses—and ideological commitment.[59]

What about instruction? With the individual student, active learning, and curricular choice paramount values in alternative schools, what teaching practices occurred? Most researchers who have studied alternative high schools have concentrated upon issues of governance, curriculum, the composition of the student body, student-teacher relationships, and organizational processes; few have paid attention to pedagogy.[60]

The little that has been done reveals diversity in teaching methods. David Moore, for example, cites the range of practices that he observed and identified from the limited research: from teacher-directed, programmed instruction to "relatively formless, collaborative investigations and activities." Discussion was the preferred teaching method, he noted. "Curiously," he writes, "lecturing happens more than one might imagine, but open talk is far more common." Frequent field trips, guest speakers, films, and groupwork were commonly used, according to Moore. Still "teachers often take the primary responsibility for designing and supplying materials for courses." His interviews with students revealed that they wanted "instructors to assume that role." Moore notes that there may be less innovative teaching practice in and of itself but that the frequency and mixture of these practices "may be new in American education."[61]

Dan Duke studied six alternative secondary schools. In grouping students for instruction, he found, all six schools created classes for teenagers of different abilities. Teachers used a variety of classroom groupings, with small-group and independent study common to all but one of the schools. When he looked at teaching practices he found that half of the schools had special rooms set aside for students to work with tutors or individually. None, however, had "creative room arrangements" (e.g., learning centers or chairs arranged to increase student exchanges). One high school had team teaching and one used older students to tutor younger ones. To evaluate student performance, three schools used fixed scales against which students were measured; however, far more stress was reportedly placed on individual, noncompetitive grading. In reporting to parents how their children were doing in school, four alternative schools used portfolios of what students had produced and held teacher-parent conferences. After reviewing the results and the history of instructional reforms, Duke concluded that "contemporary alternative schools do not constitute a pedagogical revolution."[62]

In New York City, alternative schools became an official plank in Harvey Scribner's platform to improve the city's high schools. Scribner was in charge of over 100 academic and vocational high schools enrolling over 300,000 students in the early 1970s. The academic high schools were large by any standard. Most ranged between 3,000 and 4,000 students taught by a faculty of 175 to 215 teachers. Enrollment at the smaller vocational schools was between 1,500 and 2,000 students; the larger ones in 1971 included John Jay in Brooklyn, with 5,600 students; Louis Brandeis in Manhattan, with nearly 6,000 students; and DeWitt Clinton in the Bronx, New York's largest high school, with almost 7,000 students, all male. The ethnic composition of the high schools in 1971 was: white, 50.9%; black, 29.5%; Puerto Rican, 15.1%; Oriental, 1.4%; and other groups, 3.1%. Average daily attendance for academic high schools was 77% of the student body. Almost 1 out of every 3 students read two or more years below grade level, yet nearly 8 out of 10 graduates applied to either junior or four-year colleges.[63]

The new chancellor directed a massive operation. Even before Scribner's arrival, a number of privately funded storefront schools, established through private efforts, were aimed at salvaging able students who had dropped out of regular high schools. The New York Urban Coalition and the Urban League, using funds raised from banks and corporations, established networks of these schools in low-income minority areas of the city. As the grants ended, the private groups negotiated with the Board of Education to install the storefront schools in regular high schools as minischools. Examples of such schools, which had 75 to 125 students with separate staff and rooms in main school buildings or in churches or rented facilities nearby, included Harambee Prep at Charles Evans Hughes High School in Manhattan, Wingate Prep at the school of the same name in Brooklyn, and Haaren High School, itself divided into 14 semi-autonomous minischools.[64]

Under Scribner and his successor, these minischools and separate alternative schools spread throughout the system so that by 1975 in the five boroughs of the city there were 11 alternative schools enrolling 4,000 students and 40 minischools with about 6,500 students. In addition there were a number of alternative programs, located within schools and aimed at talented students. The Executive High School Internship at Erasmus Hall's Institute of Music and Art and Julia Richman High School's Talent are examples of such programs. By 1976 these alternatives, including minischools, together enrolled almost 15,000 students, or about 5% of all high school youth.[65]

Most minischools were last-ditch efforts to save students from dropping out, to recruit truants back to school, and to upgrade academically ill-prepared yet able young men and women who found it difficult to adjust to regular high schools. Classes were small, with less than 25 students. Administrators recruited teachers who would listen to students, be demanding, and not mind being called by their first names. Other staff, sometimes called "streetworkers," were recruited to visit students at home or at work. These were some key features of minischools.[66]

The 11 alternative schools in 1976 included the City-as-School, the New York counterpart of Philadelphia's Parkway program; Harlem Prep; Middle College High School, which was linked to LaGuardia Community College; and Park East High School, a school initially founded by community groups.

Journalists who observed over a dozen classes at Wingate Prep, Harambee, George Washington Prep, and Lower East Side Prep found a range of familiar teacher approaches. Here is a sampling:

- A wide-ranging discussion on the use of drugs, the new state law on punishing drug pushers, and the impact of peer cultures intensely engaged students.
- An English class reading a Dorothy Parker short story about a blind black child spent part of the period moving around the class blindfolded before discussing the story.
- Students reading parts in a play written by a contemporary black writer paused periodically for heated discussions.
- In a disastrous history class, the teacher lectured, rambled, asked questions, and plunged on with answers to those questions; students paid little attention, talked among themselves, and ignored teacher warnings. Mercifully, the bell rang.
- A teacher wrote quadratic equations on the blackboard and students took notes silently.
- An astronomy lesson was interspersed with questions and answers on astrology and horoscopes.[67]

One reporter summed up his impressions of classroom teaching in minischools thus: "The classroom instruction and subject matter are not essentially different from what might be found in many conventional high schools." Differences in these alternatives were school size, class size, the informality of relations between teachers and students, and frequent involvement of students in governance decisions.[68]

Regular High School Classrooms

In the conventional academic high schools, patterns of instruction were like those practiced in earlier generations. I located photographs and written descriptions of 33 teachers in 13 high schools between 1969 and 1975. Spare as the sample is, the convergence in teaching patterns is striking in Figure 6.2.

In most cases, the entire class was taught as a group; the teacher talked about two-thirds of the time; there was hardly any student movement within

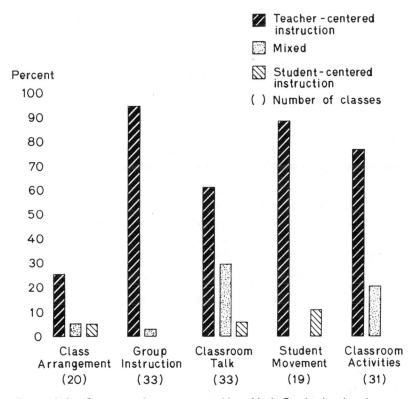

FIGURE 6.2 *Patterns of instruction in New York City high school classrooms, 1967–1975*

the room; and most class activities were built around students listening, writing, or watching. In short, teacher-centered instruction writ large.

Profiles of two high schools, including extensive classroom observations, by *New York Times* reporters offer data about additional classes. Reporter William Stevens produced an in-depth article in 1971 on John Bowne High School in Queens, a school with a faculty of 200 for 3,100 students, of whom 75% went to either two- or four-year colleges. Ethnically, Bowne was 65% white and 30% black, mostly as a result of a Board of Education desegregation plan.[69]

Stevens contrasted a radio electronics class taught by physics teacher Norman Hessel, where students individually and enthusiastically build radios piece by piece, with a math class that would give any teacher a nightmare—students throwing spitballs at one another, playing cards, walking around the room, and ignoring the teacher's directions. "This year," Stevens wrote,

"Bowne has been preoccupied with how to create more situations like that in Hessel's class and change scenes like those in the mathematics class."[70]

Bowne had nearly 500 classes a day in about 75 different subjects. The day was divided into nine 40-minute periods. Intense discussions would get going, teachers reported, only to be cut off by the bell. While scheduling of classes affects instruction, teachers also pointed out to Stevens that "traditional teaching approaches" drove students to boredom. "If we were ever to teach sex the way we teach other things," one teacher remarked, "it would go out of style." Stevens, after sitting in a number of classes, observed that "the teacher is at the front of the class attempting to interest everyone in the same subject at the same time."

Hard as that is to do, teachers did try. The social studies department chairman told Stevens that each lesson was supposed to have a specific objective and incorporate questions that provoked students to think and participate in discussions. One teacher in that department said that if one third of his class participated, he judged the lesson a success.[71]

The *Times* reporter also spent a week shadowing a Harlem ninth grader who attended John F. Kennedy in the Bronx, a newly built eight-story high school with 1,800 ninth and tenth graders whose enrollment would grow to almost 5,000 as it absorbed more grades. Fifteen-year-old Natalie Wright was part of the 40% of the school that was black. The rest of the school was equally divided between white and Hispanic students. William Stevens's reports and Wright's observations of her academic classes follow:

- *Introductory physical science.* The science teacher paired off students to work on a second run-through of an experiment on the conservation of mass. They heated sealed test-tubes of copper and sulphur, weighed them, and recorded the results. They spent two days on the experiment because the teacher was trying to get the class to graph the results. This was "very boring to Natalie," Stevens wrote, because she had learned conservation of mass in junior high school.
- *Algebra.* This was "happy class," according to Natalie. She worked on polynomial multiplication problems all period as the teacher circulated, helping individual students. After Natalie finished, she began helping other students. "I just like it," she replied to Stevens's question about her interest in algebra.
- *Social studies.* Natalie was bored on Monday. She couldn't have cared less about ancient China's civil service system or their scholar-gentry class. On Wednesday, students and teacher got into a lively discussion of civil service, social status, and class mobility.
- *Spanish.* Natalie had failed class in the first nine weeks. Teachers were switched. Monday's lesson was based upon a story of a meeting between a tourist and a hotel clerk. Using a "Peanuts" cartoon, the teacher asked questions in Spanish and the class chorused replies.
- *Creative writing.* The teacher introduced onomatopoeia. Question-and-

answer exchanges followed the teacher's explanation. When the teacher asked for examples, the class exploded with a "cacophony of bangs, meows, buzzes, bow-wows, swishes, jingles, moos, oinks. . . . Much hilarity."
- "2:45 p.m. Bell. Liberation."

Stevens summarized two entire days of classes with a laconic "Tuesday was the same as yesterday" or "Classes were the same."[72]

Except for science, where laboratory work paired Natalie with a classmate, the classes were taught as a whole group. Teachers questioning students were the primary means of exchanging information. Seatwork took up an entire period. Little student movement was apparent except in science lab. Each lesson was structured, directed, and moved along by the teacher so as to cover the content. Reliance upon a textbook was common. As another John F. Kennedy teacher put it a few years later, "I have always felt that the best teaching machine is a book."[73]

Stevens's descriptions of two high schools echo the 33 descriptions I gathered. Teacher-centered instruction dominated both conventional and minischool classes, with some variations in the degree and frequency of particular practices.

At about the time when Stevens's account appeared, Scribner announced his resignation. Within a year Irving Anker, a New York City educator with 38 years' service who had risen through the ranks (as most of his predecessors had), assumed the chancellorship. "Improving test scores" and "accountability" were the new catchphrases circulating among insiders in the mid-1970s. Automatic promotion to the next grade was abolished; students now had to meet tougher standards for reading performance before they could progress to a higher grade. Open classrooms were no longer a hot topic. With the onset of severe budget cuts in 1975, survival replaced talk about reform.[74]

The fiscal emergency that jolted New York drove public officials to severely cut funding for all government agencies, especially the public schools. Teacher layoffs crippled programs. At an Open Corridor school, P.S. 84, 26 of 52 teachers were let go. The ripple effects of layoffs shipped teachers with more seniority to vacancies in schools from which teachers with fewer years of service, many of whom were black and Hispanic, had been fired. Massive staff dislocation aborted many efforts to open up classrooms. Class sizes in elementary and secondary schools ballooned beyond the contractual limits of 32 and 34 students. Aides were let go. The numbers of counselors and special teachers were cut. Larger classes and less help combined to further lower teacher morale. The swift turn of events discouraged teacher initiatives, risk-taking, extra efforts, and innovation.[75]

Yet in 1981 P.S. 84, as well as a number of other elementary schools with a decade of experience with Open Corridors and informal education, still retained those classrooms. While there were fewer teachers and principals than a decade before, the fact that such efforts survived and even flourished in an indifferent, if not hostile, environment is a testimonial to the tenacity of committed teachers and administrators.

At the secondary level, alternative high schools and minischools, also hit hard by retrenchment, survived handily. In 1979, 11 alternative high schools were still operating, with an enrollment of 5000 students, excluding the many students enrolled in minischools lodged in senior highs (e.g., Seward Park High School, James Monroe High School, and Haaren High School).[76]

By the early 1980s, residues of informal schooling persisted across the city amid the dominant teacher-centeredness of most classrooms. As in the two North Dakota cities I visited in 1981, variations in classroom patterns were evident. Degrees of openness had penetrated numerous elementary classrooms but far fewer high school classrooms. I now turn to Washington, D.C., to see whether similar patterns emerged there.

WASHINGTON, D.C.

Veteran schoolwatchers had never seen so much happen in three months. In April 1967, the capital's teachers voted 3–2 to have the American Federation of Teachers represent them at the bargaining table. Teacher unions had arrived in a nonunion town. In June, for the first time in the history of the District schools, the Board of Education had a majority of black members, most of whom actively opposed the policies of Carl Hansen, who had been school chief for 9 years. Later in the same month, the Board released a year-long, quarter-million-dollar study by Teachers College of the entire school system. The study severely criticized the superintendent's policies and the largely ineffective and inappropriate instructional program, and called for an end to the Four-Track system of grouping students.

The very same day, Federal Judge J. Skelly Wright rendered a 183-page decision in the *Hobson v. Hansen* suit. He ordered an end to the track system, the beginning of busing black children from overcrowded schools to nearly empty white schools west of Rock Creek Park, and faculty integration. Within two weeks, the Board decided not to appeal Wright's decision and asked the superintendent to implement the court order. Instead, Carl Hansen, father both of the Amidon Plan, a tightly structured curricular program that placed the teacher at the center of instruction, and of the Four-Track system, resigned. The events of April through June 1967 shook the D.C. system, profoundly unnerving the organization in the decade that followed.[77]

One benchmark of the subsequent instability was increased superintendent turnover. During almost a half century (1920–1967), only four superintendents had served the District: Frank Ballou, Robert Haycock, Hobart Corning, and Carl Hansen. Now, in just over a decade (1968–1980), six school chiefs moved in and out of the large 12th-floor office in the downtown Presidential Building.

Demography, court decisions, and political change help explain the turmoil at the top. The school system had grown from over 90,000 students in 1940 to 150,000 in 1967, of whom more than 90% were black. In 1967, almost 8,000 teachers worked in nearly 140 schools. Washington was the largest predominantly black school system in the nation. Although the *Bolling v. Sharpe* decision, the District's counterpart to *Brown v. Board of Education,* had required desegregation of schools in 1955, when nearly two out of three children were black, whites continued to leave the school system as they had been doing since World War II. As these white students were replaced by black newcomers from the South, desegregation generated much attention from the media and civic groups. The attention was largely symbolic, since a decade after the *Bolling* decision there were only 15,000 white children in a school system of 150,000 students. By 1967, other concerns shoved aside desegregation as an issue.[78]

By the late 1960s and early 1970s, educating black children to perform well academically slowly replaced desegregation as the fundamental goal of the schools. But the goal's clarity (and its pursuit) often went astray after 1968, when Congress, in the backwash of widespread rioting triggered by the assassination of Martin Luther King, Jr., granted limited home rule to the District government. In addition, the goal was obscured by the efforts of administrators to comply with the *Hobson v. Hansen* decision, which mandated transfers of teachers in the middle of the school year to permit equitable allocation of resources to all schools. Such massive transfers of teachers disrupted school programs for the remainder of the school year.[79]

Electoral politics came to D.C. initially with an elected Board of Education in 1968. Anything connected with schools became a contested issue. The new Board's search for a superintendent to replace Carl Hansen brought William Manning from Lansing, Michigan. He lasted less than 2 years. His successor, Detroit administrator Hugh Scott, became the first black in the nation to head a big-city school system. Appointed in 1970, he arrived just as the School Board was independently arranging for Kenneth Clark (school critic, psychologist, and member of the New York State Board of Regents) to install his program design for improving education in the District's schools. The Clark Plan, an effort that focused the school system's energies on the teaching of reading and on improving academic achievement, was handed to Scott to implement. The plan met stiff resistance from the teachers' union because of testing requirements and less-than-subtle hints by school officials that teachers might be evaluated on the basis of test results. Constant bickering among school board members, union threats to strike, and bureaucratic foul-ups over executing the Wright decree buried the plan by 1972, and Scott exited less than a year later. He had lasted less than 3 years.[80]

Scott's successor, Barbara Sizemore, a Chicago school administrator, advocated active citizen participation in the governance and operation of schools, the empowerment of black people, and the positive benefits of conflict. Sizemore had the twofold distinction of being the District's first female superintendent and the first superintendent fired after a public hearing of the Board of Education. She lasted 2 years.

The swinging-door superintendency halted with Vincent Reed's appointment in 1975. An insider who had risen through the ranks, served as a high school principal, and been a top lieutenant of the three superintendents who followed Hansen, Reed re-established managerial order in a system that was in grave organizational disarray after the whiplashing of entering and exiting administrators.

In 1976, Reed launched a comprehensive program called the Competency-Based Curriculum (CBC), a massive staff development program that trained thousands of staff members to set lesson objectives, devise instructional strategies to achieve those objectives, and assess the results of classroom instruction. In-service sessions, 3-pound manuals of directions distributed to the instructional staff, elaborate explanations to the public, and tactics to boost staff morale were various strategies used in implementing the CBC. A slim majority of the Board approved Reed's direction, including the end of automatic promotion from grade to grade and the setting of minimum levels of competency that students had to demonstrate before they could move to the next grade. In 1980, after a number of public displays of superintendent-Board friction and a deep split in the Board over Reed's plan to create a high school for the gifted, as well as over other issues, he took an early retirement.[81]

This summary of organizational instability at the top between 1967 and 1980 sets the stage for examining what occurred in schools amid turbulent Board-superintendent politics and the confusion of green and red lights given to principals and teachers. A snapshot of where the entire system was in 1966–1967 (at the onset of this period of turmoil) comes from a Teachers College study, called the Passow Report after study director A. Harry Passow, who with a staff of nearly 200 conducted the yearlong survey.[82]

Passow found the schools in need of fundamental changes if Washington was to create a "Model Urban School System"—the formal title of the study. The shortcomings of the system, documented in the 593-page study, gave little comfort to Carl Hansen or his supporters when they read it in early 1967. Among its findings were:

- A low level of scholastic achievement;
- Grouping procedures that had been followed erratically;
- A curriculum that, with certain exceptions, was not suited to an urban enrollment; and
- An overly large and bureaucratic District headquarters.

Nor did any of the conclusions on the instructional program throw bouquets at school officials.[83]

For instance:

- *Teachers were "inadequately prepared."* Pressures to staff classrooms "at all costs" had led to school board to hire hundreds of temporary teachers over the years. "The presence of so many ill-qualified teachers," Passow concluded, "no doubt accounts for the many teachers who, according to classroom observers, are ritualistic, superficial in presenting subject matter, and fearful of the normal activities of teachers."[84]
- *Curriculum was narrow.* Schools "stripped subjects to their most formal and least meaningful aspects." In the teaching of reading, the narrowness reached its peak in a program that "construed reading as word-recognition and word-recognition as phonics, thus turning reading into a program of ritual code-breaking. . . ." Other elementary school subjects were "either given short shrift or detoured into further exercises in reading." Yet test results showed that "not enough children [did], in fact, learn to read well."[85]
- *Tracking was ineffective.* After reviewing student achievement, the numbers of elementary and secondary students in the various tracks, and the degree of student movement between tracks, the task force studying tracking concluded that there were "sufficient inequities, inconsistencies, and inadequacies to warrant its abandonment."[86]
- *Teaching was standardized and unimaginative.* Twenty-three experienced teachers and administrators trained in observing classrooms visited 75 teachers in nine elementary schools selected at random. "The clock seemed to be in charge of the classroom," one observer wrote. Daily schedules set who did what, when, and under what conditions. Lessons—consistent with the curriculum bulletins of the Amidon Plan—were similar from one classroom to another. There was little evidence of teachers departing from the spirit of the plan or daily schedule. "The striking characteristics of these classrooms," observers reported, "[were] the quiet and orderliness. . . . The children seem compliant, obedient, and passive." Time was spent mostly on "drill and reading and phonics, on reading for social studies information, and on working arithmetic problems." On the basis of these observations,

Passow concluded that District elementary teachers played "a highly directive role. . . . The child spent most of his day paying the closest possible attention to his teacher, following her directions, responding to her questions, obeying her rules. The children were not encouraged to talk to one another, either formally or informally. . . ."[87]

At the high school level, observations were limited and offered even less comfort to either teachers or administrators.

- Science: "The teachers lecture and the students listen. There was a minimal pupil-teacher or pupil-pupil interaction."
- Social studies: "In most classrooms, instruction seems to follow a textbook approach. . . ."
- Foreign languages: "[Teachers'] training for the textbooks, instructional resources, and the direct method . . . needs . . . massive upgrading."
- Mathematics: "Teachers observed seemed either uncomfortable with the material they were teaching or oblivious to its nuances and implications. Mathematics errors or misconceptions occurred frequently. . . . Continued organization of large mathematics classes conducted by inept teachers is a questionable policy."[88]

The Passow Study portrayed teaching practices in 1966–1967 at both the elementary and secondary levels as mostly teacher-centered. The study also referred to some promising classroom innovations under way in individual schools and programs. In the turbulent years following Hansen's resignation and the dismantling of the Amidon Plan and Four-Track system, just when public and professional interest in informal education was at its peak, opportunities surfaced to expand these infant efforts to reform classroom practices. The Model School Division (MSD) is a case in point.

Model School Division

Located in the Cardozo neighborhood of the city, an area labeled for years as a slum by newspapers and reformers, the Model School Division by 1969 became a decentralized unit enrolling 19,500 students in 5 preschools and 18 elementary and secondary schools, including Cardozo High.[89]

Between 1964 and 1975, the MSD was a holding company for almost every innovation that promised improved schooling for urban poor minority students. Established to be an experimental arm for the entire school system, by 1970, when a program inventory was taken, the MSD had implemented over two dozen curricular, instructional, and organizational innovations (e.g., Elementary School Science, English in Every Classroom, the Madison Math Project, team teaching, nongraded primaries, Language Experience in Reading). Federal, private, and local funds combined to produce in the Cardozo area a heady climate resonating with optimism and change. With the departure of Carl Hansen, the MSD had even more discretion to innovate.

One showcase effort that brought much publicity while earning the respect of many educators, both locally and nationally, was the Innovation Team. Composed of 15 experienced classroom teachers, the team began operating in 1967 under the direction of Mary Lela Sherburne, who had worked with the Education Development Center (EDC) in Newton, Massachusetts. The team's initial task was to coordinate the myriad programs that kept spinning out of federal and local reformers' heads and wallets. The team was also to help classroom teachers incorporate new ideas and materials into their daily practice.

By 1969, when a formal evaluation of the team was completed, the objectives had shifted from providing teachers with conventional in-service training and technical assistance to changing teachers' roles and making classrooms into more active places "where different learning styles, interests, and paces can be accommodated through a variety of materials and techniques." Moreover, the team's charge now included "involving teachers in schoolwide cooperative problem-solving and decision making." The team, underwritten in part by EDC, had held scores of workshops, visited hundreds of classrooms numerous times (at the request of teachers), and provisioned rooms with new math, science, social studies, and reading materials. In a small but growing number of MSD classrooms, science and math centers began to appear.[90]

While much of the vocabulary used by team members, the director, and the assistant superintendent was consistent with the language of informal education advocates, seldom was there a reference in the MSD to open classrooms. Materials from the EDC, the use of tri-wall cardboard to construct learning centers and carrels, and expanding the teacher's view of the classroom as a place where children actively learn were integral to the quiet message conveyed by the Innovation Team.

Part of the reason for so little explicit language on open classrooms may have been that the philosophy of the Team evolved in that direction between 1967 and 1970 and was stated explicitly in the latter year. The marriage of the Team's beliefs in active learning and informal education with the belief in the teacher's central role as primary decisionmaker, however, did not produce in the MSD large numbers of classrooms packaged as or labeled "open". Some did exist, and more were developing by 1970. But the Innovation Team's primary goal was not to copy open classrooms. Rather, the team existed to respond to teachers' requests for help. Moreover, teachers in the MSD endorsed the team's work, indicating repeatedly in surveys that the 15 teachers "had contributed to their effectiveness as teachers more than any other source or MSD program."[91]

In 1969, when Russell Cort completed his evaluation of the team, he said that "improving performance at the school and classroom levels will take continuous, dedicated, persistent, focussed effort." Within a year, the Innovation Team disbanded.[92]

A new superintendent, Hugh Scott, stuck with implementing the Board of Education's decision to adopt Kenneth Clark's design for academic improvement, saw other uses for the team. In just over 3 years, the team had assembled, worked with teachers, received local and national applause for its work, and dispersed. The promise of planned change embedded in the team dissolved as well.

Innovation Team members moved on to principalships or central office posts or left the system. Mary Lela Sherburne, the team's first director, and member Olive Covington helped organize the Advisory and Learning Exchange (ALE), a privately funded group of educators interested in establishing and spreading open classrooms in the Washington metropolitan area. Created as a teacher center and support group for those private and public school parents and educators seeking to explore open education and similar approaches, ALE opened its doors in a downtown Washington suite of offices in 1971. By 1974, over 600 workshops had attracted teachers and parents from the D.C. area. By 1981, however, the organization had undergone many changes and support of informal classrooms was no longer its main interest.[93]

Open Classrooms and Open Space

Elsewhere in the city, open classrooms appeared in the early 1970s. Sometimes these were promoted by groups of white parents (as they were in New York City); sometimes they were installed by eager teachers. For example, at Hearst-Eaton schools, Joan Brown, a new principal (she had been installed in 1971) and former Innovation Team member, recruited new teachers enthusiastic for informal education and exhorted the ones she had inherited to open up their classrooms. A summer workshop in 1970 trained 20 teachers to start open classrooms in 12 schools west of Rock Creek Park, a predominantly white, affluent area. Parents from schools in the area lobbied school officials in order to win support for the program. The summer workshop was led by Innovation Team members LaVerne Ford, Mary Alexander, and others.[94]

The Morgan School, the first school in the District designated by the Board of Education to be operated by an elected group of parents, began open classrooms in 1967 under the aegis of Antioch College. Young teachers, mostly white, and community aides, mostly black, all trained to use instructional materials from EDC, divided the school into teams of children by age rather than grade and embraced informal education. By 1969 Ken Haskins, the first principal, had left, and Bishop Reed, head of the Morgan Community School Board, had died. By that time Antioch College had severed its ties with the school. The few white parents who had helped establish the school and had negotiated the contract with the Board of Education that gave Morgan its autonomy had also left. A new local Board and principal set specific rules for student conduct, brought back report cards, tested students, and told teachers to stress basic skills and discipline.[95]

By 1970, most of the original teachers and open classrooms had been pushed out of the school. The principal recruited teachers from Southern black colleges to replace the ones who had left. In 1971, 17 of 30 teachers in the school were teaching for the first time. When a newspaper reporter visited the school in 1973, 6 years after it began as a parent-run public school, only two of the primary teachers still maintained informal classrooms. Most teachers "ran their classrooms along highly traditional lines and [said] they [were] appalled by what they regard[ed] as the disorganization and lack of discipline in the classes of some teachers at Morgan." Yet the few open classroom teachers in the school looked forward to the replacement of the old Morgan schoolhouse with a new open-space building in 1974.[96]

The erection of open-space buildings, like many efforts in the District requiring money, had to wait while the Board of Education, the District government, and both Houses of Congress reached agreement over the question of authorizing and then appropriating the necessary funds. As Frank Ballou found out in 1925 when his first building program was finally approved by all the necessary agencies, patience, a sense of the absurd, and a rabbit's foot helped. Often requests for building schools waited for up to 7 years before the Board was authorized to proceed with already outdated architectural plans. So it was with the replacement of old, cramped elementary buildings built before and during Superintendent Frank Ballou's tenure.

The concept of open-space schools had seized the imagination of school boards and superintendents across the country in the early 1960s as a way of revolutionizing curriculum, instruction, and the customary role of the teacher. The District was no exception. Requests for open-space schools were submitted and, after lengthy delays, were approved. By the mid-1970s open-space schools appeared at both the elementary and secondary levels (e.g., plans for replacing the old Brookland elementary school were approved in 1967; the open-space school was finally dedicated in 1974; a similar span of time marked the erection of the open-space Dunbar High School).

An open-space environment encourages teaming among teachers, varied groupings of children, nongraded arrangements, and diverse uses of space. It is consistent with, but not essential for, open classrooms. Beginning with

1971, when the Ketcham addition opened, each year brought new open-space schools, until in 1979 there were 17, costing $163 million, including the new Morgan School, which had been renamed Marie Reed.[97]

In the District the open-space concept in building was wedded to open classrooms. Between 1971 and 1974, in-service workshops for teachers who volunteered to work in open space were held. Six training cycles were sponsored by a federally funded Training Center for Open Space Schools. Few doubted that the British primary school, Lillian Weber's Open Corridors, and informal classrooms were the models that key District school officials had in mind. Those principals, supervisors, and middle-level managers who shared a passion for open classrooms sought improved ways of training teachers who had volunteered to work in the new buildings. But no board of education, and no superintendent, made a public commitment to informal education.[98]

Consider Brookland School. Two years before the new school opened, the principal and members of the six-teacher staff of the "old" school attended workshops, visited open-space schools in the Washington area, took courses at D.C. Teachers College, and spent 2 weeks touring British schools at their own expense. The staff gave workshops to parents explaining "open classrooms" as they would operate in open-space buildings. The new school opened in 1974 and was subsequently identified as the model open-space school for the District schools.[99]

The Spread of Open Classrooms

How widespread open classrooms, even broadly defined, were in Washington is difficult to estimate. As in New York City, no survey was undertaken after the Passow Report. With 130 elementary schools staffed by nearly 3,500 teachers (in 1975), an accurate estimate is hard to come by. Less than 15% of the schools were open space. It would be foolish to assume either that all teachers in open space conducted open classrooms or that open classrooms were located only in open space. There are some clues, nonetheless.

By 1974, in the last training cycle for teachers electing to teach in open-space buildings, 28% of the 200 participants reported they had opened up their classrooms. For over half of the teachers attending, the workshop was their first experience with informal classrooms. The ALE reported that in 1975–1976 over 700 D.C. elementary teachers had attended workshops. There was no indication whether the number was cumulative or represented individual teachers. Also consider the 46 classroom descriptions from 23 elementary schools that I gathered from photographs, newspaper articles, published interviews with teachers, and an evaluation report. (See Figure 6.3.) Note, however, that the percentages for student-centered instruction are probably inflated since, of the 10 schools that had learning centers, 2—Mor-

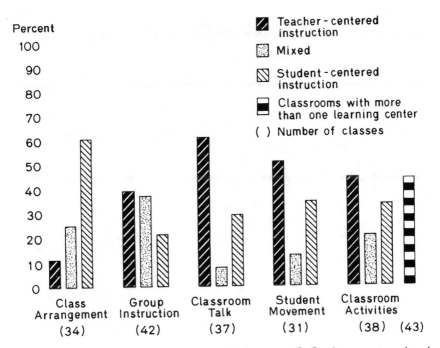

FIGURE 6.3 *Patterns of instruction in Washington, D.C. elementary school classrooms, 1967–1975*

gan and Hearst-Eaton—appeared in the narrative. These two schools accounted for almost half of the classrooms that had one or more centers.[100]

A student-centered pattern is strongest with regard to furniture arrangement (62%), learning centers (44%), and students moving around the classroom without asking the teacher's permission (35%). However, when it comes to small groups and individual activities, student participation in classroom tasks, and the prevalence of student talk, the range goes from 22% to 34%—again with the caveat that these figures may be somewhat inflated because of the small number of schools and because two schools contributed more accounts than the others. Teacher-centered patterns still registered strongly; almost half of the classrooms were taught through whole-group instruction (40%) and engaged in listening, working at desks, and responding to teacher questions (45%). In over half of the classes there was little student movement (52%), and in nearly two of every three of these classes teachers dominated verbal exchanges (62%).

All of these scattered figures provide a fragmentary, but nonetheless considered, basis for estimating that one in four or five elementary teachers did something in their classroom that could be defined as informal education.[101]

PLATE 6. 1 *Winston Elementary School, Washington, D.C., 1977*

By 1975, interest in informal education had flagged considerably. Federal funds for the Training Center had run out. City deficits produced lists of budget cuts, and protracted squabbles occurred between the Board of Education and the mayor over which agencies would bear what portions of the budget cuts. The schools retrenched by cutting aides, staff development, and other services that had nurtured open education. By 1978, a small study that compared reading achievement and other student outcomes in 372 open-space and self-contained classrooms found that "the self-contained classroom provided a better learning environment than . . . the open space classroom." [102]

More important, however, was the growing concentration on improving basic skills and the constant monitoring of progress by tests, initially through the Clark Plan (1970–1973) and later through the Competency-Based Curriculum under Superintendent Vincent Reed (after 1976). Teachers were charged to provide specific and direct instruction in skills; they had to know whether or not students had performed at the appropriate level on a given day. Testing expanded. Standards for semi-annual promotions of students were tightened and enforced. For children who were retained, remedial programs were expanded. Such measures, while not necessarily incompatible with open classrooms, were far closer in spirit to the Amidon Plan, abolished in 1967, than to informal education.

PLATE 6.2 *Friendship Elementary School, Washington, D.C., 1977*

The stress upon academic skills through CBC, the reduction of tangible support for open classrooms, and the inherently greater demands that accompany informal teaching may explain the difficulties that principals had, after 1976, in securing volunteers to staff open-space classrooms. Teachers, some of whom had been assigned to open-space schools to replace dismissed junior colleagues, threw up jerry-built walls of portable blackboards and bookcases to create self-contained rooms within open-space work areas. Learning centers gradually disappeared.[103]

In 1981–82 I spent two mornings at Bruce-Monroe and Brookland, both open-space schools. Bruce-Monroe, with 525 pupils and a staff of 20, had a principal who had worked with the Innovation Team. When it opened in 1974, Bruce-Monroe had had centers in reading, math, science, and social studies planted in "Learning Communities" of three to four teachers (also known as "pods"). In 1981, when I walked through the pods, I saw a number of centers, which, however, were used only sporadically by teachers, usually for practice activities after formal periods on reading, math, and language arts. Aides were no longer present. Special teachers did pull students out of classes for specific instruction.[104]

Of the 7 teachers I observed (out of a staff of 14 for grades 1 through 6), only 1 had children sit in rows of chairs facing the chalkboard; the other 6 teachers had students sit at tables facing one another. Children moved freely

PLATE 6.3 Gage-Eckington elementary school, Washington, D.C., 1976

as they worked on tasks, asked the teachers questions, and so on. Four of the teachers were working with the class as one group; the rest used a mixture of small and large groupings within the 2 hours I spent moving in and out of their pods. Four of the teachers had on the chalkboards the CBC objective for the day:

- Circle the beginning sounds.
- Add and subtract.
- Review plural endings.
- Use contractions

During classroom activities, 5 of the teachers gave directions to students and then had them all work at their desks on the same task, (i.e., textbook questions, copying from the blackboard) for 30–45 minutes. One teacher asked questions about math problems as the entire class sat on the floor with texts in their laps in front of her. Another teacher had divided her class into at least three groups that worked on different tasks.

Six of the seven teachers had learning centers, but these were not used daily. Teachers told me that they were used occasionally to reward students or to allow them to practice for CBC objectives when scheduled activities had been completed.

Brookland, which also opened in 1974, had 450 students in kindergarten through eighth grade. Large open spaces with few dividers made up the "learning centers," as the grades were called. As at Bruce-Monroe, aides had been eliminated. Reductions in the teaching force had brought new staff to the school while sending others elsewhere. The art, music, and home economics teachers each taught all grades. Only one classroom center was visible in the entire school the morning I visited.

I spent two hours each with six of the nine teachers in the grades that I observed. Most teachers had their students sitting at round tables, facing one another. Children moved at will in the classroom space. In five of the teachers' classes, each used the method of working with one group while the rest of the classroom sat at their tables doing assignments out of texts. One teacher had two groups working on different tasks. In four of the six classrooms where teacher-student exchanges occupied more than 10 minutes, the exchanges were in the teacher question–student answer format, with the questions drawn directly from a text or worksheet. On the walls of every classroom were charts listing CBC skills in reading, thinking, math, language arts, and other subjects. Charts listing tasks that specific students had completed hung in five of the six classrooms.

PLATE 6.4 *Takoma elementary school, Washington, D.C., 1977*

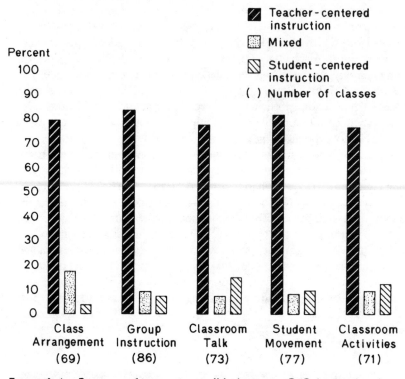

FIGURE 6.4 *Patterns of instruction in Washington, D.C. high school classrooms, 1967–1975*

In the two schools that I observed, there were many outward signs of open classrooms. The space was open. There were centers, flexible furniture arrangement, use of space, and freedom of student movement. Yet it was clear that teachers controlled who did what, when, how, and with whom. Student participation was limited to tasks assigned by the teachers. These mixed behaviors closely resemble what an earlier generation of teachers had created: a hybrid, a teacher-centered progressivism.[105]

If informal classrooms, at different levels of development and in mixed fashion, emerged in elementary schools after 1967, what happened in D.C. high schools in those years?

High School Classrooms

As in New York City and elsewhere in the country, in Washington the late 1960s saw university students' protest against their institutions' policies and actions spill over into high schools. The high schools shared the experience of Howard University except that initially student protests concentrated on racial issues, especially after the fiery riots triggered by the assassination of Martin Luther King, Jr., in 1968. The development of racial consciousness led to the establishment of the first public alternative school in the District.[106]

Freedom Annex grew out of the work of a small cadre of Eastern High School students who were dissatisfied with the quality of the schooling they were receiving. They designed the alternative school, raised money for it, chose the courses, and selected the teachers. Billed as one of the few student-run high schools in the nation, Freedom Annex was supported by George Rhodes, then assistant superintendent of secondary schools, and was approved by the Board of Education, but no public funds were allocated for it. Money came from foundations and other private sources.

Over 100 students took required courses at Eastern High School in the morning and spent the rest of the school day at a nearby church where they heard lectures and participated in discussions of black history, black literature, Swahili, black art and drama, and community organization.[107]

Two years later, after a new principal at Eastern High School had modified its curriculum and instituted a number of changes, and after the student leaders who had created Freedom Annex had graduated, the alternative school, with less than 30 students enrolled and private and foundation grants spent, closed its doors.[108]

Since the Freedom Annex made local headlines, George Rhodes, an advocate of choice, had been laying the groundwork for other alternative programs sponsored and funded by the Board. In 1970, Washington's version of Philadelphia's Parkway Program, New York's City-as-School, and Chicago's Metro Program accepted its first students. Tenth graders from all over the city applied for admission to the School-Without-Walls. In addition, Rhodes and his assistants encouraged a group of secondary teachers and administrators to establish minischools in five junior high schools. A Literary Arts and Journal Program, in which students would spend afternoons producing a citywide creative arts journal, was also established. No minischools, however, were developed at any of the 11 high schools.[109]

Like other cities, Washington had privately funded alternative schools outside the aegis of the public schools, such as the Urban League's Street Academy, D.C. Street Academy, Rap Inc., and other ventures that tried to reclaim actual and potential dropouts from District high schools and direct students toward higher education. The District of Columbia Board of Education did not, as the New York Board of Education had done, incorporate these programs into the alternative school framework that began to evolve in the early 1970s.[110]

By 1981, the School-Without-Walls, the Literary Arts and Journal Program, the Lemuel Penn Career Center, the Duke Ellington School of Performing Arts, and the newly established Banneker High School for the Gifted constituted the alternative high school program. Issues of governance, size, and instruction were seemingly subordinated to developing choices for students.

I found no evidence that classroom instruction in alternative schools differed from the range of practices in regular high schools. However, class size was smaller. Teachers had time to help individual students. Informal relations between teachers and students did exist in the smaller programs. The frequency of small groups and independent work was probably higher in the programs where specific crafts and skills were taught.[111]

In regular high schools, the picture that emerges from Figure 6.4, which is based upon data from 86 classrooms (1967–1975), is acutely familiar. As in New York City, the percentages in each category for teacher-centered patterns are uniform for 10 of the 12 high schools from which these descriptions are drawn. Nearly 8 out of every 10 high school teachers described in these accounts or depicted in photos taught in a stunningly similar fashion—so similar that on a meter measuring student participation the needle would barely have moved from zero.

Nothing here contradicts my experience as a social studies teacher and team leader in a teacher-training program during 3 years (1967–1968 and 1970–1972) at Roosevelt High School in Washington, D.C. My duties as team leader for groups of interns in the building brought me in contact with many teachers, especially in the English and social studies departments, whom I observed briefly and informally. The patterns reported here for high schools elsewhere in the District were similar to what I observed: whole-group instruction, little student movement, discussions and informal recitations, assigned seatwork, students at blackboards, and occasional student reports and panels. The textbook, the chalkboard, durable vocal chords, and a strong pair of legs were the primary teaching tools.

In 1979, Pat Lewis, a *Washington Star* reporter, spent 2 months in four high schools in the metropolitan area, among them Coolidge High School. She attended a half dozen classes and described two of them in detail. Here is her account of a U.S. history class at Coolidge:

> Fourteen don't answer roll call in room 230. . . . Ten do.
> "The test is tomorrow. Today I am going to review with you the exact questions on the test," Rita Dinnerstein tells her U.S. history class.
> "What's an act?"
> "A law," someone replies.
> "What was the National Labor Relations Act?"
> No one answers. "It's in your textbook," she says.
> "It is?" someone asks quietly.

Four students saunter into class eight minutes after it was scheduled to begin.

"Three tardies are equal to a cut," Dinnerstein yells. "And I've had it."

"The National Labor Relations Act was passed in 1935. What did it guarantee?"

Someone answers, "Collective bargaining."

There is lots of noise in the hallway. Faces appear in the windows of the wooden door and peer into the classroom.

"What's the difference between industrial and craft unions?" No one answers.

Dinnerstein raises her voice. "This is a review! We've done this!"

A student in the hallway steps into the room, holding the door open. "Mrs. Dinnerstein, someone wants to see you."

Dinnerstein marches to the door: "I'm about to explode." It is eleven minutes after class is supposed to have begun. Dinnerstein steps out into the hallway and comes right back. "You interrupted my class," she tells someone out there. "What is a union?" she asks her class. One student reads the answer from his notes. When he finishes, Dinnerstein tells another student, "If you want to play games, feel free to leave."

"Who said I'm playing games?" the student retorts. . . .

"What is a union shop?" she asks. One girl says the answer quietly.

"I can't hear you," Dinnerstein tells her.

A boy sitting next to the girl repeats the girl's answer for his own. It is correct. The class is quiet now, 20 minutes after it began. The students are listening. A few know the answers to the questions that Dinnerstein first gave them on Monday. This is Thursday. On Friday, those same questions will be on the test.[112]

The reporter suggests that the class was a disaster due to its low level of content, the amount of subject matter covered in a week, and the hallway distractions and interruptions that spilled over into the classroom. Such vignettes implicitly judge the teacher's performance and give teachers good reason to bar reporters from their classes. Since I have seen Dinnerstein teach, I know that this episode from one class does not in any way capture the overall quality of her instruction. It does embody another instance of the question-answer format, reinforced by reliance upon the text, and show how classes were being taught a few years after interest in open classrooms and alternative schools had ebbed.

THE NATIONAL PICTURE

Case studies of North Dakota, New York, and Washington, D.C., between 1967 and 1975 have established that informal schooling existed in some elementary school classrooms and that alternative formats developed in the upper grades. How typical were these instances of what was happening elsewhere in the nation? Nowhere could I find a majority of classrooms taught informally, even in the broad sense of the word, for any sustained period. The highest estimate I came across was by a researcher who claimed that 60% of the schools in Roslyn, New York, had at least *one* open classroom.

Another estimate came from a survey sent by the National Open Education Association in 1974 to superintendents in 153 cities with populations of over 100,000. Ninety-one cities (59%) responded, meaning that either the superintendent or someone else delegated to complete the task filled out the items (Lillian Weber responded for New York City). The question from which an estimate of the spread of open classrooms was constructed read: "About ___% of the classrooms in my city make substantial use of open approaches to education." [113]

Defining the words "substantial" and "open approaches" for the purposes of answering this question would involve having a central office person make a few inquiries of principals whose schools have such classes in order to find out how many teachers were using "open approaches." The mean estimate by superintendents and their designees in the 91 cities was 17%; the median was 10%. Such estimates are, at best, informed guesses laced with a large dose of hope. They are not unlike the predictions of 80% by these same administrators, who said that in the next 5 years (1975–1980) the use of "open approaches would increase in their cities." [114]

I cite these figures only to underscore how limited the spread of the movement was in public schools by 1974 even when optimism infused school officials' statements. The lack of reliable national data on the prevalence or spread of open classrooms compels me to sample scattered descriptions and studies that have appeared between 1967 and 1975 in order to support or challenge the data I have reviewed thus far.

In the late 1960s, John Goodlad and a team of researchers observed 150 primary classrooms in 67 schools in 13 states. They wanted to test whether the widely publicized educational innovations of the 1960s—team teaching, ungraded primaries, curricular reform, and individualized instruction—had entered classrooms. What they found were "remarkably similar" classroom programs in school after school, irrespective of local differences. The classrooms they observed were marked by "telling, teachers' questioning individual children in group settings, and an enormous amount of seemingly quite routine seatwork." The primary tool of instruction was the textbook, followed by workbooks and supplementary readings. [115]

The common pattern of instruction in the whole group was question-and-answer. When the teacher divided the class into groups for reading—a

PLATE 6.5 *Dunbar High School, Washington, D.C., 1977; English class*

daily activity—one group read to the teacher, one group read independently, and one group did seatwork related to current, previous, or future work. "Rarely," Goodlad wrote, "were children engaged in self-initiated and self-directed small groups or individual activity." The report concluded that in subject matter, materials, and teaching practice the 150 classrooms were "geared to group norms" rather than individual differences. "Judging from our sample," he wrote, "childhood schooling is more vanilla than . . . neapolitan."[116]

Goodlad was disappointed. In looking behind the classroom door, he and his associates found a dreary sameness—"a flatness"—at a level of schooling where promised reforms had a reasonable chance of success. Reforms were "blunted on school and classroom door." His team documented repeatedly that teachers' reports of how innovative they were differed sharply from what observers reported. "Teachers sincerely thought they were individualizing instruction, encouraging inductive learning, involving children in group processes." Observers found that this was not the case, a finding consistent with results from other researchers.[117]

Examining a somewhat longer time span, the National Science Foundation commissioned a survey of research into the curricular and instructional

PLATE 6.6 *Dunbar High School, Washington, D.C., 1977; science class*

changes that had taken place in science, math, and social studies between 1955 and 1975. The results, drawn from a synthesis of surveys, classroom observation studies, and other research, were remarkably similar for the three subjects.

Math. Summarizing the results of seven studies of elementary and secondary teachers' verbal behavior in classrooms between 1968 and 1976, authors Suydam and Osborne found that, on average, the teacher talked about two-thirds of the time, and that teachers tended to use a direct, rather structured approach. Regarding classroom practice, the authors cited eight studies (including Goodlad's) done between 1959 and 1977 and concluded that (a) telling and questioning, usually involving the whole class, was the prevailing teaching practice; (b) tell-and-show and seatwork at the elementary level and homework–lecture–new homework at the secondary level were the dominant patterns of instruction.[118]

Social studies. A review of two decades of research, including studies in the early 1970s disclosed, as with math, a pattern that one researcher summarized almost sadly:

"The students' social studies classes will be strikingly similar to those that many of us experienced as youngsters: textbook assignments followed by recitation led by a teacher who, in his or her own way, likes students and tried to show concern for them. . . ."[119]

Science.   Summarizing the results of nine studies of elementary school science teaching (1963–1976), reviewers found that:

There is more use of 'hands on' and laboratory types of instruction. . . . However, a substantial number of teachers do not emphasize laboratory activities. Lecture-discussion is the most common learning activity, followed by student demonstration. Reports and surveys indicate a substantial number of teachers (probably about 30–40 percent) teach science largely as a reading/lecture class. At the secondary level, there is less lecture and more 'student-centered activity' than there used to be but lecture and discussion is the predominant method used by teachers.[120]

Focusing on high school English classrooms, James Squire and Roger Applebee examined 158 schools with reputed programs in English. Trained teams of observers from the University of Illinois visited 1,600 classrooms between 1963 and 1966. The researchers discovered that lecture and recitation dominated classroom talk. Student-teacher discussions occurred 23% of the time, with few instances of groupwork.[121]

Another body of literature that allows a glimpse of existing practice is the studies of failed innovations—that is, descriptions and analyses of individual schools where a systematic and intentional effort to open up classrooms occurred and, for a number of reasons, failed. Louis Smith and Pat Keith's "Kensington," a pseudonym for a St. Louis–area elementary school in the mid-1960s, was to be a child-centered, staff-led operation in a new building. "Cambire School," another pseudonym, was a Boston elementary school where Gross and his colleagues, in 1966–1967, documented how an inept administrator and the staff's unclear expectations for classroom innovations produced an educational disaster. At the Attucks-Lincoln program in New Haven (1968–1969), described by Barth, open classrooms staffed by bright, young, but inexperienced white teachers in a predominantly black school sank from sight within 2 years, again for a variety of reasons. All of these studies show how hard it was to plan and implement changes in teachers' classroom behavior.[122]

A few points are clear. That various degrees of openness in classrooms existed and that such informal practices spread among some teachers is, as the evidence I gathered from North Dakota, New York City, Washington, D.C., and scattered sites around the country shows, undeniable. At any given time, in any given setting a tiny minority of teachers were involved in fundamentally restructuring their classrooms. Many more teachers chose some techniques associated with informal education and incorporated these novel approaches into their more traditional routines. Yet teacher-centered practices remained prominent in most classrooms between 1967 and 1975. Unless data surface to throw the above statements into doubt, I conclude that an overwhelming majority of teachers stayed with what can comfortably be called teacher-centered practices.

SUMMARY AND CONCLUSIONS

For a second time in the same century, reform-minded practitioners, administrators, and policymakers undertook, between the late 1960s and mid-1970s, intense and widespread efforts across the nation to fundamentally alter the topography of the self-contained classroom. I will now compare the patterns of instruction that emerge from the data I collected in North Dakota, New York City, Washington, D.C., and elsewhere to see whether what occurred in those settings in the 1960s and 1970s is comparable to what occurred during the years 1920–1940, when the tides of progressivism ran strong in school systems.

1. *A core of informal practices did emerge.*
Like the progressive approaches of a generation earlier, certain teaching practices that can be labeled informal were evident in a considerable number of elementary school classrooms, especially in the primary grades. Artifacts of open classrooms included learning centers, tables clustered so that students could speak and work together, increased use of small groups for instruction, and students' relative freedom to move about without securing the teacher's permission. Seldom did more than a fourth of a given district's staff adopt these new approaches. Even fewer teachers employed other informal approaches such as allowing students to decide what to study and how much time to spend on particular topics, or using learning centers as the primary means of instruction.

Comparisons between the interwar decades and the 1960s and 1970s reveal a general similarity in the extent of the spread of certain teaching practices. While a few teachers tried to institute fully child-centered classrooms, most elementary school teachers who adopted informal practices were selective in what they incorporated into their daily routines. These mixtures of informal and formal practices resemble the hybrid forms of teacher-centered progressivism that I described earlier. One major difference, however, was that—unlike Denver and New York City in the 1920s and 1930s—at none of the sites I studied were formal board-superintendent alliances or organizational mechanisms constructed to incorporate open classrooms into teachers' instructional repertoire.

2. High school instruction in regular and alternative settings changed little.

As in the 1920s and 1930s, a higher percentage of student-centered practices was found in the lower than in the higher grades. There is some evidence to demonstrate that during both periods student-centeredness peaked in the primary grades and dwindled to a tiny fraction of that level in the senior high school. While academic subject matter in the secondary schools was revised to link content to events in students' lives or to heighten interest, and while class discussions tended to be informal, the basic instructional sequences and patterns reported earlier remained in place.

For alternative high schools, the categories of instruction (and here the evidence is indeed sparse) show no substantial difference in the range of techniques used by teachers, although the frequency of some approaches involving students, especially discussions and classroom informality, resembles elementary patterns for student-centered instruction. The picture of high school teaching that emerges from these accounts is unmistakably teacher-centered and remarkably akin to what had existed three to four decades earlier.

3. The tradition of teacher-centered instruction continued to dominate elementary and secondary classrooms.

At least two forms of teacher-centeredness emerged as a consequence of efforts to introduce student-centered instruction. The pure form—whole-class instruction, teachers talking most of the time while students listen, activities limited in range and performed by the entire class (e.g., those involving the textbook or worksheets), and little voluntary student movement—characterized the high school. The other form was a mixture of practices drawn from the two traditions of teaching. Such hybrids contained diverse classroom groupings for instruction and allowed more informality in instructional talk, student movement, and organization of space than did the pure form.

What appeared as a direction by 1940 emerged clearly as a pattern by 1975. Certain child-centered practices became increasingly common in elementary school classrooms: flexible seating patterns, students moving freely within the classroom, and the use of varied groupings. Other practices, such as learning centers and small-group work, showed up less frequently but often enough to be worth noting. These changes suggest that the elementary school classroom of the 1970s was decidedly more informal than that of 1900.

But these changes, important as they are, occurred at the periphery of the classroom. The core of classroom practice in all grades, anchored in the teacher's authority to determine what content to teach and what methods to use, endured as it had since the turn of the century. Hybrids developed. Far more informality now existed in teaching and in relationships between the teacher and students, but the growth of hybrids and sociability in the elementary school, particularly the lower grades, should not mask the persistence of deeply embedded patterns of instruction. In the academic organization of the classroom, whole group instruction, reliance upon the textbook for authoritative knowledge, and homework assignments still captured the majority of high school teaching practices in the 1970s.[123]

CHAPTER 7

Local and National Snapshots of Classroom Practices, 1975–1990

I was stunned when I walked into the classroom of Carmen Wilkinson at Jamestown Elementary School in 1975. In my first year as Arlington County superintendent, I had already seen over 300 elementary classrooms. This was the only one I had seen that had mixed ages (grades 1 through 4) and learning stations in which students spent most of the day working independently and moving freely about the room; they worked in small groups and individually while Wilkinson moved about the room asking and answering questions, giving advice, and listening to students. Called "The Palace," by parents, children, and staff, the class used two adjacent rooms. Wilkinson teamed with another teacher and, at that time, two student teachers. She orchestrated scores of tasks in a quiet, low-key fashion.

Had Lillian Weber, Vito Perrone, Charles Silberman, William Kilpatrick, Harold Rugg, and Elizabeth Irwin been looking over my shoulder as I watched Wilkinson and her colleague work with the 50 children that April morning, I am sure they would have been pleased with the presence of the Palace at Jamestown. Had they walked the halls with me and looked into the other 17 self-contained classrooms, they would have seen only one other classroom similar to the Palace.[1]

Over the years I served as superintendent, I visited Wilkinson, who had taught for 32 years (as of 1980), at least 10 more times and saw her classroom change into a one-grade, self-contained room, one that nevertheless retained flexible groupings and learning centers that were integrated into the instructional day. Wilkinson's informal classroom was unusual at Jamestown and compared to those of 500 other Arlington elementary teachers between 1975 and 1980.

Also unusual was Bobby Schildt's social studies classroom in 1975 at Hoffman-Boston, an alternative junior high school in Arlington. When I saw Schildt's room during my visits in my initial year as superintendent, there was no class for me to see. Schildt had individualized her courses into a series of projects, contracts, and learning stations that she collectively called a "social studies laboratory." For each course, students would gather once a week as a class to discuss some topic. For the rest of the week, students worked at various tasks and centers, completing contracts they had negotiated with Schildt. She spent class time asking questions of individual students, helping those who were stuck on problems, and reading and commenting on work that would be placed into student cubbies along the wall. Teacher-made, teacher-gathered, and commercial materials abounded in the room.

As with Wilkinson, I saw Schildt a number of times over the years. When I last saw her in 1981, she was still teaching social studies to seventh through ninth graders in an alternative school that had merged with another alternative school to become a 7–12 secondary school. But the laboratory was no more. The high degree of independent and individual work through contracts and learning stations was now integrated with more whole-class discussions, simulations, role-playing, and small-group work.

The subtle changes that occurred in these Arlington classrooms mirror, in a number of important ways, what happened nationally to efforts aimed at reforming teaching practices. In this chapter, I sketch the swift shift in attention from informal education to a renewed and intense preoccupation with the teaching of basic skills, minimum competencies, and accountability, a trend that swelled in the mid-1970s and spilled over into the 1980s. Then I try to reconstruct what happened in classrooms both nationally and in one school district—Arlington County, Virginia,—before, during, and after this abrupt shift.

The swiftness with which media and popular interest in informal classrooms vanished was breathtaking. Within a brief period, roughly between 1968 and 1974, open classrooms and alternative schools attracted national attention, became a *de rigueur* innovation, and then began to lose the public's attention. Mirroring the rise and fall of public and professional interest are the number of references to newspaper articles, trade books, television programs, journal articles, academic research, and research notes on the subject in the *Readers' Guide, Educational Index, New York Times,* and *Washington Post* indices and other similar listings.

While other school reform impulses have surfaced and coalesced into movements, as this one had, their lifespans have usually stretched over a few decades. Somehow this impulse toward informal education and alternative schools was compressed into less than a decade (allowing for regional and local differences). It seemed that in the early 1970s the public and school professionals, for any number of reasons, switched channels, so to speak, to another station. By 1975, the climate surrounding open classrooms and alternative schools had changed substantially. Obviously, such generalizations about a country with over 15,000 school districts, almost 100,000 schools, and millions of teachers and children cannot hold for all schools in the 1970s. Yet while an incoming tide seldom arrives evenly, there is still a high tide.

Exactly when and why the shift occurred is uncertain. One scholar marked it in a series of events that began in the late 1960s and continued through the mid-1970s: the establishment of experiments in which private firms contracted with schools to raise student test scores; President Richard Nixon's education message to Congress in 1970, in which he called for reduced expenditures, more research, and accountability for student performance; and the business community's growing demand that financial support for schools be tied to their productivity. One reporter marked the end of the passion for informal schools in the founding of alternative schools committed to traditional approaches. Pasadena, California, established its John Marshall Fundamental School in 1973; in the same state, Palo Alto, a leader in informal education, created the Hoover Contemporary School in 1974 with a program, according to its brochure, that concentrated upon "academic skills and subject matter and the establishment of good study habits . . . in a quiet and orderly environment. . . . A majority of the school hours will be devoted to the teaching of reading, writing, spelling, language and arithmetic." Many school districts established "basic alternative schools," as Prince George's County, Maryland, did in 1975. Arlington's entry came in 1978 with the Page Traditional Alternative School. "Back to the basics," a phrase conveying more political baggage than affection for the familiar trinity of basic skills, became a rallying slogan throughout the mid-1970s.[2]

No one can say with confidence whether the stiffening of academic standards was a knee-jerk reaction to the perceived changes that had occurred in schools and classrooms and that were often labeled "permissiveness"—a code word borrowed from an earlier generation of critics blasting progressivism. It could also have been caused by persistent reports of declining test scores, increasing school vandalism, disrespect for teachers, or the educational version of the newly conservative political climate.

Whatever the explanation, there was a renewed passion for orderliness, stability, and academic skills captured in symbols that plucked nostalgic strings within the hearts of teachers, parents, and taxpayers: rows of desks facing the blackboard, the teacher in front of the room, required homework, detentions, dress codes, spelling bees, letter grades on report cards, tougher promotion standards, and schoolwide discipline rules.

Implicit in these slogans and symbols was a belief that most teachers had either converted or threatened to convert their classrooms into places where children decided what they should do, standards were undefined, basic skills were neglected, and discipline was problematic. This misperception of informal classrooms, in both their character and pervasiveness, is clear in the light of the evidence. As the limited data I gathered from 1967 through 1975 in New York City, Washington, D.C., and North Dakota suggest, open classrooms did indeed turn up in numerous and unpredictable places, but at no point did the brief passion for the reform ever capture more than a minority of teachers and schools. The slogans reveal less about what actually occurred in classrooms than about the historical vulnerability of public schools to social and political impulses in the culture, which in turn are reshaped by newspapers, magazines, and, nowadays, television.

To assess the rapid shift from a strong interest in informal education to an equally strong interest in direct instruction in basic skills, tougher academic courses, and making sure that students do well on standardized tests, I will look at the policies and practices of the Arlington, Virginia, public schools and then review recent national studies of teaching practices.

ARLINGTON, VIRGINIA, 1974–1981

In turning to this school district, I am no longer a historian collecting data, evaluating sources, sifting the evidence, and drawing inferences from scattered fragments of information, all filtered through my values and experience as a teacher and administrator. When I write about Arlington, I write as a participant.

In 1974, I was appointed superintendent. I served nearly 7 years and left in 1981 to begin writing this study and teach at Stanford University. The 7 years I spent in Arlington were both exhilarating and exhausting. Viewing a school system from the cockpit of the superintendent's office, however, is a narrow perspective. While in the narrative I will try to broaden the view beyond what I saw, I mention my position to signal to readers that other accounts of Arlington would probably vary in both detail and emphasis.

Few people, professional or lay, have automatic access to as many classrooms as a superintendent does, should he or she choose to use this privilege. I did. My visits to classrooms began weeks before I formally assumed my post. The School Board agreed to my request to spend a month and a half visiting schools and sitting in classes so as to become acquainted with principals and teachers before I assumed my formal duties. The Board, staff, and community knew that my last job before becoming Arlington's superintendent had been that of a social studies teacher in a Washington, D.C., high school. Because the Board and I agreed that improving students' academic performance was one of our top priorities, it was reasonable that I spend time with principals and teachers.

My 7-year routine for school visits was set in those initial 6 weeks. I would go unannounced to a school, stop in the principal's office, chat with him or her for a few minutes, and then begin to walk through the building, stopping in classrooms at random. Most often my stay in a classroom lasted from 15 minutes to a half hour; usually it spanned about 20 minutes. In a folder I jotted notes about what the teacher and students were doing, the arrangement of the classroom, any unusual activity I noticed in class, and student-teacher exchanges. If it was possible to speak with the teacher without disrupting the class, I did. If I could, I would often ask questions about the tasks students were working on, the materials the teacher was using, and any special activities about which the teacher wanted me to know. As the years went by, teachers grew accustomed to these visits and would often take the time to mention items on their personal agenda for the school, the district, parents, and the union.

In a cryptic shorthand I took notes so that I could write to teachers thanking them for answering my questions, praising something I had liked about their classes, or simply expanding on a point that we had been discussing. While I did not write a note after every single visit, notes from me were common. The purpose of my visiting classrooms and writing notes was explicitly stated and repeatedly reaffirmed in the articles I wrote in local newspapers, in speeches to the staff, and in statements at public meetings: I believed that teachers should know that the superintendent was as concerned about and interested in instruction as they were. One of the few ways I had of demonstrating that concern was to allocate my time—roughly one and a half days a week—to listening, watching, and answering questions in face-to-face exchanges with teachers, principals, and students. In addition, at least twice a year, I taught workshops for teachers and administrators interested in improving thinking skills through the use of questions. All of these activities brought me in touch with a substantial number of teachers. A brief description of the school district and community in these years will establish the setting for my examination of classrooms.[3]

The Setting

Arlington, Virginia, is located across the Potomac River from Washington, D.C. Once a quiet, middle-class white suburb with segregated schools, by the early 1970s it had become a city with a flourishing multi-ethnic population. In those years Arlington's population simultaneously became smaller, older, and more culturally diverse. The facts are plain: population dropped from almost 180,000 in 1966 to about 160,000 in 1978; there were fewer and smaller families with school-age children; and the number of young singles and adults over age 55 jumped sharply. Simultaneously with these changes, scores of different nationalities moved into the county, swelling the minority population, but in insufficient numbers to counteract the other shifts.[4]

The impact of these demographic changes upon schools was dramatic. Enrollment shrank from 26,000 in 1968 to 14,000 in 1982. The number of schools fell from nearly 40 (including 3 high schools) in 1968 to 31 in 1982. The number of minority pupils doubled—from less than 15% of all students in 1970 to over one third in 1980. The sharpest jump was in the number of non-English-speaking minorities, particularly Hispanic, Korean, and Vietnamese children.[5]

If demographic changes were one pincer squeezing schools, the other was the rising cost of schooling. Having to spend more to buy less was as much a fact of life for a school system as it was for families in the mid- to late 1970s. With diminishing revenue intersecting with inflation, the pincers tightened.

Since the appointed five-member School Board was fiscally dependent upon the elected five-member County Board, state and federal revenue shortfalls combined with inflation to unravel school budgets in these years, precisely while the cumulative effects of the demographic changes were being felt. The arms of the pincers closed.

What prevented the pinch from crippling Arlington schools was the wealth of the county, measured by family income and assessed valuation of property. That wealth somewhat eased the county's painful transformation from suburb to city during a recession. Arlington's prime location—close to Washington, and improved further by the installation of a subway system—and the County Board's cautious fiscal policies gave it the lowest tax rate in the metropolitan area (1980). Nonetheless, the County Board had to struggle with the politics of retrenchment. Irate property owners, most of whom no longer had children in school, wanted lower taxes. Their demands competed with requests from citizens who wanted higher school budgets, subsidies for the elderly, and improved policing forces, recreation, and social services.

Like everyone else during recessions, county officials tightened belts, and the County emerged from the mid-1970s' recession with most services intact, the lowest tax rate in the metropolitan area, and a school system that had become an annual target for holding costs down and reducing expenditures.

County politics were changing too. There had been a gradual but persistent shift from a Republican County Board to one composed of a coalition of Independents and Democrats. By 1971, this liberal bloc had attained complete control of the County Board. By 1978, however, three Republicans had been elected to the five-member Board, thereby reasserting a majority they had enjoyed a decade earlier. Since the County Board appointed School Board members, those who served on the School Board throughout the 1970s had been appointed by the liberal majority. Due to the lag between the Republicans' attaining a majority on the County Board (1978) and appointments to the County Board, not until 1980 did the School Board have a three-member Republican majority. By the mid-1980s, the liberal majority was back in control.[6]

The political shift in the 1970s brought changes in the School Board's relationship with its superintendent. Previous Republican School Boards in the 1960s had left operational decisionmaking to the Board's executive officer. Liberal appointees to the School Board, however, intervened more actively on what most superintendents would have considered their turf. Inevitably, friction developed between a superintendent who had been appointed in 1969 by a Republican-dominated School Board content to let their hired expert transact school business and the new, far more activist liberal School Board. In 1974, the superintendent resigned. I was appointed that year.

I find it difficult to summarize my tenure as superintendent without succumbing to such temptations as listing achievements, cloaking errors, or telling battlefield stories. To avoid these obvious pitfalls, while risking a tumble into less evident traps, I will try to summarize my agenda and that of the School Board as it changed over the period in question, and the issues that seized substantial amounts of our attention.

The Board that appointed me in 1974 was concerned with the consequences of shrinking enrollment, declining test scores, and an experienced instructional staff that was either unaware of the need for or resistant to changes prompted by the growth of an increasingly diverse student population. In the first few years my staff and I spent much time in establishing a process by which the Board and community could determine in an orderly manner whether or not to close schools and, if schools were to close, which ones. By 1975, the decisionmaking process for school consolidation was in place and the trauma from the closing of the first elementary school reverberated through the affluent portion of the county. By 1980, five elementary schools and two junior highs had been merged with nearby schools. Moreover, a secondary reorganization that moved the ninth grade to the high school and retained four intermediate schools (seventh and eighth grades) had been approved by the School Board. The merger process appeared resilient enough to weather the controversy that erupted periodically over school closings.

Our other time-consuming task was creating an organizational framework for improving student academic performance. By 1976–1977, a framework for instructional improvement was in place. It contained the following elements:

- The School Board established a set of instructional goals for the system (e.g., improving reading, math, writing, and thinking skills; improving students' understanding of the humanities and of human relations).
- The superintendent and staff established organizational devices for converting those goals into school and classroom priorities:

  1. Each school's staff, with advice from parents, drew up an annual school plan that concentrated upon the Board's goals.
  2. The superintendent reviewed each school plan, met with each principal at midyear to discuss progress and make changes, and, at the end of the year, received an assessment of the plan.
  3. Each year the superintendent and principals discussed face-to-face a school academic profile, created by the superintendent, that listed test scores and other student outcomes linked to the Board's goals.
  4. Administrator and teacher evaluation forms and procedures were revised to incorporate the objectives of the annual school plan into each professional's formal evaluation.
  5. Revisions in curriculum objectives for grade 12 in all subjects and skill areas were undertaken to align them with one another and link them to School Board goals. Instructional materials, including textbooks, were reviewed and modified to conform to curriculum objectives. Districtwide tests were constructed to assess the aims of the revised curriculum and to determine their fit with the materials in use. Analyses of test items missed on districtwide curriculum-based tests and national standardized achievement tests were completed and shared with principals and teachers annually to determine areas needing improvement.

In short, over a 3-year period a major effort was made to tighten the generally loose linkages among system goals, district curriculum, school goals, texts and materials, tests, and normal evaluation procedures in order to concentrate the instructional staff's attention on fewer, more worthwhile targets. In doing so, the School Board and I hoped to generate a positive climate for academic improvement.

Test scores—the coin of the realm in Arlington—at the elementary level climbed consistently for 7 straight years. Though plateaus and a few gains occurred at the junior and senior high schools, progress was much less evident there. In 1978 the staff identified for the School Board and community sub-stantial gaps in academic achievement between minority and white students and began to work on closing those gaps. Other performance indicators, such as the number of students continuing their education, the number dropping out of school, districtwide test scores, and Scholastic Aptitude Test scores, also reflected well on the efforts of the teachers and administrators.

This reconstruction of organizational processes instituted since 1974 suggests that events and decisions involving the Board and superintendent flowed smoothly. Far from it. Unexpected events proved to be disruptive and complex, often producing unexpected consequences. Consider, for example, how the transfer of a veteran principal from the district's mother high school produced a political controversy that trailed the School Board and superin-tendent for 7 years, leaving in its wake a court suit, the election of one of the transferred principal's advocates to the County Board, and, when the Repub-licans secured a majority on that Board, the appointment of that very princi-pal, by then retired, to the School Board.

Another unexpected crisis occurred in 1976, when the Governor of Vir-ginia sued the Arlington School Board and County Board for having uncon-stitutionally conducted collective bargaining since 1967. The Governor lost in the local court but won an appeal in 1977 in the State Supreme Court. After a decade of bargaining and establishing personnel procedures with four different unions (including all administrators), the School Board found it was now illegal to sit down with teacher or administrator representatives to ne-gotiate salaries or working conditions.

Simultaneously with the 1977 Virginia Supreme Court decision, a num-ber of retrenchment measures were forced onto the schools by the County Board, itself coping with a reduced flow of revenues. Reductions in teaching positions and specialist categories occurred throughout the 1970s. With 85% of the district's budget allocated to salaries, and with inflation soaking up existing funds, teachers saw their salaries lag behind a relentlessly spiraling cost of living. After the collapse of collective bargaining, teachers received a 2% salary increase that they interpreted as a slap in the face. Resentment over this increase erupted in subsequent years, with the union calling for a work-to-the-rule action and a majority vote of the membership asking for my res-ignation in 1979.

Take a volatile political setting where Arlington-style liberals and con-servatives periodically switch control of county offices, often using the schools as a community punching bag; add economic changes that yielded less revenues for county services; and mix in a new direction charted by the School Board and superintendent that caused staff changes and concentration on different agenda items. What resulted made for flashy headlines, 7 years of long evening meetings, and a volatile climate for organizational change.[7]

Schools and Classrooms

I turn now to the schools. In 1975 the county had 36 schools (25 elementary, including 1 alternative; 6 junior high; and 3 senior high, excluding 2 alternative secondary schools). Of the elementary schools, 6 were completely open-space and 9 contained substantial additions of open space to buildings with traditional corridors and classrooms. Teachers were experienced (over half were at the top of a 15-step salary schedule) and highly educated (52% had a master's or higher degree). Average class size ranged between 22 and 26 students at all school levels throughout the 1970s. Books, materials, and supplies were adequate and, in some cases, abundant. Per-pupil expenditure—a large proportion of which went to teacher salaries—rose from nearly $2,000 in 1974 to $3,000 in 1981. By that year, five elementary schools and two junior high schools had been closed, the two secondary alternative schools had been consolidated into a single program (grades 7 through 12), and a reorganization had pushed the ninth grade into the high schools, leaving the former junior highs as two-grade intermediate schools.[8]

Professional acceptance of innovation and responsiveness to most school problems were high. Harold Wilson, an associate superintendent of instruction during the 1960s, had developed networks of teachers and administrators proud of and loyal to Arlington schools as educational trendsetters. Under his leadership, throughout the 1960s, the school district had either adopted or at least considered numerous innovations, including team teaching, individually prescribed instruction, computer-assisted instruction, new curricula (social studies, science, and math), alternative schools, open space, and, of course, informal education. No formal School Board or superintendent mandate to innovate accompanied these new efforts. There was, however, an implicit expectation that professionals be familiar with whatever novel approaches were being tried elsewhere in the nation and that they investigate their appropriateness for Arlington. As in an archeological dig, traces of previous innovations could be seen at various strata within the organization when I became superintendent in 1974.

So it was with open classrooms. In the June 1969 issue of "Profile," a publication sent to all staff members, two of the five pages described the new "Learning Center Approach." Acknowledging that the "experiment" had proved "exciting and creative" to teachers in Arlington and across the nation, teachers at four elementary schools who had implemented informal education in previous years offered enthusiastic endorsement of the practice. Workshops were held to train teachers in setting up centers, stocking them, and establishing management systems to track student performance in the centers.

Variations in the use of centers had already emerged by 1968–1969:

PLATE 7.1   *Glebe elementary school, Arlington public schools, 1975*

Some teachers prefer to have one or two centers for smaller groups while they work with a larger group. . . . There are those who prefer to have their students involved in learning centers for the entire class day while others will spend a portion of the day dealing with the entire class in a traditional manner and then allot the rest of the time for the students to pursue projects in the centers.[9]

Tempering enthusiasm with caution, teachers recognized that "learning centers demand a great deal of work and creativity on the part of the teacher." Teachers who were interviewed saw the workload as "impossible without the help of teacher aides." Others were skeptical. Bessie Nutt at Henry Elementary School said:

I'm still wondering in my own mind if this is a new trend in education or just another gimmick. Meanwhile, I am keeping an open mind and experimenting a bit.[10]

Three years later at Jamestown, where Carmen Wilkinson had embraced informal education in 1966, 50 fifth and sixth graders were being team-taught by three teachers who were jointly responsible for eight learning centers in science, social studies, math, and language. All three said that they spent part of each weekend preparing center materials and activities for the following week.

I cannot ascertain how widespread the use of learning centers, an index of informal classrooms, was in the schools in the early 1970s. Wilkinson, who traveled to various schools in the county to give workshops and had a steady stream of visitors to her classroom, estimated that two or three teachers in each building opened up their classrooms to various degrees. The Drew Elementary School, an alternative school, introduced centers, nongraded primaries, and team teaching when it opened in 1971. By 1975, when I visited all of the elementary teachers at least once, I located about 25 teachers who used centers daily, permitted students to move freely, and organized their instruction for small groups and individuals, with some time set aside for large-group teaching. That teachers who chose to establish centers in their rooms varied in their fervor for open classroom practices is evident from the quotations. That teachers could choose to do so in a climate of acceptance is also clear.[11]

Between 1975 and 1981, I informally observed, two or more times, 280 elementary school classrooms, or almost 50% of the teachers who served in those years. The results of those visits are displayed in Table 7.1 along with the results of my observation of 63 classrooms in two North Dakota cities.

TABLE 7.1 *Patterns of elementary school instruction, 1975–1981*

	Teacher-centered instruction		Mixed		Student-centered instruction		Number of classes	
	Arl. %	N.D. %	Arl. %	N.D. %	Arl. %	N.D. %	Arl. %	N.D. %
Classroom Arrangement	42	43	18	30	39	27	223	63
Group Instruction	49	62	50	25	1	13	215	63
Classroom Talk	45	60	52	23	2	16	215	63
Student Movement	60	37	0	0	40	63	125	63
Class Activities	34	59	64	30	2	11	213	63
Classrooms with one or more centers					23	32	209	63
Classrooms observed in at least two school years with one or more centers					8		150	

The Arlington figures indicate considerable, but not exclusive, reliance upon a teacher-centered configuration. Student-centered patterns registered substantially in two areas: arrangement of space and student movement. A mixed pattern in instructional groupings (large, small, and individual), classroom talk, and activities suggests higher levels of student participation. Just under one in four classrooms contained learning centers. On closer inspection of those classrooms with centers one finds that a half dozen teachers used centers as an integral part of the instructional day. In most cases, the centers were used for enrichment, skills practice, or freely chosen activities before and after formally scheduled lessons (e.g., at the end of the reading period, before lunch, after recess). I did track a dozen teachers (8%) who had centers when I visited classrooms during two different school years. Among all the teachers who had at least one center in the classroom, there was no consistent relationship between the presence of the center and the kind of space the teacher taught in (i.e., open-space or self-contained), except for one school, where 7 of the 11 classrooms had learning centers. The school had been built as open-space but teachers had put up bookcases and temporary partitions to divide the space into self-contained rooms.

Examine the figures for the Grand Forks and Fargo teachers whom I observed briefly in 1981. While the percentages are not comparable in either sample size or duration of observation, the visits occurred in a similar time period and in settings that were much like Arlington with regard to class size, history of responsiveness to innovations, and the presence of experienced and highly trained staffs.

The comparison shows a twofold similarity—in the strength of teacher-centered instruction, albeit to a higher degree in the two North Dakota cities, and in the less noticeable presence of student-centered instruction, particularly in Arlington. Two student-centered categories, however, show surprising strength: classroom arrangement and student movement. These figures are quite similar to what occurred in Washington, D.C., classrooms in 1967–1976 in the use of classroom space and in New York City in 1967–1976 in student mobility.

In visiting elementary school classrooms during nearly 7 years I came to expect a number of constants. Almost half of the teachers (43%) put up a daily schedule on the blackboard. If it was time for reading, the teachers would work with one group and assign the same seatwork or varied tasks to the rest of the class. If the subject was math, social studies, science, or language arts, the teacher would generally work from a text, with the entire class answering questions from it or from dittoed sheets or workbooks. These regularities in alloting time and grouping students were common except for those teachers who selected student-centered teaching practices such as learning centers, using grouping in subjects other than reading, and assigning different tasks to different students. If these patterns emerged at the elementary school level, which ones, if any, emerged in Arlington secondary schools?

High School

In the early 1970s, Arlington was no different than many communities in experiencing the growing concern expressed by students, teachers, and parents over the curriculum's irrelevance to problems teenagers faced, over disciplinary rules that made 17-year-olds feel like 2-year-olds, and over students' lack of opportunity to do independent work in or out of school. The search for a type of education where students assumed responsibility for learning drove a small group of teachers and students at Wakefield High School to experiment with different classes and students' choosing what they wanted to study for a week. These experiments led to a drive for a separate alternative high school.[12]

A group of teachers and students at Wakefield designed a new school and presented their design to the School Board. Concerns for the size of high schools, student decisionmaking, electives, and a variety of instructional practices produced a plan for a small (225-student) alternative high school that would be open to any 10th- to 12th-grade student on the basis of a lottery.

PLATE 7.2 Swanson intermediate school, Arlington public schools, 1979

The School Board approved the venture and Woodlawn opened its doors in a converted, abandoned elementary school in 1971. Two years later an alternative junior high, prompted by similar impulses, was also endorsed by the School Board and was placed in the former all-black secondary school, Hoffman-Boston. In 1979, both schools were consolidated into one alternative secondary school, called H-B Woodlawn and incorporating grades 7 through 12. With an enrollment of over 400 students and a waiting list of parents hoping to enroll their children, the school sustained its popularity (that is, its voluntary enrollment) throughout the 1980s.[13]

Like other alternative schools that opened in the early 1970s, H-B Woodlawn had a head teacher and a town meeting to govern itself, informal relationships between adults and teenagers, small classes, and a remarkable acceptance of differences within its school community that made it unique in Arlington. Students and teachers were on a first-name basis; a bulletin board near the front doors became an instant communication center pinned with notes, announcements, and pleas for help to find a missing textbook or get the name of a tutor for flute lessons. Students designed elective courses with teachers, and teachers found internships in schools and agencies in Arlington and nearby Washington, D.C. During the day, there was frequent student traffic in and out of the building to attend courses at other Arlington high schools (some courses were unavailable at the alternative school) and work at internships or regular jobs.[14]

Teaching in such a school was a novel experience, according to Amos Houghton, a veteran teacher who volunteered to work in the Woodlawn program when it began:

> Teaching here is infinitely more challenging than in a traditional school. I'm putting in more hours. I've never read so much in my life. But the ultimate reward is the depth in which you get to know the student personally in a school of 200 instead of 1,600. Oh, I've had some adjusting to do. This is not a neat and tidy school. But I've been able to learn from my own son that this is not as important as a relaxed atmosphere. . . .
>
> We don't have rules like hall passes that must be signed by a teacher for a student to leave the room. We've dropped the authoritative aspect in the teacher-student relationship and we find that kids are not tensed up, don't feel persecuted and are more amenable to our ideas.[15]

Discussions, student reports, lectures, independent study, textbooks, projects—all were used by various Woodlawn teachers. How different their classroom practices were from mainstream teachers is suggested by Table 7.2.

Between 1967 and 1976, regular high school teaching practices in Arlington closely resembled those of New York City and Washington, D.C. The nature of high school teaching in Arlington matches what I have described

TABLE 7.2 *Comparison of patterns of instruction in a regular high school and H-B Woodlawn, 1975–1981*

	Teacher-centered instruction		Mixed		Student-centered instruction		Number of classes	
	H.S. %	H-B.W. %	H.S. %	H-B.W. %	H.S. %	H-B.W. %	H.S.	H-B.W.
Class Arrangement	85	61	10	0	1	31	91	11
Group Instruction	94	36	6	45	0	18	87	11
Classroom Talk	72	33	27	33	1	33	85	12
Student Movement	96	27	1	0	2	73	85	11
Class Activities	72	25	26	42	0	33	86	12

previously: rows of tablet-arm chairs facing a teacher who is talking, questioning, listening to student answers, and supervising the entire class for most of the period—a time occasionally punctuated by a student report or a film.

I sat in regular high school classes and listened to discussions, recitations, and, on occasion, student reports. I watched teachers send students to the chalkboard, use the overhead projector, give tests, and run movie projectors. The range and sequence of activities, I discovered, was predictable: The teacher took attendance, made an assignment from the text, collected homework done on the previous day, picked up a point from the previous lesson or the homework, and questioned students on items in the textbook or the homework. Periodically, a film, a test, student reports, or a field trip would interrupt the above activities. The sequence of activities might differ from subject to subject (e.g., science labs or language tapes, assignments given at the end of the period rather than the beginning), but the sequence of teacher activities listed above captured about 90% of what I observed teachers and students do in classrooms. The universe of classroom tasks was finite and dominated by regularities that seemed to be as predictable as the next day's sunrise and sunset.

As this study has shown, teaching repertoires in Arlington in the 1970s differed little from those in New York City and Washington, D.C. and looked considerably like the teaching of colleagues a generation earlier across the country.

PLATE 7.3   *Washington-Lee High School, Arlington public schools, 1974;
math class*

H-B Woodlawn was an exception in that, while practices were similar,
there seemed to be more variety in the mixing of classroom techniques, particularly student participation. Mixed and student-centered patterns in each
of the categories appear as frequently used alternatives to the familiar teacher-
centered instruction.

Between 1974 and 1981, a middle-sized district underwent substantial
demographic changes under the aegis of a school board and superintendent
trying to steer a course of action aimed at improving students' academic performance. The classroom teaching showed traits common to earlier periods
when impulses for instructional reform had weakened or disappeared. Forms
of teacher-centered instruction dominated classrooms. The tediously familiar
pattern of some variety in elementary teaching practice within a teacher-

centered and mixed configuration narrowing into a pristine version of teacher-centeredness at the high school level is apparent in Arlington.

Certain informal practices did penetrate Arlington's elementary school teachers' repertoires, producing hybrid forms of informal teacher-centered practice. No such cross-fertilization seemed to have occurred at the high school level in Arlington, except for the occasional teacher in a regular school or among the faculty at H-B Woodlawn.[16]

NATIONAL DATA ON CLASSROOM PRACTICE, 1975–1990

Arlington is a single school district. It is fair to ask whether classroom practice in Arlington in the 1970s and early 1980s was unique. Comparisons with 63 elementary classrooms in two North Dakota cities in 1981 suggest a general convergence in patterns, with the differences a matter of degree rather than kind. Other data collected in the late 1970s offer points of comparison and contrast: two National Science Foundation (NSF) studies, completed in 1978, and John Goodlad's nationwide investigation, reported in *A Place Called School*.

The NSF Case Studies in Science Education (CSSE) sent writers and researchers into 11 districts across the nation in 1976–1977. Concentrating on science, math, and social studies programs in 11 high schools and their feeder schools, the field researchers constructed from interviews, documents, and observations richly textured case studies of urban, rural, large, small, wealthy, poor, white, and black schools. To corroborate the findings emerging from the case studies, NSF commissioned a survey of over 7,000 teachers, principals, central office administrators, and state supervisors.[17]

No clear portrait of elementary classroom teaching emerges from the details in the case studies. The full range of teaching practice is described, sometimes in painful detail, when the observer takes the reader through a class discussion that isn't going anywhere and tedium blankets the reader's eyes, or, on occasion, when the prose about a gifted teacher wraps itself seductively around the reader and won't let go until the last paragraph.[18]

The mass of detail, however, overwhelms. Sorting out any regularities in instruction is difficult since frequency counts were beyond the scope of the writers' task and were alien to doing case studies. Nonetheless, amid the variety of practices the observers described there were some general patterns. Principal investigator Robert Stake found teachers to be central to all classroom activity in the 11 cases. Moreover, the textbook was the primary authority of knowledge in math, science, and social studies; it was "presented as what experts had found to be true."[19]

In high schools, observers, after mentioning the occasional superb math or science teacher who hooked students' attention and steered it elegantly for 50 minutes, commented on the remarkable similarities in teaching that cut across subject matter, class size, and teacher experience. A sampling from the cases makes this point:

- Researcher Rob Walker quotes a math teacher at Central High School (all names of schools are pseudonyms) in a Houston, Texas suburb: "I am a very traditional teacher. I use a chalkboard, a textbook, and handouts." Walker comments: "If half the faculty did not say this precisely, they came close. I believe it is a fair representation of the faculty's pedagogical style. . . ."
- Researcher Mary Smith reported on Fall River High's science program in a small Colorado city: "Introductory Biology—instructional methods are largely lectures, lab investigations, review sheets, and occasional films and guest speakers. The text used is from the Biological Sciences Curriculum Study (green version). Chemistry—the text *Modern Chemistry* is used but the approach is traditional. The vast majority of class time is spent in lectures and laboratory experiments."
- Researcher Louis Smith reported on science in Alte High School in a St. Louis suburb. He jotted down a number of statements that summarized what he saw "across schools, levels, disciplines, and departments":

  1. "In most classrooms, a section of the blackboard with assignments for each day of the week.
  2. Teachers' grade books literally full, cell by cell, of pages of numbers.
  3. Teachers carrying a stack of laboratory notebooks home to be graded (in the evening) or into class to be returned (in the early morning before school)
  4. Lab books full of red ink comments.
  5. Frequent classroom byplay around the question, "Does it count?"
  6. Reviews before tests, taking of quizzes and tests, returning and checking of tests."[20]

If numbers appear infrequently in the volume of case studies, they are densely packed onto every page of another NSF volume, this one reporting the results of a 1977 national survey. Stratified by geography, socioeconomic status, and other variables, almost 5,000 questionnaires from teachers were returned at a response rate of 76%. Teachers reported their classroom techniques and manner of grouping students for instruction. In Tables 7.3 and

TABLE 7.3 *Use of selected math and science techniques for grades k–3, 4–6, and 10–12*[a]

	Math			Science			Social studies		
	K–3 %	4–6 %	10–12 %	K–3 %	4–6 %	10–12 %	K–3 %	4–6 %	10–12 %
Lecture	47	58	90	40	66	87	56	59	80
discussion	86	88	87	76	90	89	88	91	95
Individual assignment[b]	80	83	61	18	42	46	27	52	42
Teacher demonstration	71	64	53	35	37	41	NA	NA	NA
Students at blackboard	81	78	58	12	18	10	10	13	6
Tests or quizzes	45	64	78	7	30	62	20	38	60
Students use lab materials or manipulatives	66	34	14	37	36	72	31	30	11
Student reports or projects	12	10	5	19	18	23	21	27	22
Sample number	297	277	548	287	271	586	254	281	490

[a]Frequency is defined as a technique reported by teachers to be used daily or at least once a week

[b]"Teacher supervises students working on individual activities."

7.4, I have selected those teaching practices that approximate the ones I have used throughout this study.[21]

A number of commonalities are obvious from the self-reports. First, teachers favored lectures and discussion throughout the grades, except for elementary math. Second, certain teaching practices—lecture, discussion, tests, and quizzes—increased in frequency as students moved through the grades into high school, except for high school science teachers' use of lab equipment. Third, classroom practices associated with student-centered classrooms, such as student reports and projects or use of manipulatives and lab materials—either decreased as students got older (again, except in science classes) or did not exceed a reported 25% in use.[22]

In Table 7.4, which shows how teachers reported grouping their students, even more familiar patterns reassert themselves. Teaching the entire class at the same time becomes more common in the higher grades, according to teacher responses, so that by high school, regardless of subject, over half of

TABLE 7.4 *Average percentages of subject of time spent in various instructional groupings for grades k–3, 4–6, and 10–12*

	Math			Science			Social studies		
	K–3	4–6	10–12	K–3	4–6	10–12	K–3	4–6	10–12
Entire class	36	38	54	52	52	52	59	50	68
Small groups	29	25	22	18	18	19	15	15	11
Students working individually	36	38	24	30	30	30	26	35	21
Sample number	293	271	539	272	262	576	254	281	453

class time is spent on whole-group instruction. Teaching small groups decreases in practice as the students move through the grades, except in science. Small-group instruction, however, did not exceed one fourth of the time spent on the three subjects at any level, except for K–3 math. The meaning of working "individually" is ambiguous since the question included answers of teachers who assigned the entire class the same task and also assigned students to work independently on different tasks.[23]

This national cross-section of teachers' self-reports in 1977 shows regularities in practice generally consistent with those in Arlington: teacher-centered patterns in total-group instruction, classroom talk, and class activities converged with teacher self-reports of frequent use of lecture-discussion and whole-group instruction. Furthermore, the patterns of increasing teacher-centeredness as students move from elementary to high school converge.

A Place Called School

A final set of data come from John Goodlad's team of researchers, who collected classroom information throughout the 1970s in what was initially called "A Study of Schooling." In 1981 Kenneth Sirotnik published a technical report of observations in over 1,000 elementary and secondary classrooms in 38 schools across the nation, representing different regions, school sizes, and student racial, socioeconomic, and ethnic backgrounds. Although the study, later published as *A Place Called School,* covered the goals of schools, parent and student views of what schools do, student expectations of the curriculum, and other issues, I will concentrate on the report that dealt with what observers recorded in classrooms.[24]

Classroom data were elaborate. Trained observers did Five-Minute Interactions (FMI), using an instrument to count the number of classroom events that occurred within 5 minutes, and doing this 4 times daily during high school classes and 16 times daily in elementary classrooms. The observers concentrated on how teachers spent time on different tasks and on exchanges between students and teacher. These periodic observations offered a continuous picture of classroom exchanges. Another information pool came from socalled Snapshot data: Brief descriptions were taken in each classroom to locate what activity was going on, who directed the activity, and the form of grouping used for the activity.[25]

From both sets of data on over 1,000 elementary and secondary classrooms, Ken Sirotnik, who headed this portion of Goodlad's "A Study of Schooling," noted the following:

- Approximately half of the time is devoted to teacher talk. . . . Relatively speaking, teachers "out-talk" students by a ratio of about three to one.
- The model classroom configurations which we observed . . . looked like this: the teacher explaining/lecturing to the total class (or a single student), asking direct, factual-type questions or monitoring or observing students; the students' "listening" to the teacher or responding to teacher-initiated interaction.
- The majority of students at all schooling levels—nearly two-thirds in elementary and three-fourths in secondary—work as a total class. . . . Less than 10% are found working in small group configurations.[26]

In Sirotnik's tables, the data for a number of specific activities closely match other data included in this study. For example, observers found that, of 129 elementary classrooms, 39% had at least one learning center. No explanation of how the centers were used appeared in the report, however. From one table of activities in elementary and high school classrooms, I included in Table 7.5 and 7.6 a number of familiar classroom tasks already discussed at length in this study.[27]

For about two-thirds of each class, elementary and high school students spent their time on only five activities—ones generally labeled as teacher-centered. These figures are generally consistent with the 1977 NSF survey data, which tallied teacher responses for frequently used techniques, and with the Arlington figures for regular high schools in the category "Class Activities." Percentages from this report, however, exceed by a considerable margin Arlington's figures for these tasks. In comparing the various sets of data for another category—grouping for instruction—one should keep in mind that

TABLE 7.5 *Percentage of time teachers used for selected activities*[28]

	Elementary	High School
Preparation for assignments or instructions; cleanup	12.1	13.2
Explain, lecture, read aloud	18.9	25.8
Discussion	6.8	5.2
Work on written assignments	29.1	15.2
Taking tests or quizzes	2.6	5.6
Totals	69.5	65.0

TABLE 7.6 *Forms of instructional grouping of elementary and high school class sizes*[a]

	Entire class		Small group–Individual[b]	
	% Elementary	% High School	% Elementary	% High School
Study of schooling	63	71	9	15
National Science Foundation survey	48[c]	58	26	21
Arlington	49	94	1	0
North Dakota cities	62	NA	13	NA

[a]All percentages are rounded off.

[b]A "Study of Schooling" has a category "Medium/Large" group, not included in this table, that accounts for the remainders of percentages.

[c]NSF separated math, science, and social studies. The percentages I used are means for the three subjects.

two of the sets of data come from direct observation (albeit with vastly different instruments) and from teacher reports in dissimilar settings.

Degrees of difference in the figures are apparent. Frequencies vary for any number of reasons ranging from the nature of the data survey and direct observation to the instruments used or actual differences in classrooms. What does appear significant in the face of differing methodologies, settings, and research designs are the commonalities in grouping for instruction (i.e., whole-group teaching is frequently used, whereas small-group and individual instruction are much less common). By now the nature of teaching practices in the 1970s should be familiar to the reader; teacher Ellen Glanz's experience as a student may help to fill in more of the blanks.

Teacher Playing Student

Ellen Glanz spent 1978–1979 as a student at the high school in which she taught. She took her teacher's perspective and put it behind a student's desk, facing the teachers, her colleagues. Her 1-year experience illuminates classroom instruction in an unusual manner.[29]

When she had been a social studies teacher for 6 years at Lincoln-Sudbury Regional High School in Sudbury, a suburb 20 miles from Boston, Glanz proposed to her superintendent a project that would enable her to find out what it was like to be a student in high school. The superintendent gave her permission to take courses like any other student, provided the teachers, Glanz's colleagues, agreed to her being in class. Glanz enrolled as a senior. Her schedule included advanced expository writing, calculus, Russian history, advanced French, drawing, and trampoline.[30]

Glanz kept a journal of her experiences and thoughts. Successful in being accepted as a student by classmates after the novelty wore off, she attended classes, did homework, took tests, and, as she remarked with a touch of pride, was even "kicked out of the library for talking." Periodically, she met with teachers to share her observations and, by the end of the project, wrote two reports for the high school staff, parents, and students. Her observations from the perspective of a teacher-turned-student reiterate a number of points that both the text and tables made earlier.[31]

"I was curious," Glanz writes, "to discover how different other teachers' classes were from those I attended as a child and a teenager." What she found out was that they "were not very different."

> Most teachers teach in much the same way they were taught—in an essentially didactic, teacher-centered mode. . . . The teacher knows the material and presents it to students, whose role is to 'absorb' it.

The system, she said, nurtures "incredible passivity." In class after class, "one sits and listens."

> In one class during my second week as a student, I noticed halfway through the hour that much of the class was either doodling, fidgeting, or sleeping. Before long, I found my own mind wandering too.

Yet this teacher was touted as one of the finest in the school. "I realized," she said, "that what was boring was not what the teacher was saying but the very act of sitting and listening for the fourth hour in a row."[32]

When it comes to teaching methods, Glanz observed, most techniques teachers use "promote the feeling that students have little control over or responsiblity for their own education." She pointed out that the agenda for the class is the teacher's. He or she plans the tasks and determines who does what to whom, when. There is, she found, little opportunity for students to "make a real difference in the way a class goes, aside from their doing their home-work or participating." She described how her English teacher surprised the class one period by letting two students lead a discussion. After some practice, "students were far more attentive and the teacher learned when and how to intervene to lead the discussion . . . without taking control." [33]

After completing the year, writing the reports, and returning to teaching five classes a day, Glanz pondered the regularities in teaching practices that she saw. She concluded: "We must realize that in all likelihood, despite the problems I've described, classes will remain basically as they are right now." She explained that academic content—French, math, anatomy, history— "dictates an essentialy didactic class model since the subject matter is not known intuitively by students and must be transmitted from teacher to stu-dent. And the ultimate authority and control will and should remain with the teacher." [34]

Glanz's description of her life as a student in 1978–1979 is consistent with the figures presented above. Have teaching practices in the 1980s dif-fered from those in the 1970s?

TEACHING PRACTICES IN THE 1980s

Beginning in the early 1980s and extending into the 1990s, another ma-jor movement to improve teaching got under way. Federal and state commis-sions, foundation- and corporate-sponsored reports, and state laws inundated the nation with a sea of words and waves of policies about the imperative need to raise academic standards, extract more effort from both students and teachers, and bolster the economy. A president and 50 governors announced goals for the nation's schools. Corporate leaders volunteered time and dollars to lobby for and enact school reform. Foundations opened their wallets wide to school reformers. A reform vocabulary reflecting vastly different goals and calling for major shifts in the routine behaviors of educators infiltrated the discourse on schools: effective schools, curricular alignment, choice, cooper-ative learning, empowered teachers, critical thinking, restructuring, disman-tling school bureaucracies, school-based decisionmaking, and national exams.

Some words became policies. State requirements for graduation in-creased. Goals, curricula, texts, and tests were fitted together like the cogs of gears to move a machine. Students took more achievement tests. Teachers took competency tests. States allowed parents to send their children to schools outside their neighborhoods. Districts enacted new programs that permitted schools to decide on their priorities and allocate their funds. New math and science curricula promoted by national commissions found teachers and administrators eager to experiment. Principals and teachers launched program initiatives to increase student academic performance. Spending for schools rose in the 1980s but declined in the early 1990s.[35]

Whether these recent reform ideas came from presidents, governors, and corporate leaders anxious to improve the economy through better schools, child-centered instruction advocates eager to reassert their belief in the whole child, technologically inspired reformers who envisioned pupils using microcomputers in every classroom, enthusiasts dedicated to the remote control of classrooms by setting standards, getting teacher proof materials into student hands, and revising mandated tests, or researchers intent upon spreading the results of studies of effective teaching—the unchanging target was moving the classroom teacher from one set of practices to another.

By the late 1980s, a small but growing body of scholarship based upon direct observation of classrooms and on interviews with teachers and students drawn from national, regional, and local studies had revealed patterns in teaching practices strikingly similar to the findings of studies of earlier efforts to reform teaching. The three patterns I had identified earlier persisted through the 1980s: the dominant practical pedagogy of teacher-centered instruction for most teachers, a steady growth in the numbers of teachers who blended the two pedagogical traditions, and a small number of teachers who continued to adopt student-centered practices.

Ideology of Effectiveness in the 1980s

The spirit of the effective schools movement that began in the late 1970s, harnessed to research findings about what constitutes effective teaching, have offered a strong justification for the methods of teachers (especially many located in big-city schools enrolling low-income black and Hispanic pupils) who practiced their craft well within the teacher-centered tradition. The ideology of the effective schools movement (e.g., high expectations for students, aligning instruction with curricular materials and tests, frequent monitoring of performance), wedded to decades of classroom research findings on teacher effectiveness (as measured by gains on standardized achievement tests), provided a broader, more socially acceptable rationale for teacher-centered instructional practices.

Over the last half century, researchers and school policymakers have sought to pin down precisely what teaching effectiveness is, which teachers have it, and how they got it. Findings drawn from a number of correlational studies of certain teaching practices at the elementary level have yielded strong, positive relationships to student test scores on standardized achievement tests in reading and math. The following practices have proven effective:[36]

- Teacher focuses clearly on academic goals.[37]
- Teacher allots class time to instructional tasks rather than socializing.[38]
- Teacher presents information clearly, organizing instruction by explaining, outlining, and reviewing, and covers subject matter extensively.[39]
- Teacher monitors student progress toward instructional objectives, selecting materials and arranging methods of increasing student success.[40]
- Teacher paces instruction to fit students' capabilities.[41]
- Teacher feedback is quick and targeted on content of instructional tasks.[42]
- Teacher's management abilities prevent disturbances by encouraging cooperation.[43]

Barak Rosenshine, reviewing a number of studies, specified six instructional "functions" that have repeatedly been shown to produce improved academic achievement, as measured by test scores:

1. Checking previous day's work;
2. Presenting new content/skills;
3. Initial student practice (and checking for understanding);
4. Feedback and correctives (reteaching, if necessary);
5. Student independent practice; and
6. Weekly and monthly reviews.[44]

These findings have been attacked. Criticisms of correlational research have concentrated on how the design isolates certain teacher behaviors, links them to high student test performance at a given moment, and then uses these relationships as a basis for instructional improvement efforts or changes in teacher education curriculum.[45]

Aside from such criticisms, the sample listed here resembles the stable core of teaching practices that, as this study has demonstrated, have persisted since the end of the last century. The similarity, of course, is not wholly accidental. Teaching practices that scholars carefully counted and compared in effectiveness through pre- and post-tests are themselves activities that have been used for decades by teachers confident in their efficacy.

These practices identified as effective are not associated only with teacher-centered classrooms. Open classrooms, in their various incarnations, employ most of these practices, as was seen in the New York City Activity

Program and in the North Dakota and Washington schools. I said that these teaching behaviors resemble teacher-centered instruction to avoid any premature leap to inferences linking what I detailed as durable teaching practices and these specific teaching behaviors labeled by recent studies as effective. Beyond the substantive methodological issues associated with correlational research, there are a host of contextual variables, often absent from such investigations, such as teachers' beliefs, students' socioeconomic status, school size, the number of students in each class, grade level, and time of observation, that influence outcome measures.[46]

The core of practices that teachers have learned to use over this century gained in stature in the 1980s. Administrators prescribed the findings of teacher effectiveness research as a sensible formula to follow, while policymakers saw opportunities for retaining long-distance control over the classrooms, especially in inner cities, in the apparent precision of isolated teaching behaviors that could be counted and evaluated, competency-based curricula, and daily objectives scrawled on chalkboards.

Because they were officially encouraged to do so, many teachers relied even more heavily than before on the practical pedagogy that they had always used. Both national and local evidences suggest a strengthening of teacher-centered instruction in the 1980s.[47]

A few national studies were conducted in the early 1980s, but they concentrated upon high schools and steered clear of quantitative descriptions of schooling or teaching practices, as John Goodlad's study had done in the 1970s. Theodore Sizer's *Horace's Compromise* and Arthur Powell, Eleanor Farrar, and David Cohen's *Shopping Mall High School* were part of a large-scale study sponsored by the National Association of Secondary School Principals and the National Association of Independent Schools.[48]

These scholars investigated public and private high school organizations, curriculum, and instruction. They sent observers into schools and classrooms to watch teachers teach and to listen to staff, students, and parents recount their experiences. They found schools and teachers faced with the dilemma of providing an equal education to students from diverse backgrounds, and of doing this with inadequate funds and insufficient time. The "treaties," as they called the compromises to these dilemmas, resulted in a trade-off: a victory for democracy in high retention rates, diverse opportunities, and general "customer" satisfaction weighed against a dreadful intellectual mediocrity. These public and private bargains struck by administrations and faculty showed up in the curriculum, the organization of the school, and classroom instruction.

For the classroom descriptions, Sizer created a composite teacher called Horace from the many teachers he interviewed and observed. He portrays his 53-year-old prototypical high school teacher as someone who has the highest academic standards. As a 28-year-veteran of teaching, Horace cares deeply about his work, but faces five classes a day, the grading of nightly homework, 120 essays a week, and an after-school job in a liquor store. He tries to figure out how he can survive such impossible demands upon his emotions, intellect, and energy while still having something left for himself, his wife, and his family. Horace's work, although admired by his colleagues, is a series of humbling compromises that leave him tired and frustrated. Horace's classes are teacher-centered, Sizer suggests, largely because of the dilemmas of the high school work setting, which drive him to make bargains simply in order to survive.[49]

Between 1981 and 1982, Powell, Farrar, and Cohen and their colleagues spent 2 to 3 weeks at each of 11 public high schools across the country, representing a cross-section of urban and rural, wealthy and poor, mostly white and mostly minority. Almost 20 vignettes of teachers in academic classes, gleaned from chapters describing what teachers do in their classrooms, encompass the range from teacher-centered instruction to hybrids of the two traditions. Except for a few of the vocational classes, there was no description of a student-centered class. The work's major theme is the numerous classroom treaties negotiated between teachers and students at all levels of the school as compromises to the conflicting goals of a comprehensive high school: offering equal opportunities to students while steering them to occupy diverse socioeconomic niches as adults.[50]

Another national study of high schools, authored by Ernest Boyer and sponsored by the Carnegie Foundation for the Advancement of Teaching, collected data over a 20-day period from each of 15 high schools in 1980– 1982, again by sending teams of observers into communities, schools, and classrooms.[51]

In the chapter devoted to classroom teaching, "Instruction: A Time to Learn," the vignettes focus entirely on teacher-centered instruction. Teachers tell, tell, tell. They concentrate on covering content, asking questions of students who listlessly reply with information gleaned from the text or the teacher's talk. What Boyer describes as "good" classes of "star" teachers are ones where the teacher has a strong grasp of subject matter, uses questions to elicit thinking from the students, listens carefully, and injects enthusiasm and humor into exchanges with students—in short, another version of teacher-centered instruction.[52]

Later in the decade, Rexford Brown and a team of researchers visited schools and classrooms in seven districts enrolling mostly poor ethnic and racial minorities. In 1987–1988, he and his colleagues went to schools and spent brief amounts of time in classrooms that had a reputation for cultivating thoughtfulness in their students. In a series of vignettes from two rural districts in Louisiana and two city school systems (one has a pseudonym and the other is Pittsburgh), Brown describes 26 classrooms (10 elementary and 16 secondary) in these four districts. Brown was dismayed by the similarity across rural and urban, elementary and secondary schools, in teachers' relying on question-answer recitations, moderate to heavy use of seatwork, whole-group activities, and very little focus on stimulating students to think about the content they studied. There were exceptions: Two secondary school teachers used small groups as the main vehicle of instruction, and three others stimulated student thought by artful use of questions, pauses, and listening to what students had to say.[53]

Another source of national data, one that does not depend upon scholars, informed observers, or journalists sitting in classrooms and reporting what they see, is evidence drawn from students describing teaching practices. The National Assessment of Educational Progress (NAEP) regularly collects elementary and secondary school students' reports of how their teachers teach mathematics, science, U.S. history, and writing. Questions ask about lecturing, about use of textbooks, chalkboard, and worksheets, and about memorization. "Across subjects," the authors of a summary of 1984 and 1986 data conclude, "the most frequently-used instructional approaches that students report are teacher presentations to the class as a whole, textbook reading, and the completion of individual exercises presented in workbooks or dittos." Moreover, the authors point out:

> Relatively small proportions of students are regularly asked by their teachers to engage in small group work, perform laboratory experiments, prepare reports, or engage in projects that provide experience in problem solving. Even in science classes, where laboratory work is a common instructional activity, 41 percent of the eleventh graders and 60 percent of the seventh graders reported that they were never asked to write up a science experiment independently.[54]

Aside from the above sources, national data on teaching practices (and, as the above instances illustrate, I have stretched somewhat the notion of "national") remain skimpy. State and local data are contained in doctoral dissertations, scholarly monographs, and occasional reports from both researchers and observers.

There is also the literature of teacher self-reports, books written about and by gifted teachers, and popular articles about teacher-invented innovations. Such a literature includes personal stories that reveal average-to-remarkable teachers displaying teacher- and student-centered forms of instruction and imaginative mixes of both. An Eliot Wigginton teaching for over two decades in Rabun Gap, Georgia, where each generation of students continues to produce another *Foxfire,* might bring a smile to John Dewey's face, were he alive. A Jaime Escalante prodding, cultivating, and motivating

Garfield High School, Los Angeles, students to take Advanced Placement calculus works well within the tradition of teacher-centered instruction where the teacher knows best, knowledge of subject matter is central, and students absorb the knowledge, rework it, and apply it. Chris Zajacs in Holyoke, Massachusetts, teaches fifth grade in a teacher-centerd manner with much dedication and a touch of flair to a group of children spanning multiple abilities and cultures.[55]

The mid-1980s saw a resurgence of interest in neoprogressivism: the integration of reading, writing, and thinking into "whole-language" instruction; the middle school movement that called for team teaching, core curriculum, and cultivating student interests in academic tasks; small-group instruction; active learning by students through use of math and science materials; the teaching of practical and critical reasoning; and stronger links between what is learned in school and what occurs in the immediate community. Educational journals, conferences, and in-service workshops advocated classroom activities and teaching practices that an earlier generation would have recognized as the trappings of student-centered instruction.

Policies were adopted, programs launched. Teachers were trained. The spread of these new programs into classrooms remains as yet hard to trace beyond their initial entry into some schools and occasional testimonials by teachers and administrators. How many tried out new techniques or materials and dropped them after a short period is unknown.[56]

Nonetheless, there has yet been no clustering of research findings or written observations to challenge the picture of the enduring dominance of teacher-centered instruction, of some teachers inventing hybrids of both teaching traditions, and of those gifted teachers who simply go their own way. I end this section on teaching practices in the 1980s by turning to the most populous state in the nation, a trendsetter in school reform since the election of a vigorous, accountability-minded state superintendent in 1982. The following glimpses of three California classrooms in the 1980s contrast with the national picture sketched above and raise puzzling issues that will be taken up in the next chapter.[57]

Some California Classrooms

In 1983–1984, Elliot Eisner and a group of graduate students and high school teachers studied four San Francisco Bay area high schools. They observed the classrooms of six teachers for 2 weeks. They interviewed students and staff. But they also shadowed 21 students for their entire school day for 2 weeks, which in effect gave the researchers a broader view of teaching practices in the whole school. Having an observer (some of whom were high school teachers) trail a student for 6 to 7 periods a day for 2 entire weeks and then discuss each day's events is an unusual allocation of research time and adds a certain heft to this study.[58]

Eisner acknowledged the many forms of teaching they encountered in the four high schools, especially in nonacademic subjects. He underscored that the team saw instances of inspired teaching that leaned heavily upon student involvement and thoroughly engaged both teacher and teenagers. But when it came to subjects such as mathematics, science, and history, Eisner concluded:

> In general the teacher provides information as a supplement to what the textbook provides. The most salient feature of such teaching is its didactic character: teachers do a great deal of telling and assigning. Some also spend a great deal of time showing movies that are seldom adequately discussed. Indeed, perhaps the most obvious absence within the instructional patterns we have seen is the lack of dialogue between teacher and student and student and student.[59]

Although the findings are familiar, Eisner's study from an "insider's" perspective gives an unusual glimpse of teaching practices in four northern California high schools.

Another glimpse of Californian teaching practices comes from a district almost 200 miles away from the Bay Area. Between 1983 and 1987 I served as a consultant to a school board–appointed committee of parents and staff charged with improving the district's two high schools. This High School Study Committee held its first meeting just as the *Nation at Risk* report was published, and met as the legislature debated and finally pased an omnibus school reform bill that was signed by the governor. Within that political context, the committee generated recommendations aligned with the *Nation at Risk* advice and in compliance with the new legislation. The committee's recommendations were largely accepted by the superintendent and his cabinet and approved by the school board. One of my tasks as a consultant was to visit each high school, interview the principal and teachers, and observe classrooms, and make a "state of the schools" report to the Committee. I did that in 1983. Over the next 2 years, the Committee investigated various aspects of the high schools and held hearings for parents and teachers. By the spring of 1985, the Committee had made over two dozen recommendations on curriculum, school organization, and instruction; my work was largely finished.

In 1987, the associate superintendent who had worked with the Committee called me and asked whether I could return to the district to see whether the committee recommendations approved by the School Board had been implemented in the two high schools. I agreed to do so and secured permission from the administration and School Board to repeat my visits to the schools to interview staff and observe classrooms. I spent a total of 4 days in the two schools interviewing students and staff. I visited 32 classes (16 teachers in each school, out of about 40 on each faculty) in college preparatory and general curricula. What did I see?

- Most classes were busy. Rarely did I note that a class was straying from the teacher-assigned tasks. The busy-ness frequently consisted of completing worksheets, doing homework in class, and taking quizzes.
- In the academic subjects, all but 4 teachers (87%) taught the entire class as one group.
- Twenty-eight of the 32 teachers (87%) used the common trio of classroom activities while I sat in the room: lecture/discussion, seatwork, and review of either homework or test. Five of the 32 showed either a film or a videocassette either for part of the period or for the whole session.
- Of the 26 teachers who engaged students in question-and-answer for a portion of the period, all but 6 (74%) depended largely upon factual recall questions from the text, worksheet, homework, or previous lecture. Seldom did a student in these classes (whether college-bound or non-college-bound) recite answers more than a few words in length. The 6 teachers who probed student answers by asking for explanations, elaboration, or evidence to support statements did so in small groups, individually, and, on occasion, with the whole class.[60]

Reformers' obsessive concentration on high schools throughout the 1980s is mirrored in these two studies. One investigation, however, focused on the teaching of math in California elementary schools. As part of the state's school reforms, a thorough revision of the "Mathematics Framework," a set of curricular guidelines, occurred in 1985. Departing from the previous stress on learning rules and procedures for doing math, the new framework aimed at having students acquire a deep understanding of math concepts through active involvement with materials and problem solving. Memorization was out; thinking was in. The new vision of math teaching and learning embodied in the California "Framework" was well ahead of curricular and instructional reform elsewhere in the nation.

A group of Michigan State University researchers led by Penelope Peterson and David Cohen chose three districts for study. Two were identified as pacesetters in implementing the "Framework," while the third was considered "average." Two schools in each of the pacesetter districts were identified as clearly engaged in teaching math for understanding, while in the "average" district two schools reflecting that level of math teaching were chosen. Twenty-three teachers at the six sites were interviewed and observed for 3 days during the 2-week-long site visits in late 1988 and early 1989. From these 23 teachers, the researchers elicited five in-depth descriptions of second- and fifth-grade teachers teaching math.[61]

The five descriptions yield a mixed picture. The investigators describe two teachers who favored the new "Framework" and believed that they had substantially altered their teaching to be consistent with it. Two other teachers maintained their style of teaching while adapting to a minor degree some of the "Framework's" concepts. The fifth teacher continued to teach as he had, ignoring the new "Framework." Thus, three of the five teachers made little or no adjustments to fit the new framework and continued their familiar form of instruction, called "traditional" in the various descriptions,—that is, whole-group instruction, use of the recitation format for questioning students, heavy reliance upon the text, and so on.[62]

It is in the two instances where the researchers and teachers together noted substantial modifications in teaching practices that puzzling anomalies arise. For example, the "Framework" calls for extensive use of small-group instruction (called "cooperative learning" in the "Framework"). The idea is that students can help one another learn, instead of being totally dependent upon the teacher for content, skills, and direction. One teacher who viewed herself as innovative organized the desks and tables to encourage small-group work. Yet when the teacher engaged the class in discussion about math concepts, she conducted the exchange as a whole-group quasi-recitation, with the usual teacher-centered volleying of questions and answers. The teacher seldom left small groups of students to discuss a point among themselves or answer questions. Small groups were used by the teacher to pass out and collect materials and assignments, but for learning concepts she used the groups in a teacher-centered manner. She would call on individual children within a group, for example, to come to the board to complete a graphing exercise, rather than having the group work it out together and produce a graph. So the paradox emerges of a teacher who perceives herself as innovative and uses a student-centered form of classroom organization (small-group instruction in math), yet engages in teacher-centered forms of discussion even while using the new form.[63]

In another class the teacher had embraced the "Framework" and considered that he had made important changes in his teaching. Joe Scott had students drawing pictures to represent math concepts (e.g., fractions) and solving problems involving real-life uses of math information. Yet Joe was still the drill-sergeant, asking the whole class questions and getting answers, even in problem-solving situations. He taught problem solving as a series of rules that students had to memorize and follow. Here, again, is the anomaly of a teacher viewing himself as making important changes yet transforming those innovations into previous practices.[64]

SUMMARY

These puzzling contradictions in the work of two teachers who view themselves as being responsive to the state's policy directions for teaching math point to some persisting paradoxes and dilemmas facing policymakers, practitioners, and researchers who wish to determine how teachers really taught. For policymakers, the paradox is that the teacher is both the source of the problem and its solution. Teachers are the problem because they continue to teach math as a set of rules to memorize and apply; they lack the knowledge and skills to teach math for understanding. Yet it is teachers who teach children, and without enlisting faculty in the effort to alter past practices, without putting different ideas in their heads, without transforming old beliefs, and without building new skills, little will improve in classrooms.

Practitioners face the dilemma of deciding whether to adopt all, part, or none of a new curricular policy and the cost of implementing the changes in their classrooms. In making such choices, teachers must determine how much value to attach to what they already do, how much changes will help their students, and how much energy and time they can invest to make the changes, given the organizational and personal constraints that they face daily.

Researchers face the dilemma of deciding whether changes that teachers make are sufficient to indicate that a policy has been implemented successfully, or are only distracting blips on a policymaker's radar screen. What does the researcher make of the teacher who says with confidence that she has made a 180-degree shift in her teaching and cites the evidence of different teaching practices that the researcher has observed, when the researcher sees those very same changes as modest alterations of the teacher's existing repertoire of practices?

Such paradoxes and puzzles are confusing and need further elaboration, if not reconciliation. They go beyond the initial question I asked in the Introduction: How did teachers teach? Chapters 1 through 7 offer one historian's answer to the question. The second question—Why have teachers taught the way they have?—requires an analysis of competing explanations. That is the task of the next chapter. The final chapter will take the answer I construct and return to these paradoxes and dilemmas that face policymakers eager to improve teaching, practitioners desiring more autonomy and support, and researchers trying to make sense of the confusing evidence about the dominance of teacher-centered practices, the changes that teachers have made in shifting toward student-centered practices, and the presence of mixtures of both traditions.

PART III

Constancy and Change
in the Classroom,
1890–1990

CHAPTER 8

Explaining How They Taught: An Exploratory Analysis

> I must show the school as it really is. I must not attack the school, nor talk overmuch about what ought to be, but only about what is.
> —Willard Waller, *The Sociology of Teaching*

Do you remember the metaphor of the hurricane—images of storm-tossed waves on the ocean surface, turbulent waters a fathom down, and calm on the ocean floor? The image lent itself well to describing agitated squabbles over curricular theories, textbooks, and classroom instruction. The years after impulses toward student-centered instruction pumped new languages, ideas, policies, and practices into public schools, revealed that trying to reform teaching was a huge task and that one could not generalize about classroom instruction simply based on the quantity of policy talk among educators or the dominance of reform ideas and language in professional journals and popular magazines.

But the metaphor was not entirely apt. Not all was calm and unchanged on the ocean floor while the hurricane whipped up waves on the surface. After all, incremental and even fundamental changes in teaching have occurred over the past century, especially in elementary schools. The metaphor now needs to be set aside for a more detailed look at how school reforms develop and how they affect classroom practices.

PHASES AND LEVELS OF SCHOOL REFORM

School reforms unfold unevenly, unmechanically, in identifiable phases, less like an auto engine piston pumping up and down within a cylinder than like a large weather front of uncertain origin moving erratically and unpredictably across the nation. The following are the phases of reform:

- Social, political, and economic changes in objective conditions of life or in ideologies create situations that opinionmakers in society define as problems. An example is a change in a country's economic standing in the world community, as when the German economy and military expanded rapidly in the 1890s or when Japanese products seized large sectors of the U.S. market in the 1980s, fueling a growing perception that changes were needed in the American economy and particularly in the schools producing graduates for the workplace.
- Policymakers, academics, and opinionmakers such as journalists and top corporate officials—outsiders to the educational enterprise—talk about the problems as they see them, and a consensus begins to develop about what the problems are and what solutions are feasible.
- Groups and individuals (elite entrepreneurs, foundation presidents, special-interest groups, prominent public officials, community organizations, etc.) outside the schools develop policy proposals and programs to solve the perceived problem.
- Through various mechanisms (e.g., state and federal legislation, district school board decisions, foundation-funded pilot projects), groups and individuals connected to the educational enterprise come to be known as reformers and press insiders (school board members, superintendents, principals, and teachers) to adopt and implement reforms.
- Some policies do get adopted in the form of legislation, school board decisions, and the like. Superintendents, principals, and teachers attempt to implement these policies. Efforts to incorporate the deliberate reforms into routine practice get under way within districts, schools, and classrooms.
- Growing criticism of educators' seemingly slow or halfhearted efforts to implement reforms gives way to shrinking attention to whether schools are solving the problem that had been defined earlier. Disappointment sets in.
- Social, economic, or demographic conditions in society again shift and the cycle begins anew. . . . [1]

These identifiable phases do not occur at regular intervals; moreover, they often overlap. Even amid the adoption of reform policies in many districts across the nation, new social conditions elsewhere (e.g., major shifts in population) may result in calls for different reforms. The pace of each phase varies according to the nature of the proposed reforms, when they occur, the region of the nation being affected, the power of any political coalitions involved, the caliber, training, and inclinations of the educators implementing the reforms, and—most important—the extent to which the reform permeates popular and professional media.

These phases of a school reform underscore four important points illustrated in the previous chapters on attempts by child-centered progressives and open classroom promoters to alter the dominant mode of teacher-centered instruction. The initial impulse for reform most often (but not always) comes from outside the schools; the impulse is converted into a shared and politically acceptable definition of what the problem is and how schools and teachers can solve that problem; the policies and programs that get adopted are partially implemented as they unevenly and erratically travel through the different levels of schooling (state, district, school, and classroom); and, finally, the institution of schooling, with its varied levels, bends reforms to its purposes. The journey from policy talk at the national and state levels to what occurs in schools and classrooms is long, some road markers are missing, and the unpredictability of the weather makes arrival at the destination uncertain.

In earlier chapters, I have roughly mapped school change, highlighting reformers' words, intentions, and public policies but concentrating upon the classroom. These maps of classrooms have revealed the danger of inferring that policy talk about reforming teaching practices mirrors what occurs in classrooms. The maps have also displayed the limitations of the hurricane metaphor in characterizing the multilayered policymaking process.

The preceding seven chapters have charted a few salient features of that classroom terrain. I have collected data in five categories, embracing an important portion of the visible teaching behaviors that educators label "instruction." Note, however, that these categories hardly convey the richness or complexity of classroom life. They do not capture the artistry of teachers who can individualize instruction with the nod of a head, the wink of an eye, and a friendly arm around a shoulder, or the abundant exchanges between students and teachers that produce a classroom culture complete with traditions to be honored and roles to be played. Instead, the study concentrates upon those practices in which teachers engage regularly.

Drawn from a large number of varied sources in diverse settings over nearly a century, the data show striking convergence in broadly outlining two traditions of teaching (teacher-centered and student-centered) that have persisted for centuries.

We can now answer the question of how teachers taught by drawing on a substantial body of evidence, both direct and contextual, from the 1890s to the present. This evidence clearly shows that the dominant teaching tendency was toward varied forms of teacher-centered instruction. In elementary schools that prevailing tendency was modified by clusters of hybrids mixing student-centered teaching practices with more familiar ones. In high school academic subjects, fewer hybrids existed and the dominant tendency emerged clearly.

Although precision in methodology and in sampling historical sources was limited, descriptions of and results from studies of 7,000 classrooms in diverse settings revealed the durability of teacher-centered practices since the turn of the century. This historical inquiry into classroom instruction and the imperfect methods used were in the spirit of another researcher who said, "far better an approximate answer to the right question, which is often vague, than an exact answer to the question, which can always be made precise."[2]

But previous chapters also disclosed that the student-centered tradition of teaching was alive and well. Changes in teaching practices did indeed occur. Some pedagogical reforms moved from the drawing board to the school board and ended up on the chalkboard.[3] A tiny fraction of elementary school teachers created their versions of child-centered classrooms where students could move about freely to work in activity centers, where clustered desks made it easy for students to work together, and where teacher-student planning occurred daily. Subjects were correlated and students spent ample time working in small groups or independently on projects.

Other teachers—a much larger number, especially in elementary schools, but still a minority—spent perhaps part of a day or a session a week on certain student-centered practices which they felt would benefit children and not unsettle existing classroom routines. Some began grouping students for certain periods a day; others established a science or reading center in a corner of the room. Some pulled desks into a circle or into groups of four so that children could talk to one another as they worked; others chose a unit, say, on the Pilgrims and Thanksgiving, and tried to integrate many subjects into the 3 weeks spent on the project. These practices, well within the tradition of student-centered instruction, and often implemented on a consciously selective, piecemeal basis, were incorporated slowly into daily instructional routines. Thus did practice alter.

The modification of teacher practices that produced hybrid forms of teacher-centeredness occurred in substantial numbers of elementary school classrooms during the interwar years and after the late 1960s. By the 1980s, most elementary and some secondary school classrooms were far less formal places than they had been a century earlier. Interactions between teachers and students were more relaxed. Moreover, varied grouping procedures, learning centers, student mobility, and certain kinds of noise were acceptable. But far fewer teachers jointly planned with students what content to teach, which activities to use, and how much class time to allocate to each activity in lesson plans.

Why did these different patterns in the two traditions of teaching emerge? To ask "why" is to look for causes, yet unambiguous cause-effect relationships seldom march up to scholars and tap them on the shoulder. Moreover, because of some excesses in previous writings, historians have been leery of dealing openly with causes, preferring to substitute for the word such nouns as "factors," "influences," and "elements." Yet historians, in my judgment, cannot escape trying to explain what they have documented.

Let me state plainly what I mean by "why," since the word can be used in several ways. In asking why the dominant form of instruction continued to be teacher-centered and why hybrids of teacher-centered progressivism and informal education developed more in elementary than in high school classrooms, I might:

- Seek out motives (i.e. of reformers, teachers, and administrators);
- Lay blame (i.e., on intransigent teachers or penurious school boards);
- Justify the status quo (i.e., that's how the system has always been); or
- Seek to understand why new patterns of behavior developed and existing ones endured.

This last way of asking why—seeking to understand the sources of continuity in teacher-centeredness and the development of hybrids—can, I believe, lead to knowledge that policymakers, scholars, and school officials can use. My search for explanations, then, inquires into the determinants of classroom instruction in the hope of producing a foundation of reliable knowledge upon which informed policies can be built.

This exploratory effort to explain patterns in classroom instruction requires criteria to help evaluate varied explanations. Obviously, given the data and its inevitable gaps, there is no one single, comprehensive, or final explanation. Explanations that might meet certain criteria would be, at best, suggestive and provide only further hunches to explore. After all, historical explanations are arguments anchored in evidence. My criteria for selecting explanations-as-arguments are drawn directly from patterns that emerged from the evidence:

1. Does the argument explain the strong, clear pattern of teacher-centered instruction in both elementary and high school classrooms?
2. Does the argument explain why some instructional changes occurred at the elementary and not at the high school level?
3. Does the argument explain why teachers selected particular progressive and informal practices and not others?

These criteria exclude, for now, the possibility that there are separate explanations for separate questions that may be also mutually exclusive. I exclude these possibilities now in the hope of initially finding straightforward answers rather than complex ones. Yet these possibilities exist.

I return now to the six explanations (using the words argument and explanation interchangeably in this context) that I sketched out briefly in the

Introduction, in order to review them and add more detail where relevant. Each plausibly explains either the persistent regularity or the change in teaching practices. No doubt all of these explanations, "like buckets put out in the rain, catch some truth. But none of them catches all of the truth."[4]

The danger of building weak arguments in order to present the correct one is inherent in this approach. I have tried to avoid that trap by distilling from the literature on stability and change in schooling those arguments that are consistent with evidence presented in the previous chapters and fit the issues of pedagogy raised in this study. In presenting each explanation, I argue as if I were an advocate of the position. I then analyze the strengths and flaws of each. In short, I have tried hard to make each bucket carry some truth.

Explanations

1. *Cultural beliefs about the nature of knowledge, how teaching should occur, and how children should learn are so widespread and deeply rooted that they steer the thinking of policymakers, practitioners, parents and citizens toward certain forms of instruction.*

Millennia ago formal schooling was instituted in religious institutions to spread the word of the particular gospel and to study its meaning. Books were rare. Teaching and learning in church-related schools and colleges depended on those who were informed telling the uninformed what was important to know. Knowledge was a body of stable beliefs, facts, procedures, and opinions that were true and unquestioned. Ten centuries ago in Europe, for example, educated men worked from laboriously copied handwritten books, sacred texts, from which others could read and teach. The contents of these books were memorized and reverently repeated to the ignorant. Such reverence for written knowledge gave books an authority that would persist in succeeding centuries. The very origins of these educational institutions in western and nonwestern cultures established norms about the socially accepted meanings of knowledge, teaching, and learning.

Embedded in these tasks and roles were implicit theories of teaching and learning: Teachers who have acquired bodies of knowledge are authorities who convey that knowledge to those lacking it; because students lack the teacher's knowledge, their task is to absorb information and wisdom from those who possess it and to periodically display what they have learned. Teaching, then, demands that teachers acquire formal knowledge, find efficient ways of sharing it, and determine whether pupils have learned what was taught. Instruction depends upon the teacher. Learning, on the other hand, depends upon students' attention, study, and hard work. If teachers are active and central to instruction, students are a passive audience for teachers.

Over time, such popular notions, anchored in the origins of formal education in Asia, India, Africa, and Europe, became accepted as culturally appropriate. That is, both the educated and uneducated came to believe in the absolute integrity of certain bodies of knowledge that had to be passed on to the next generation. Teaching became a familiar set of behaviors, with teachers spending most of their time telling youth what was important to know and finding out if they knew it. To spend time on what the culture defined as play (e.g., walking in the woods observing animals, painting a picture, singing, working together in groups), where the dispensing of knowledge was not central to the activity, was, simply put, neither teaching nor learning. Learning was hard, requiring sustained work and little play. If students were having fun, they must not be learning.

The ideas of 17th- and 18th-century European educators such as John Comenius, Jean-Jacques Rousseau, and Johann Pestalozzi, who saw the child as the proper focus of education and the teacher's primary role as guiding the unfolding of the child's talents, are recent developments in a history of schooling that stretches back millennia. Nineteenth-century American reformers who appreciated their European forebears, such as Edward Sheldon, Francis Parker, and John Dewey, were eager to develop a "New Education" and a student-centered focus in public schools. Twentieth-century reformers have introduced the kindergarten and other child-centered practices into public schooling. These changes have come very slowly and have often been transformed by the dominant cultural norms deeply buried in these schools.

Thus, it should come as no surprise that most descriptions of classrooms continue to portray the persistence of a dominant tradition of teacher-centered classrooms with minor inroads from a small and more recent, but insistent, tradition of student-centered instruction. The prevailing mode of teaching is consistent with the traditions of a time when men and women lived their brief lives by the rhythms of the sun and land, guided by a deep reverence for the accumulated wisdom of their elders, who tried to make sense of the mysteries of life. After all, transforming a cultural inheritance is not as easy as bulldozing, grading, and paving a new road.[5]

2. *The organization and practice of formal schooling function to socialize and sort students into varied socioeconomic niches.*

The school stands between the family and the marketplace. The overriding purpose of the school, not always explicit but nonetheless evident, is to inculcate into children the prevailing social norms, values, and behaviors that will prepare them for economic, social, and political participation in the larger culture. How schools are organized (bureaucratic, age-graded, grouping students by ability in elementary schools and tracks in secondary schools), what knowledge is highly valued (e.g., American history and literature, grammar, math and science), administrator and teacher beliefs and attitudes toward cultural differences, and certain pedagogical practices (recitation, homework, tests, lecturing, etc.) mirror the norms, beliefs, and practices of the larger socioeconomic system. Schools and the adults who staff these institutions distribute dominant cultural knowledge, inculcate mainstream values, and channel students into socioeconomic niches.

Teaching practices that concentrate on particular bodies of content and on skills have to be learned such as student obedience, conformity, productivity, and other traits. These skills and content are required for minimal participation in social, bureaucratic, and industrial organizations. Mainstream beliefs and values need to be taught; children from other cultures who bring to classrooms their own languages, habits, and attitudes need to be transformed into model American citizens. There is a standard English that has to be mastered; there are ways to line up to go from class to class; there are proper ways of getting adult attention; there is a school etiquette of behavior to be learned that is different from what is practiced on the street and in the home.

Students who have already learned the necessary lessons and etiquette at home fit the expectations of the teachers and tend to adjust to the school's demands. Such students know what is expected of them behaviorally and academically and follow both the overt and covert rules. They are placed in advanced reading groups and, in the higher grades, college preparatory tracks.

Other students, who come from cultures or socioeconomic backgrounds where these school demands are unfamiliar, find it initially harder to adjust. Some do adjust, and seek more schooling than their peers—even entrance into college, the turnstile to economic advancement. But many more of these students are labeled by teachers and administrators as "slow" or as misfits and are assigned to particular groups within a classroom or to separate programs. Over time, such students receive a different education: The content they learn, the skills they acquire, and the teaching practices they experience vary significantly from what students labeled as "average" or "above-average" receive. Many of these students leave school before graduating and enter the job market at the lowest levels or join the ranks of the unemployed.

Teaching practices for the two groups vary. For children who come from a low socioeconomic background and minority groups certain teaching practices prevailed: arranging classroom desks into rows to secure uniform behavior; using textbooks, a primary source of knowledge endorsed by the teacher, to yield reams of homework; giving tests and quizzes to permit the teacher to sort students by their achievement or lack of it; and having students follow teacher-directed procedures for seatwork, recitation, and reports. These dominant teacher-centered practices endure because they enable schools to socialize and sort these students to meet the requirements of the larger society.

Student-centered pedagogy, on the other hand, nourishes individual choice, expressiveness, group learning skills, derivation of knowledge from many sources, joint student-teacher decisionmaking, and student participation in both the verbal and physical life of the classroom. Such classroom practices and student behaviors fit the requirements of the university and the marketplace; they are tailored for future professionals, managers, and executives. Such a fit helps to explain why student-centered changes and open classrooms are often associated more with private schools and upper-middle-class, highly educated parents living in affluent neighborhoods than with public schools in blue-collar and welfare-recipient-dominated communities.

This argument about schools as socializing and sorting mechanisms of the larger society is another explanation for the stability in pedagogical practices since the turn of the century.[6]

3. *If educational policymakers had effectively implemented reforms aimed at changing what teachers routinely do, changes in instructional practices would have occurred.*

When policymakers systematically and thoroughly executed policies aimed at the classroom, involving teachers in both understanding and enacting what had to be done, teaching behaviors did change. But where policy efforts were ill-conceived and haphazardly involved teachers in putting new ideas into practice, teachers largely ignored the mandates and dreams of reformers.

Thus, a core of teacher-centered instructional approaches endured because reform efforts to alter those approaches were ineffectually executed. Had thoughtful, systematic, and comprehensive efforts been undertaken to implement instructional changes, far more numerous progressive and informal educational practices would be apparent in the 1990s. Where implementation succeeded, teaching practices altered. It is the inattention of policymakers to the details of implementing reforms aimed at making classrooms more student-centered that explains the persistence of teacher-centered instruction.

Except for Denver and New York in the 1930s, few school districts developed conscious strategies for applying new ideas about teaching. Where classroom reforms were adopted, they invariably stemmed from a decision made at the top administrative level. Implementation was given little thought beyond issuance of a batch of directives and briefings for principals and teachers. Indeed, seldom were teachers directly and continuously involved in determining how to convert policies made by others into classroom practice except, again, interwar Denver (which still remains unique among school districts).

Instances where formal, top-level endorsement occurred. The few organized efforts to put progressive or open classroom approaches into practice include the Child Development Program instituted in Washington, D.C., in 1938; expansion of the experimental Activity Program to encompass all New York City schools in 1941; and, in the same year, Denver's decision to mandate general education courses and apply the results of the Eight-Year Study to all high schools. These decisions became exercises in paperwork compliance, with few intended changes filtering down into classrooms.

A Darwinian approach to implementing policies characterized middle-sized and large school systems after the superintendent and school board embraced instructional reforms. Individual advocates or bands of partisans favoring one policy change or another in a school system would fight doggedly for a niche (i.e., resources) to last a couple of years. If they were successful, the district grapevine and sporadic contacts with like-minded professionals and parents would spread word of the change. Perhaps, if conditions were just right, formal notice of the successful reform by a top administrator, superintendent, or board of education would lead to its expansion. Serendipity, more than planning, often accounted for the spread of a reform. Absent, more often than not, were administrative mechanisms to disperse information, organizational linkages between school practices and districtwide goals, and teacher participation in the process.

Student-centered approaches, then, infrequently penetrated classrooms because of the unwillingness or inability of school officials to convert a policy decision or formal approval of an instructional change into a comprehensive and systematic process that would not only gain teachers' support for classroom adoption but also enhance their capacity to make changes. This argument contains within it the adage implementers are fond of using: It was a terrific idea; it is a shame that it wasn't ever tried.[7]

4. *The organizational structure of the district, school, and classroom shaped teachers' dominant instructional practices.*

Organizations influence the ideas and behavior of those who work within them. How an organization such as a school is put together—its goals, policies, roles, and processes—shapes that work. Thus, district and school structures drove teachers to adopt certain instructional strategies that varied little over time.

The classroom, as an organization located within the larger school like a small Russian wooden doll nested within a larger one, is a crowded setting. A teacher has to manage 25 to 40 or more students of approximately the same age who involuntarily spend—depending upon their age—anywhere from 1 to 5 hours daily in one room. Amid continual exchanges with individual students and groups—up to 1,000 a day in an elementary classroom, according to Philip Jackson—the teacher is expected to maintain control, teach prescribed content, awaken students' interest in the subject matter, vary levels of instruction according to student differences, and show tangible evidence that students have performed satisfactorily.

Within these overlapping school and classroom structures, teachers rationed their energy and time in order to cope with multiple and conflicting demands, and invented teaching practices that have emerged as resilient, imaginative, and efficient compromises for dealing with a large number of students in a small space for extended periods of time.

So, for example, movable desks arranged in rows let the teacher scan the class for disorder. Located in a visually prominent part of the room near a chalkboard, the teacher's desk quietly underscores who determines what the class will do each day.

Teaching the entire class together is an efficient and convenient use of the teacher's time—a valuable and scarce resource—to cover the mandated content and maintain control. Lecturing, recitation, true-false and multiple-choice questions on tests, point systems to calculate grades, and homework drawn from texts are direct, uncomplicated ways of transmitting knowledge and assessing what has been learned by the groups. Given the constrictions placed upon the teacher by the daily school schedule, and the requirements that a course of study be completed by June, the above instructional practices permit the teacher to determine quickly and efficiently whether students have learned the material.

Student-centered approaches for organizing space, instructing small groups, integrating subject matter, encouraging expressiveness, and student decisionmaking generate noise and movement, lessen the teacher's authority, and make a shambles of routines geared to handling large groups of students. These approaches are incompatible with existing school and classroom structures and would require a complete overhaul of basic modes of classroom operation. When the entire burden of change is placed upon the shoulders of the teacher, it should come as no surprise that few teachers are willing to upset their intimate world for the uncertain benefits of a student-centered classroom. Hence, the practical pedagogy of teacher-centered instruction continues to dominate schooling because of the organizational pressures of the school and district upon the classroom.[8]

5. *The cultures of teaching that have developed within the occupation tilt toward stability in classroom practices.*

The occupational norms are conservative. This conservatism—that is, a preference for stability and a cautious attitude toward change—is rooted in the nature of the craft, in the people recruited into the profession, in how they are informally socialized, in how they are evaluated, and in the school and classroom cultures of which teaching itself is a primary ingredient.

Teaching is people-changing work. Unlike in psychotherapy, social work, medical practice, and other endeavors where clients are often expected to take a large share of the responsibility for their improvement, teachers are largely responsible for student performance, yet they are utterly dependent on their students for successful results. Furthermore, there is much uncertainty and disagreement in the larger society about what the desirable outcomes of teaching are. Given these constraints unique to the practice of teaching, there is a decided reluctance to take risks by instituting new teaching practices, particularly student-centered instructional reforms, which rely even more upon students for results.

People attracted to teaching seek contact with children, appreciate the flexible work schedule, and, while acknowledging the limited financial rewards, still embrace the service mission built into the occupation. Newcomers are usually young people who are already favorably disposed toward schools, having been students for many years. Moreover, among new teachers women outnumber men, who often leave the classroom in search of administrative posts and higher salaries. Work schedules permit teachers with family obligations to make flexible arrangements. Male and female teachers, for different reasons, have little incentive to transform occupational norms of structures. Recruitment, then, brings into the occupation people who tend to reaffirm rather than challenge the school's role and its current organizational structures.

Even before their formal entry into teaching through the required but brief training program, informal socialization has tilted newcomers' attitudes toward favoring continuity. Consider that as public school students for 12 years (over 13,000 hours), entering teachers were in close contact with their teachers. Teaching is one of the few occupations one can observe firsthand while sitting a few yards away, year after year. Hence the familiar assertion that teachers teach as they were taught.

Similarly, the act of teaching within a self-contained classroom, isolated from colleagues, fosters conservatism. The first-year teacher, after a brief apprenticeship, is thrust into the classroom with the same responsibilities as a 20-year veteran. The private and lonely anguish of the sink-or-swim ordeal that usually consumes the newcomer's first few years is alleviated by occasional advice and sharing of anecdotes by experienced colleagues. From the very first day, facing the complicated process of establishing routines that will induce a group of students to behave in an orderly way while learning subject matter that the teacher is still unfamiliar with, the teacher is driven to use practices that he or she remembers seeing used or that veterans advise using. By taking such advice, entrants absorb through a subtle osmosis the school's norms and expectations about what it takes to survive as a teacher. The folklore, occupational gimmicks, norms, and daily teaching reinforce existing approaches rather than nourish skepticism, especially if one wishes to continue in the job.

Thus, teacher-centered classroom practices tend to be stable over time. After all, homework assignments, discussion, seatwork, tests, and an occasional film to interrupt the routine were all methods familiar to newcomers in their own schooling and, more often than not, seemed to keep the class moving along. To use such practices in their own classrooms would preserve what some of their exemplary teachers and esteemed college instructors had used. Rather than making fundamental changes—such as teaching in small groups, integrating varied content into units, planning lessons with students, and letting class members choose what to do—tinkering with an occasional new method, polishing up routine techniques, and introducing variations of existing ones would be consistent with the basic conservatism of the occupation.[9]

6. *Teachers' knowledge of subject matter and their professional and personal beliefs about the role of the school in society, classroom authority, and children's ethnic and socioeconomic status shape classroom practices.*

What teachers know about the subjects they teach and how they use that knowledge with students, the beliefs they have about how children learn and develop, and the social attitudes they bring to their classroom shape how they teach.

Consider the subject knowledge that teachers have and how they convert that knowledge into language and formats children can understand. The science teacher who knows that fifth-grade children have trouble understanding the concept of natural selection uses examples of giraffes and pelicans, redwood trees and Venus flytraps to make the abstraction concrete. A social studies teacher may use the metaphor of a bitter divorce to convey to eighth-grade students the intensity of feelings surrounding the Civil War.

If a teacher's knowledge of subject matter and ability to convey it count, so does how long the teacher has taught the subject. Experienced history teachers, for instance, thoroughly familiar with the causes of the American Revolution, will use different images and analogies to convey the underlying causes for the separation of the colonies from the mother country than will novice teachers.

Teachers' professional and personal beliefs about subject matter and about how children learn also intersect. A math teacher who believes, for example, that children cannot do geometry until they have learned what proofs are and know the basic ones by heart will teach a different lesson than will a math teacher who believes that students can learn the essentials of geometry by planning and laying out a school garden on an oddly shaped lot in the back of the building. The teacher who conceives of block building as an exercise to develop muscles in 5-year-olds will plan that task differently than one who views the exercise as play that distracts children from getting ready for the first grade. Finally, the teacher who looks for connections between textbook content and daily events because he or she believes that knowledge related to a context will be learned by students, will depart from the text far more often than others to explore these connections. Coverage of subject matter will be sacrificed in a trade-off that offers students deeper understandings than dates, numbers, or similar facts could convey.

Teachers' beliefs about the nature of knowledge and the role of the school in conveying that knowledge also shape behavior. Many teachers, especially in the secondary school, believe that the role of the school in society is to develop the mind and instill social values. Moreover, certain bodies of knowledge must be passed on to all students. Many also believe that students learn best in well-managed, noiseless classrooms where teachers set the limits, prize academic rigor, and enforce rules fairly. Many further believe that the teacher's authority, rooted in institutional legitimacy and knowledge, must be respected. These and similar beliefs are held by many teachers, especially in high schools. They account for the perseverance of such teaching practices as reliance upon textbooks, limitations on student movement, and a concern for noiseless classrooms.

Finally, those teachers whose social attitudes lead them to prize contacts and relationships with higher- rather than lower-status children and with children whose ethnic, racial, or religious background is more similar to their own will address decisions of what content to teach, how to manage the classroom, and how to structure activities differently when teaching low-income black or Hispanic pupils than when teaching affluent white or Asian-American students.

The knowledge, beliefs, and attitudes that teachers have, then, shape what they choose to do in their classrooms and explain the core of instructional practices that have endured over time.[10]

APPLYING THE CRITERIA TO THE ARGUMENTS

Earlier I posed three criteria:

- Does the argument explain the strong, clear pattern of teacher-centered instruction in both elementary and high school classrooms?
- Does the argument explain why some instructional changes occurred at the elementary and not at the high school level?
- Does the argument explain why teachers chose particular progressive and informal practices and not others?

All six arguments meet the first criterion of explaining the durability of teacher-centered instruction in elementary and high school classrooms. The other two criteria, however, are not always met.

The first argument of a cultural inheritance is compelling in explaining the persistence of school and classroom practices, especially the durability of teacher-centered instruction. After all, beliefs about the nature of knowledge, what teaching is, and how learning should occur stretch back millennia. Contrary notions that knowledge is not absolute but constructed, relative, and ever-changing or that teaching spans an array of activities beyond lecturing and explaining are fairly recent additions to debate about the proper conduct of education. This argument falls short, however, of meeting the other two criteria. The argument fails to explain why more changes seemingly penetrated elementary schools than secondary ones and why some practitioners rejected tradition and chose to introduce student-centered approaches.

The strength of the second argument, about the socializing and sorting functions of schools, is in its connecting the larger social order to routine school and classroom activities. Such school structures as, for example, grade levels, time schedules, curricular tracks, and having one teacher for 30 students help teachers and administrators place "achievers" and "non-achievers" into appropriate niches. Persistent instructional practices such as grouping children by socioeconomic status also have social meaning—they are not simply coincidences or artifacts created independently or detached from their social context.

Yet substantial evidence over the last century that practitioners acted in contrary ways weakens the argument. For example, during both periods when progressive and open classroom methods were in fashion, groups of elementary school teachers and administrators established student-centered classrooms in schools enrolling large numbers of children of low socioeconomic status. Nor does the argument account for those individual teachers and administrators (e.g., Leonard Covello in New York City in the 1930s) who believed that poor, nonwhite children could learn as well as white, more affluent students. The argument also does not clarify why hybrids of teaching approaches arose and thrived among elementary school teachers in settings that the argument would not have predicted over the last century. Such instances weaken the socializing and sorting functions argument.

The third argument, about the lack of effective implementation, for example, explains why so few changes in teaching practice penetrated classrooms (except in New York City and Denver) during the 1930s even though concerted organizational efforts were undertaken. But the argument fails to account for why student-centered practices occurred among grade school teachers but rarely spread among high school staff. Nor does the interpretation account for teachers' choosing to implement some approaches but not others.

The argument about a teacher culture explains the durability of a core of teacher-centered instructional practices and accounts for high school classrooms retaining the look, smell, and activities of classrooms of previous generations, but its usefulness is limited. Evidence that teachers, singly and in groups, established student-centered classrooms in various places during both periods when progressive and open classroom ideologies were in vogue reveals that large numbers of teachers, while shaped by that occupational culture, did break away from its confining limits. Nor does the argument help in understanding why hybrids of approaches developed among teachers.

The fifth argument, about school and classroom structures, is also initially compelling. Organizational structures such as 30 students to a class, 5 classes a day, and multiple preparations do shape school and classroom practices. But to say this assumes that elementary and high schools are similar in structure. The fact is that the two organizations differ markedly in their size, goals, formal structure, complexity of content students face in classrooms, in allocation of time to instruction, and in external arrangements imposed upon high schools by other institutions.

Children in elementary grades learn basic writing, reading, and math skills. Content is secondary and often used as a flexible vehicle for teaching skills. But in the upper grades of elementary school, and certainly in the secondary school, not only are more sophisticated skills required of students but these skills are embedded in complex subject matter that in and of itself must be learned. Literary criticism, historical analysis, solving advanced math problems, quantitative analysis in chemistry—all require knowledge of complicated facts and their applications. High school teachers continue to use didactic methods because subject matter drives methodology in the classroom.[11]

Also, student-teacher contact time differs markedly between the elementary and high school levels. In the former, the self-contained classroom remains the dominant form of delivering instruction. Generally, teachers spend 5 or more hours with the same 30 or more students. They see far more of a child's strengths, limitations, capacities, and achievements than a high school teacher who sees five groups of 30 students for less than an hour a day. Over a year, the elementary school teacher sees a class of 30 children for nearly a 1,000 hours; a high school teacher sees any one class for no more than 200 hours during the year, or about one fifth of the time that elementary school colleagues spend with pupils. Contact time becomes an important variable in considering issues of grouping, providing individual attention, varying classroom tasks and activities, and rearranging furniture. In elementary schools, the *potential* to make changes in these and other areas is present because the teacher has more contact time with the same children; such potential is absent when one sees 25 students within a 50-minute period. Whether such changes occur in the lower grades, is, of course, an entirely separate issue, but the difference in allocation of instructional time allows for possible changes in elementary school classrooms.[12]

Finally, external pressures from accrediting associations, college entrance requirements, and job market qualifications have a far more direct and unrelenting influence upon high schools than upon lower grade classrooms. In the high school, the students are under strong pressure to meet the demands of Carnegie units, tests (e.g., College Boards, Scholastic Aptitude, and Advanced Placement tests, and state and national standardized achievement exams), certifying agencies, and other external factors that push teachers to prepare students and complete the textbook by June, and drive students to prepare for exams, seek jobs, and take the proper courses for graduation.

While some pressure is exerted on teachers and students in the lower grades, especially in getting students ready for the upper grades, flexible responses are possible. Two consecutive grades can be merged. Groups within a class can include a range of ages and performance. Whole days and even weeks can be set aside for special concentration on particular academic or other areas.

These three structural differences—emphasis on subject matter, contact time, and external pressures—may well account for why classroom changes occurred rather frequently in elementary schools and much less so in high schools.

While this argument meets most of the criteria and also explains teacher-centered instruction as a series of teacher-engineered inventions designed to cope with the *physics,* the organizational forces, of school and classroom structures, there is still the final hurdle of explaining why teachers selected certain student-centered practices and not others. Here this argument falls short. It does not offer a plausible reason for why those teachers who embraced new practices chose ones that produced hybrids of teacher-centered and student-centered classrooms (e.g., unconventional arrangements of classroom furniture, more student movement, learning centers, projects, or various groupings wedded to teacher-centered approaches).

The sixth explanation, which concerns the power of teachers' knowledge, beliefs, and attitudes, is robust because it implies that teachers can change. While beliefs and attitudes are deep-seated, they can be altered, and new ones learned and even integrated with others into a unique synthesis. Changes in what teachers know, in their ideas and attitudes, occur slowly. Hence, changes in teacher practice may follow shifts in knowledge and in beliefs among teachers.

This argument meets two of the criteria: It accounts for the durability of teacher-centered instruction, but it also explains variations in teaching behavior. Teachers may have selected from among pedagogical practices because they had modified their beliefs as social attitudes and belief systems in the larger society shifted. Individual teachers moved by new knowledge may give a novel technique a limited trial in their classrooms. Because classrooms are unforgiving crucibles for testing ideas, a few of these novel approaches may meet the rigors of daily instruction; while others are relegated to the grave-yard of attempted school reforms.

But the argument for the power of teachers' knowledge, beliefs, and attitudes fails to explain why teacher-centered instruction dominated secondary schools while student-centered instruction turned up more often in elementary schools.

Thus, none of the six explanations completely meets the three criteria. Nevertheless, one could carve from these six perspectives a number of reasonably coherent explanations that would meet all three criteria. I offer a synthesis of these arguments, again acknowledging that it is one of many possible ones. This explanation suggests why teacher-centered instruction persevered, why elementary classrooms changed more than those in high schools, and why mixed versions of progressivism and informal education developed.

SITUATIONALLY CONSTRAINED CHOICE

Teacher-centered instruction over the past century has been largely shaped by two overlapping contexts. Long-term cultural beliefs about the nature of knowledge, what teaching and learning should be, and the social setting (the ethnic, racial, and social backgrounds of the children attending school) established the outer context. The school and classroom organizational structures formed the inner context within which individual teacher beliefs and an occupational ethos worked their influences in shaping a durable practical pedagogy called teacher-centered instruction. Intertwined as these situational influences are, disentangling them and assigning a relative weight to the influence of each is impossible.

The constraints, pressures, and channeling that the outer and inner contexts generate are an invisible, encompassing web of influences upon classroom teachers that few can explicitly identify or recognize. Seymour Sarason, in an attempt to see the school differently, used the device of a visitor from outer space asking basic questions about school structure. This required imagination. To contrast the image of a superb teacher working with, for example, a wealthy, highly-motivated student daily for 2 hours in the teacher's living room with that of an eighth-grade U.S. history class of 30 low-income minority students in a school of 1,500 students is to see two starkly different settings. The cultural and historical baggage of notions and expectations that accompanies the tutor-student and teacher-class relationships into the teacher's living room or the self-contained classroom in that school of 1,500 students suggests the overriding importance of considering the less apparent, social and cultural contexts and more apparent organizational contexts within which teachers work.[13]

Consider, for example, that the familiar rows of desks, recitations, whole-group instruction, worksheets, and textbook assignments can be viewed as inventions for reconciling the daily problems of managing a score or more of students while they acquired the information and values prized by community and teacher. These unsentimental compromises worked out by teachers made it possible to maintain control while trying to get students to learn. Pure forms of this practical pedagogy, as researchers have noted, often appear in schools serving large numbers of immigrant children. Thus, the outer and inner contexts merge in shaping how teachers teach.[14]

Within these interacting outer and inner contexts, the occupational ethos of teaching funnels both newcomers and veterans into rituals that the wisdom of the craft reinforces as essential for classroom survival. In an occupation where every practitioner faces the class alone, there is less opportunity for teachers to cooperate to alter these rituals.

What leavens the deterministic drift of this argument for situational constraints is the potential for change associated with teachers' changing knowledge, beliefs, and attitudes. Here, teachers create a margin of choice. Certainly, the larger social milieu shaped belief systems. I have provided evidence that documents the pervasive influence upon practitioners of prevailing social beliefs. For example, new and different ideas about children's development, how they learn, and the purposes of schooling (beyond that of cultivating minds) permeated the larger culture and penetrated educators' thinking. Child-rearing manuals were influenced by developments in psychology. Newspapers, films, and magazines touted the New Education. Popular media helped shape different attitudes toward children and schools. Too often one forgets that while parents and citizens absorbed these ideas, teachers—as both parents and professionals—did also. Ideas, once embraced, are not easily abandoned. You cannot unring a bell.

Moreover, new and deeper knowledge of subject matter—be it math, biology, history, or literature—means revising familiar ways of treating routine topics and experimenting with new ones. Student descriptions of certain teachers at Washington, D.C.'s Central High School in the 1920s and Denver's East High School in the 1930s suggest that some teachers altered aspects of their teaching as they gained more content knowledge and revised long-held notions of why they taught their subject matter.

This argument of situationally constrained choice, one of a number that could have been constructed, accounts for both constancy and change in teaching practice. More important, it suggests that teachers had some autonomy to make classroom choices derived from their belief systems.

The issue of teacher autonomy weaves in and out of any explanation about classroom change. Of the six arguments I set forth, three suggested that teachers were gatekeepers for any pedagogical reforms, choosing what they would do in their classrooms once they closed the door. The argument that

stressed policymakers' reckless implementation assumed that if certain organizational mechanisms were in place, teachers would be either coerced by formal authority or persuaded by incentives to try out certain instructional reforms. This remote control of teachers through sanctions and incentives,
according to the implementation argument, was torpedoed both by inept execution of policy changes and by the power that teachers had to decide what
to bring into their classrooms. The other argument, about granting teacher
discretion, focused upon teachers' knowledge, beliefs, and attitudes, which
might change were teachers exposed to different ideas about subject matter,
pedagogy, and how children learn. A third explanation argued that teachers
had a little choice when they invented practical ways of coping with school
and classroom imperatives. They built a pedagogical scaffold that conformed
to the contours of a demanding classroom terrain.[15]

In the remaining three explanations, teachers' freedom to alter what is
done in classrooms is greatly diminished by adaptations to the cultural and
social belief systems and structures outside the school or to the professional
culture itself. Because the zone of discretion that teachers have, be it narrow
or broad, is crucial in determining how big a role individual teachers play in
continuing or changing classroom practices, I now turn to the issue of teacher
authority and autonomy.

Teacher Autonomy

Teacher-bashing—blaming teachers for resisting instructional
changes—is a common response to the tenacity of teacher-centeredness.
Faulting teachers for refusing to change places reformers in the unenviable
position of seeing teachers as the both the problem and the solution.

Why can't teachers simply change their shoes, pull up their socks, and
get on with the changes, for God's sake? reformers may ask. Such bashing
assumes that most teachers are free to adopt changes, if they merely chose to.
When they do not, it is because they are stubborn or fearful of classroom
consequences. Attributing to teachers the personal power to halt or divert
change is a common tendency of those who locate explanations for events in
individual action rather than assessing the potent influence of the situational
contexts or a blend of many influences.

Junior high school teacher James Herndon once asked the key questions
that strike at the core of what teachers can and cannot decide:

> If a teacher comes into his room, who decides that there are going to be 35
> chairs in that room?. . . . Who decided 35 kids are going to come in there?
> Who decided that there would be 35 textbooks in there? Who decided that
> they are going to go to school from 9:25 to 3:30 or whatever it is, and that
> periods are going to be so and so many minutes long? Who decides that

fourth graders in one state learn about South America whereas they learn about South America in the fifth grade in another state?[16]

To extend James Herndon's point, consider the basic decisions directly affecting instruction that for decades have been made by authorities outside the classroom:

1. How many and which students should be in the class?
2. Which students should leave the class because they are not profiting from instruction?
3. What extra instructional help should students get?
4. How long should the school day or class period be?
5. Should teachers' daily schedule include planning time, and, if so, how much and when?
6. What texts should be used for each subject?
7. What grades or subjects should each teacher teach?
8. What should be the format and content of the report card?
9. What standardized tests should be given?
10. What subjects and courses should the teacher teach?

The results of these decisions made outside the classroom placed severe limits upon teachers' authority and established sharp organizational boundaries for what they could do in their classrooms.

The point here is to differentiate between those organizational decisions affecting instruction over which teachers have had little influence and those classroom decisions that teachers could indeed make. The latter include the following:

- How should classroom space and furniture be arranged [once portable furniture was installed in rooms]?
- How should students be grouped for instruction?
- Who should talk and under what circumstances?
- To what degree and under what circumstances should students participate in classroom activities?
- What tasks are most appropriate to get students to learn what is expected?
- What instructional tools (texts, television, film, computers, etc.) are most conducive to reaching classroom goals?
- What topics within the subject matter should be taught and in what order?

Most teachers had authority to answer these questions; their answers constituted the margin of choice available to them. Yet these teachers' decisions were inescapably colored by their knowledge of how to convey subject matter and their attitudes toward students, their families, and other outside influences, such as the demand that teachers maintain order in their classrooms and get students to learn the required curriculum.

The issue of how much authority and how much autonomy teachers had in making school and classroom decisions is fundamental to any analysis of instruction and curriculum, since what policymakers and school administrators assume teachers can and cannot do is often built into decisions touching classrooms. Is the teacher a captive of social and organizational processes that inexorably shape what happens in classrooms? Is the teacher a leader who determines what needs to be done within the classroom and who does it? Or is the teacher part leader, part follower?

The argument of situationally constrained choice stresses that social, cultural, and organizational influences were sufficiently potent to maintain teacher-centered practices, especially in high schools. But once teachers closed their classroom doors, they had limited discretion to alter their routines. This limited freedom increased for those teachers who, for any number of reasons, expanded and deepened their knowledge of subject matter and embraced different beliefs about children, learning, and what schools should do. These teachers believed that new and different ideas could be introduced to their classrooms and forged ahead in a trial-and-error fashion.

Few changes that teachers introduced, however, were sharp departures from mainstream practice. More often, these teacher-made reforms were hybrids of the old and new. What I have yet to explain is why these hybrids of teacher-centered progressivism and informal education appeared.

Recall that informality in seating, student movement within the classroom, and a softening in language and tone of the formal relationships between teachers and students increased in elementary classrooms over the years. Teachers began dividing classes into two or three groups for reading, math, or other activities. Many teachers increased their attention to individual students and reduced the chilly formality and fear that marked so many teacher-student exchanges. The climate and social organization of the classroom changed.

Yet fewer changes occurred in the academic organization of the classroom. Surely, substantial numbers of teachers started using activity centers and projects in one generation and in a later one, learning centers. Some teachers lectured less, conducted fewer recitations, and assigned less seatwork. But why did those teachers who chose to tinker with the academic work of the classroom introduce some innovations but not others, such as student-teacher planning of content and the daily schedule or student choice of activities? Teacher selectivity in innovating is a puzzle to which I now turn.

Why Did These Hybrids Develop?

This question can be divided into two: Why did teachers who chose to introduce new techniques limit what they selected? Why did teachers choose some student-centered approaches and not others?

To answer these questions, I will divide teachers since 1900 into three general groups. The largest group, possibly two of every three teachers (including over 90% of high school teachers), chose to continue teacher-centered instruction in a manner to which they were accustomed—or, as I have argued, were shaped by the larger cultural inheritance of beliefs about schooling, organizational structures, and occupational culture. A second and considerable group of teachers—probably up to 25% of the teacher population—accepted some of the student-centered instructional ideas but tried out only a few, limiting themselves to particular techniques. Finally, a fraction of teachers, probably in the 5–10% range and concentrated in elementary schools, believed in progressivism and informal education. They introduced as faithful a replica of those ideas as they could, tailoring it to their classrooms and the available resources. The last two groups, I estimate, added up to at least one third of all teachers (though they mostly represented elementary schools). These teachers developed mixed versions of progressivism and open classrooms. It is to these teachers that the two questions I ask apply.

Why did teachers limit their choices? Two reasons dulled teachers' appetites for fundamental classroom changes: the personal cost in time and energy and the lack of help to put complex ideas into practice. Teaching ordinarily requires a major investment of time and emotional, if not physical, energy. Planning content and figuring out how to translate it into understandable terms, interacting with children, continually handling unexpected events as they arise, making hundreds of small decisions daily while in front of the class, marking papers, managing disputes between children, and a dozen other activities—all these require work. Effectively doing these tasks spells the difference between maintaining a harmonious class with a direction or watching an unorganized garden party in the room. To incorporate any departures from routine practice, especially if they entail revising the customary role of teacher, demands a large personal investment of time, energy, and effort while posing a threat to classroom routines.

Consider what often appears to policymakers and reformers as a fairly simple change: getting teachers to use new and varied materials (e.g., math manipulatives like Cuisenaire rods or readings that permit the best readers and those who can barely sound out words to study the same topic) to better match students' interests and performance with classroom tasks and learning theory. To do so requires that teachers find new materials in the school or district or, if they are not available there, then elsewhere. Otherwise, teachers must make the materials themselves. Recall rural Vermont teacher Mary Stapleton and to what lengths she went in 1932 to create instructional materials similar to those she heard were being used in the Winnetka, Illinois, schools. Or imagine how much time and work goes into starting learning centers for the first time, much less the continuing work of changing them weekly. Or consider the emotional energy and managerial skills that go into operating a class where children move about doing many varied tasks simultaneously while the teacher listens to a child or speaks to a small group.

Monitoring what children are doing, determining what skills they need to work on, and resolving unexpected problems as they arise demand that the teacher develop top-notch classroom management skills. Having students decide on classroom rules or what topics will be studied requires of the teacher skills in democratic decision making, far more patience in anticipating, responding to, and accepting diverse classroom noises and student activity than they have known, and, most important, an ideological commitment to delegate authority to students.

Previous chapters contained many examples of different versions of classroom student-centeredness. Such changes in classroom traditions imposed a direct, unrelenting obligation upon the teacher to invest far more time and effort than was invested by teacher-centered colleagues. If there is any continuous theme in what teachers have said about opening up their classrooms or introducing progressive practices, it is that these innovations require more of teachers. They must often spend afternoons and evenings preparing materials and marking papers, or come to school early in the morning, before the children arrive, in order to rearrange centers and set up activities for the day. Arlington's Carmen Wilkinson, with over 30 years' experience, told me:

> We have a lot of work. The curriculum is overloaded and we have so many assessments to do. So much paperwork. Yet I teach Spanish in the first grade. That's not in the curriculum. Every other Friday, we cook. That's not in the curriculum. But I feel that they need these extras. Teachers need to expand their own thinking and their own creative ideas.[17]

Anyone reading even a small portion of teacher accounts describing what they have done in their classrooms would come away impressed with the amount of extra work that has to be done to alter even a few routine classroom practices.

Help was also essential to altering one's way of teaching. Teachers often needed another pair of hands, another person to work with individuals and small groups, grade papers, prepare seatwork, and so on. Teachers needed advice from trusted peers in developing materials and building centers, managing students engaged in six different classroom tasks, distinguishing between instructional and disruptive noise, coping with distractions, and helping pupils work through decisions. Teachers needed time alone and together with colleagues to discuss, plan, and work through some of the thornier classroom issues of control, management, implementing curriculum, and risking one's self-esteem in trying something new. Many student-centered classrooms in the 1970s had student teachers, aides, or parent volunteers to help in open classrooms. The Innovation Team (Washington, D.C.), the New School's support team (North Dakota), and the Workshop Center for Open Education (New York City) are instances of the awareness that teachers needed help in implementing reforms.

Most teachers who endorsed progressive and informal educational ideas lacked access to that kind of help or already felt overloaded with existing classroom demands. In a sink-or-swim fashion, most teachers who ventured into progressive and informal practices had to learn these skills by themselves, or from like-minded colleagues either in school or elsewhere, or from books or summer courses. New York City's Dorothy Boroughs, the P.S. 198 fourth-grade teacher, took a course in open classrooms, visited a school where two teachers had created open classrooms without any outside help, and even placed a math center in one corner of the room. Yet doing all she had to do to keep abreast of her students, school requirements, and her expectations of what was necessary to get her class to read on grade level left her little time and few emotional resources for implementing changes in her classroom.

All of this is to say that adopting student-centered teaching practices requires rethinking daily classroom events, what materials must be secured, how to use time differently, and what new activities children are to do. The time-and-effort burden falls solely upon the teacher's shoulders. No professor, reformer, principal, or superintendent had to stay after 4 p.m. to construct learning centers. Unsurprisingly, teachers would ask themselves: What organizational recognition and incentives are there to spend less time with my family while increasing the amount of work taken home? What new problems would I have with students, other colleagues, and school administrators as a result of making these classroom changes? Are the satisfactions of teaching worth the potential aggravation and additional work? No unambiguous answers existed to these questions. Perhaps this is why teachers willing to make changes limited their choices of student-centered techniques to just a few.[18]

But why did they choose some techniques over others? During the surges of reform to introduce student-centered instruction, why did a substantial number of teachers specifically choose to increase informality through rearranged classroom space and furniture, permit more student movement in the classroom, introduce less formal ways of relating to students, develop projects and learning centers, and use varied groupings? Although partisans of child-centered schools three generations ago and open classrooms a quarter century ago might wince at these superficial choices, these artifacts of pedagogical reform, still, an informed observer whose lifespan permitted sampling classrooms at the turn of the century and in the 1990s could easily conclude that the social organization of the classroom had largely changed from formal to informal.

Teachers are, as Philip Jackson puts it, "kindlier, friendlier, less strict, less formal—in a word more humane—in their dealings with students than they once were. . . . The scowls and frowns of teachers past . . . have gradually been replaced by the smiles and kindly looks of teachers present." He argues, however, that this informality may be deceptive. Studying a group of 50 elementary teachers identified as "superior" in suburban Chicago in the early 1960s, he found them informal but made some careful distinctions:

> "Informal," as these teachers use the term, really means less formal rather than not formal, for even in the most up-to-date class-rooms, much that goes on is still done in accordance with forms, rules, and conventions. Today's teachers may exercise their authority more casually than their predecessors, and they may unbend increasingly with experience, but there are real limits to how far they can move in this direction. As a group, our interviewees clearly recognized and respected those limits. For them, the desire for informality was never sufficiently strong to interfere with institutional definitions of responsibility, authority, and tradition.[19]

Jackson's comments echo John Dewey's earlier observations that substantial changes had occurred in the "life conditions" of the classroom but that such "atmospheric" modifications had not "really penetrated and permeated the foundations of the educational institution." Moreover, Dewey continued, "the fundamental authoritarianism of the old education persists in various modified forms." The key that might unlock the puzzle of teacher selectivity in choosing particular student-centered practices is what both Jackson and Dewey mention—teacher authority in maintaining the academic organization of the classroom.[20]

The state legally delegates through a local school board and its administrative hierarchy formal authority to the teacher to transmit knowledge and skills to students in an orderly manner. Maintaining classroom control, an essential exercise of that formal authority, is a necessary precondition for instruction. Maintaining classroom control, however, is a complex venture that involves a teacher's negotiation with students to secure compliance and cooperation. It can be expressed in a number of forms ranging from coercively blunt to charmingly subtle. Still, to the teacher, managing a group of students in a harmonious manner is paramount.

An asymmetrical power relationship in the classroom permits the teacher to establish conventions that demonstrate his or her power: calling the roll, giving assignments, changing students' seats, asking questions, interrupting students to make a point, giving directions, telling students to perform tasks, drinking coffee in front of the class, giving grades, reprimanding students, and praising individual effort. These actions reinforce daily the teacher's prerogatives, making it plain who is in charge of the classroom. Yet, though this appears as a straightforward exercise of legitimate authority, it is the students who ultimately consent to be managed.

While teachers and students weekly engage in hundreds of behaviors that certify the teacher's power, there are, nonetheless, key discretionary decisions that touch the very core of the academic organization of instruction and the teacher's authority. Who, for instance, allots time for each of the many tasks assigned daily? Who determines what content will be studied? Who determines what instructional methods will be used? These and other decisions can be arrayed in a series of squares with those closer to the center representing the core of instructional authority. (See Figure 8-1).

Many teachers decide what will occur in each square, from seating charts for students, to grading assignments, to which students will knock dust from the erasers. Such teachers view cautiously student participation in any decision in the outer areas. At the beginning of this century, all decisions were made solely by the teacher. As progressive ideas about children's development and learning entered the thinking of educators, increased student talk, movement, and participation in the life of the classroom became professionally acceptable adjuncts to teaching.

Substantial numbers of teachers, concerned with maintaining order and limiting classroom noise, yet attracted to the new ideas about children and their development, struck compromises between what were viewed as essential teacher prerogatives (i.e., the inner core) and the new beliefs. Controlling students shifted from obvious coercive techniques—slaps, spankings, rapping of knuckles, threats of bodily harm—to indirect approaches that leaned heavily upon the teacher's personality and the budding relationships with students, but still sought the same order and distribution of power.[21]

Most experienced teachers, for example, establish student loyalty and compliance in the initial weeks of the school year. They can then count on students' consistently responding to their requests. In such a setting, a teacher who introduces such changes as rearranging desks, permitting students' to move around, establishing learning centers, or dividing pupils into groups is not threatened by such changes, since the teacher's authority, though less manifest, is still felt by students. Not only are such increments of student involvement in the classroom less menacing once the teacher's mandate is accepted by students, but they offer the best of both worlds: Social control of student behavior is maintained through the routines established by the teacher, but this occurs within an informal, relaxed atmosphere.[22]

Thus, John Dewey's observations about the limited penetration of child-

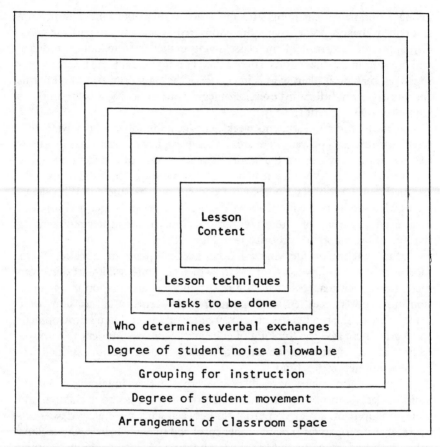

Lesson
Content

Lesson techniques

Tasks to be done

Who determines verbal exchanges

Degree of student noise allowable

Grouping for instruction

Degree of student movement

Arrangement of classroom space

FIGURE 8.1 *Classroom decisions made by the teacher. (I make no special case for the order in which I have arranged the decisions. The point is that the closer to the center one gets, the more the decisions touch the core of the teacher's authority.)*

centered practices in classrooms are consistent with the evidence I have gathered. So, also, is the notion that the hybrid forms of progressivism and open classrooms that emerged in this century may well have strengthened the teacher's authority in the elementary school, making it congruent with shifts in society's attitudes toward spanking, child-rearing, individual expression, and participation in decision making.

These answers to questions about the development of teacher-centered forms of progressivism and informal education derive from an explanation that I fashioned from six other arguments. How persuasive my explanation of situationally constrained choice is depends upon each reader's judgment based on the evidence I have arrayed, the logic of its presentation, its veracity, and the authenticity of my voice in presenting both argument and evidence. Let us assume that the argument, if not compelling, is at least plausible. What are its implications for current and future efforts to alter how teachers teach? The final chapter takes up this question.

CHAPTER 9

So What?
Implications for Policymakers, Practitioners, and Researchers

What have I found as a result of my investigation into teaching practices since the 1890s?

1. *Overall, the tradition of teacher-centered instruction continues to dominate elementary and secondary classrooms, but a hybrid version of student-centered practices, begun in the early decades of this century, has spread and is maturing.*

At least two forms of teacher-centeredness emerged as a consequence of determined efforts to introduce student-centered instruction on at least two occasions in this century. The pure form—whole-class instruction, teachers talking most of the time while students listen, a limited range of activities done by the entire class (such as using the textbook or worksheets), and little voluntary student movement—has persisted in the high school. The other form was a mixture of practices drawn from the two traditions of teaching. Such hybrids involved diverse classroom groupings for instruction and allowed for more informality in instructional talk, student movement, and organization of space than did the pure form. Hybrids occurred most often in elementary schools.

What appeared as a direction by 1940 emerged clearly as a pattern by the 1980s: teacher-centered instruction dominating high school classrooms and the increasingly frequent appearance of hybrids of instruction, mostly in elementary school classrooms but occasionally in the upper grades as well.

2. *High school instruction has largely remained teacher-centered.*

While academic subject matter in secondary schools has been revised frequently to link content to events in students' lives or to heighten interest, and although class discussions have become less formal and more frequent, the basic instructional sequences and patterns in the core academic subjects have remained teacher-centered since the turn of the century. A modest relaxation in formal relationships between high school students and their teachers has occurred, but dominant classroom practices across academic subjects have continued to be teaching-centered. There have been, of course, instances where teachers, occasional departments, and even entire schools have introduced hybrids of student-centered teaching in particular subjects, but they have been short-lived.

3. *A core of student-centered teaching practices has developed over the last century in a substantial number of elementary school classrooms.*

Some student-centered teaching practices have emerged in a considerable number of elementary school classrooms, especially in the primary grades. They include learning centers, tables clustered so that students can speak and work together, increased use of small groups for instruction, and relatively free student movement. Teachers who selected and adapted new ideas have seldom comprised more than a fourth of the staff in any district. Few teachers have used other student-centered approaches such as having students decide what to study and how much time to spend on particular topics or using learning centers as the primary means of instruction.

In trying to explain these developments in teaching practice over the last century, I constructed an explanation deeply rooted in the contexts (the outer context of cultural beliefs about knowledge, teaching, and learning and the inner context of school and classroom structures) that all teachers learn to negotiate when they enter and stay in classrooms. While contexts shape practice, they do not steer it. Teachers have a limited autonomy to choose what they teach and how they teach. Thus, situationally constrained choice helps to explain the practical pedagogy that teachers hammered out daily in their classrooms and also the substantial changes that many teachers decided to make in their routines.

What do these findings and interpretations of teaching practices over the past century have to do with those who make school policy, teach in classrooms, and systematically study the practice of schooling? Before answering the "so what?" question, I will review the puzzles, dilemmas, and paradoxes that face policymakers, practitioners, and scholars trying to improve teaching.

Federal, state, and local policymakers determined to improve public schooling face a paradox in viewing the teacher as both the cause of school problems and the indispensable source of a solution. In the view of some policymakers, teachers cause problems because many of them continue to teach math, for example, as a set of rules to memorize and apply; they may lack the motivation, knowledge, and skills to teach math for understanding. Yet those very teachers are essential to any improvement. Unless those teachers are enlisted in the effort to alter past practices, unless they understand new knowledge, unless their beliefs are transformed, and unless they develop new skills, little will improve in classrooms. Beyond the paradox of teachers' being both the problem and the solution, policymakers face a dilemma in having at their disposal limited tools for making desired classroom changes. Their only tools for penetrating the several layers that separate them from classroom teachers who make situationally constrained choices are policies harnessed to incentives and sanctions.

Among the many dilemmas practitioners face is having to decide, from time to time, whether to adopt all, part, or none of a new curricular or instructional policy in the midst of competing demands for their attention, energy, and time. In making such classroom choices, teachers determine how much value to attach to what they already do, how much any changes that they make will help their students, and how much energy and time they have to make the changes.

Researchers, in turn, face the predicament of deciding whether changes that teachers make in their classrooms are fundamental or incremental, and whether the evidence indicates that a policy has been implemented completely, moderately, or hardly at all. What does the researcher make of the teacher who says with confidence that she has made a 180-degree shift in her teaching of science to her fourth graders and cites as evidence the different materials and practices that she uses? Yet the researcher sees those very same new materials and practices being used in ways that undermine the purposes intended by designers of the reform.

For historians of schooling, these dilemmas and paradoxes facing policymakers, practitioners, and researchers are further complicated by the debates among historians themselves over the practice of their craft. Historians who write about institutions and the changes that occur within them, for example, still quarrel over how to write about the past, whether or not to explain it, and the wisdom of trying to connect the past they have recreated with the present and future.

Many historians relish the story. They construct narratives that unfold a complex chronicle of intertwined people and events, caring little for explaining what it all means. The pleasure is in the detail, the vignette, and the narrative; the story, as it is organized and unwinds, contains meaning. No more is necessary.

Other historians, and I am one of them, also use narrative but go further in analyzing events, people, and circumstances; they construct various explanations for institutional policies, changes, and actions. Most are anchored in individual actions (e.g., if it had not been for Franklin Delano Roosevelt, the Great Depression would have destroyed American democracy), the pervasive influence of the immediate setting upon individuals (e.g., to understand why early-20th-century asylums for the mentally ill became warehouses, one needs to examine the institution's goals, structures, and policies, and the roles and motives of the administrators and staff), or the underlying forces embedded in the larger environment (e.g., the capitalist economic system drives the political and social structures of the nation).

These modes of explanations are not, of course, mutually exclusive, and most historians have employed combinations of all three. Persisting debates over historical explanations are, more often than not, disputes over the relative weight given to one or another of these categories or the ignoring of a particular influence in explaining what happened. In trying to explain the constancy and change I observed in how teachers taught, I blended the individual, organizational, and societal into my explanation of situationally constrained choice.

Historians also debate the "uses of the past": that is, how to connect explanations of past events, policies, and changes to the present. Some scholars seek the pleasures of narrative and history for its own sake, avoiding at all cost the use of history as a rearview mirror to assist those who currently research, create, and implement policy. Other historians, closely allied to the social sciences, believe that solid generalizations mixed from the sand and gravel of facts will yield rock-hard truths about change and stability that policy researchers, analysts, and implementers may find useful now or in the future.

Yet other historians enjoy both telling stories and borrowing from the social sciences. They argue that policymakers, practitioners, and researchers already have strong views of the past uninformed by historical evidence, that they already have detailed notions of what changes have occurred and what has remained the same. Since these people help form and execute policy, historians ask, why not speak to them? I belong to this group of historians.[1]

In addressing academics, policymakers, and practitioners, this historical study of classroom instruction in public schools combines fact gathering, concept building, and narrative. My interpretations about constancy and change in how teachers taught are constructed out of the facts I have found, the concepts I have used, and the personal and professional experiences I have had as a policymaker, administrator, teacher, and scholar. I know the risks involved in projecting the present into the past. I know the dangers of tailoring versions of the past to fit the present. I know the traps of grafting personal values onto interpretations. I also know that others mining the same ore could just as easily have discovered different nuggets and ignored the gold dust that I found, perhaps even calling it fool's gold.[2]

Still, even given the risks of writing a history that walks the tightrope between the past and present, between facts and values, and that is intended for diverse audiences, what binds my fellow diggers and me is *how* we go about digging the ore and extracting what is valuable, how we discover facts, find varied sources, analyze evidence, and tell stories or construct arguments (or both), and how openly we tell our readers about our values and the limits of the evidence we use.

What also binds historians together is our common interest in analyzing change and stability. Because time is the sea historians swim in, we record and try to understand planned and unplanned changes, traditions that evolve, and the puzzling inertia that marks individual biographies, institutions, and societies. To policy researchers, public officials, and practitioners who implement policy, a history of how teachers taught that displays evidence of classroom changes and continuities offers a perspective that most scholars and policy actors lack, since they commonly rely on memories of their own experiences in classrooms or on contemporary data. In what ways, then, does this study of a century's constancy and change in teaching speak to diverse audiences about the persistent efforts to improve classroom instruction?

OVERALL IMPLICATIONS FOR THOSE WHO SEEK TO REFORM CLASSROOM TEACHING

In the past century of American schooling, there have been at least three national efforts to alter what occurs in classrooms. This study has concentrated upon the school reforms of the progressive decades at the turn of the 20th century, upon the brief decade of the mid-1960s to early 1970s, when informal education was promoted, and upon the state-driven reforms of the 1980s that, if anything, strengthened the tradition of teacher-centered instruction. These reform movements, especially the first two, aimed to break the hold of teacher-centered instruction upon American teachers. These movements contained far more policy talk than they did programs that altered what teachers did. Still, I documented that some changes had occurred.

In this study I argued that there were two traditions of teaching rooted in practices that were millennia old. While I have personal preferences, I have avoided judging the quality, value, or effectiveness of any instructional reform over the last century. Thus, I did not assume automatically that a proposed change was superior to the practice it was intended to replace. Nor did I assume that stable teaching practices were ineffective in getting students to learn and therefore should have been changed. I did assume, however, that there were organizational, economic, political, and social limits to any reforms aimed at altering classroom behavior. Those limits to reforming teaching practices became evident by the early 1990s and are embedded in my argument that teachers practice situationally constrained choice.[3]

For one thing, it is clear to me that as long as the public schools' dominant social role in the culture (i.e., to bolster the economy and national defense, to solve major social ills, and to select those students who can succeed academically) remains unchanged, and as long as schools remain organized as they currently are (as age-graded schools, with hierarchical authority flowing down from the top, etc.), teacher-centered instruction will remain pervasive but not unchallenged. Given the above caveats and extensive neoprogressive rhetoric, I do not expect, in the short term, any major shift by the majority of teachers to student-centered instruction. All of the above constraints are high fences to leap for reformers devoted to student-centered instruction.

I do expect that more and more teachers will slowly but deliberately incorporate into their repertoires various student-centered instructional practices, particularly ones that affect the informal relationships and climate of the classroom, thereby continuing the slow blending of the two teaching traditions. It became clear from the evidence I collected and analyzed that even with heavy curbs upon teacher autonomy many teachers, especially in elementary schools, still found room to make modest or even substantial changes in classroom organization. The steady growth of hybrid versions of these two traditions in each reform movement, particularly in the early grades of elementary schools, convinced me that teachers will continue to modify their teacher-centeredness and will move, albeit slowly, toward a more student-centered classroom organization.

These teacher-invented mixtures of teacher-centeredness and student-centeredness varied from classroom to classroom, from subject to subject, from school to school, and from district to district. Such mixtures seldom satisfied ardent reformers fighting for student-centered instruction. Slight modifications in routine practices appeared as failures to these reformers. Yet the steady increase in these hybrids in elementary schools is a clear trend that has emerged over the last 100 years. Without major shifts in the social role of public schooling or fundamental changes in organization structures, I would expect the trend to continue.

If these hunches prove accurate, what implications are there for policymakers, practitioners, and scholars?[4]

Implications for Policymakers

At least three basic questions face national, state, and district policymakers. First, what forms of public schooling and teaching are best for both children and society? Second, where should limited resources be directed? Third, what strategies should be pursued?

The first question—about the purpose of schooling—is seldom asked explicitly by national, state, or district policymakers and is rarely, if ever, connected to the forms of teaching. The ideas of Plato, St. Augustine, Rousseau, Adam Smith, John Mill, Jeremy Bentham, and John Dewey weave in and out of the assumptions that policymakers hold about the purposes of schooling but infrequently enter public discourse.

Mainstream policymaking about schooling in the 20th century is anchored in premises and a vision that encourage pragmatic, fair, and utilitarian policies—that is, policies intended first to serve efficiently the economic, social, and political purposes of the larger society, and next to serve equitably the largest possible number of children. Such policies get debated within the narrow range of these purposes when curricular issues (e.g., multicultural textbooks, vocational education, more arts in the curriculum, national exams) get discussed by professionals and touch the public nerve. Seldom, however, is the curriculum-in-use—that is, the actual content and pedagogy that teachers use—ever get examined in depth.

To the degree that school organization and teacher-centered instruction have in the past stressed and continue to stress the teacher as the sole source of intellectual authority in the classroom, student acquisition of certain bodies of knowledge, obedience to school-made rules, learning that is frequently tested through homework and exams, classroom competition and ranking of performance, and teaching that is mostly telling rather than listening—to that degree, the existing organization of the classroom serves the unexamined, implicit social purposes of schooling that policymakers pursue. Continued support of those purposes would call for policies that encourage incrementalism to improve existing teaching practices. No fundamental restructuring of teaching practice would be necessary.

Were policymakers deeply interested in pursuing forms of schooling that aimed at cultivating the intellectual, social, and economic powers of individual children while creating democratic communities in schools, they would see that current classroom organization discourages students from learning from one another, limits the growth of independent reasoning and problem solving, restricts opportunities for student decision-making at the classroom and school level, and largely ignores the contributions that the community can make to the students and that students can make to the community. To the degree that policymakers sought such ends, they would encourage the increase of hybrid forms of teaching and nudge schools to experiment with student-centered forms of instruction. Such policymakers would see that existing school organization and teacher-centered instruction would have to undergo fundamental alterations in the interlocking structures of school governance, the graded school, instruction and curriculum, and university linkages. Increases in mixtures of student- and teacher-centered instruction aimed at altering the classroom's organization could incrementally move a district toward transforming existing structures.[5]

To the second question of where to concentrate resources, I would answer, in the light of the historical evidence, that policymakers interested in strengthening teacher-centered instruction and resisting the spread of hybrids should continue policies that allocate more staffing, more funds, and larger facilities to high school. Such policies will ensure that teacher-centerdness will persist into the 21st century.

Policymakers interested in encouraging mixtures of student- and teacher-centered instruction should, on the contrary, allocate more resources to both teachers and pupils in elementary schools. According to the findings of this study, elementary schools offer a much higher rate of return in terms of teachers' implementing pure and hybrid versions of student-centered instruction than do high school.

The structural features of elementary schools offer a potentially rich arena for reform. Yet scant notice is paid to this level by those national and state policymakers who make the difference between dreamy intentions and fully funded programs. The results of this study are unambiguous, at least on the subject of how much teacher change is possible: The potential for change in the practical pedagogy that teachers have constructed is far greater in the lower grades than in high school classrooms.

Middle schools (units that bring together children ages 10 or 11 through 13 or 14) that have embraced elementary school-based approaches such as longer periods of instruction, teaching different subjects together (e.g., math and science, English and social studies), or having the classroom teacher advise students are also promising candidates for investment of resources to cultivate hybrids of student-centered teaching.

If the social purposes of high schools and their current structure, which is consistent with those purposes, persist, high schools will continue to be the graveyard of serious attempts to move classrooms toward student-centeredness. Throwing dollars and people at those institutions in an effort to create a student-centered pedagogy will work for some teachers (but not the majority), occasionally even for an entire school for perhaps as long as 3 to 5 years, but will ultimately fail because of the combined weight of the high school's social purposes, its organizational roles, structures, and processes that buttress those purposes, and deeply buried cultural attitudes toward knowledge and teaching.[6]

Regarding the question of strategies, there are many routes toward a system of schooling that ties together broad policies and classroom realities. After all, what policymakers do is look downward and figure out how they can tickle the system from the top (by adopting policies and procedures), in the middle (by supervising administrators in state and district offices), and at the bottom (by monitoring school principals and classroom teachers) to produce desired outcomes. There is no one best route. The choice of strategies depends upon the notions that federal, state and local policymakers hold about the social role of schools in the larger culture, their views of planned change, and the links among their notions, their beliefs about change, and their preferences regarding forms of classroom instruction. Amid the political and economic constraints within which they work, these notions and beliefs enter into the choices policymakers make. Their tools are policies, regulations, incentives, and sanctions. Federal, state, and district policymakers can establish and nurture the school-site conditions needed to implement their vision, especially if it is clear and endorsed by teachers. But they can do little else. Policymakers are limited by the actions of school administrators and classroom teachers. What strategies, then, make sense?

Historically, policymakers have pursued change strategies that have been incremental, piecemeal, and expedient—in a word, tinkering—although often the language used to describe modest additions has contained phrases that sound revolutionary. For example, public officials joined by corporate executives beat the drums in the 1980s for more desktop computers in classrooms because they would bring "radical" changes to classroom instruction. But placing computers in classrooms and training teachers to use them is no more than tinkering, since the basic structures of schooling remain as they are.

Not since the mid-19th-century introduction of the age-graded school, which doomed the one-room school and was a truly fundamental change in delivering schooling to masses of children, have top federal or state public officials or educational leaders in major policymaking roles had a *comprehensive* and *systematic* vision of fundamental changes to existing structures of schools and classroom instruction. There have been, of course, recommendations for fundamental changes that have been aimed at a particular school structure (e.g., parent-controlled schools, site-based management by teachers and principal, vouchers, open classrooms, multicultural texts, teacher education programs in the university) but have ignored the potential relationships among reforms. They are also enhanced, 21st-century versions of what already existed (e.g., reform proposals of the early 1990s, such as the nation's governors agreeing to six goals to reach by the next century).[7]

Policymakers who lean toward teacher-centered instruction as the preferred mode of teaching need only tinker with existing goals, structures, roles, and processes of schooling. Tougher curricula and textbooks for students, more tests, and similar measures continue the strategy of top-down policies pursued in trendsetting states such as California, New York, Florida, and Texas since the mid-1970s, or expand their reach to include the entire country through proposed national goals, exams, and curriculum tied to those exams, as occurred in the late 1980s. In the early 1990s, such highly touted reforms as "outcome-based education" and computerized curricular and instructional systems for schools strengthen current teacher-centered instructional practices.

For policymakers whose vision of schooling leans toward more student-centered instruction and alterations in the academic organization of the classroom, a top-down strategy sensitive to local differences that focuses on building the capacities of teachers to work together and blend teacher-centered and student-centered approaches in either elementary or secondary schools would make sense. Features such as cooperative learning and whole-language instruction, for example, encourage student-centered teaching practices and have been introduced into many elementary school classrooms. Such a strategy has a far greater likelihood of success than does one targeted at creating classrooms with wholly student-centered practices.[8]

For such a strategy to succeed, reforms aimed at altering teacher routines need to secure the teacher's commitment. Teachers need to be persuaded that a change will be better for children, that it will not undercut their authority, and that it can be adapted to the particular setting. Where modest changes have occurred, they have occurred because teachers have absorbed rival beliefs competing with existing ones.

I have argued that changing teachers' attitudes needs to be closely bound to tangible school and classroom help in putting new ideas into practice. Because most instructional reforms make increased demands upon the teacher's limited time and energy, help from outside the classroom is essential. While there are some Vivian Paleys, Eliot Wiggingtons, and Jaime Escalantes in the classrooms, most teachers, like other professionals, fall in the middle range and therefore need help in implementing any alteration in basic classroom practices. The instances I cited in discussing the earlier reform movements, such as the Washington, D.C., Advisory Network, Liaisons, and Innovation Teams, and New York City's Workshop Center for Open Education in the 1970s, permitted teachers to plan and talk together. Such institutions seem to be preconditions for modifying classroom routines. Current research on teacher collaboration and the literature on school-based improvement involving teachers buttress this point.[9]

Because policymakers use data to initiate and justify proposed and existing policies, they might profit from reconsidering their notions of what constitutes success in modifying classroom practice. Recall New York administrator Joseph Loftus's generous estimate in 1941 that 25% of the system's teachers had initiated activity methods "in some degree." Loftus hinted that he was proud of that percentage. He, in effect, acknowledged that it was hard to make teachers alter their daily practices, but asserted that many teachers had indeed moved toward student-centeredness. Yet how could he be proud with three quarters of the staff continuing in the dominant teacher-centered instructional patterns—approaches that he found wrongheaded?

In view of the powerful social, political, organizational, and cultural constraints on teacher behavior and the difficulty in capturing teachers' attention, 25% may well be viewed as a victory. That perhaps one out of four teachers incorporated some new practices into their repertoires suggests the influence of situationally constrained choice within classrooms. Such figures certainly would be a victory in other highly competitive arenas. If Nielsen television ratings, for example, register that large a viewing audience for a program, the show is judged a winner. Or, if a textbook publisher gains a 25% share of the school market, it has scored a coup. Direct mail executives would jump for joy over even a 5% response rate from recipients of their mailings.

The point is that judging the effectiveness of an instructional reform requires an acute awareness of the limits within which teachers work. The usual standards of defining the success of a reform in altering teaching practices need to be revised in the light of evidence demonstrating that large numbers of teachers invented and used mixed versions of teacher- and student-centered instruction.

Finally, federal and state policymakers might consider the linkages between university teacher education and what happens in classrooms. Again, for policymakers interested in continuing the dominance of teacher-centered instruction, little change need occur in the creaky, ill-coordinated relationships between the preparation of teachers and their entry into schools as novices. John Goodlad's studies of teacher education are devastating critiques of the conditions that prevail in the nation's colleges and universities for those preparing to teach.[10]

For policymakers interested in increasing the numbers of teachers who use student-centered approaches or blends of the two traditions, Goodlad and others offer coherent strategies for change in higher education. These scholars urge closer, integrated links between schools and colleges in order to reform schools and help teachers to teach differently.

Implications for Practitioners

Practitioners, too, make policy when they are asked to implement the decisions of others outside their classrooms. In deciding, for example, whether to adopt all, part, or none of a new curricular or instructional mandate approved by the district or state school board, teachers must consider the competing demands for their attention, energy, and time by the subjects they teach, the students who appear each day, and the continuing requirements of the school, district, and state.

What implications might this study's findings and interpretations have for them as classroom policymakers? First, the knowledge that for over a century other men and women in their occupation have wrestled with similar dilemmas puts in perspective the classroom choices of teachers in the 1990s. Teachers often ask, and have always asked, tough questions: What changes should I adopt in my classroom? How much of what I am expected to change can I actually change in the face of other demands? Will these changes enhance or hinder helping Janice and Joe while keeping the rest of the class on track? Will the proposed changes make it easier or harder to decide whether I cover the information that will be on the test today or spend time helping students understand the concepts involved? These hard choices, many of them involving unattractive trade-offs, derive from the very character of the organization within which teachers work and the roles that they are expected to play. Knowledge of how past generations of teachers coped with change at least removes the feeling of self-reproach, even failure, that often accompanies the practice of teaching; such knowledge offers an historical perspective that is often missing from teacher education and from the practical wisdom of the occupation.

Second, using the vocabulary of policymaking to discuss teachers in their classrooms is another way of saying that teachers are leaders. In previous generations many teachers were classroom leaders when they decided to make modest or even substantial changes in their daily practice. Using the language of policymaking and leadership in connection with teaching gives a very different tone to discussions among practitioners about what can and cannot occur in their classrooms. As the evidence shows, many teachers over the past century, faced with large classes, many responsibilities unrelated to teaching, and innumerable social and cultural constraints, took risks in initiating incremental and fundamental changes. Thus, many teachers, as solo practitioners, were indeed leaders in their isolated, self-contained classrooms in the age-graded school. That knowledge should reassure and encourage practitioners.

Even though the historical evidence of teacher leadership in classrooms is ample, note again that this leadership is nonetheless constrained. Teachers can invent and create, but only within certain limits imposed by organizational structures and by cultural values and beliefs. The margin of freedom that teachers enjoy in their situationally constrained choice may be small, but it is significant, as the historical evidence has demonstrated. Of course, that margin can expand or shrink, depending on whether administrators and policymakers see as their task the cultivation or repression of teachers' capacities to lead both inside and outside the classroom.

Finally, in studying the evidence of how teachers taught, practitioners can realize anew that reform talk applies not only to the state, district, and local school but also to their classroooms. Teachers can lead within their classroom, and, if they choose, also at the school, district, and state levels. Because the choices they have at the classroom are situationally constrained, teacher action at the school and district levels to, for example, lighten or remove organizational constraints can expand their autonomy within the classroom, creating even more opportunities for change. For this to occur, teachers at the school, district, state, or national levels need to agree collectively on what kinds of reforms they seek.

Implications for Researchers

The nature of this study and its findings also suggest many issues and directions that scholars of schooling may consider. I chose the four questions I pose here because they are especially thorny: Why do so few researchers investigate teaching practices? Is there a danger that studies of classrooms and schools will become teacher-centric and ignore students' voices? When has a change in teaching practice been implemented fully enough to be called a change, and who can determine that such a change has occurred? Are some hybrids better than others?

1. *Why do so few researchers investigate teaching practices?*
With the object of so many school reforms the transformation of teaching from what it is to what it ought to be, the scarcity of studies on how teachers have taught and do teach is surprising. Knowing what the common teaching practices are before trying to change them seems, at the least, a reasonable position from which to begin. Yet the scarcity of such studies is self-evident.

Barbara Finkelstein argues that most historians of education have studied the ideas of reformers and pioneers who have influenced schooling, and have either assumed that those ideas penetrated the classroom and shaped teaching practices or argued that they should have. She also points out that what happens in classrooms is a "silent history." Written sources such as student recollections, teachers' diaries, evaluation records, and student papers recapture the daily routines of thousands upon thousands of classrooms of a generation or even a century ago, but they are scattered in various local and state archives, in school basements, or in descendants' attics. Faced with the apparent inaccessibility of sources, scholars find popular textbooks, teaching manuals, superintendents' reports, and educational journals of the times far more accessible. Similarly, the enormous investment of time and money involved in visiting contemporary classrooms for extended periods often dissuades researchers from observing how teachers teach.[13]

As a consequence, the "how" of teaching has been neglected for the "what." When subject matter is emphasized over pedagogy, the effects of how something is taught get lost in the intense concentration upon content. The history of school reform has been marked by an intense preoccupation with curriculum because the community's values are displayed in choices of what should be learned in schools. But that preoccupation with content has diminished the crucial role of pedagogy in making content engaging or deadly, understandable or incomprehensible, and connected to or removed from the lives of students. Some researchers indirectly stress the power of pedagogy when they describe and analyze effective teachers whose personalities, harnessed to particular styles of instruction, influence students. Other investigators have shown that two teachers teaching the same course (even from the same textbook) end up teaching subject matter very differently.[14]

The "how" and the "what" of teaching and learning are married. To know one well and the other only marginally is to understand only partially what happens in classrooms.

A few historians have plunged into the swamp of district and school sources to locate personal accounts, documents, and records that might shed light on what teachers and students thought and did in long-forgotten classrooms. William Reese, William Johnson, and Lawrence Zilversmit, for example, are mining primary sources in their current work on 19th- and 20th-century schools and classrooms.

Future historians will have some advantages over current ones studying schools and classroom of the late 19th century and the early decades of this century. The slow accumulation of classroom ethnographies, studies of individual teachers and students, and schoolwide portraits since the 1950s will aid the next generation of historians seeking to understand teaching practices since the mid-20th century.[15]

Nonetheless, histories of teaching that use multiple classroom sources remain rare. Policy debates about what schools were like a generation or more ago or what students did in their classrooms in earlier times are seldom informed by historical scholarship. Notions of a "golden age" of teaching and learning persist. Historians do offer a perspective on change that social scientists and scholars in the humanities lack. By studying phenomena over time and the context within which events occur, we can see the quirks of the moment or what appear to be jolting changes as part of long-term trends or short-term rumblings. Such historical studies are needed.

Also needed are cross-institutional studies. Seldom do researchers examine the similarities and differences in teaching among public elementary and secondary schools, private schools, and colleges and universities. Superficial evidence suggests many similarities in teaching between, say university and secondary school instruction (whole-group instruction, lectures, infrequency of student questions, etc.). Yet university professors' freedom from the constraints faced by high school teachers would suggest far more variability in teaching practice than seemingly exists. Similarly, comparisons between teaching practices in all-black parochial schools and nearby all-black public schools might challenge prevailing views of private versus public schooling. Cross-institutional studies are yet another mirror for examining the nature of teaching.

Also, cross-national studies of pedagogy can suggest fruitful comparisons and contrasts. Studying elementary school classrooms in urban China and U.S. cities reveals cultural, organizational, social, and political differences. Yet in what respects is the teaching similar, and how is it different? A cursory review of evidence drawn from classrooms observations in European, African, Latin American, and Asian schools suggests similarities that cut across profoundly different cultures. Such evidence might raise intriguing questions for scholars, whether about the pervasiveness of particular teaching practices or, conversely, about their culture-bound nature.[16]

2. *Is there a danger that studies of classrooms and schools will become teacher-centric and ignore students' voices?*

Even though no flood of such studies is imminent, were they to increase, the answer would be yes. Although this inquiry into how teachers have taught since the 1890s is intended to be teacher-centric, I have pointed out what is missing from the study: information about classroom climate, the impact upon students of different forms of instruction, teacher-student relationships, and the students' perspective on teaching.

David Cohen raises the point of the absence of student perspectives on teaching and learning. It is easy to slip into believing that what teachers say students learned or think is the whole truth. A small but growing literature on student perspectives on what teachers taught and student misperceptions and misconceptions of knowledge suggests that another world of meaning exists within classrooms. Reading student-written 1-minute summaries of a class that I just taught or listening to students tell me what they learned from my class has jolted me more times than I care to recall. Without students' views of what occurred in their classes, only part of the story of classroom teaching is told.

If historians and social scientists who study schooling have difficulty in locating sources about teaching, the difficulties increase exponentially for uncovering what students felt, thought, and learned. As David Cohen points out, the materials are there, unused and undiscovered, but the questions that researchers must ask before seeking out sources have yet to be asked.[17]

3. *When has a change in teaching practice been implemented fully enough to be called a change, and who can determine that such a change has occurred?*

Researchers, like policymakers and practitioners, have great difficulty in wrestling with the ambiguity of change. One of the clear findings from research into organizational change is that a reform journeying from invention to adoption to implementation to incorporation into daily routine will get transformed in the process. Thus, if the design for a change in pedagogy gets modified as teachers implement it in their classrooms, has the reform occurred? And whose perspective on the change counts more: the researcher's or the teacher's? Thus far, the answer has been clear: The researcher's view of change counts far more among policymakers than the teacher's view.[18]

Deborah Ball, Suzanne Wilson, Penelope Peterson, David Cohen, and other researchers have investigated changes that elementary school teachers have made in teaching math. Their studies, which combined interviews and classroom observation and were cited in Chapter 7, pointed out the varied changes teachers made. A few teachers thoroughly immersed themselves and their students in trying to understand math rather than simply learning rules. A larger group selectively implemented portions of the approach and created a mixture of the old and new practices. A third, smaller group largely ignored the proposed changes. Did teachers change? Yes. Were the changes consistent with the intentions of the designers of math reforms? Yes and no. Were the changes meaningful to the teachers? Often, yes. To the researchers? Much less so. To the students? No one knows.[19]

Many reforms that researchers study aim at fundamental changes in pedagogy—for example, moving a math classroom from drill-and-practice to a setting where students are encouraged to estimate, work on real-life situations, think aloud about the problems they create, and question the teacher. So when researchers come into classrooms for a week, a month, or, in rare instances, a year and observe only fragments of the fundamental change in action, they may conclude that these are additions to former practices, not fundamental changes.

What complicates the task of researchers is that they often underestimate the impact of the workplace and prior constraints upon teachers and overestimate the power of the innovation to alter teaching and learning. Moreover, even when changes are made, researchers may imply that the changes teachers made were insignificant. That teachers even initiate incremental changes in the face of considerable constraints speaks of their strong impulses toward improvement. For many teachers, voluntarily switching textbooks, deciding to use a computer in a classroom, or introducing small-group instruction into a class once a week is a sharp departure from routine and therefore may be considered a substantial change. To researchers, however, who may have forgotten their own experience as teachers or never taught in public schools, such changes appear insubstantial or even trivial. Since researchers publish and most teachers do not, it is the researcher's voice that gets heard, not the teacher's. When one considers the places that researchers call home—universities—and considers the limited reach, slow pace, and questionable quality of organizational, curricular, and instructional change in those institutions, one might conclude that perhaps a touch of humility among scholars about the stubborn realities of classroom change might infuse more respect for what teachers face.[20]

4. *Are some hybrids better than others?*

I end with this question for researchers because it brings me back to a central finding of this study, namely, the tendency for teachers to create hybrids of teacher- and student-centered instruction, especially in the social relationships within the classroom.

All of this, however, avoids the issue of which hybrids are better. This question turns us again to the issue of effectiveness of instruction and can be answered in numerous ways. It may be useful to speak about researchers' apparent preferences for certain forms of instruction over others, preferences that spring from their core values, disciplinary perspectives, and experience.

For example, many researchers, particularly those who are cognitive psychologists or are strongly drawn to the insights generated by such scholars, have since the mid-1970s had great affection for forms of teaching that are thoughtful, engage students in active learning, explore ideas, combine different subjects, challenge student beliefs, and offer chances for students to be self-directed. Such scholars tend to be critical of forms of teaching that are less thoughtful, call for passive learning, focus on developing behavioral conformity, and are geared toward enabling students to score higher on standardized achievement tests.

Other scholars prefer forms of teaching that are highly structured, well-organized, and focused on building students' academic skills. And so on. Rather than continue to sketch out the range of ideological convictions about effective teaching among researchers, I will simply reiterate that researcher's notions about what is effective teaching need to be acknowledged openly as they strive to understand the nature of teaching and learning in classrooms. In short, no consensus can be reached about which forms of teaching are objectively more effective than others without (a) gaining a consensus on the role of public schooling in a democratic society and what students should learn and (b) dealing explicitly with scholars' personal teaching preferences.

Such a consensus has yet to be achieved either among researchers, practitioners, and policymakers or among the general public. Public discourse throughout the 1980s and in the early 1990s has vibrated between linking slipping test scores to the nation's eroding economic productivity and calling on the schools to provide essential social services to students and their families. There is, then, no answer that I can now offer on the worth of some hybrid forms of teaching over others other than the personal one I offered from my experiences as a teacher.

I end with an unanswered question a chapter that has explored the implications of this study's findings for policymakers, practitioners, and researchers. I have posed other questions and have answered some of them to the degree that the evidence permitted. Other questions have gone unanswered. Beyond questions and answers, however, is an attitude, a predisposition, among practitioners, policymakers, and scholars about improving schools. Does the evidence I offer in this study of constancy and change in teaching practices encourage pessimism or optimism about the future in the hearts and minds of key players in the game of classroom reform?

I can speak for myself. My impulses tend toward optimism. After all, one does not become a high school teacher, a superintendent, and a professor without believing strongly in improving schools. Yet I have never felt that my optimism soared unreasonably or was unanchored in realistic expectations. Unlike the Grand Academy of Lagado where Gulliver saw workers trying to extract sunshine from cucumbers, turning ice into gunpowder, and weaving cloth from spiderwebs, I have a cautious but nonetheless buoyant view of the possibility of improving schools.[21]

The data can, however, be easily interpreted as an unrelentingly pessimistic picture of failed attempts to fundamentally change teaching practices or yield anything beyond tatters of change that are at best marginal and at worst irrelevant. I do not interpret the data in this manner.

Another way of avoiding the trap of choosing between optimism and pessimism is to ask: What can schools and teachers do? Recall the comparison of schooling to farming, where the essential point is learning to work with an ancient, unchanging process of growth by building one's efforts around what seeds, plants, insects, and climate are likely to do. By understanding the nature and limits of this process, farmers can improve the yield of crops. But these organic forces, over which a farmer has limited control, have to be worked with, not ignored.

This study shows that schools and classrooms contain analogs of organic processes like seeds and climate—for example, organizational constraints and other factors—that need to be taken into account in order to improve what happens within school buildings. Self-contained classrooms and time schedules are made by human hands, not by wind, locusts, and drought. Yet until the handmade structures are fundamentally changed, they blow like a wind, endure like the land, and help create the outlines of a practical pedagogy. Reformers bent on channeling those "organic" forces need first to understand them.

I draw my optimism from these metaphors and from the findings of this study, because they suggest strongly that even within the seemingly unbendable structures of schooling built by previous generations a substantial minority of teachers made both incremental and fundamental changes in their teaching practices. Hybrids developed over time in many elementary school classes, for example. If more of these changes are to occur among teachers in their classrooms, if teachers' zone of discretion is to expand rather than contract, then the organizational conditions, the forms of education that teachers receive, and the occupational cultures within which they work must also change. That may be a fragile basis for feeling optimistic, but it gets closer, at least in the mind of one practitioner-scholar, to capturing realistically the conditions within which teachers work.

Appendix

The categories that I use to capture dominant instructional patterns are: classroom arrangements, group instruction, classroom talk, student movement, and classroom activities. I recognize that these categories in no way capture the totality of teaching. They are, at best, windows of the classroom; they are visible to observers. They describe the terrain of the classroom while accounting for some of the time that teachers and students spend together. And, most importantly, these categories are within the power of teachers to determine for their classrooms: how space should be arranged, who should talk, what homework to assign, where students should go within the room, etc.

The issue is whether or not certain patterns in these categories cluster together to create regularities in classrooms. I argue that they do. My reasons for arguing that the categories reflect regularities follow.

1. *Organization of space in the classroom.* If movable desks or student chairs are arranged in rows facing either the blackboard or teacher's desk then there is a high probability that the instruction is teacher-centered. The rationale for the assertion is:

a. Such an arrangement is intentional (except for the classrooms where desks were bolted to the floor). Furniture arrangement is seldom mandated by a school board, superintendent, or principal. The teacher decides (or accepts prevailing norms) how to use classroom space. Furniture placement, consciously or not, expresses the teacher's views of how best to teach, maintain order, and get students to learn.

b. When all students face the teacher or blackboard where directions, assignments, tests, or class recitation occurs, whole-group instruction is encouraged. Teacher-student exchanges gain higher priority and legitimacy than ones between students.

c. Surveillance is easier for a teacher with space arranged in this manner.

Threats to classroom order can be seen quickly and dealt with expeditiously.

d. Such a configuration of classroom space limits students' movement within a classroom to that which the teacher permits.

Note, however, that in the early decades of this century when desks were fixed to the floor, there were teachers who introduced student-centered practices into the classroom and ingeniously overcame that obstacle. Such furniture may have discouraged many teachers but it did not prevent some from altering their teaching practices. With movable desks and chairs, other arrangements became possible.

If desks are arranged into a hollow square, horseshoe, or tables scattered around the room, thus permitting students to face one another and talk, student-centered instruction becomes a much stronger possibility. But far more information about what happens in the classroom would be needed, since teacher-centered instruction can, and often does, occur in these seating arrangements (Getzel, 1974; Weinstein, 1979; Sommer, 1969).

2. Instructional grouping and classroom activities. If class space is organized into student-centered arrangements, e.g., tables and desks where students can face one another, carrels, or rug-covered area for a reading corner, then the researcher looks for evidence of student movement, student participation in verbal discourse, diverse grouping patterns, and the extent of project activities (or learning centers). Projects (a common term used in the 1920s and 1930s to describe a child-centered activity) and learning centers (a phrase used often in movements to install informal education after 1967) operated on the assumption that students can learn effectively as individuals or in small groups while making decisions independent of the teacher.

Thus, the external signs of a student-centered classroom would include furniture arrangements that encourage face-to-face exchanges and small group meetings; work stations in the classrooms (project areas or learning centers) where individual and small groups of students operate in a self-directed manner, and evidence of students moving about without securing the teacher's permission. The teacher's desk is no longer front and center; often, the room lacks a discernible front (Barth, 1972; Silberman, 1971; Busis, et al., 1976; Perrone, 1972, 1977).

I would add that the simple presence of a project corner or learning centers, like tables scattered around the room, does not make a classroom student-centered. Much of the literature on such settings in the 1920s and 1970s focused upon a process of learning and the teacher's grasp of the underlying principles in child development and learning. Seating arrangements, projects, and centers are visible signs of student-centered instruction, but in no way guarantee that the process will occur or that the teacher understands the principles involved. To suggest that only the physical arrangements and available artifacts described and depicted in written accounts and photographs represent what a William Kilpatrick or Harold Rugg of the 1920s espoused, and a Lillian Weber and Vito Perrone of the 1970s advocated, would trivialize complex processes.

3. *Classroom Talk.* The evidence that teachers talk far more than students in classrooms dates back to Romiett Stevens' work at the turn of the century. That pattern of teacher talk consuming most of the instructional discourse in the form of telling, explaining, and questioning is a proxy for a teacher-centered classroom. Student talk in such a classroom is generally confined to responding to content questions from the teacher, asking procedural questions (e.g., will it be on the test?), and covert conversations with classmates. The teacher determines what questions have to be asked, who should be asked, and the quality of the student response. It is a classroom discourse that contains implicit rules that students come to learn over time (Mehan, 1979; Stevens, 1912; Hoetker and Ahlbrand, 1969).

These categories, then, contain the pieces that teachers arrange into instructional patterns. Organizing the classroom space, grouping for instruction, classroom talk, student movement, and classroom activities as they materialize in schools point to a variety of teaching patterns. These categories, I believe, can extract from the data dominant instructional patterns in classrooms.

NOTES

INTRODUCTION

1. Cuban, 1979a.
2. I take up the question of how historians have viewed stability and change in schools and classrooms in Chapter 1.
3. I drew these ideas from Watzlawick, Weakland, & Fisch, 1974. In their book, they use the term "first-order" for changes that I call "incremental" and "second-order" for changes that I call "fundamental."
4. Atkin & House, 1981; Stake & Easley, 1978; Suydam et al., 1977. For other instances of incrementalizing fundamental reforms, see Wolcott, 1977; Popkewitz, Tabachnik, & Wehlage, 1982; Malen & Hart, 1987; Edelfelt, 1972.
5. Spindler & Spindler, 1988.
6. Powell, Farrar, & Cohen, 1985.
7. Meyer, 1986; Meyer & Rowan, 1978. See also Cuban, 1992.
8. James, 1958; Katz, 1968; Jackson, 1986.
9. The rationale for using these indicators is in the Appendix.
10. Stephens, 1967, p. 11. David Tyack pointed out to me that progressive reformers Ellwood Cubberley and Franklin Bobbitt used both metaphors. For other images of schools and classrooms, see Marshall, 1989; Firestone, 1980.
11. Fischer, 1970, p. 134.

CHAPTER 1: TEACHING AT THE TURN OF THE CENTURY: TRADITION AND CHALLENGE

1. Fuerst, 1900, pp. 106–107.
2. Cremin, 1961; Tyack, 1974; Finkelstein, 1970. Finkelstein revised her dissertation and included essays on the nature of schooling and historians' treatment of that schooling in *Governing the Young: Teacher Behavior in Popular Primary Schools in 19th Century United States* (New York: The Falmer Press, 1989).
3. *Report of the Commissioner of Education, 1890–1891* (Washington, D.C.: Government Printing Office, 1894), Vol. 1, p. 43 and Vol. 2, p. 792; *1900–1901* (Washington, D.C.: Government Printing Office, 1902), Vol. 1, p. xi; *1911* (Washington, D.C.: Government Printing Office, 1912), Vol. 2, pp. xxvi, xxviii.
4. Department of the Interior, Biennial Survey of Education, 1920–1922 (Washington, D.C.: Government Printing Office, 1924), Vol. 1, pp. v, 2, 4; Bennett, 1940, pp. 41–43, 125.
5. Report of the Commissioner of Education, 1911 (Washington, D.C.: Govern-

ment Printing Office, 1912), Vol. 2, p. xxix. For the lower levels of state spending on black students and teachers as compared to spending on whites, see Harlan, 1968, pp. 11–27; DuBois & Dill, 1911.

6. Finkelstein, 1970, pp. 22, 86.

7. Finkelstein, 1974, pp. 81–82, 84.

8. Finkelstein, 1970, pp. 174–175, 179; Kaestle, 1983. The shift from urban monitorial schools to age-graded schools suggests that many changes did, indeed, occur in how teachers handled students' recitation. Use of young monitors listening to small groups of students recite gave way to whole-group instruction. See, for example, David Hamilton's (1989) chapter on British and Scottish schools moving from the monitorial model of Joseph Lancaster to "simultaneous" instruction in self-contained classrooms under the eye of one teacher in *Towards a Theory of Schooling*. William Johnson is completing a history of teaching and teacher education in Maryland in the 19th and 20th centuries. His work points out that teachers dramatically adjusted their manner of instruction in response to the constant student turnover and large numbers of students they faced in moving from monitorial schools to multiclassroom buildings in mid-19th-century Baltimore.

9. Fuerst, 1900, pp. 8, 132. For a description of teaching types in rural schools at the turn of the 20th century, see Wayne Fuller (1982), *The Old Country School*.

10. The Frances Benjamin Johnston collection of photographs is lodged at the Library of Congress; other photographs are reproduced in Tyack, 1974; Tyack & Hansot, 1990; and Davis, 1976.

11. Rice, 1969.

12. ibid., pp. 139–140.

13. ibid., p. 32.

14. Cubberley, 1916, pp. 116, 118.

15. ibid., p. 119.

16. Thayer, 1928, pp. 7, 9–12.

17. ibid., p. 12.

18. Folger & Nam, 1967, pp. 84–85; Rice, 1969, pp. 58–59, 76, 159–160.

19. *Report of the Educational Commission of the City of Chicago, 1898* cited in William Bagley, "The Textbook and Methods of Teaching," National Society for the Study of Education, *The Textbook in American Education*, Part 2 (Bloomington, IL: Public School Publishing Co., 1931, p. 8; see also various issues of *New York Teachers Monographs* (1900–1904) in which teachers describe how they use their courses of study.

20. Hoffman, 1981; see selections from Margaret Haley's speech to the National Education Association in 1904; selection from an anonymous teacher in *Atlantic Monthly* (July, 1896).

21. Krug, 1964, pp. 5, 14, 169; Sizer, 1964, pp. 5, 39, 53; Tyack & Hansot, 1990, p. 114.

22. Sizer, 1964, pp. 44, 46; New York State Department of Education, p. 55.

23. Sizer, 1964, pp. 45, 53; see also Buffalo survey.

24. Sizer, 1964, p. 66; Tyack, 1978, p. 3.

25. Dayton, Ohio, Public Schools, 1896, pp. 13, 49; insert after p. 250.

26. Dayton, Ohio, Public Schools, 1896, p. 250.

27. Dayton, Ohio, Public Schools, 1896, pp. 13, insert after pp. 250, 274.

28. ibid., pp. 58–59.

29. ibid., pp. 59–60.

30. ibid., p. 64.

31. ibid., p. 65.

32. ibid., pp. 76–77.

33. Romiett Stevens, 1912.

34. ibid., pp. 11, 15–17.

35. ibid., p. 11.

36. ibid., p. 25.

37. Buffalo survey, p. 127.

38. ibid., pp. 132–133.

39. ibid., p. 134.

40. ibid., pp. 140–142.

41. ibid., p. 138.

42. Callahan, 1962, chaps. 1–5; Tyack, 1974, pp. 39–59.

43. Thayer, 1928, p. 7.

44. Thayer, 1928, pp. 7–8; see Dearborn (1925, pp. 159–169) for 13 lessons taken from Sheldon's *Elementary Instruction.*

45. Dearborn, 1925, p. 97; Cremin, 1961, p. 129.

46. Patridge, 1889, p. 657; Campbell, 1967, p. 78; Cremin, 1961, p. 130, citing an 1879 report by Parker; Heffron, 1934, p. 25.

47. Marler, 1965, p. 108; Campbell, 1967, p. 119.

48. Marler, 1965, p. 179; Campbell, 1967, pp. 130–132.

49. Marler, citing a report from J. M. Greenwood, "A Visit to Colonel Parker's School in December, 1892."

50. Dewey, "In Memoriam, Colonel Wayland Parker," June, 1902 in *Elementary School Teacher and Course of Study,* Vol. 2, 1902, pp. 704–708.

51. Mayhew & Edwards, 1936, pp. 80–84.

52. ibid., pp. 84–85.

53. ibid., pp. 228–232.

54. ibid., p. 405.

55. ibid., p. 395.

56. Rice, 1969, p. 184.

57. ibid., pp. 207, 229.

58. The Gary schools during Wirt's tenure became a showplace of pre–World War I progressivism. Merging the impulse toward economy with the child-centered school, Wirt created student communities out of schools by scheduling students in different parts of a school building. Half of the school met in regular self-contained classrooms and the other half in manual arts shops, on playgrounds, in the gymnasium, or in other spaces. Then the students would switch sites. Called "platoon schools," Wirt's innovations were promoted by journalists and aroused great interest in many school districts across the nation.

Because of the political controversy triggered by the Gary Plan's abortive implementation in New York City in 1917, the Gary School Board and Superintendent Wirt asked a foundation to conduct an impartial survey of Gary Plan schools. The survey team, directed by Abraham Flexner, inspected each of the innovations, including classroom instruction, and produced an eight-volume report. Finding much merit in the Gary Plan, Flexner nevertheless concluded that classroom instruction in the academic subjects taught in the grades from elementary through high school was mechanical. See Flexner & Bachman, 1918, pp. 77, 79, 80–83, 160. For the long-term effects of Wirt's efforts, see W. Lynn McKinney and Ian Westbury, "Stability and Change: The Public Schools of Gary, Indiana, 1940–1970" in William Reid and Decker Walker (eds.), *Case Studies in Curriculum Change* (London: Routledge and Kegan Paul, 1976); for a detailed description and analysis of the social context of Gary, Indiana, from the early 1900s through the 1960s, see Ronald Cohen, *Children of the Mill* (Bloomington, IN: Indiana University Press, 1990).

59. Dewey & Dewey, 1915, preface; see also Nearing, 1915.

CHAPTER 2: BEHIND THE CLASSROOM DOOR: NEW YORK, 1920–1940

1. DeLima, 1925, pp. 21–31. All quotations are from DeLima's observation. I have paraphrased the description of the classroom.

2. Tyack, *One Best System*, pp. 182–98; Katz, 1971, pp. 117–120; Cremin, *Transformation of the School*, pp. 179–239. See also Graham, 1967, ch. 4; Cohen, 1964, ch. 1–4; Bowers, 1969, chs. 1–4; Tyack & Hansot, 1982, pp. 105–166.

3. Graham, 1967, p. 46.

4. Graham, 1967, chs. 3–4; DeLima, 1925, chs. 4, 9; Cremin, *Transformation of the School*, pp. 201–34.

5. *Time*, October 31, 1938, p. 31.

6. Historians, however, disagree upon the degree of progressive ideas' impact upon classroom practice. Of the dozen historians who have written about progressivism and schools, at least six have dealt with the issue of changes in teaching practice. Lawrence Cremin, Joel Spring, and Diane Ravitch assert, for very different reasons, that teaching behavior changed.

Cremin, in *The Transformation of the School* (1961), cites Robert and Helen Lynd's "Middletown" studies in 1925 and 1935, to illustrate how a conservative strain of progressivism in Muncie, Indiana, classrooms might have been typical of schools in the pedagogical mainstream, noting that for every Winnetka there were probably schools "that must have taught McGuffey and little else well into the thirties." Nonetheless, he goes on to state that the reformers left unmistakable footprints in classrooms.

> The character of the classroom changed markedly, especially at the elementary level, as projects began to compete with recitations as standard pedagogical procedure. Students and teachers alike tended to be more active, more mobile, and more informal in their relationships with one another. (pp. 305, 307)

Cremin modified this view in *American Education: The Metropolitan Experience, 1876–1980* (1988), in which he reviewed the research on classroom practices during the progressive decades and concluded that the "language of education probably changed more rapidly than the practice of education, and small, specific, concrete changes in practice tended to be adopted more rapidly than larger, more general ones" (p. 239).

In *Education and the Rise of the Corporate State* (1972), Joel Spring traces the movement of the ideas of Dewey, Kilpatrick, and Colin Scott on groupwork into classrooms as evidence of elite social groups' imposing their views upon schools and classroom practices. Spring isolates specific teaching methods: the "socialized recitation," where students assume the role of teacher and review the lesson; the project methods; and other group activities in the classroom. To demonstrate their impact upon the classroom, Spring cites the abundance of articles on these methods, the books written by advocates of each, and the appearance of courses on these topics in teacher education curricula. "Group learning experiences in the form of cooperative projects and socialized recitations," he concludes, "prepared the individual to be what David Riesman called in later years 'other directed'" (pp. 49–61). Spring modified his views in *The American School, 1642–1985* (1986). "At times," Spring concludes, "there has been little relationship between the expressed goals of education and actual educational practices. . . . Elites and educational leaders might have wanted the school to expand as a social agency to provide order and discipline and training and control of future workers, but these desires were often countered by students and parents who wanted to use the schools as a means of gaining upward mobility and greater political power and by teachers who had other social objectives. Therefore, although the educational system may have been structured to exert social control, that goal may have been modified by other social forces" (p. 181).

Diane Ravitch claims in *The Troubled Crusade: American Education, 1945–1980* (1983) that by the 1940s "the ideals and tenets of progressive education had become the dominant American pedagogy" (p. 43). For evidence Ravitch leans heavily upon the ideas of progressive educators, the widespread revision of official curricula, and a series of dissertations written at Teachers College during and immediately after the height of progressive school reforms in the 1930s and 1940s documenting changes that had occurred in schools (see pp. 43–80 and citations on pp. 333–336).

Dissent from these views of reformers' impact upon teaching practice comes from economists Samuel Bowles and Herbert Gintis and historians Michael Katz, David Tyack, and Arthur Zilversmit. In *Schooling in Capitalist America* (1976), Bowles and Gintis argue that a coalition of business leaders and liberal professionals spearheaded successful reforms that changed the public schools' administration and curriculum (for example, the comprehensive high school, standardized testing, ability grouping, vocational education, and the concentrating of authority in school professionals). However, they say, "the schools have changed little in substance in the exchange between teachers and students." Because pedagogical reformers lacked popular support and avoided criticizing corporate capitalism, Bowles and Gintis argue, they "worked in vain for a humanistic and egalitarian education." No direct evidence of classroom instruction is offered except for what other researchers cited (pp. 43, 181, 200).

Michael Katz argues in *Class, Bureaucracy, and Schools* (1971) that instructional reform stopped at the classroom door because the movement itself was essentially conservative in outlook and aimed at bureaucratic changes. Katz refers to Robert & Helen Lynd's *Middletown* to support his arguments. He does acknowledge that historians cannot learn what happened in schools by studying what leading theorists wrote and said. Whether teaching changed during the progressive years, Katz wrote in 1971, cannot yet be answered by historians (pp. 113–25).

David Tyack shares a similar perspective on how bureaucracy impeded change in teaching practice. In the *One Best System* he surveyed progressive reform and its consequences, both anticipated and unanticipated, between 1890 and 1940. Distinguishing among the varied strains of progressivism, Tyack described the success administrative progressives had in changing the structure and governance of public schools. Coalitions of professors, superintendents, foundation executives, and lay reformers possessing a vision of a "one best system" based upon scientific school management changed the landscape of American schooling through the strategic use of formal surveys of school systems, writings, conferences, and close contact with networks of influential educators. Reformers did seek to eliminate inefficient classroom practices such as a uniform course of study, whole group instruction, and formal recitation, according to Tyack (pp. 126–198). Using more primary sources on schools and classrooms than other researchers studying this period, Tyack drew on city school surveys, teacher accounts, newspaper articles, cartoons, and autobiographies to conclude that the dreams of Dewey and his followers about exciting classrooms for children had foundered on the very successes of the administrative progressives, especially in the cities:

> A gifted teacher in a one-room school house might alone turn her class into Dewey's model of social learning, but changing a large city system was more difficult for Dewey's ideas of democratic education demanded substantial autonomy on the part of teachers and children—an autonomy which . . . teachers commonly lacked. Predictably, the call for a "new education" in urban school systems often brought more, not less red tape and administration, more forms to fill out and committees to attend, more supervisors, new tests for children to take, new jargon for old ideas. The full expression of Dewey's ideal of democratic education required fundamental change in the hierarchical structure of schools—and that was hardly the wish of those administrative progressives and their allies who controlled urban education. (pp. 197–198)

In subsequent research, Tyack, Elisabeth Hansot, and Robert Lowe have examined classrooms in studies of the effects of the Great Depression upon schooling. In *Public Schools in Hard Times: The Great Depression and Recent Years* (1984), they document how progressive rhetoric on child-centered pedagogy hardly penetrated most classrooms (pp. 163–167).

Prior to my study, Arthur Zilversmit had been the only historian to focus upon classroom changes in order to determine how widespread progressive practices were in American elementary schools. His verdict: They were not.

Zilversmit relied upon three indicators of acceptance of progressive pedagogy. First, he argued, the curriculum of pre-1940 teacher training institutions should be expected to mirror the extent of instructional reform since a skilled, alert, and knowledgeable teacher is essential to a progressive classroom. In three national surveys of teacher education curricula, he found that progressive ideas had made only minimal inroads into normal and college training courses of study. Second, Zilversmit examined classroom furniture. Progressive educators took as a given the importance of movable desks and chairs for flexible seating and classroom workspace, yet, as Zilversmit pointed out, in 1934 stationary school desks still accounted for almost 40% of new desks sold, not to mention the millions of old desks firmly bolted to the floor. Third, the mental health of children, he argues, was a serious concern of progressive educators, committed as they were to the whole child. Yet, according to Zilversmit, school systems hired few specialists (i.e., social workers and school psychologists) to promote mental health.

For evidence on what occurred in the classroom, Zilversmit relied upon the Regents' Inquiry, an intensive evaluation of New York state schools between 1935 and 1938. Using two of the 12 volumes, he quotes extensively from each one's conclusions about the traditional instruction that evaluators found in urban, rural, and suburban classrooms across the state. He concludes that the progressive ideas of the child-centered school left few marks on elementary schools (Zilversmit, 1976, pp. 252–261).

The research cited above and this study challenge the premise that progressive ideas heavily influenced teaching practices. For scholars inquiring into what happened in classrooms, the evidence used has been sparse and leans heavily upon the *Middletown* research or selected studies. Moreover, historians trying to assess the spread of progressive practices in classrooms often take an all-or-nothing approach, and, except for Zilversmit, ignore the critical point of the extent of penetration.

7. New York [City] Board of Education, *Thirty-Second Annual Report of the Superintendent of Schools (New York: Board of Education, 1930), p. 485; New York [City] Board of Education, The First Fifty Years: A Brief Review of Progress, 1898–1948* (New York: Board of Education, 1949), p. 86. The last two comparisons about the size of the school system are mine.

8. Cohen, 1964; Ravitch, 1974; Ravitch & Goodenow, 1981.

9. Cohen, 1964, p. 153.

10. On Maxwell as superintendent, see Abelow, 1934; Berrol, 1968; Ravitch, 1974, pp. 111–186.

11. *Who's Who in America, 11,* 1921, p. 895; New York [City] Board of Education, 1949, p. 92; Cohen, *Progressives & Urban School Reform,* p. 110.

12. New York [City] Board of Education, *Thirtieth Annual Report of the Superintendent of Schools* (New York: Board of Education, 1928), p. 53.

13. See New York [City] Board of Education, *Progress of the Public Schools, 1924–1929* (New York: Board of Education, 1929); O'Shea, 1927, pp. 99–103.

14. Cohen, 1964, pp. 129–132.

15. Cohen, 1964, pp. 159–160. While it is beyond the scope of this study, Campbell's embrace of the Activity Program remains an intriguing puzzle that deserves exploration: Why does a superintendent who has characterized himself as an educational conservative decide, in the midst of economic retrenchment, to launch the largest experiment ever undertaken in the nation's history to reform a city's elementary public school curriculum and instruction?

16. Snyder, "A Stupendous Schoolhouse Problem," *American School Board Journal,* 66 (February, 1923), pp. 59–61; also see same journal volume 65 (October, 1922), pp. 60–61.

17. New York (City) Board of Education, *All The Children,* 1935–1936 (New York: Board of Education, 1936), p. 120.

18. *New York Times,* May 18, 1930, p. 9.

19. New York (City) Board of Education, *Thirty-Third Annual Report of the Superintendent of Schools, 1930–1931* (New York: Board of Education, 1931), p. 615.

20. Campbell, 1935, p. 139; *Thirty-Eighth Annual Report,* 1935–1936, p. 83.

21. *Report of Survey of Public School System, City of New York,* 1924 (New York: Board of Education, 1929), p. 306.

22. ibid., pp. 1265–1292.

23. ibid., pp. 1292–1296, 1309.

24. *The First Fifty Years,* pp. 94–95.

25. O'Shea, "Progress of Public Schools," pp. 29–31; New York [City] Board of Education, 1949, p. 95; "Report of the Investigation of Regents Examinations by the First Assistants' Committee," *High Points,* 21 (December, 1939), pp. 14–29; "Report of the Regents Examination Committee," *High Points,* 22 (April, 1940), pp. 8–16.

26. *Twenty-Eighth Annual Report,* 1925–1926, pp. 176–177.

27. New York (City) Board of Education, Junior High School Report Card, 1925; *The Handbook of Evander Childs High School, 1927–1928,* pp. 124.

28. *High Points,* 3 (December, 1921), pp. 30–1; *Practical Suggestions For Teachers* (Bronx), 1926, pp. 28–31; *High Points,* 12 (October, 1930), pp. 52–55; *High Points,* 14 (April, 1932), pp. 44–48.

29. New York Principals Association, *The Principal,* November 14, 1921, (n.p.)

30. New York (City) Board of Education, *The Teachers' Handbook: A Guide For Use in the Schools of the City of New York* (New York: Board of Superintendents, 1921), p. 27.

31. ibid., pp. 22–31.

32. *Survey,* 1924, pp. 841–849.

33. Tenenbaum, 1940, pp. 28–29.

34. The comparison with driving and rules for the road comes from Barr & Dreeben, 1977, p. 114.

35. Berrol, 1981, pp. 108, 110; Ravitch, 1974, p. 169.

36. Tyack, 1974, p. 231.

37. Ravitch, 1974, p. 234; Berrol, 1981, p. 106.

38. Covello, 1958; Montalto, 1981, pp. 69–75; New York City Board of Education, *All the Children, 43rd Annual Report, 1941–42* (New York: Board of Education, 1942), p. 16.

39. Jersild et al., 1939, p. 166; Loftus, 1940, p. 117.

40. *The Activity Program: The Report of a Survey* (Albany, New York State Department of Education, 1941), pp. 20–21.

41. Loftus, 1936, p. 2.

42. *The New York Times.* July 9, 1941.

43. Loftus, 1940, p. 117.

44. Jersild, et al., 1941, pp. 299, 301.

45. ibid.

46. Jersild, 1939, p. 196.

47. *The Activity Program: Report of a Survey,* p. 47.

48. ibid., p. 41.

49. ibid., p. 53.

50. ibid. See also Tyler, 1976, pp. 36–37.

51. Morrison, 1943, p. 28; *All the Children, 1940–1941,* p. 62.

52. *The New York Times,* May 18, 1930, p. 9.

53. ibid., February 16, 1940, p. 2. Also see the use of the word "progressive" in Superintendent O'Shea's Progress of The Public Schools, 1924–1929.

54. New York (City) Board of Education, *Exploring a First Grade Curriculum* (New York: Bureau of Reference, Research, and Statistics, 1947), foreword pp. 1–7, 86–90.

55. *Activity Program: Report of a Survey,* p. 143.

56. See, for example, "An Experiment With the Dalton Plan in the Wadleigh High School," *Survey,* 1924, pp. 205–207; *High Points,* 9 (March 1927), pp. 26–27.

57. Briggs, 1935, pp. 745–752.

58. Rosenthal, 1940, pp. 21–39.

59. ibid.

60. ibid., pp. 31–39.

CHAPTER 3: BEHIND THE CLASSROOM DOOR: DENVER, 1920–1940

1. Mira Scott Frank, "Dedication of Valverde Elementary School," mimeo, 1951, n.p.

2. *Taxpayers' Review,* October 12, 1934.

3. *Who's Who in America, 1936–1937,* 19 (Chicago: Marquis Co., 1937), p. 1814; Denver Public Schools, "Classroom interests," April 21, 1936, p. 3; Threlkeld, 1937, pp. 164–166.

4. School District of Denver, *Twenty-Eighth Annual Report of Superintendent of Schools, 1930–1931* (Denver, Colorado, 1931), p. 45; *Thirty-Eighth Annual Report, 1940–1941,* p. 63; *Twenty-Sixth Annual Report, 1928–1929,* pp. 33–36.

5. *Twentieth Annual Report, 1922–1923,* p. 64; Denver Public Schools, *School Review,* June, 1934, p. 3.

6. U.S. Office of Education, *Statistics of City School Systems, 1933–1934,* Bulletin, 1935, No. 2 (Washington, D.C.: Government Printing Office, 1936), p. 6.

7. Newlon, 1917, p. 267.

8. ibid., p. 266.

9. Denver Public Schools, *Denver Program of Curriculum Revision,* Monograph No. 12 (Denver Board of Education, 1927), pp. 17–21; Newlon & Threlkeld, 1926, pp. 231–233.

10. *Denver Program of Curriculum Revision,* p. 14; Newlon & Threlkeld, 1926, p. 232.

11. *Denver Program of Curriculum Revision,* pp. 22–27.

12. ibid., p. 28.

13. ibid., pp. 30–31.

14. Denver Public Schools, "General Information and Courses: Senior High School Courses of Study," 1929 (Denver, 1929), p. 28.

15. Newlon & Threlkeld, 1926, p. 235.

16. Denver Public Schools, *School Review,* March, 1929, p. 2.

17. *Thirty schools tell their story,* 1942, p. 146.

18. See chapter on Denver schools in *Thirty schools tell their story,* 1942, pp. 146–212, and Spears, 1948, pp. 243–273.

19. Spears, 1948, pp. 268–269.

20. Denver Public Schools, "North High School Master Schedule, 1938–1939;" also the 1938 and 1939 *Thunderbolt* and *Viking,* student yearbooks for Manual Training and North High Schools, respectively.

21. Denver Public Schools, "Handbook for the Application of Progressive Education Principles to Secondary Education," mimeo. September 1936, pp. 45–46, 50.

22. Giles et al., 1942, 2, pp. 320–328.

23. Cremin, 1961, pp. 253–256.

24. Denver Public Schools, "Classroom Interests," January, 1934, p. 11.

25. East High School Core Classes. "Our Education," 1938, pp. 12–13.

26. *Thirty schools tell their stories,* 1942, p. 182.

27. Cushman, 1938, pp. 316–317.

28. *Thirty schools tell their story,* 1942, p. 210.

29. North High School. "Master Schedule," 1938–1944, mimeo; East High School. "History of East High School," 1948, pp. 112–113.

30. *Denver Post,* October 13, 1954, p. 25.

CHAPTER 4: BEHIND THE CLASSROOM DOOR: WASHINGTON, D.C., 1920–1940

1. District of Columbia. *Report of Board of Education, 1921–1922* (Washington, D.C.: Government Printing Office, 1922), pp. 96, 97, 103.

2. *Who's Who in America, 1936–1937,* 19 (Chicago: Marquis Co., 1937), p. 230.

3. *Report of Board of Education, 1921–1922,* p. 137.

4. *Report of Board of Education, 1929–1930,* p. 71; Report of Board of Education, "School Achievements in Twenty Years," June 30, 1941, pp. 106–108.

5. *Report of Board of Education, 1910–1911,* p. 35.

6. Garnet C. Wilkinson, "Washington is Easily the Foremost Center of Negro Education in America," *School Life,* cited in Constance Green, *The Secret City* (Princeton, N.J.: Princeton University Press, 1967), p. 211.

7. Hundley, 1965; Thomas Sowell, "Black Excellence: A History of Dunbar High School," *Washington Post,* April 28, 1974, p. C3.

8. Frazier, 1967, pp. 100–111; Borchert, 1980, pp. 146–150.

9. Green, 1967, pp. 245–246.

10. Frazier, 1967, p. 97.

11. *Report On Survey of the Public School System of the District of Columbia by the Bureau of Efficiency, 1928* (Washington, D.C.: Government Printing Office. 1928), pp. 50–5; Strayer, 1949, p. 388.

12. Strayer, 1949, pp. 401–403.

13. *Report of Board of Education, 1929–1930,* p. 107; Strayer, p. 444.

14. *Bureau of Efficiency Survey,* 1928, p. 69.

15. ibid., p. 70; Strayer, 1949, pp. 439–441.

16. ibid., pp. 438–439.

17. ibid., p. 441.

18. *Bureau of Efficiency Survey,* 1978, p. 94.

19. *Report of Board of Education,* 1929–1930, pp. 79–80.

20. Strayer, 1949, p. 409.

21. King, 1936, p. 28.

22. Strayer, 1949, pp. 81–82.

23. *Report of the Board of Education, 1923-1924,* pp. 92–97.

24. Mayme Lewis, "Report of Visit to Horace Mann School, New York," *The Journal of the Columbian Educational Association,* May, 1925, pp. 28–29; Minor, 1939, pp. 11–12. See issues of *Journal of the Columbian Educational Association* for July, 1925 and February, 1926.

25. *Washington Post,* April 3, 1938 and October 27, 1940; Hahn, 1933, pp. 206–210.

26. Handorf, 1962, p. 190.

27. Strayer, 1949, pp. 427–428, 443–447.

28. ibid., p. 407.

29. ibid., p. 458.

30. ibid.

31. Central High School, *Handbook,* 1926, pp. 43–44.

32. Central High School, *The Bulletin,* all issues from 1925–1938.

33. Hundley, 1965, p. 66; Sowell, 1974.

34. For background on the concept of the Talented Tenth, see Thomas Sowell's article for a description of how it was cultivated at Dunbar High School prior to 1954; also see the essay by W. E. B DuBois, "Talented Tenth," in *Negro Problems* (New York: James Pott Co., 1903, pp. 33–75; and his "Education and Work," 1930 in Herbert Aptheker (ed.), *The Education of Black People* (Amherst, MA.: University of Massachusetts Press, 1973), pp. 61–82.

35. Dunbar High School, *Crimson and Black Handbook,* 1924–1925, pp. 11, 15, 47–48, 70, 81.

36. See Eastern High School, *The Easterner,* February, 1921, pp. 8–21.

37. *Report of the District of Columbia Board of Education,* 1919–1920, pp. 372–373; Dunbar High School, *Liber Anni,* 1929–1930 (student yearbook); *Dunbar Observer,* January 28, 1932.

CHAPTER 5: RURAL AND URBAN SCHOOLS, 1920–1940

1. *Changes in Classroom Teaching Made During 1937-1939 in One-Room Rural Schools in the Area of the Michigan Community Health Project* (Battle Creek, MI.: W. K. Kellogg Foundation, 1940), p. 129.

2. *Time,* October 31, 1938, p. 31.

3. Dworkin, 1959, pp. 129–130.

4. Otto et al., 1942, pp. 1, 5.

5. Otto et al., 1942, p. 3; *Changes in Classroom Teaching,* foreword. Because three of the teachers were listed as anonymous, I have used 190 reports in the analysis.

6. Hermine Marshall. "Open Classrooms: Has the Term Outlived Its Usefulness," *Review of Educational Research,* 51 (Summer, 1981), pp. 185–186.

7. *Changes in Classroom Teaching,* pp. 50–51.

8. E. Dewey, 1919; Ellsworth Collings, *An Experiment with a Project Curriculum* (New York: Macmillan Co., 1923); Dunn & Everett, 1926.

9. Report of the Committee on Experimental Schools, *What Schools Are Doing* (New York: Progressive Education Association, 1937), pp. ii, 3–5, 10, 19, 31, 42–43, 50.

10. Taplin & Pearson, 1938, pp. 114–115.

11. Department of the Interior, *Biennial Survey of Education, 1920–1922.* Bulletin 1924, Vol. 1 (Washington, D.C.: Government Printing Office, 1924), p. 125.

12. Department of the Interior. "Status of the Rural Teacher in Pennsylvania," Bulletin 1921, No. 34. (Washington, D.C.: Government Printing Office, 1922), pp. X–9, 21, 33; *Biennial Survey, 1920–1922,* pp. 143–145.

13. *Biennial Survey, 1920–1922,* p. 127; Fannie W. Dunn, Modern Education in Small Rural Schools," *Teachers College Record,* 32(5), 411–412.

14. McGuffey, 1929, pp. 10–13.

15. "Status of Rural Teacher in Pennsylvania," pp. 18, 33.

16. ibid., p. 20.

17. Texas Educational Survey Commission, 1924, pp. 321, 365.

18. ibid., 1924, pp. 307, 368, 376.

19. ibid., 1924, pp. 378–379.

20. Berg, 1929, pp. 19–20.

21. Uggen, 1938, pp. 195–202.

22. *Grade Teacher,* 48 (October, 1930), p. 159.

23. ibid., (December, 1930), p. 316.

24. Louisiana Educational Survey, 1924, Section B, "The Negro Public Schools," pp. 57–58.

25. ibid., pp. 164–165.

26. ibid., p. 56.

27. Hoetker & Ahlbrand, 1969, pp. 145–167.

28. Koos & Troxel, 1927, p. 343; Hughes & Melby, 1930, pp. 285–289; Barr, 1929, pp. 84, 103; Bursch, 1930, p. 128.

29. U.S. Office of Education, *National Survey of Secondary Education. Summary,* Monograph No. 1 (Washington, D.C.: Government Printing Office. 1934), pp. 126, 129.

30. Wrightstone, 1936, pp. 21–22, 48–49, 59, 76, 184–185. See also Dora V. Smith's examination of English courses of study in 127 cities in 35 states. She found a mix of progressive approaches and teacher-centered instruction in these courses and in the 70 schools she visited. *Instruction in English,* Office of Education Bulletin 1932, No. 17, Monograph No. 20 (Washington, D.C.: Government Printing Office, 1933).

31. This estimate is drawn from the following sources: the descriptions and photographs I collected of classrooms instruction; the analysis of 190 teacher self-reports

in rural Michigan (1937–1939); accounts about 55 teachers at Central High School in Washington, D.C. (1925–1938); Joseph Loftus's estimate in New York City at the height of the Activity Program's implementation; and reports from Krause and Bagley, who tried to estimate the degree of teacher use of different practices in the 1930s.

    32. Dworkin, 1959, pp. 129–130.

CHAPTER 6: INFORMAL EDUCATION, 1965–1975

    1. Vito Perrone et al., 1977, 1–20.

    2. Jackson, 1968b, p. 4.

    3. For histories of public schools since World War II, see Ravitch, 1983; Powell, Farrar, & Cohen, 1985, ch. 5; and Hampel, 1986.

    4. Cremin, 1973, p. 171.

    5. ibid., pp. 2–3.

    6. Perrone, 1976, pp. 186–187; Perrone, 1972, pp. 10–11.

    7. Barth, 1972; Featherstone, September 11, 1971, pp. 20–25; Featherstone, September 25, 1971, pp. 17–21.

    8. Featherstone, September 11, 1971, p. 20.

    9. Roland Barth, 1973, p. 59; for examples of checklists, see New York State Education Department, *Information and Planning Kit for Use in Developing Open Education Programs* (Albany, N.Y.: Task Force on Open Education, 1971); Anne Bussis, 1976. For warnings about too rapid an embrace of open classrooms, see Roland Barth's article in *Saturday Review;* Perrone's Phi Delta Kappan Fastback; Ruth Flurry, "Open Education: What Is It?" in Ewald Nyquist and Gene Hawes (eds.), 1972, pp. 102–110; Charles Silberman, 1973, pp. 297–298.

    10. Horwitz, 1979, pp. 72–73; Kathleen Devaney, 1973, pp. 3–5; Perrone, 1972, pp. 12–21.

    11. Silberman, 1973, pp. 297–298.

    12. For example, see *Newsweek,* 77 (May 3, 1971), p. 65; Resnick, 1971, pp. 67–69; *The New York Times,* October 11, 1970, p. 68.

    13. Resnick, 1971, pp. 67–68; Silberman, 1970, chs. 7 and 11; Vito Perrone and Warren Strandberg, "The New School" in Nyquist and Hawes (eds.), 1972, pp. 275–291; The North Dakota Statewide Study of Education, 1973, pp. 6–9; Michael Patton, 1973, p. 7.

    14. Patton, 1973, p. 21.

    15. Devaney, 1974, pp. 209, 211.

    16. Landry, 1975, p. 5.

    17. Devaney, 1974, p. 219.

    18. Vincent Dodge, 1974, Item VI, pp. 1–5; *Fargo-Moorhead Forum,* October 4, 1970; October 25, 1970; November 29, 1970.

    19. *Grand Forks Herald,* August 26, 1969; Larry Hoiberg, "We're Putting It All Together at Washington Elementary School" (Grand Forks, N.D.: Washington Elementary School, 1971), mimeo, pp. 1–51.

    20. *Final Report, Title III, Elementary and Secondary Education Act:* "The Impact

of the Teacher and His Staff" (Grand Forks, N.D.: Grand Forks Public Schools, 1970), mimeo, p. 56.

21. Silberman, 1970, pp. 290–297; Silberman (ed.), 1973, pp. 43–52; *Life,* October 1, 1971; *Today's Education,* February, 1973, p. 35.

22. Marshall, 1981, p. 180.

23. Patton, 1973, p. 7.

24. Landry, 1975, p. 14.

25. Ronald Kutz, 1977, pp. 21, 37.

26. A distinction needs to be made between "open-space" and "open classrooms." The former refers to the physical facilities that contain "pods," or large blocks of space with much portable furniture that can be easily rearranged into smaller spaces by accordion-like partitions, portable walls, and other easily movable wall-like mechanisms. The conventional building, on the other hand, usually has a series of self-contained classrooms arrayed along corridors that house around 30 students per room with different larger spaces set aside for many students (e.g., cafeteria, auditorium, library, gymnasium). Open-space schools permit both self-contained spaces to be created but also space that encourages teachers to work together with larger numbers of children. Thus, diverse groupings of pupils become possible. Open-space permits children of different ages to come easily together to work in areas set aside as "commons" for children to congregate. Open-space, then, establishes the necessary physical conditions for "open classrooms" to occur, should teachers wish to initiate the changes in curriculum and instruction, as well as their roles, in embracing the principles of informal education. See Weinstein, 1979; Getzels, 1974, pp. 527–540.

27. New York [City] Public Schools, *Facts and Figures,* 1977–1978. (New York: Board of Education, 1978), pp. 1, 5, 11.

28. Ravitch, 1981, p. 239; Ravitch, *Great School Wars,* p. 261.

29. For a sampling of the diverse literature written about New York City schools in the 1960s and 1970s, Ravitch, 1974, Rogers, 1968; Wasserman, 1970; Maurice R. Berube and Marilyn Gittell (eds.), 1969; Fuchs, 1969.

30. Center for Urban Education, 1970, pp. 11–12.

31. Charles Silberman pointed out that in the midst of writing *Crisis in the Classroom* he had met Weber, read her manuscript about British primary schools, and wrote "our work took a new direction. We went off to England to see for ourselves." Ruth Dropkin, 1978, p. 48.

32. Alberty, 1979, pp. 6–7; Karunkakaran, 1978, p. 30.

33. David Rogers, 1977, p. 82–84.

34. Dropkin, 1978, p. 51.

35. Some examples of open classrooms across the city are reported in the *New York Times,* January 8, 1973 on P.S. 24 (Bronx) and P.S. 27 (Bronx) in the January 17, 1973 issue; New York City Board of Education, *Staff Bulletin,* May 15, 1972 on P.S. 92 (Bronx); *United Teacher,* June 25, 1972, pp. 15–16 has a description of P.S. 35 (Queens). In addition, there are accounts written by teachers such as Kohl, 1967; Channon, 1970. Masters' theses from teachers enrolled in the Bank Street College of Education detail classroom experiences. See theses written by Donna C. DeGaetani, "Beginning an Open Classroom in a Public School" (1974); Mamie Gumbs, "Humanizing Learning Through Open Classroom Procedures and Self-Discovery Meth-

ods" (1974); Helen Haratonik, "A Descriptive Study of an Approach to Teaching Reading in an Open Classroom" (1973); Alice Montalvo, "Diary of an Open Classroom" (1972); Helaine R. Meisler, "Educational Change in a School Mandated 'Open' As Seen Through the Eyes of an Advisor" (1977).

36. *The New York Times,* January 8, 1973.

37. *The New York Times,* July 25, 1970; State Department of Education, "Vermont Design for Education" in Nyquist and Hawes, 1972, pp. 55–62; Joseph Lelyveld, "The Most Powerful Man in the School System," *The New York Times Magazine,* March 21, 1971, p. 31; *The New York Times,* July 25, 1970.

38. *The New York Times,* January 30, 1971.

39. Ibid., February 7, 1971; December 20, 1970; and January 24, 1971 (a paid advertisement).

40. ibid., January 8, 1973.

41. Chittenden, et al., 1973; Dropkin, 1978, pp. 51–53.

42. Karunkakaran, 1978, pp. 205–207.

43. Gerald Levy, 1970, chs. 4 and 7.

44. Channon, 1970, pp. 23–24.

45. ibid., p. 116.

46. DeGaetani, master's thesis, p. 4.

47. Ibid., pp. 14, 36.

48. Montalvo, master's thesis, pp. 4–5, 33, 57.

49. Joseph Lelyveld, "Class 4-4: Educational Theories Meet Reality," *The New York Times,* October 9, 1970, p. 39; November 16, 1970, p. 39; November 25, 1970, p. 39; December 20, 1970, p. 49; January 8, 1971, p. 33; January 16, 1971, p. 31; January 22, 1971, p. 41; March 11, 1971, p. 41; May 29, 1971, p. 25; July 1, 1971, p. 49.

50. Ibid., October 9, 1970, p. 39.

51. Ibid., March 11, 1971, p. 41.

52. Ibid.

53. Ibid., May 29, 1971, p. 25.

54. Ibid.

55. Lopate, 1975, pp. 24, 29.

56. For background on the alternative school movement, I used Deal & Nolan (eds.), 1978; Graubard, 1973; Fantini, 1973; Duke, 1978; Kozol, 1972; Raywid, 1981, pp. 551–557; Moore, 1978; Lewis, 1991, unpublished doctoral dissertation.

57. Raywid, 1981, p. 551; Moore, 1978, pp. 21–22.

58. Deal and Nolan, 1978, p. 3.

59. Deal & Nolan, "Alternative Schools: A Conceptual Map," *School Review* (November, 1978), p. 33; Flaxman & Hanstead (eds.), 1978.

60. Swidler, 1979; McBride, 1979.

61. Moore, 1978, pp. 9–10.

62. Duke, 1978, pp. 40, 44–46, 51.

63. New York City Public Schools, *School Profiles,* 1970–1971 (New York: Division of System Planning, 1971), Appendix A, p. 6.

64. Rogers, 1977, pp. 10–11; Divoky, 1971, pp. 60–67.

65. Rogers, 1977, pp. 22–25. The schools I cover exclude Bronx High School of

Science, Beach Channel High School, John Dewey High School and others that are citywide, have themes of special interests, and usually have entrance requirements. These schools, in the broad sense, are alternatives but they differ markedly from other alternative schools in size, ideology, student involvement in governance, etc.

66. *The New York Times,* November 1, 1971; November 17, 1971; July 1, 1975; Divoky, 1971, pp. 60–67.

67. Rogers, 1977, pp. 14–22.

68. Divorky, 1971, pp. 60–67; *The New York Times,* November 1, 1971 and July 1, 1975.

69. *The New York Times,* November 1, 1971.

70. Ibid., May 24, 1971, p. 33.

71. Ibid.

72. Ibid.

73. Ibid.

74. *The New York Times,* January 8, 1973, p. 57.

75. Ibid., September 8, 1975; January 15, 1975; November 16, 1975.

76. New York [City] Board of Education, *Directory of the Public Schools, 1978–1979* (New York: Board of Education, 1979), pp. 5, 27, 39, 51, 122–29.

77. Hansen, 1968, pp. 91–106; Cuban, 1975, pp. 15–37.

78. Hansen, 1968, chapters 1–5; Green, 1967, ch. 13; A Harry Passow, 1967, chs. 2, 4, 5.

79. Cuban, 1975, p. 35.

80. Cuban, 1974, pp. 8–32.

81. *Washington Post,* October 13, 1980, p. C-3; Vincent Reed, "An Introduction to the Competency-Based Curriculum," *Journal of Personalized Instruction,* 3, (Winter, 1978), pp. 199–200.

82. Passow, "Executive Summary," Toward Creating a Model Urban School System (New York: Teachers College, 1967), p. 1.

83. ibid., p. 3.

84. ibid., p. 265.

85. ibid., p. 255.

86. ibid., p. 235.

87. ibid., pp. 275–276.

88. ibid., pp. 295, 305, 312, 322.

89. District of Columbia Public Schools, "Model School Division in a Capsule" (Washington, D.C.: Model School Division, 1969). In 1950, the all black Cardozo High School moved into the recently closed building that used to house the all white Central High School.

90. Cort, 1969, pp. 7–8.

91. ibid., pp. 227–228, 240; I also had frequent contacts with the Innovation Team, its initial director (Mary Lela Sherburne), and Assistant Superintendent Norman Nickens while I directed the Cardozo Project in Urban Teaching—one of two dozen programs in the Model School Division—and later, when I administered the district-wide staff development program.

92. Cort, 1969, p. 240.

93. Kaya, 1974, pp. ii-iii.

94. *Washington Star,* August 16, 1970; Theresa H. Elofson, 1973, pp. 8–154.

95. *Washington Post,* May 13, 1973, C3.

96. Lauter & Howe, 1968, pp. 235–262; *Washington Star,* March 1, 1970; *Washington Post,* July 6, 1971 and May 13, 1973.

97. *Washington Post,* December 11, 1979.

98. Behavioral Service Consultants, 1974.; "Brookland School Plan," February, 1974.

99. "Brookland Plan," n.p.; *Washington Post,* December 11, 1979.

100. Behavioral Service Consultants, 1974, pp. 21, 47.

101. District of Columbia Public Schools, *Data Resume Book* (Washington, D.C.: Division of Research and Evaluation, 1976), pp. 28, 32; Kaya, 1974, p. 9.

102. District of Columbia Public Schools, "Open Space vs. Self-Contained Classrooms" (Washington, D.C.: Division of Research and Evaluation, 1980).

103. *Washington Post,* December 11, 1979; I observed teachers' efforts to close off open space when I visited Bruce–Monroe and Brookland schools in 1981.

104. Notes from my visit; Behavioral Service Consultants, 1974, pp. 60, 71.

105. In addition to my observations, reporter Judy Valente of the *Washington Post* wrote a series of articles on second-grade teacher Dorothy Porter of Bruce–Monroe. See October 13, 1980 and May 24, 1981 issues.

106. As in New York City, I exclude continuation schools for potential or actual dropouts (e.g., the Spingarn program), the Capitol Page, and separate vocational schools. Admission criteria, governance, size, and other features differed markedly in these schools from the alternatives I describe in the text.

107. *Washington Daily News,* November 14, 1968; *Washington Post.* November 22, 1968.

108. *Washington Post,* November 1, 1970.

109. Rhodes, G., Jr., 1970, pp. 21–22, 24; *Washington Daily News,* March 9, 1971; *Washington Post,* March 9, 1971.

110. Barbara Sizemore, Superintendent Memorandum to School Board, "Procedures for Alternative Programs," June 19, 1974, p. 4.

111. I had visited the Literary Arts program at the Lemuel Penn Career Center; I had had discussions with teachers at the Duke Ellington School of Performing Arts. Also see *Washington Post,* March 9, 1971.

112. *Washington Star,* December 31, 1979.

113. *The New York Times,* April 20, 1975; *Opening Education,* 2 (Summer, 1975), p. 5.

114. ibid. p. 36.

115. John Goodlad, et al., 1974, pp. 78–79, 81.

116. ibid., pp. 82–83.

117. ibid., p. 97.

118. Suydam & Osborne, 1977, pp. 54–55.

119. Shaver, et al., 1979, p. 7.

120. Helgeson, et al., 1977, pp. 31–32, 34.

121. Applebee, 1974, pp. 210–213.

122. Smith & Keith, 1971; Gross, et al., 1971. See also Herriot & Gross (eds.), 1979.

123. Beginning in the mid-1970s and extending into the 1980s, a series of books, national reports, and articles argued that informal education caused a breakdown in the teacher's authority, curricular permissiveness, and test score decline. See, for example, Cooperman, 1978; 1977; National Commission on Educational Excellence, 1983. These critics assumed that most schools adopted open classrooms. This assumption was embedded in the massive state legislation of the early 1980s that strove to raise academic standards and arrest test score decline. The evidence presented here strongly suggests that was not the case even in places where the talk of informal education was enthusiastic. Here is another instance where school reform policies were based upon unexamined assumptions of what occurred in classrooms. For a careful and compelling examination of the test score decline in the 1970s and a rebuttal to the above critics, see Carl Kaestle, *Literacy in the United States: Readers and Reading since 1880* (New Haven, CT: Yale University Press, 1991), pp. 129–145.

CHAPTER 7: LOCAL AND NATIONAL SNAPSHOTS OF CLASSROOM PRACTICES, 1975–1990

1. In 1966, Wilkinson asked whether her principal, Kitty Bouton, could secure a larger room for her effort to introduce informal teaching practices. Bouton received approval to have a wall knocked out between two classrooms thereby creating a large double room with ample space. Seeing it for the first time, Wilkinson exclaimed: "It's like a palace!" She told me that the word took on a negative meaning among her peers in the early 1970s. Interview with Carmen Wilkinson, March 22, 1982.

2. Applebee, 1974, pp. 233–234; *The New York Times*, September 15, 1974.

3. Over the 7 years, it was, of course, these informal and frequent classroom observations that produced the puzzling questions that prompted me to do this study. The research proposal that the National Institute of Education (NIE) approved in 1980 omitted Arlington as a site to study. It was after I left the post and began collecting data in Denver, Washington, New York City, and rural schools in the interwar decades and for the early 1970s that I saw the merit of examining a school district that, in the mid-to-late 1970s, had already experienced the surge of enthusiasm for informal education and open-space buildings. Because I had not included Arlington in the original proposal, I requested permission from NIE to add the district and they agreed. Thus notes taken for one purpose were sifted to see how applicable they would be for another purpose. Most were; many were not.

After I left Arlington, to protect the confidentiality of the teachers I visited, no individual was identified except for those who had consented or had published articles themselves. The two teachers I described in the opening pages of this chapter, for example, agreed to be included by name. The data I present then were aggregated by elementary and high school.

4. Cuban, 1979, pp. 367–935.

5. ibid., p. 368; Arlington closed Drew Elementary, its last all-black elementary school, in 1971. The school reopened as a county-wide alternative school. Students interested in attending the school that was advertised as using informal approaches were bussed to Drew. A number of slots were held for black students in the Drew neighborhood.

6. Without getting caught in the nuances of what "liberal" means in the context of Northern Virginia politics in the 1970s, I use it because it was the label the press attached to the coalition, and was often used by members of the group itself.

7. For a more in-depth personal account of my years as superintendent, see *The Managerial Imperative: The Practice of Leadership in Schools* (Albany, NY: State University of New York Press, 1988), ch. 6.

8. Arlington Public Schools, *School News,* January, 1980, n.p.

9. Arlington County Public Schools, *Profile,* June, 1969, p. 3.

10. ibid., pp. 3–4.

11. This estimate is taken from my notes written during my first year as superintendent, when I visited elementary classrooms. Interview with Carmen Wilkinson, March 22, 1982.

12. *Northern Virginia Sun,* September 7, 1971; *Washington Post,* May 31, 1971.

13. Superintendent Memorandum to School Board, "Status Report on Alternative Schools," June 15, 1979, p. 22.

14. *Arlington Journal,* February 14, 1974; I visited Woodlawn numerous times and observed classrooms, listened to students, and, in general, was familiar with the details of the school and its ethos.

15. ibid.

16. In *Practical Ideology and Symbolic Community* Robert Everhart (1988) studied three urban alternative schools in 1980–1981 on the west coast. He found that the "realities of everyday practice" (grading, tests, teacher providing information to students) persisted despite the child-centered intentions of the staff, the creation of student-centered decision-making (through contracts), much affiliation with the local community, and a norm of informality.

17. Stake & Easley, 1978.

18. ibid., pp. 3–61, 62, 63, 64, 65.

19. ibid., "The Project," n.p.; pp. 3–90, 91.

20. ibid., pp. 3–90.

21. National Science Foundation, 1978.

22. ibid., pp. B-56, 57, 59, 60–61, 63–65, 67, 110.

23. ibid., p. 110.

24. Goodlad, 1984; Sirotnik, 1981. For an in-depth analysis of classrooms in 12 junior high schools that participated in Goodlad's "Study of Schooling," see Tye, 1985. Data were collected in 1977. Similarly, for further examination of high school classrooms in 13 high schools, using the same data set, see Tye, 1985. See also Stodolsky, Ferguson, & Wimpelberg, 1981, pp. 121–130.

25. ibid., pp. 2–5.

26. ibid., pp. 8, 10, 14.

27. ibid., Table 1, n.p.

28. ibid., Table 3, n.p.

29. Glanz, 1979. One anthropologist passed as a student to investigate life in high schools. See Cusick, 1973.

30. ibid., pp. 1–4.

31. ibid., 5.

32. ibid., pp. 12–13.

33. ibid., pp. 14–15.

34. ibid., pp. 25.

35. Murphy, 1990; Firestone, Fuhrman, & Kirst, 1989.

36. For reviews of the literature on teacher effectiveness, see Gage, 1977, chs. 1 and 3; Dunkin & Biddle, 1974, chs. 5–10; Brophy & Good, 1986.

37. Barak Rosenshine, 1979.

38. ibid.; See also Good, 1979, pp. 52–64.

39. Rosenshine; Tikunoff & Ward, n.d., n.p.

40. ibid.

41. ibid.

42. ibid.

43. Good & Grouws, 1979.

44. Rosenshine, 1982, p. 5.

45. Doyle, 1981, p. 3; Fenstermacher, 1978, pp. 157–183.

46. Communication from Kim Marshall, Boston Public Schools; the idea that the persistence of particular teaching practices occurred simply because they worked, i.e., efficiently solved classroom problems, was mentioned also by Tommy Tomlinson, 1981, "The Troubled Years: An Interpretive Analysis of Public Schooling Since 1950," *Kappan*, 62 (January), pp. 373–376.

47. See, for example, Darling-Hammond & Wise, 1985, pp. 315–336; Wilson & Corbett, 1990.

48. Sizer, 1984; Powell, Farrar, & Cohen, 1985.

49. Sizer, pp. 9–21.

50. Powell, Farrar, and Cohen, 1985, ch. 2. For further elaboration of the notion of classroom bargains struck between teachers and students, Cusick, 1983; Sedlak, Wheeler, Pullin & Cusick, 1986; McNeil, 1986.

51. Boyer, 1983.

52. Ibid., pp. 141–153.

53. Brown, 1991, chs. 1, 2, 4, 6.

54. Applebee, Langer, & Mullis, 1989, pp. 35–37.

55. For a sampling of the literature written by and about teachers, see: Nehring, 1989, written by a secondary school social studies teacher in the New York metropolitan area; Sachar, 1991, is about a journalist-turned-new teacher who writes of her experiences at Walt Whitman Intermediate School in Flatbush, Brooklyn, New York; Wigginton, 1985 is written by a Cornell graduate who goes to teach English in Appalachia and stays for a quarter-century. Wigginton writes about teaching in the Deweyan tradition; Welsh, 1987, is written unsparingly and irreverently by an English teacher at T. C. Williams High School in Alexandria, Virginia; Kidder, 1989, is about Chris Zajacs, an elementary school teacher in Holyoke, Massachusetts; Freed-

man, 1990, is about Jessica Siegel, a journalism teacher at Seward Park High School in the Lower East Side of New York City; Mathews, 1988, is about a Bolivian immigrant who transforms the expectations of Mexican-American youth who have strong aptitude but mild interest in math at Garfield High School in Los Angeles.

56. For a sampling of the scholarly and practitioner literatures on small-group instruction, active learning, the development of pro-social attitudes in children, and other student-centered approaches that were published in the 1980s, Brandt, 1989, pp. 1–66; Bossert, 1988, pp. 225–250; Slavin, 1984; Mathematical Sciences Education Board, National Research Council, 1990; and Epstein & McPartland, 1990, pp 436–469.

57. For example, Mary Haywood Metz and her colleagues studied eight high schools (two were private ones) in midwestern metropolitan areas in the mid-1980s. In investigating similarities and differences between high schools enrolling students from diverse socioeconomic backgrounds, she spent one school day in one teacher's class in each school, and also followed students around for one day as they attended classes. She concluded: "Instruction was conducted through lecture, recitation, discussion, and seatwork, with occasional use of student reports, filmstrips, movies, and videotapes." See Metz, 1991, pp. 75–91. Reba Page conducted a study of eight lower-track classrooms in two high schools in another mid-western city. Her direct observations of classrooms and interviews with teachers and students produced a picture of teacher-guided recitations, seatwork, and teacher-directed games. See Page, 1991.

58. Eisner, 1986.

59. ibid., pp. 67–68.

60. Cuban, "Report on Implementation of The High School Study Committee's Recommendations," April, 1987. Copy in author's possession.

61. Peterson, 1990a, pp. 257–261.

62. Ball, 1990, pp. 263–276; Peterson, 1906, pp. 277–296; Wiemers, 1990, pp. 297–308; Suzanne Wilson, 1990, pp. 309–326; Cohen, 1990, pp. 327–346.

63. Cohen, 1990, pp. 336–337.

64. Wiemers, 1990, pp. 306–307. For other instances of similar mixes of the routine and novel in science and English classrooms in the 1980s, see Carter, 1990; Hawthorne, 1987; Applebee & Langer, 1984. For another instance of math teaching that displays some of the characteristics mentioned in Wiemers and Cohen, a researcher interviewed and observed an experienced teacher who belongs to the Cleveland (Ohio) Collaborative for Mathematics Education and believes in the importance of teaching high school math for understanding to low-income, black youth. He tells the interviewer that his commitment to teaching math has become more professional and far deeper than it was prior to his involvement with the Collaborative. Yet in the Algebra 1 classroom, he practices a pure version of teacher-centered instruction. Mr. Engle assigns bellwork—text problems to be completed prior to and after the tardy bell rings. After the bell, Mr. Engle calls on students to give their answers to the text problems. Following this, he points to the chalkboard where he has written a list of homework problems for the students to do. He also has an overhead projector display a transparency on the wall with already worked-out equations taken from the text. He explains each step of the problem and what procedures to use to solve the equation.

After asking for questions and getting one which moves him to repeat the explanation for the last equation, he tells the class to finish the problems on the chalkboard in the remaining time. See Bruckerhoff, 1991, pp. 158–177.

CHAPTER 8: EXPLAINING HOW THEY TAUGHT: AN EXPLORATORY ANALYSIS

1. Downs, 1972, pp. 38–50; see essay on reform cycles and trends in David Tyack and Larry Cuban, *Tinkering Towards Utopia* (in press).

2. Tukey, 1962, pp. 13–14.

3. I thank Nicole Holthius, a graduate student, for coining this phrase in 1990 in the course "A History of School Reform."

4. This metaphor for multiple explanations comes from Scott Russell, "Fathers, Sons, Sports," *Harpers,* June, 1991, vol. 282, no. 1693, p. 32. Alternative models of explaining puzzling questions is common. Nonetheless, I want to acknowledge the many discussions I have had with David Tyack over the years about the uses of multiple perspectives as a tool for attaining deeper understandings of complex historical phenomena. He uses this mode felicitously in "Ways of Seeing: An Essay on the History of Compulsory Schooling," *Harvard Educational Review,* 46 (August, 1976), pp. 355–389.

5. This argument of a cultural inheritance about teaching, learning, and knowledge that got deposited into schools as deeply embedded scripts to be played out combines ideas and information from Aries, 1962; Jackson, 1986; Finkelstein, 1989; Cohen, summer, 1987, pp. 159–163; Cohen, 1989; Meyer & Rowan, 1977, pp. 340–363; Metz, 1990.

6. Readers will note that this argument is a blend of major points raised by anthropologists, psychologists, linguists, sociologists, historians, and other scholars who have investigated the processes of schooling and sought ways of explaining why schools function as both socializing and sorting agents for the larger society. For some scholars these functions can be located in the pervasive demands of the economic system itself. Other scholars locate the dominant functions assigned to schooling in the inevitable clashes of conflicting cultures (e.g., school vs. ethnic culture) that occur within this institutional arena. And other scholars locate these functions of sorting and assimilating in the social beliefs and attitudes of administrators and teachers who accommodate the organizational imperatives of schooling. I take up each of the scholarly strands that I have woven into this argument.

Various strains of a neo-Marxist argument point out that as schools sort out immigrants, the poor, and the caste-like minorities from the middle- and upper-classes they provide recruits for the bottom, middle, and top floors of American business enterprises. Thus, schools are beneficial to capitalism and the prevailing social order. That schools serve the existing array of social classes is in of itself sufficient evidence that schools and classroom pedagogies reproduce socioeconomic distinctions. For unvarnished versions of this argument see Bowles & Gintis, 1976; Anyon, 1980, pp. 67–92; Nasaw, 1980; Everhart, 1983.

Some scholars whose work derived from the above but who have been critical of simplistic applications of Marxist ideas to schooling have concentrated upon knowl-edge as a socially-produced commodity. They argue that culturally-dominant knowl-edge is constructed by social elites in concert with large private organizations and delivered through teachers, texts, and tests unequally to students depending upon their socioeconomic status. This interpretation leaves open the possibility that those inside the system—teachers and students—could alter what occurs. See, for example, Bernstein, 1971; Apple, *Ideology and Curriculum* (Boston: Routledge and Kegan Paul, 1979) Apple & King, 1977, pp. 341–369; Apple, 1986. For an argument that urges teachers to resist being tools of social elites in passing on this culturally-dominated knowledge and even emancipating themselves and students from this cul-tural cage, see Giroux, 1983.

Some historians have tried to connect the introduction of particular pedagogies to the values of particular social classes and larger social and economic forces. See, for example, Hamilton, 1989. He argues that shifts in teaching practices in the United States (oral instruction in the early nineteenth century; the introduction of the recita-tion into the age-graded school, and the recasting of that recitation to a more demo-cratic and informal participation) followed the economic and social changes that the United States underwent in the 19th and 20th centuries (Hamilton, ch. 6). Also see Lazerson, 1971, who documents the history of the kindergarten and its unique peda-gogy as it became incorporated into the urban elementary school. Michael Katz in his *Irony of Early School Reform* argues that middle-class school reformers like Horace Mann and Cyrus Pierce imposed certain ways of teaching upon the school to better socialize working class children for the economic changes that awaited them when they left for the workplace. See Part II of Katz. For a fuller historiographical analysis of different scholars' approaches to the social roles of schools and teachers, see Finkel-stein, 1970, pp. 5–32.

Anthropologists and sociologists have stressed the socializing functions of schools (and the cultures embedded in the schools) for decades. They have written numerous accounts of how schools perform these functions for the larger society even in the face of conflicts over the cultural baggage students bring with them and what the school wants them to discard and pick up. Hollingshead, 1949; Henry, 1963; Heath, 1983; Willis, 1977; Wolcott, 1974; Ogbu, 1982, pp. 290–307; Fordham, 1988, pp. 54–84.

Finally, there are scholars who locate the socializing and sorting functions of schooling not solely in the capitalist system nor in its culturally-dominant knowledge, nor even in the clash of cultures that occur in the crucible of schooling, but in how school organization and the social beliefs and values of the adults who staff those schools merge into practices that sort pupils by their socioeconomic backgrounds. Studies of how teachers' expectations steer poor black children into "slow" reading groups or how counselors and administrators track Hispanic and black students into non-academic classes, for example, have documented the influence of staff's social at-titudes upon student futures. Studies of the content and skills that are taught in col-lege preparatory classes and "average" classes for the non-college bound claim that administrators, counselors, and teachers view students through socioeconomic lenses and, as a consequence, treat students from higher-status groups seeking to attend col-lege differently from lower-status ones who just want to graduate. For scholars who have written in this vein, see Oakes, 1985; Metz, 1991; Jackson, 1981, pp. 39–58; Rist, 1973. For a more complex treatment of how school culture, tracking, and teacher beliefs about students and the community interact, see Page, 1991.

A few studies have examined how teachers' social expectations modified by the demands of the organization have interacted with and been shaped by students' cultural views of what knowledge is, what are appropriate teaching practices, and what makes a classroom a classroom. These studies get directly into pedagogical practice and reveal the power of student expectations upon teaching behavior. See Wolcott, 1974; Metz, 1990; Cusick, 1983; Powell, Farrar, & Cohen, 1985; McNeil, 1986. For examples of studies of British schools along similar lines, see Willis, 1977 and Jones, 1989, pp. 19–31.

In variations on the above teacher-student interaction, some policymakers and practitioners tailor their pedagogy and choice of curriculum to what they view as the classroom needs of poor and ethnic students for stability, to counter their disorganized, unstable family and neighborhood lives. For decades black teachers and administators have been convinced that what low-income black students need in their schooling is strengthening of basic skills, rather than student-centered options that foster creativity, expression, and individual growth. This conflict over appropriate educational goals for black students dates back to the late 19th century when Booker T. Washington and W. E. B. Dubois and others argued publicly on the directions that educating the race should take. Since then, minor versions of that historic argument have split educators and social activists. Recall the divisions that developed among informal education advocates during the late 1960s and early 1970s over the place of teaching basic skills to poor black students. See, for example, Kozol, 1972. More recently, the same internal conflict over approaches to the teaching of writing to black children can be seen in Delpit, 1986, pp. 379–385. Also see Bruckerhoff, 1991, pp. 158–177. More recently, the furor over whether an Afrocentric curriculum (as opposed to what some critics have labeled the traditional Eurocentric curriculum in schools) should be installed into all-black public schools reveals anew the splits among black political and educational leaders over what are appropriate educational goals for black students and what curricula and pedagogy best achieve those aspirations.

7. This argument comes from a variety of sources on rational planning, top-down implementation, and the huge gaps that exist between macro-level planning and micro-level execution in classroom. For evidence that top-down reforms, especially ones from the 1980s designed by states have, indeed, penetrated to the school site (they provide no evidence of classroom effects) see, Fuhrman, Clune, & Elmore, 1988, pp. 237–257; Odden & Marsh, 1987. For a synthesis of the research on planned change and its strengths and limitations at federal, state, and local levels, see Fullan, 1982; for evidence that planned changes can occur at the school site if certain conditions are in place, see Huberman & Miles, 1984.

The literature of policy failures and feckless implementation has become broad and deep over the last three decades. Most of this failure analysis come from in-depth case studies of particular policies that have been aimed at altering routine school and classroom operations. See, for example, Gross et al., 1971, chs. 4–5, 7, 8; Smith & Geoffrey, 1968, chs. 1, 5, 7, 9–11; Wolcott, 1977; Goodwin, 1977, ch. 6; Wildavsky

& Pressman, 1973; McLaughlin, 1987, pp. 171–178; McLaughlin, 1976, pp. 339–351; Elmore & McLaughlin, 1988; Cohen, 1982, pp. 474–499.

    8. For the influence of the physical setting upon teaching see Getzels, 1974, pp. 527–540 and Weinstein, 1979, pp. 577–610. Recent architectural designs of classroom space in New York City for the 1990s and early 21st century have moved from a square classroom, a shape which was standard since 1898, to a design that takes the square and reshapes it like this:

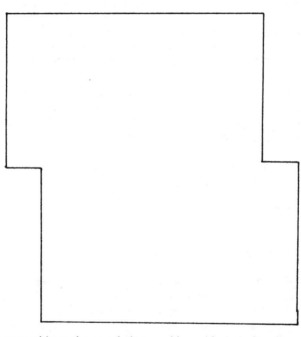

According to one architect, the new design would provide space for a bay window for more light, space for independent study groups or a place for a computer. "But at the same time," Peter Samton said, "the teacher would remain the real focus of the room." *New Yorker, 67,* no. 25, August 12, 1991, pp. 22–23.

    For the impact of the social, organizational, and cultural imperatives buried in the structures of classroom and school life see Jackson, 1968, ch. 1; Sarason, 1971, chs. 1, 7, 10, 11; Smith & Geoffrey, 1968, chs. 3–4; Meyer & Rowan, 1978.

    For a closer examination of district, school, and classroom policies and practices that shape teaching, see Johnson, 1990, chs. 1, 3, 5, and Dreeben, 1973; Dreeben & Barr, 1983; Mehan, 1979.

    For microanalysis of classroom structures and activities shaping pedagogy, see Doyle, 1986; and Cazden, 1988; Bossert, 1979.

    The notion of a practical pedagogy where teachers imaginatively cope with the demands of difficult physical and organizational arrangements had come to me directly from reflections upon my teaching, observations of colleagues, and reading other scholars, especially Philip Jackson, Seymour Sarason, Walter Doyle, and Michael Lipsky. For the latter two, see, for example, Doyle & Ponder, 1977–1978, and Lipsky, 1980. Since the first edition of *How Teachers Taught* was published, I discovered that other scholars here and in Britain had already arrived at a similar interpretation. My ignorance of their work prevented me from acknowledging their scholarship. I wish to do so now. See Westbury, 1973, pp. 99–121; Woods, 1977; Hargreaves, 1978; Denscombe, 1982, pp. 249–265.

More recently, other scholars have noted the powerful structures in school and classroom settings that influence how teachers teach. See, for example, Cusick, 1983; Sizer, 1984; Sedlak, Wheeler, Pullin, & Cusick, 1986; Page, 1991; McNeil, 1986; Flinders, 1987. Flinders calls the pragmatic tactics of teachers coping with the demands of a crowded classroom, "conservation strategies"; also see Grant & Sleeter, 1985, pp. 209–220.

9. The original formulation of this argument about cultures of teaching came from reading Willard Waller, 1965, Sarason, 1971, and Lortie, 1975. David Cohen's essays on the nature of teaching practice and its change have been most helpful to me. His critiques of the arguments I have advanced have forced me to think through with greater attention the consequences of my reasoning. See, in particular, Cohen, 1988; 1989; and 1987, pp. 153–170.

My growing awareness of occupational cultures and the power of socialization prior to and during teaching helped me understand in a different way many experiences I had as a novice learning the craft and the 14 years of teaching with colleagues in three different high schools. The argument was enhanced and further expanded over the years by reading Jackson, *Life in Classrooms;* Metz, 1978; McPherson, 1972; Judith Little, 1982, pp. 325–340. Rosenholtz, 1989, points out the impact that school culture can have on teacher attitudes and behavior in the classroom. I also found the chapter by Sharon Feiman-Nemser and Robert Floden ("The Cultures of Teaching") in Merle Wittrock (ed.), *The Handbook of Research on Teaching* (New York: Macmillan, 1986) most helpful in summarizing the literatures on various dimensions of cultures in schools. Anthropologists may have reservations on the generic use I make of the term "culture," even as applied to an occupation. For an anthropologist's view on using the term, see Erickson, 1987, pp. 11–24.

10. This argument on knowledge, beliefs, and attitudes of teachers is anchored in the assumption that what is in the teacher's head bears a strong relationship to what the teacher does and does not do in the classroom. While this appears similar in some respects to the argument about socializing and sorting functions of the school and the role that teachers' social beliefs play, it is different in a key way: the degree of choice available to practitioners to act.

In enacting the socializing and sorting functions of the school, teachers serve as unwitting agents of the larger social order, as when they unconsciously display their expectations for what students of low socioeconomic status can do, and select which students go into advanced and slow reading groups. But in the argument offered here, the teacher's knowledge, beliefs, and attitudes are not hopelessly chained to social classes or cultural elites in the larger society. Teachers may be influenced by distant social forces and by closer organizational ones but the argument here grants more individual discretion on the part of teachers to act consistently or inconsistently with these beliefs, attitudes, and knowledge. In effect, rather than a teacher as an unaware messenger of the larger society, the image in this argument is teacher as gatekeeper deciding what will and will not be taught.

In constructing this argument for the original manuscript, I found the following works most helpful: Jackson, 1968; Fenstermacher, 1978, pp. 177–182; Lortie, 1975; Bussis, Chittenden, & Amarel, 1976.

For this edition, I have found the work of Gary Fenstermacher, Lee Shulman, and Donald Schön most helpful. See Fenstermacher, 1986; Schon, 1983. Lee Shulman's work is cited below. The synthesis of the research that I found most helpful is Clark and Peterson, 1986. Also see Pajares, 1992.

What was missing from this argument in the first edition was the subject-matter knowledge of the teacher and the role that a teacher's view and handling of that content played in influencing the manner of instruction. The work of Lee Shulman and his colleagues at Stanford University on how teachers transform the subject matter that they know into teachable language and activities has added to this argument an important dimension that was missing from the first edition. See Shulman, 1987, pp. 1–22. The work of Pam Grossman, Sam Wineburg, Suzanne Wilson, and Sigrun Gudmundsdottir, in particular, I have found most helpful. See Grossman, Wilson, & Shulman, 1989; Grossman, 1989, pp. 24–32; Wilson & Wineburg, 1988, pp. 525–539; and Gudmundsdottir, 1988. Also see Stodolosky, 1988.

An explosion of writings on the impact of teachers' professional and personal beliefs and values upon classroom practices has occurred in the last two decades. Those writings that have influenced me most in constructing this argument I have already mentioned. There have been, however, particular studies that have strengthened in my mind the importance of teacher beliefs in making classroom decisions about pedagogy and pupils. See, for example, Elbaz, 1983; Clandinin, 1985, pp. 361–385; Gudmundsdottir, 1991, pp. 44–52; and Schwille, Porter, & Gant, 1980, pp. 21–40.

Two dissertations done at Stanford in the mid- to late 1980s I have found especially useful: Hawthorne, 1989, and Carter, 1990. Other dissertations I have found helpful in providing rich case studies of teacher views shaping practice: Bliss, 1986, and Bickmore, 1991.

Also, particular accounts written by or about teachers who report their deepest beliefs and describe what they do with and for children in their classrooms have strengthened the argument. See, for example, Paley, 1989, and Freedman, 1990.

11. Metz, 1978, pp. 250–251.

12. Lortie, 1975, p. 147.

13. The analogy of the visitor from outer space comes from Sarason, 1971, p. 63; for another examination of interacting contexts that influence secondary school teaching, see McLaughlin, Talbert, & Bascia, 1990, pp. 1–14.

14. One of the enduring puzzles of teaching is the familiar phenomenon of scholars finding so many schools located in poor, minority neighborhoods having almost hyper-versions of teacher-centered instruction, where the management of learning (whole-group instruction, large quantities of seatwork, frequent assessment, etc.) and constant stress on uniform behavior were dominant both in the school and especially in classrooms, even though there was substantial evidence of student alienation. See

Cusick, 1983; Boyer, 1983; Sizer, 1984; and Goodlad, 1984. Researchers and practitioners also saw these super-enriched versions of teacher-centered instruction in more affluent, white settings but there they had a softer, less sandpapery edge. Some scholars saw these differences as either educational expressions of a larger socioeconomic order, in which students were being prepared for their later positions in the job market, or further evidence that the cultural capital of the social order were being differentially and unwittingly distributed by teachers and administrators to passive, inert students.

Another view, and one that I find persuasive, is that these super-enriched, teacher-centered classrooms and schools in poor, ethnic neighborhoods are attempts to create what a Real School is. Real School, that is, the historic, cultural, and social notions of what knowledge, teaching, and learning should be, is what is desired in this nation. It is desired that even in the slums of the largest cities of America, where dropouts are highest, where the worst influences of neighborhood perversity threaten to overwhelm the school, at least one institution create an island of social calm, one that resembles what other Americans in more favored settings achieve. In these fortified arenas, at least lessons in basic skills and acceptable behaviors can be taught. According to Mary Metz and others, there are cultural scripts for the All-American High School, to cite an example, and these scripts are so deeply embedded that regardless of their seeming irrelevance or even absurdity for a particular location, they will be pursued nonetheless. See Metz, 1990, and Meyer & Rowan, 1977.

15. What continually intrigued me as I worked through the data was the recurring phenomenon of veteran elementary teachers, many of whom had taught for more than a decade, who ventured to teach newly-learned knowledge not in their texts, creating for the first time classroom learning centers, different seating arrangements, projects, varied groupings, etc. Leona Helmick in rural Michigan (1937), Mrs. Spencer (1924) and Gloria Channon (1969) in New York City, Carmen Wilkinson (1981) in Arlington, and others who were often trained in mainstream approaches and socialized by years in the classroom, exposed themselves to new knowledge and skills about subject matter and children's development. They adopted, partially or wholly, another way of teaching. They generated hybrid versions of teacher- and student-centered instruction. Generally, a small number of teachers in a district (and mostly in elementary schools) were the ones who persisted in maintaining these mixed types of instruction long after the initial enthusiasm for the activity method, projects, learning centers, and open classrooms ebbed and colleagues returned to their familiar practices.

These teachers had developed professional and personal beliefs different from their fellow teachers about how children learn and what classrooms should be. Within the organizational structure of the elementary school, where heavy external pressures were less evident, larger blocks of time were available, and skills were stressed more than content, a hospitable haven for different pedagogical practices existed for these teachers.

Researchers might profitably explore this phenomenon since it suggests renewed attention upon experienced teachers who already manage their classrooms well, yet wish to try out different approaches. Were there substance to this idea, it would question a current notion that experienced teachers hold unchanging, entrenched beliefs and are poor candidates to innovate in their classrooms. Furthermore, it might give substance to the point I suggested earlier, that teachers who combined both teacher- and student-centered approaches were pathfinders. Such teachers created hybrids of instruction that coped with classroom complexities.

16. Woods, 1979, p. 12; See Ross, 1977, pp. 173–220. Also see Herndon, 1972, p. 23.

17. Interview with Wilkinson, March 22, 1982.

18. In concentrating on the physical, emotional, and cognitive demands placed upon teachers, I have not stressed the deeper philosophical meanings that teachers embracing Deweyan notions of knowledge, action, and students' interest would have to consider. The fundamental changes in teachers' outlooks pose even another demand upon them that goes unmentioned in the text. See Schwab, 1959, pp. 139–159.

19. Jackson, 1986, p. 29.

20. Dworkin, 1959, pp. 129–130.

21. On the issue of the teacher's limited authority and reach, I found Willard Waller's (1965) work a useful starting point. Also see Muir, 1986; Grant, 1983, pp. 599–609; and Elmore, 1987, pp. 60–78.

A number of writers have stressed that a teacher's authority in a class commonly is negotiated with students. No exercise of formal authority is ever uncompromised or unvarnished by bargaining. Even drill instructors in boot camp and police officers stopping vehicles for inspection end up negotiating to some extent with recruits and drivers. Teachers also bargain, usually implicitly and, on occasion, explicitly, about what behavior and amount of work will be acceptable in classes. In schools where enrollments draw from low-income, ethnic families, teachers and students negotiate how much homework is tolerable and what classroom behavior is acceptable to both teacher and students. See Cusick, 1983; Sizer, 1964; and Powell, Farrar, & Cohen, 1985.

22. This point is made often in Swift (1971). As teaching drifted toward hybrids of student-centered and teacher-centered classroom practices, it is well to note that John Dewey sought hybrids of his own. The frequent distortions of John Dewey's position on striking a balance between subject-matter and a child-centered pedagogy haven't helped either. Contrary to what many of his followers believed about child-centered teaching, Dewey prized subject-matter and sought a hybrid position of his own between a content-centered and learning-centered approach. He used the example of carpentry to make his point

> The customs, methods and *working* (original emphasis) standards of the calling constitute a 'tradition' and initiation into the tradition is the means by which the powers of learners are released and directed. But we should also have to say that the urge or need of an individual to join in an undertaking is a necessary prerequisite of the tradition's being a factor in his personal growth in power and freedom; and also that he has to *see (original emphasis)* on his behalf and in his own way the relations between means and methods employed and results achieved. Nobody else can see for him, and he can't see just by being 'told,' although the right kind of telling may guide his seeing and thus help him see what he needs to see.

From "Individuality and Experience," cited in Westbrook, 1991, p. 505.

CHAPTER 9: SO WHAT? IMPLICATIONS FOR POLICYMAKERS, PRACTITIONERS, AND RESEARCHERS

1. Hansot & Tyack, 1982; Silver, 1990, especially chs. 1, 2, and 10.

2. See Tyack, 1989; Cohen, 1989.

3. I have avoided judging the quality or effectiveness of these forms of teaching practice for two reasons. First, determining what are the dominant forms of teaching that have endured and what changes, if any, have occurred in these mainstream practices is an essential first step prior to recommending how teachers ought to teach. Ignoring what has persisted over time in order to prescribe improvements has been a reliable recipe for the failure of both school and classroom reforms. Scholars, practitioners, and policymakers, determined to improve the quality of teaching, have ignored persistently the difference between what *is* and what *ought to be*. I have worked hard to avoid that error.

Second, my experience as a teacher, teacher educator, and superintendent who observed hundreds of classrooms yielded a core of ideas about teaching effectiveness. That experience, and the entire literature on teaching effectiveness over the last quarter-century, converge into a few concise statements: there is no one, best, way of teaching students content, skills, and values; depending on which student outcomes are stressed (high standardized achievement test scores; moral development; critical thinking; self-esteem, emotional maturity, a commitment to caring for others, etc.) there are different activities, tasks, and classroom structures that teachers can assemble and use to achieve those outcomes; a teacher's personality, experience, attitudes, and behaviors are critical variables in achieving desired outcomes with students; students backgrounds, abilities, beliefs, and preferences affect greatly teacher effectiveness. For comprehensive reviews of teaching effectiveness literature, see Brophy & Good, 1986, and Walberg, 1986.

In the Introduction I described how I developed a hybrid version of teacher-centered instruction over the fifteen years I taught high school, beginning in the 1950s, through the early 1970s, and for a brief time in 1988–1989. The pattern was one of increasing use of student-centered practices (small-group work, learning centers for individual work, etc.) harnessed to the familiar array of teacher-centered techniques (mini-lectures, whole-class discussions, etc.). I also carried this hybrid of changes into my graduate classes in the School of Education at Stanford University over the last decade. Perhaps my blending of the two traditions of teaching in classrooms over the last thirty-five years is another way to express, even personify, the slow growth of hybrids. Such blends, by their very nature, contradict the notion of one best way to teach.

4. I would advance the argument that this clear trend in teachers' adopting increasingly mixed versions of the two traditions is a decided advantage for students, even without considering whether such hybrids produce student outcomes desired by others.

What hybrids offer are more varied ways of reaching students. They extend to students whose personal ways of learning might be enhanced by active involvement, small group-work, and other techniques an opportunity to understand the content and skills teachers offer, one that would be denied them were only a standard version of a teacher-centered approach to be used. The reason that there is no one best way of teaching for students is that there is no single way that students learn. It is this eclecticism in teaching practices that make it possible for teachers to respond to the inevitable variety in students' learning styles, backgrounds, and hidden strengths that they bring to a classroom. Using the criterion of diversity among students in ability, motivation, and background factors, such as ethnicity and socioeconomic status, blended forms of teaching hold promise for increasing student engagement in and motivation for learning—two conditions necessary for achieving desired student outcomes.

This argument, of course, is not plucked from thin air. I have constructed it out of my experience; text and footnotes have repeatedly invoked my classroom experience, my research and others' scholarship. If it is not compelling or even persuasive, it is, at the least, defensible. Harvard University professor Howard Gardner has written extensively of multiple intelligences and the necessity of schools and teachers to construct activities and materials that respond to the diverse ways of learning among individual students. See *The Unschooled Mind* (New York: Basic Books, 1991).

5. I have profited greatly from discussions with Joe Kahne, who is writing a dissertation on mainstream policymakers' implicit purposes and assumptions about key public issues in schooling, and their unwitting shunting to the margins of other purposes for public policy. He has helped me clarify often confusing national policy debates about improving schools. For other sources that make the point that fundamental changes in structures need to be interrelated, see Sarason, 1990, Sizer, 1984; Hargreaves, 1990; Smith & O'Day, 1990; David, 1990; and Richard Elmore, 1990.

6. Considering the enormous body of literature that has investigated the social, organizational, political, and educational obstacles embedded in trying to reform high schools, it is a goofy but politically defensible logic that drives policymakers consistently to concentrate their limited resources on moving high schools to make fundamental changes in their routine ways of organizing instruction, teaching, and directing the lives of teenagers. What has invariably accompanied these campaigns to alter high schools is inflated rhetoric about basic changes and, over time, incremental modifications creeping into the organization. See, for example, Powell, Farrar, & Cohen, 1985.

One exception to this generalization is the work of Theodore Sizer and his colleagues in creating and sustaining the Coalition of Essential Schools and holding volunteer schools in the Coalition to their core principles. This reform effort is one instance of trying to alter in fundamental ways the structures and practices of mainstream high schools. Whether the energies of the promoters of this reform will continue to run high and whether private and public funds will continue to underwrite one of the few national efforts to alter the character and shape of American high schools is uncertain.

7. Sarason, 1990; Smith & O'Day, 1990.

8. Elmore & McLaughlin, 1988; McLaughlin, 1990, pp. 11–16.

9. See, for example, Rosenholtz, 1989; Huberman & Miles, 1984; and Elmore, 1990.

10. Goodlad, 1990; Goodlad, Soder, & Sirotnik (eds.), 1990.

11. See Clifford & Guthrie, 1988.

12. On the point of teacher leadership, see the chapter "Teaching as Institution-alized Leadership" in Waller, 1965. Also see chapter "From Images and Roles to Leadership" in Cuban, 1988.

13. Finkelstein, 1970, pp. 34–36. Also see Cohen, 1989, pp. 399–401, for his views on why historians seldom have studied teaching.

14. For examples of teachers teaching the same course yet displaying very different pedagogies, see Page, 1991; Wilson & Wineburg, 1988, pp. 525–539. Also see Stanford University dissertations by Kathy Bickmore, Beverly Carter, and Rebecca Hawthorne.

15. To cite just a few examples of such studies, see, Barker & Wright, 1951; Henry, 1963; Smith & Geoffrey, 1968; Varenne, 1977; Grant, 1986; and Page, 1991.

16. See, for example, comparisons between Beijing, China and Chicago, Illinois schools and classrooms in Stevenson, Lee, Chen, Stigler, Hsu, & Kitamura, 1990.

17. David Cohen raises the issue of a teacher-centered history clearly and cogently in "Practice and Policy." For an engaging synthesis of the research on students' attitudes, beliefs, and perspectives about what they experience, see Erickson & Shultz, 1992. For an imaginative exploration of what college students learn from an unusual class taught by a professor of history, see McDiarmid, Wiemers, & Fertig, 1991.

18. March, 1981, pp. 563–577; McLaughlin, 1987, pp. 171–178.

19. The Center for the Learning and Teaching of Elementary Subjects at the College of Education, Michigan State University has done a superb job of investigating teachers' knowledge and beliefs as they are enacted in practice across subject areas in elementary schools. I have found their work most helpful. I cited earlier the work of Deborah Ball and David Cohen that was published in *Educational Evaluation and Policy Analysis* (1990). See Peterson, Putnam, Vredevoogd, & Reineke, 1991; Knapp & Peterson, 1991; Remillard, 1991; also see Wood, Cobb, & Yackel, 1991, pp. 587–616.

20. See, for example, the discussion among a group of researchers who have been studying pedagogical changes among math teachers. Peterson & Fennema (eds.), 1989.

21. Sisk, 1981, p. 70.

References

Abelow, S. P. (1934). *Dr. William H. Maxwell, the first superintendent of schools of the city of New York*. Brooklyn: Scheba.

Alberty, B. (1979). *Continuity and connection: Curriculum in five open classrooms*. New York: City College Workshop Center for Open Education.

Aldrich, H. E. (1979). *Organizations and environments*. Englewood Cliffs, NJ: Prentice-Hall.

Anyon, J. (1980). Social class and the hidden curriculum of work. *Journal of Education, 162*(1), 69–92.

Apple, M. (1979). *Ideology and curriculum*. Boston: Routledge and Kegan Paul.

Apple, M.(1986). *Teachers and text*. London: Routledge and Kegan Paul.

Apple, M., & King, N. (1977). What do schools teach? *Curriculum Inquiry, 6*(4), 341–369.

Applebee, A. (1974). *Tradition and reform in the teaching of English: A history*. Urbana, IL: The National Council of Teachers of English.

Applebee, A., Langer, J., & Mullis, I. (1989). *Crossroads in American education: A summary of findings*. Princeton, NJ: Educational Testing Service.

Applebee, A., & Langer, J. (1984). Moving towards excellence: Writing & learning in the secondary school curriculum. Washington, D.C.: National Institute of Education.

Aries, P. (1962). *Centuries of childhood*. New York: Knopf.

Arlington County Public Schools. Profile (June 1969).

Arlington County Public Schools. *School News* (January 1980).

Arlington County Public Schools. Newspaper Clip Files in Public Information, 1972–1981.

Atkin, J. M., & House, E. (1981). The federal role in curriculum development. *Educational Evaluation and Policy Analysis 3*(5), 5–36.

Bagley, W. C. (1931). The textbook and methods of teaching. In National Society for the Study of Education, *The textbook in American education* (pp. 10–25). Bloomington, IL: Public School Publishing Co.

Ball, D. (1990). Reflections and deflections of policy: The case of Carol Turner. *Educational Evaluation and Policy Analysis, 12,* 263–276.

Barker, R., & Wright, H. (1951). *One boy's day*. New York: Harper Brothers.

Barr, A. S. (1929). *Characteristic differences in the teaching performance of good and poor teachers of the social studies*. Bloomington, IL: Public School Publishing Co.

Barr, R., & Dreeben, R. (1977). Instruction in classrooms. In L. Shulman (Ed.), *Review of research in education*. Itasca, IL: F. E. Peacock.

Barth, R. (1972). *Open education and the American school*. New York: Agathon.

Barth, R. (1973, November 6). Should we forget about open education? *Saturday Review*.

Behavioral Service Consultants. (1974). Final evaluation report: Training Center for Open-Space Schools, ESEA Title III Project. Greenbelt, MD: Author.

Bennett, H. E. (1940). Fifty years of school seating. *American School Board Journal, 100* (March), 41–43, 125.

Berg, A. C. (1929). *A daily program for the one-room schools of North Dakota*. Unpublished master's thesis, University of North Dakota, Grand Forks, ND.

Berliner, D. (1980). Studying instruction in the elementary classroom. In R. Dreeben & A. Thomas (Eds.), *The analysis of educational productivity*. Cambridge, MA: Ballinger.

Bernstein, B. (1971). On the classification and framing of educational knowledge. In M. Young (Ed.), *Knowledge and control*. London: Collier-Macmillan.

Berrol, S. C. (1968). William Henry Maxwell and a new educational New York. *History of Education Quarterly, 8*, 215–228.

Berube, M., & Gittell, M. (Eds.). (1969). *Confrontation at Ocean Hill–Brownsville*. New York: Praeger.

Bickmore, K. (1991). *Practicing Conflict: Citizenship education in high school social studies*. Unpublished doctoral dissertation, Stanford University, Stanford, CA.

Blauch, L., & Powers, J. (1938). *Public education in the District of Columbia*. Washington, DC: Government Printing Office.

Bliss, T. (1986). *Small group work in high school social studies*. Unpublished doctoral dissertation, Stanford University, Stanford, CA.

Borchert, J. (1980). *Alley life in Washington: Family, community, religion, and folklife in the city, 1850–1970*. Urbana, IL: University of Illinois Press.

Bossert, S. (1979). *Tasks and social relationships in classrooms: A study of instructional organization and its consequences*. New York: Cambridge University Press.

Bossert, S. (1980). Cooperative activities in the classroom. In E. Rothkopf (Ed.), *Review of Research in Education* (pp. 225–252). Washington, DC: American Educational Research Association.

Bowles, S., & Gintis, H. (1976). *Schooling in capitalist America*. New York: Basic Books.

Boyer, E. (1983). *High school*. New York: Harper and Sons.

Brandt, R. (1989). Cooperative learning. *Educational Leadership, 47*(4), 1–66.

Briggs, T. (1935). The practices of best high school teachers. *School Review, 43* (December), 745–752.

Brophy, J., & Good, T. (1986). Teacher behavior and student achievement. In M. Wittrock (Ed.), *Handbook of research on teaching*. New York: Macmillan.

Brown, R. (1991). *Schools of thought*. San Francisco: Jossey-Bass.

Bruckerhoff, C. E. (1991). The Cleveland Collaborative and the pursuit of mathematics curriculum reform. *Educational Policy, 5*(2), 158–177.

Bursch, C. W. (1930). *The techniques and results of an analysis of the teaching process in high school English and social science classes.* Unpublished doctoral dissertation, Stanford University, Stanford, CA.

Bussis, A. M., Chittenden, E., & Amarel, M. (1976). *Beyond the surface curriculum: An interview study of teachers' understandings.* Boulder, Co: Westview.

Campbell, H. (1935). Class sizes in New York City. *The School Executive, 55* (December), 138–139.

Campbell, J. (1967). *The children's crusader: Colonel Francis W. Parker.* New York: Teachers College Press.

Campbell, R. (1974). *The chasm.* Boston: Houghton Mifflin.

Carter, B. (1990). *The limits of control: Case studies of high school science teachers' responses to state curriculum reform, 1981–1987.* Unpublished doctoral dissertation, Stanford University, Stanford, CA.

Cazden, C. (1988). *Classroom discourse: The language of teaching and learning.* Portsmouth, NH: Heinemann.

Center for Urban Education. (1970). *Open door: New York City.* New York: Center for Urban Education.

Changes in classroom teaching made during 1937–1939 in one-room rural schools in the area of the Michigan Community Health Project. (1940). Battle Creek, MI: W. L. Kellogg Foundation.

Channon, G. (1970). *Homework.* New York: Outerbridge and Dienstrey.

Chittenden, E., et al. (1973). *First year evaluative study of the Workshop Center for Open Education.* New York: Workshop Center for Open Education.

Clandinin, J. (1985). Personal practical knowledge: A study of teachers' classroom images. *Curriculum Inquiry, 15*(4), 361–385.

Clark, C., & Peterson, P. (1986). Teachers' thought processes. In M. Wittrock (Ed.), *Handbook of Research on Teaching.* New York: Macmillan.

Clifford, G., & Guthrie, J. (1988). *Ed school.* Chicago: University of Chicago Press.

Cohen, D. (1987). Educational technology, policy, and practice. *Educational Evaluation and Policy Analysis, 9,* 153–170.

Cohen, D. (1988). Teaching practice: Plus que ça change. In P. Jackson (Ed.), *Contributions to educational change.* Berkeley, CA: McCutchan.

Cohen, D. (1989). Practice and policy: Notes on the history of instruction. In D. Warren (Ed.), *American teachers: Histories of a profession at work.* New York: Macmillan.

Cohen, D. (1990). A revolution in one classroom. *Educational Evaluation and Policy Analysis, 12*(3), 327–346.

Cohen, R. (1990). *Children of the mill: Schooling and society in Gary, Indiana, 1906–1960.* Bloomington, IN: Indiana University Press.

Cohen, S. (1964). *Progressives and urban school reform.* New York: Teachers College, Columbia University.

Collings, E. (1923). *An experiment with a project curriculum.* New York: Macmillan Co.

Cooperman, P. (1978). *The literacy hoax: The decline of reading, writing, and learning in the public schools and what we can do about it.* New York: William Morrow.

Cort, H. R. (1969). *An evaluation of the Innovation Team.* Washington, DC: Washington School of Psychiatry.

Covello, L. (1958). *The heart is the teacher.* Totowa, NJ: Littlefield, Adams.

Cremin, L. (1961). *Transformation of the school*. New York: Vintage.

Cremin, L. (1973, October). The free school movement: A perspective. *Notes on Education*.

Cremin, L. (1988). *American education: The metropolitan experience, 1876–1980*. New York: Harper and Row.

Cuban, L. (1974). Reform by fiat: The Clark Plan in Washington, 1970–1972. *Urban Education, 9* (April), 8–33.

Cuban, L. (1975). Hobson v. Hansen: A study in organizational response. *Educational Administration Quarterly, 11* (Spring), 15–37.

Cuban, L. (1979a). Determinants of curriculum change and stability, 1870–1970. In J. Schafferzick & G. Sykes (Eds.), *Value conflicts and curriculum issues* (pp. 139–196). Berkeley, CA: McCutchan.

Cuban, L. (1979b). Shrinking enrollment and consolidation: Political and organizational impacts in Arlington, Virginia, 1973–1978. *Education and Urban Society, 11* (May), 367–395.

Cuban, L. (1988). *The managerial imperative: The practice of leadership in schools*. Albany, NY: State University of New York Press.

Cuban, L. (1992). Stability and change in curriculum. In P. Jackson (Ed.), *The handbook of research on curriculum*. New York: Macmillan.

Cubberley, E. P. (1916). *The Portland Survey*. Yonkers-on-the-Hudson, NY: World Book.

Cushman, C. L. (1938). Conference Appraises Denver Secondary Program. *Curriculum Journal, 9* (November), 317–318.

Cusick, P. A. (1973). *Inside high school*. New York: Holt, Rinehart and Winston.

Cusick, P. (1983). *The egalitarian ideal and the American high school*. New York: Longman.

Darling-Hammond, L., & Wise, A. (1985). Beyond standardization, state standards, and school improvement. *Elementary School Journal, 85*(3), 315–336.

David, J. (1990). *Results in education: State actions to restructure schools: First steps*. Washington, DC: National Governors' Association.

Davis, O. L., Jr. (1976). *Schools of the past: A treasury of photographs*. Bloomington, IN: Phi Delta Kappa Educational Foundation.

Dayton, Ohio Public Schools. (1896). *Annual report of the Board of Education, 1895–1896*. Dayton, OH: Board of Education.

Deal, T., & Nolan, R. (1978). *Alternative schools: Ideologies, realities, guidelines*. Chicago: Nelson-Hall.

Dearborn, N. H. (1925). *The Oswego Movement in American education*. New York: Teachers College, Columbia University.

DeLima, A. (1925). *Our enemy the child*. New York: New Republic.

Delpit, L. (1986). Skills and other dilemmas of a progressive black educator. *Harvard Educational Review, 56*(4), 379–385.

Denscombe, M. (1982). The "hidden pedagogy" and its implications for teacher training. *British Journal of Sociology of Education, 3*(3), 249–265.

Denver Public Schools. (1927). *Denver Program of Curriculum Revision*. Monograph 12. Denver, CO: Author.

Denver Public Schools. (1929). *General information and courses of study: Senior high schools*. Denver, CO: Author.

Denver Public Schools. (1936). Handbook for the application of progressive education principles to secondary education. Denver, CO: Author.

Denver Public Schools. (1948). *History of East High School*. Denver, CO: East High School.

Denver Public Schools. (1920–1945a). *Angelus*. Denver, CO: East High School.

Denver Public Schools. (1920–1945b). *Thunderbolt*. Denver, CO: Manual Training High School.

Denver Public Schools. (1920–1945c). *Viking*. Denver, CO: North High School.

Denver Public Schools. (1921–1938). *Classroom interests*. Denver, CO: Denver Teachers.

Denver Public Schools. (1920–1940a). *School Review*. Denver, CO: Author.

Denver Public Schools. (1920–1940b). Newspaper clip files in Public Information Office. Denver, CO.

Denver Public Schools, School District Number 1 in the City and County of Denver. (1919–1941). *Annual report*. Denver, CO: Author.

Denver Public Library. (1916–1940). Newspaper clip files on public schools.

Devaney, K. (1973). Developing open education in America: A review of theory and practice in the public schools. Pamphlet. Washington, DC: U.S. Department of Health, Education, and Welfare.

Devaney, K. (1974). *The New School of Behavioral Studies in Education*. Grand Forks, ND: Center for Teaching and Learning.

Dewey, E. (1919). *New schools for old*. New York: E. P. Dutton.

Dewey, J. (1902). In Memoriam, Colonel Wayland Parker, 2, pp. 704–708.

Dewey, J., and Dewey, E. (1915). *Schools of tomorrow*. New York: E. P. Dutton.

District of Columbia Board of Education. (1908–1941). *Annual report to the Commissioners of District of Columbia*. Washington, DC: U.S. Government Printing Office.

District of Columbia Board of Education. (1941). *School achievements in twenty years*. Washington, DC: Author.

District of Columbia Board of Education, Cardozo High School. (1965–1975). *Purple wave*. Washington, DC: Author.

District of Columbia Board of Education, Central High School. (1919–1926). *Handbook*. Washington, DC: Author.

District of Columbia Board of Education, Central High School. (1919–1950). *Brecky*. Washington, DC: Author.

District of Columbia Board of Education, Central High School. (1925–1938). *Bulletin*. Washington, DC: Author.

District of Columbia Board of Education, Dunbar High School. (1920–1940; 1965–1975). *Liber anni*. Washington, DC: Author.

District of Columbia Board of Education, Dunbar High School. (1925). *Crimson and black*. Washington, DC: Author.

District of Columbia Board of Education, Dunbar High School. (1942). *The Dunbar news reel*. Washington, DC: Author.

District of Columbia Board of Education, Eastern High School. (1925–1940). *The Easterner*. Washington, DC: Author.

District of Columbia Board of Education, Roosevelt High School. (1965–1975). *The roughrider*. Washington, DC: Author.

District of Columbia Board of Education, Woodrow Wilson High School. (1939–1945). *Woodrow Wilson*. Washington, DC: Author.

District of Columbia Public Library. (1919–1981). Newspaper clip files in Washingtonia Room.

Divoky, D. (1971). New York's mini-schools. *Saturday Review*, 18, pp. 60–67.

Dodge, V. (1974). The Fargo-Madison School Program: A Cooperative School-University Effort. Pamphlet. Grand Forks, ND: Center for Teaching and Learning.

Donovan, J. (1921). *School architecture*. New York: Macmillan.

Downs, A. (1972). Up and down with ecology—the issue-attention cycle. *Public Interest, 2* (3).

Doyle, W. (1981). Research on classroom contexts. *Journal of Teacher Education, 32* (November–December), 35–50.

Doyle, W. (1986). Classroom organization and management. In M. Wittrock (Ed.), *Handbook of research on teaching*. New York: Macmillan.

Doyle, W., & Ponder, G. (1978). The practicality ethic in teacher decision-making. *Interchange, 8*(3), 1–12.

Dreeben, R. (1973). The school as a workplace. In W. Traver (Ed.), *The second handbook of teaching*. New York: Rand McNally.

Dreeben, R., & Barr, R. (1983). *How schools work*. Chicago: University of Chicago Press.

Dropkin, R. (Ed.). (1978). *Changing schools*. New York: City College Workshop Center for Open Education.

DuBois, W. E. B. (1903). Talented tenth. In *Negro Problems* (pp. 60–61). New York: James Pott.

DuBois, W. E. B., & Dill, A. (1911). *The common school and the Negro American*. Atlanta, GA: Atlanta University Press.

Duke, D. L. (1978). *The retransformation of the school*. Chicago: Nelson-Hall.

Dunkin, M., & Biddle, B. J. (1974). *The study of teaching*. New York: Holt, Rinehart and Winston.

Dunn, F., & Everett, M. (1926). *Four years in a country school*. New York: Teachers College, Bureau of Publications.

Dunn, F. (1931). Modern education in small rural schools. *Teachers College Record, 32* (5), 411–423.

Dworkin, M. (Ed.). (1959). *Dewey on education*. New York: Teachers College Press.

Eddy, E. (1967). *Walk the white line*. New York: Doubleday.

Eisner, E. (1986). What high schools are like: Views from the inside. A Report to the School of Education, Stanford University, Stanford. In The Schools Project: Curriculum Panel Report, January, 1986.

Elbaz, F. (1983). *Teacher thinking: A study of practical knowledge*. London: Croom Helm.

Elmore, R. (1978). Organizational models of social program implementation. *Public Policy, 26*(2), 185–228.

Elmore, R. (1987). Reform and the culture of authority in schools. *Educational Administration Quarterly, 23*(4), 60–78.

Elmore, R. (1990). *Restructuring schools: The next generation of educational reform.* San Francisco: Jossey-Bass.

Elmore, R., & McLaughlin, M. (1988). *Steady work.* Santa Monica, CA: Rand.

Elofson, T. (1973). Open education in the elementary school: Six teachers who were expected to change. Urbana, IL: Center for Instructional Research and Curriculum Evaluation.

Epstein, J., & McPartland, J. (1990). Education in the middle grades: A national survey of practices and trends. *Phi Delta Kappan, 69*(6), 436–469.

Erickson, F. (1987). Conceptions of school culture: An overview. *Educational Administration Quarterly, 23*(4), 11–24.

Erickson, F., & Shultz, J. (1992). Students' experiences of the curriculum. In P. Jackson (Ed.), *Handbook of research on curriculum.* New York: Macmillan.

Everhart, R. (1983). *Reading, writing, and resistance: Adolescence and labor in a junior high school.* Boston: Routledge and Kegan Paul.

Everhart, R. (1988). *Practical ideology and symbolic community.* New York: The Falmer Press.

Fantini, M. (1973). *Public schools of choice.* New York: Simon and Schuster.

Fargo-Moorhead Forum. (1967–1975). Fargo, ND: Author.

Featherstone, J. (1971, September 11). The British and us. *The New Republic,* 17–21.

Featherstone, J. (1971, September 25). Tempering a fad. *The New Republic,* 17–21.

Feiman-Nemser, S., & Floden, R. (1986). The cultures of teaching. In M. Wittrock (Ed.), *Handbook of research on teaching.* New York: Macmillan.

Fenstermacher, G. (1978). A philosophical consideration of recent research on teacher effects. *Review of Research in Education, 6,* 157–185.

Fenstermacher, G. (1986). Philosophy of research on teaching. In M. Wittrock (Ed.), *Handbook of research on teaching.* New York: Macmillan.

Final Report, Title III. (1970). Elementary & Secondary Education Act. The impact of the teacher & his staff. Grand Forks, N.D. Grand Forks Public Schools, mimeo.

Finkelstein, B. *Governing the young: Teacher behavior in American primary schools, 1820–1880.* Unpublished doctoral dissertation, Teachers College, Columbia University, New York.

Finkelstein, B. (1974). The moral dimensions of pedagogy. *American Studies 5* (Fall), 79–91.

Finkelstein, B. (1989). *Governing the young: Teacher behavior in popular primary schools in 19th century United States.* New York: The Falmer Press.

Firestone, W., & Herriott, R. E. (1981). Images of schools and patterns of change. *American Journal of Education* (August, 1980), 459–487.

Firestone, W., Fuhrman, S., & Kirst, M. (1988). *The progress of reform: An appraisal of state education initiatives.* New Brunswick, NJ: Rutgers University, Center for Policy Research in Education.

Flaxman, A., & Hanstead, K. (Eds.). (1978). *1977–1978 national directory of public alternative schools.* Amherst, MA: National Alternative Schools Program at School of Education, University of Massachusetts at Amherst.

Flexner, A., & Bachman, F. (1918). *The Gary schools.* New York: General Education Board.

Flinders, D. (1987). *What teachers learn from teaching*. Unpublished doctoral dissertation, Stanford University, Stanford, CA.

Folger, J., & Nam, C. (1967). *Education of the American population*. Washington, DC: Government Printing Office.

Fordham, S. (1988). Racelessness as a factor in black students' school success: Pragmatic strategy or Pyrrhic victory? *Harvard Educational Review, 58* (1), 54–84.

Fox, L. K. (1948). *The rural community and its school*. New York: King's Crown Press.

Frank, M. S. (1951). *Dedication of Valverde elementary school*.

Frazier, E. F. (1967). *Negro youth at the crossways*. New York: Schocken.

Freedman, S. (1990). *Small victories*. New York: Harper and Row.

Fuchs, E. (1969). *Teachers talk*. New York: Anchor Books.

Fuerst, S. M. (Ed.). (1900). Methods in New York schools. *New York Teachers' Monographs, 2* (June), 106–107.

Fuhrman, S., Clune, W., & Elmore, R. (1988). Research on education reform: Lessons on the implementation of policy. *Teachers College Record, 90*(2), 237–257.

Fullan, M. (1982). *The meaning of educational change*. New York: Teachers College Press.

Fuller, W. (1982). *The old country school*. Chicago: University of Chicago Press.

Gage, N. L. (1977). *The scientific basis of the art of teaching*. New York: Teachers College Press.

Getzels, J. W. (1974). Images of the classroom and visions of the learner. *School Review, 82* (4), 527–540.

Giles, H. H., et al. (1942). *Exploring the curriculum*. New York: Harper Bros.

Giroux, H. (1983). *Theory and resistance in education: A pedagogy for the opposition*. South Hadley, MA: Bergin and Garvey.

Gladstone, C. (1975, March). What constitutes a remedial reading lesson. *High Points*, 29–33.

Glanz, E. (1979). *What are you doing here?* Washington, DC: Council for Basic Education.

Good, T. L. (1979). Teacher effectiveness in the elementary school. *Journal of Teacher Education, 30,* 52–64.

Good, T. L., & Grouws, D. A. (1979). The Missouri mathematics effectiveness project. *Journal of Educational Psychology, 71,* 355–362.

Goodlad, J., et al. (1974). *Looking behind the classroom door*. Worthington, OH: Charles Jones.

Goodlad, J. (1984). *A place called school*. New York: McGraw-Hill.

Goodlad, J. (1990). *Teachers for our nation's schools*. San Francisco: Jossey-Bass.

Goodlad, J., Soder, R., & Sirotnik, K. (Eds.). (1990). *Places where teachers are taught*. San Francisco: Jossey-Bass.

Goodwin, D. (1977). *Delivering educational service: Urban schools and schooling*. New York: Teachers College Press.

Graham, P. (1967). *Progressive education: From Arcady to academe*. New York: Teachers College Press.

Grand Forks Herald. (1967–1975). Grand Forks, ND: Author.

Grant, C., & Sleeter, C. (1985). Who determines teacher work: The teacher, the organization, or both? *Teaching and Teacher Education, 1*(3), 209–220.

Grant, G. (1983). The teacher's predicament. *Teachers College Record, 84*(3), 599–609.

Grant, G. (1986). *The world we created at Hamilton High.* Cambridge, MA: Harvard University Press.

Graubard, A. (1973). *Free the children.* New York: Pantheon.

Green, C. M. (1967). *The secret city: A history of race relations in the nation's capital.* Princeton, NJ: Princeton University Press.

Greene, M. F., & Ryan, O. (1965). *The school children.* New York: Pantheon.

Gross, N., et al. (1971). *Implementing organizational innovations.* New York: Basic Books.

Grossman, P., Wilson, S., & Shulman, L. (1988). Teachers of substance: Subject matter knowledge for teaching. In M. C. Reynolds (Ed.), *Knowledge base for the beginning teacher.* New York: Pergamon Press.

Grossman, P. (1989). A study of contrast: Sources of pedagogical content knowledge for secondary English. *Journal of Teacher Education, 40*(5), 24–32.

Gudmundsdottir, S. (1991). Values in pedagogical content knowledge. *Journal of Teacher Education, 41,* 44–52.

Gudmundsdottir, S. (1988). *Knowledge use among experienced teachers: Four case studies of high school teaching.* Unpublished doctoral dissertation, Stanford University, Stanford, CA.

Hahn, J. (1933). Some whys & hows of the activity program. *Childhood Education, 9* (January), 206–210.

Hamilton, D. (1989). *Towards a theory of schooling.* New York: The Falmer Press.

Hampel, R. (1986). *The last little citadel.* Boston: Houghton Mifflin.

Handorf, G. G. (1962). *An historical study of the superintendency of Dr. Frank Ballou in the public school system of the District of Columbia.* Unpublished doctoral dissertation, American University, Washington, DC.

Hansen, C. (1968). *Danger in Washington.* West Nyack, NY: Parker.

Hansot, E., & Tyack, D. (1982). A usable past. In A. Lieberman & M. McLaughlin (Eds.), *Policymaking in education.* Chicago: National Society for the Study of Education.

Hargreaves, A. (1978). The significance of classroom coping strategies. In L. Barton & R. Meighan (Eds.), *Sociological interpretations of schooling and classrooms.* Driffield, England: Nafferton.

Hargreaves, A. (1990). *Restructuring restructuring: Postmodernity and the prospects for educational change.* Ontario, Canada: The Ontario Institute for Studies in Education.

Harlan, L. (1968). *Separate and unequal.* New York: Atheneum.

Hart, C. (1946). *Memories of a Forty-niner.* Philadelphia: Dunlap.

Hawthorne, R. (1987). *Classroom curriculum: Educational criticisms of teacher choice.* Unpublished doctoral dissertation, Stanford University, Stanford, CA.

Heath, S. B. (1983). *Ways with words: Language, life, and work in communities and classrooms.* London: Cambridge University Press.

Heffron, I. (1934). *Francis W. Parker.* Los Angeles: Ivan Deach.

Helgeson, S., et al. (1977). *The status of pre-college science, mathematics, and social science education: 1955–1975.* (Vol. 1). Columbus, OH: Center for Science and Mathematics Education.

Henry, J. (1963). *Culture against man.* New York: Random House.

Herndon, J. (1972). Who shapes the curriculum? *Urban Review, 5*(3), 22–25.

Herriot, R., & Gross, N. (Eds). (1979). *The dynamics of planned educational change.* Berkeley: McCutchan Publishing Co.

Hoetker, J., & Ahlbrand, W. (1969). The persistence of the recitation. *American Educational Research Journal,* 6 (March), 145–167.

Hoffman, N. (1981). *Woman's "true" profession.* New York: McGraw-Hill.

Hoiberg, L. (1971). We're putting it all together at Washington Elementary School. Pamphlet. Grand Forks, ND: Washington School.

Hollingshead, A. B. (1949). *Elmstown's youth: The impact of social classes on adolescents.* New York: Wiley.

Horwitz, R. A. (1979). Psychological effects of the open classroom. *Review of Educational Research, 49* (Winter), 71–86.

Hoy, W. (1969). Pupil control ideology and organizational socialization. *School Review, 77.*

Huberman, A. M., & Miles, M. (1984). *Innovation up close.* New York: Plenum.

Huebner, T. (1939). Suggested standards in the supervision of foreign languages. *High Points, 21*(9), 5–13.

Hughes, J. M., & Melby, E. O. (1930). A cross-section of teaching in terms of classroom activities. *Educational Method, 10* (October), 285–289.

Hundley, M. (1965). *The Dunbar story.* New York: Vantage.

Jackson, P. (1968a). *Life in classrooms.* New York: Holt, Rinehart and Winston.

Jackson, P. (1968b). *The teacher and the machine.* Pittsburgh, PA: University of Pittsburgh Press.

Jackson, P. (1981). Secondary schooling for the children of the poor. *Daedalus, 110*(4), 39–58.

Jackson, P. (1986). *The practice of teaching.* New York: Teachers College Press.

James, W. (1958). *Talks to teachers.* New York: Norton.

Jersild, A., et al. (1939). An evaluation of aspects of the activity program in the New York City public elementary schools. *Journal of Experimental Education, 8*(2), 166–207.

Jersild, A., et al. (1941). Studies of elementary school classes in action. *Journal of Experimental Education, 9*(4), 295–302.

Johnson, S. M. (1990). *Teachers at work.* New York: Basic Books.

Jones, A. (1989). The cultural production of classroom practice. *British Journal of Sociology of Education, 10*(1), 19–31.

Kaestle, C. (1981, October 3). *Ideology and American educational history.* Paper presented at the meeting of the History of Education Society, Pittsburgh, PA.

Kaestle, C. (1983). *Pillars of the Republic.* New York: Hill and Wang.

Kaestle, C. (1991). *Literacy in the United States: Readers and reading since 1880.* New Haven, CT: Yale University Press.

Karunkakaran, C. (1978). *Life & work in several communities: A case study of open education.* Chicago: Center for New Schools.

Katz, M. (1968). *The irony of early school reform.* Cambridge, MA: Harvard University Press.

Katz, M. (1971). *Class, bureaucracy, and schools.* New York: Praeger.

Kaya, E. (1974). An evaluation and description of the advisory and learning exchange, 1973–1974. Pamphlet. Washington, DC: Advisory and Learning Exchange.

Kidder, T. (1989). *Among schoolchildren.* Boston: Houghton Mifflin.

King, A. (1936, June). Evolution of the study group. *Journal of the Education Association of the District of Columbia, 28–29.*

Knapp, N., & Peterson, P. (1991). What does CGI mean to you? Teachers' ideas of a research-based intervention four years later. East Lansing, MI: Center for the Learning & Teaching of Elementary Subjects, Michigan State University.

Kohl, H. (1967). *36 children.* New York: New American Library.

Koos, L. V., & Troxel, O. L. (1927). A comparison of teaching procedures in short and long class periods. *School Review, 35.*

Kozol, J. (1972). *Free schools.* New York: Bantam.

Krause, L. W. (1941). What principles of modern and progressive education are practiced in intermediate-grade classrooms. *Journal of Educational Research, 35* (December), 252–259.

Krug, E. (1964). *The shaping of the American high school* (Vol. 1). New York: Harper and Row.

Kutz, R. (1977). An analysis of the use of math manipulative materials in North Dakota. Pamphlet. Grand Forks, ND: Bureau of Educational Research and Services.

Landry, R. (1975). *Comparative and longitudinal analyses of teaching intern classrooms on selected dimensions of openness: Third year.* Grand Forks, ND: Center for Teaching and Learning.

Lauter, P., & Howe, F. (1968). The short, happy life of Adams-Morgan Community School. *Harvard Educational Review, 38*(3), 235–262.

Lazerson, M. (1971). *Origins of the urban school.* Cambridge, MA: Harvard University Press.

Levy, G. (1970). *Ghetto school.* New York: Pegasus.

Lelyveld, J. (1970, October 9). Class 4-4: Educational theories meet reality. *The New York Times,* p. 39.

Lelyveld, J. (1971, March 21). The most powerful man in the school system. *The New York Times Magazine,* pp.

Lewis, M. (1925). Report of visit to Horace Mann School, New York. *The Journal of the Columbian Educational Association, 1*(2), 28–29.

Lewis, P. (1991). *Private education and the subcultures of dissent: Alternative/free schools (1965–1975) and Christian fundamentalist schools, 1965–1990.* Unpublished doctoral dissertation, Stanford University, Stanford, CA.

Lipsky, M. (1980). *Street-level bureaucracy: Dilemmas of the individual in public services.* New York: Russell Sage Foundation.

Little, J. W. (1982). Norms of collegiality and experimentation: Workplace conditions of school success. *American Educational Research Journal, 19*(1), 325–340.

Loftus, J. (1936). The nature of the Activity Program. (September 9, 1936).

Loftus, J. (1940). New York's large-scale experimentation with an activity program. *Progressive Education, 17* (2), 116–124.

Lopate, P. (1975). *Being with children.* New York: Bantam.

Lortie, D. (1975). *Schoolteacher.* Chicago: University of Chicago Press.

Louisiana Educational Survey, Section B. (1924). *The Negro Public Schools.* Baton Rouge, LA: Louisiana Educational Survey.

Lynd, R., & Lynd, H. (1929). *Middletown.* New York: Harcourt, Brace.

March, J. (1981). Footnotes to organizational change. *Administrative Science Quarterly, 26* (December).

Marler, C. D. (1965). *Colonel Francis W. Parker: Prophet of the "new education."* Unpublished doctoral dissertation, Stanford University, Stanford, CA.

Marshall, H. H. (1981). Open classrooms: Has the term outlived its usefulness? *Review of Educational Research, 51* (1), 181–192.

Marshall, H. H. (1988). Work or learning: Implications of classroom metaphors. *Educational Researcher, 17*(9), 9–16.

Marshall, K. (1972). *Law and order in Grade 6-E.* Boston: Little, Brown.

Mathematical Sciences Education Board, National Research Council. (1990). *Reshaping school mathematics: A philosophy & framework for curriculum.* Washington, DC: National Academy Press.

Mathews, J. (1988). *Escalante: The best teacher in America.* New York: Henry Holt.

Mayhew, K. C., & Edwards, A. C. (1936). *The Dewey school: The Laboratory School of the University of Chicago.* New York: Appleton-Century.

McBride, M. (1979). *Five alternative schools.* Unpublished doctoral dissertation, University of Maryland, College Park, MD.

McDiarmid, G. W., Wiemers, N. J., & Fertig, L. (1991, April). *Bounded by their pasts: Exploring the relationship between understandings of history and the views of teaching and learning of history among majors in a historiography seminar.* Paper presented at the annual meeting of the American Educational Research Association, Chicago.

McGuffey, V. (1929). *Differences in the activities of teachers in rural one-room teacher schools and of grade teachers in cities.* New York: Teachers College, Columbia University.

McLaughlin, M. (1978). Implementation as mutual adaptation in classroom organizations. In D. Mann, *Making Change Happen* (pp. 19–31). New York: Teachers College Press.

McLaughlin, M. (1979). An exploratory study of school district adaptation. Pamphlet. Los Angeles: Rand.

McLaughlin, M. (1987). Lessons from past implementation research. *Educational Evaluation and Policy Analysis, 9*(2), 171–178.

McLaughlin, M. (1990, December). The RAND change agent study revisited: Macro perspectives and micro realities. *Educational Researcher, 19,* 11–16.

McLaughlin, M., & Talbert, J. (1990). The contexts in question: The secondary school workplace. In M. McLaughlin, J. Talbert, & N. Bascia (Eds.), *The contexts of teaching in secondary schools: Teachers' realities.* New York: Teachers College Press.

McNeil, L. (1986). *Contradictions of control: School structures and school knowledge.* London: Routledge and Kegan Paul.

McPherson, G. (1972). *Small town teacher.* Cambridge, MA: Harvard University Press.

Mehan, H. (1979). *Learning lessons.* Cambridge, MA: Harvard University Press.

Metz, M. H. (1978a). Clashes in the classroom: The importance of norms for authority. *Education and Urban Society, 11* (1), 13–49.

Metz, M. (1978b). *Classrooms and corridors.* Berkeley, CA: University of California Press.

Metz, M. (1990). Real school: A universal drama amid disparate experience. In D. Mitchell & M. Goertz. (Eds.), *Education politics for the new century* (pp. 75–92). New York: The Falmer Press.

Metz, M. (1991). How social class differences shape the context of teachers' work. In M. McLaughlin & J. Talbert (Eds.), *The secondary school workplace.* New York: Teachers College Press.

Meyer, J. (1986). The politics of educational crises in the United States. In W. Cummings, E. R. Beauchamp, W. Ichikawa, Y. N. Kobayashi, & M. Ushigi (Eds.), *Educational policies in crisis* (pp. 44–58). New York: Praeger.

Meyer, J., & Rowan, B. (1977). Institutionalized organizations: Formal structures as myth and ceremony. *American Journal of Sociology, 83*(2), 340–363.

Meyer, J., & Rowan, B. (1978). The structure of educational organizations. In M. Meyer (Ed.), *Environments and organizations* (pp. 78–109). San Francisco: Jossey-Bass.

Minor, P. (1939, May). A Unit in Creative Writing. *National Educational Outlook Among Negroes, 11*–12.

Moore, D. T. (1978). Alternative schools: A review. Pamphlet. New York: Institute for Urban and Minority Education, Teachers College.

Morrison, J. C. (1943). The curriculum experiment with the Activity Program and its implications for the further study of education. In *New York Society for Experimental Study of Education yearbook* (pp. 15–30). New York: Thesis Publishing.

Muir, W. K. (1986). Teachers' regulation of classrooms. In D. Kirp & D. Jensen (Eds.), *School days, rule days: The legalization and regulation of education.* New York: The Falmer Press.

Murphy, J. (1990). The educational reform movement of the 1980s: A comprehensive analysis. In J. Murphy (Ed.), *The educational reform movement of the 1980s: Perspectives and cases* (pp. 3–56). Berkeley, CA: McCutchan.

Nasaw, D. (1980). *Schooled to order.* New York: Oxford University Press.

National Commission on Educational Excellence. (1983). *A nation at risk.* Washington, DC: Government Printing Office.

National Science Foundation. (1978). *Report of the 1977 national survey of science, mathematics, and social studies education.* Washington, DC: Author.

National Society for the Study of Education. (1926). *Curriculum making: Past and present.* 26th yearbook. Part 1. Bloomington, IL: Author.

National Society for the Study of Education. (1931). *The textbook in American education.* 30th yearbook. Part 2. Bloomington, IL: Author.

National Society for the Study of Education. (1934). *The activity movement.* 33rd yearbook. Part 2. Bloomington, IL: Author.

Nearing, S. (1915). *The new education.* Chicago: Row, Peterson.

Nehring, J. (1989). *Why do we gotta do this stuff, Mr. Nehring?* New York: Fawcett Columbine.

New York [City] Board of Education. (1910–1942). *Annual report of the Superintendent of Schools.* New York: Author.

New York [City] Board of Education. (1921). *The teachers' handbook: A guide for use in the schools of the City of New York.* New York: Author.

New York [City] Board of Education. (1929a). *Progress of the public schools, 1924–1929.* New York: Author.

New York [City] Board of Education. (1929b). *Report of survey of public school system, City of New York, 1924.* New York: Author.

New York [City] Board of Education. (1937). *Working together: A ten year report.* New York: District 23 and 24 Principals.

New York [City] Board of Education. (1947). *Exploring a first grade curriculum.* New York: Bureau of Reference, Research, and Statistics.

New York [City] Board of Education. (1949). *The first fifty years: A brief review of progress, 1898–1948.* New York: Author.

New York [City] Board of Education. (1971). *School profiles, 1970–1971.* New York: Division of System Planning.

New York [City] Board of Education. (1978). Facts and figures, 1977–1978. New York : Author.

New York [City] Board of Education. (1918–1975). *High points.* New York: Author.

New York [City] Board of Education. DeWitt Clinton High School. (1920–1975). *Clintonian.* New York: Author.

New York Principals' Association. (1921, November 14). *The Principal.*

New York State Department of Education. (1941). *The Activity Program: The report of a survey.* Albany, NY: Department of Education.

Newlon, J. (1917). The need of a scientific curriculum policy for junior and senior high schools. *Educational Administration and Supervision, 3* (5), 253–268.

Newlon, J., & Threlkeld, A. L. (1926). The Denver curriculum revision program. In *Curriculum making: Past and present.* 26th yearbook. Part I (pp. 229–240). Bloomington, IL: National Society for the Study of Education.

North Dakota Statewide Study of Education. (1973). *Educational development for North Dakota, 1967–1975; An overview.* Grand Forks, ND: Center for Teaching and Learning.

Nyquist, E. & Hawes, G. (1972). (Eds.) *Open education.* New York: Bantam Books.

Oakes, J. (1985). *Keeping track.* New Haven: Yale University Press.

Odden, A., & Marsh, D. (1987). *How state education reform can improve secondary schools.* Berkeley, CA: Policy Analysis for California Education.

Ogbu, J. U. (1982). Cultural discontinuities and schooling. *Anthropology and Education Quarterly, 13*(4), 290–307.

O'Shea, W. (1927). What are the progressive steps of the New York city schools? *Educational Review, 74*(1), 99–103.

Otto, H., et al. (1942). *Community workshops for teachers in the Michigan Community Health Project.* Ann Arbor, MI: University of Michigan Press.

Page, R. (1991). *Lower-track classrooms: A curricular and cultural perspective.* New York: Teachers College Press.

Paley, V. (1989). *White teacher.* Cambridge, MA: Harvard University Press.

Pajares, F. (1992). Teachers' beliefs and educational research: Cleaning up a messy construct. *Review of Educational Research, 62*(3), 307–332.

Passow, H. A. (1967). *Toward creating a model urban school system.* New York: Teachers College Press.

Passow, H. A. (1976). *Secondary education reform: Retrospect and prospect.* New York: Teachers College Press.

Patton, M. (1973). *Structural dimensions of open education.* Grand Forks, N.D.: Center for Teaching & Learning.

Patridge, L. E. (1889). *The Quincy methods illustrated.* New York: E. L. Kellogg.

Perrone, V. (1972). Open education: Promise and problems. PDK Fastback. Bloomington, IN: Phi Delta Kappan Educational Foundation.

Perrone, V. (1976). A view of school reform. In R. Dropkin & A. Tobier (Eds.), *Roots of open education in America.* New York: The Workshop Center for Open Education.

Perrone, V., et al. (1977). *Two elementary classrooms: Views from the teacher, children, and parents.* Dubuque, IA: Kendall/Hunt.

Perrone, V., & Strandberg, W. (1972). The new school. In E. Nyquist & G. Hawes (Eds.), *Open Education* (pp. 275–291). New York: Bantam Books.

Peterson, P. (1990a). The California Study of Elementary Mathematics. *Educational Evaluation and Policy Analysis, 12*(3), 257–261.

Peterson, P. (1990b). Doing more in the same amount of time: Cathy Swift. *Educational Evaluation and Policy Analysis, 12*(3), 277–296.

Peterson, P., Putnam, R., Vredevoogd, J., & Reineke, J. (1991). Profiles of practice: Elementary school teachers' views of their mathematical teaching. East Lansing, MI: Michigan State University.

Powell, A., Farrar, E., & Cohen, D. (1985). *The shopping mall high school: Winners and losers in the educational marketplace.* Boston: Houghton Mifflin.

Ravitch, D. (1974). *The great school wars: New York City, 1805–1973.* New York: Basic Books.

Ravitch, D. (1983). *The troubled crusade: American education, 1945–1980.* New York: Basic Books.

Ravitch, C., & Goodenow, R. (Eds.). (1981). *Educating an urban people.* New York: Teachers College Press.

Raywid, M. A. (1981). The first decade of public school alternatives. *Kappan, 62*(8), 551–557.

Reed, V. (1978). An introduction to the competency-based curriculum. *Journal of Personalized Instruction, 3*(Winter), 199–200.

Remillord, J. (1991). *Abdicating authority for knowing: A teacher's use of an innovative mathematics curriculum.* East Lansing, MI: Center for Learning & Teaching of Elementary Subjects, Michigan State University.

Report on survey of the public school system of the District of Columbia by the Bureau of Efficiency, 1928. (1928). Washington, DC: Government Printing Office.

Resnick, H. (1971). Promise of change in North Dakota. *Saturday Review, 54,* 67–69.

Rhodes, G., Jr. (1970). *Action programs in progress in the secondary schools.* Washington, DC: District of Columbia Board of Education.

Rice, J. (1969). *The public school system of the United States.* New York: Arno Press.

Rist, R. C. (1973). *The urban school: A factory for failure.* Cambridge, MA: MIT Press.

Rogers, D. (1968). *110 Livingston Street.* New York: Random House.

Rogers, D. (1977). *An inventory of educational improvement efforts in the New York City schools.* New York: Teachers College Press.

Rosenholtz, S. (1989). *Teachers' workplace: The social organization of schools.* New York: Longman.

Rosenshine, B. (1979). Content, time, and direct instruction. In P. L. Petersen & H. Walberg (Eds.), *Research on teaching* (pp. 28–56). Berkeley: McCutchan.

Rosenshine, B. (1982, February). *Teaching functions in instructional programs.* Paper presented at the NIE Conference, Airlie House, VA.

Rosenthal, B. (1940). A case study of a lesson in American history. *High Points, 22*(9), 21–39.

Ross, L. (1977). The intuitive psychologist and his shortcomings: Distortions in the attribution process. *Advances in Experimental Social Psychology, 10,* 173–200.

Rugg, H. (1928). *The child-centered school.* Yonkers-on-the-Hudson, NY: World Book Co.

Sachar, E. (1991). *Shut-up and let the lady teach.* New York: Poseidon Press.

Sarason, S. (1971). *The culture of the school and the problem of change.* New York: Allyn and Bacon.

Sarason, S. (1990). *The predictable failure of school reform.* San Francisco: Jossey-Bass.

Schildt, R. (1982, March 22). Unpublished interview.

Schon, D. (1983). *The reflective practitioner.* New York: Basic Books.

Schwab, J. (1959). The "impossible" role of the teacher in progressive education. *School Review, 67* (2), 139–159.

Schwille, J., Porter, A., & Gant, M. (1980). Content decision making and the politics of education. *Educational Administration Quarterly, 16*(2), 21–40.

Sedlak, M., Wheeler, C., Pullin, D., & Cusick, P. (1986). *Selling students short: Classroom bargains and academic reform in the American high school.* New York: Teachers College Press.

Shaver, J., et al. (1979). An interpretive report on the status of pre-college social studies based on three NSF-funded studies. In National Science Foundation, *What are the needs in pre-college science, mathematics, and social science education?* Washington, DC: National Science Foundation.

Shulman, L. (1987). Knowledge and teaching: Foundations of the new reform. *Harvard Educational Review, 57*(1), 1–22.

Silberman, C. (1970). *Crisis in the classroom.* New York: Random House.

Silberman, C. (Ed.). (1973). *The open classroom reader.* New York: Vintage.

Silver, H. (1990). *Education, change, and the policy process.* New York: The Falmer Press.

Sirotnik, K. (1981). What you see is what you get: A summary of observations in over 1,000 elementary and secondary classrooms. Technical Report No. 29. Los Angeles: UCLA Graduate School of Education.

Sizer, T. (1964). *Secondary schools at the turn of the century.* New Haven, CT: Yale University Press.

Sizer, T. (1973). *Places for learning, places for joy.* Cambridge, MA: Harvard University Press.

Sizer, T. (1984). *Horace's compromise: The dilemma of the American high school.* Boston: Houghton Mifflin.

Slavin, R. (1984). Students motivating students to excel: Cooperative incentives, cooperative tasks, and student achievement. *Elementary School Journal, 85,* 53–64.

Smallwood, J. (Ed.). (1976). *And gladly teach: Reminiscences of teachers from frontier dugout to modern module.* Norman, OK: University of Oklahoma Press.

Smith, D. (1933). *Instruction in English.* U.S. Office of Education Bulletin no. 17, Monograph 20. Washington, D.C. Government Printing Office.

Smith, L., & Geoffrey, W. (1968). *The complexities of an urban classroom.* New York: Holt, Rinehart and Winston.

Smith, L., & Keith, P. (1971). *Anatomy of an educational innovation.* New York: Wiley.

Smith, M., & O'Day, J. (1990). *Systematic school reform* (Report). Stanford, CA: Stanford University, School of Education.

Snyder, C. B. J. (1922). A stupendous schoolhouse problem. *American School Board Journal, 65,* 59–61.

Sommer, R. (1969). *Personal space.* Englewood Cliffs, NJ: Prentice-Hall.

Sowell, T. (1974). Black excellence: A history of Dunbar High School. Washington *Post,* April 28, C3.

Spears, H. (1948). *The emerging high school curriculum.* New York: American Book Co.

Spindler, G., & Spindler, L. (1982). Roger Harker and Schönhausen. In G. Spindler (Ed.), *Doing the Ethnography of Schooling.* New York: Holt, Rinehart and Winston.

Spodek, B., & Walberg, H. (Eds.). (1975). *Studies in open education.* New York: Agathon.

Spring, J. (1972). *Education and the rise of the corporate state.* Boston: Beacon Press.

Spring, J. (1986). *The American school, 1642–1985.* New York: Longman.

Stake, R., & Easley, J. (1978). *Case studies in science education* (Vol. 1). Urbana, IL: Center for Instructional Research and Curriculum Evaluation.

State University of New York. (1916). *Examination of the public school system of the City of Buffalo.* Albany, NY: Author.

Stephens, J. M. (1967). *The process of schooling.* New York: Holt, Rinehart and Winston.

Sterling, P. (1972). *The real teachers.* New York: Random House.

Stevens, R. (1912). *The question as a measure of efficiency in instruction.* New York: Teachers College, Columbia University.

Stevenson, H., Lee, S. Y., Chen, C., Stigler, J. W., Hsu, C. C., & Kitamura, S. (1990). *Contexts of achievement: A study of American, Chinese, & Japanese children.* Chicago: University of Chicago Press.

Stodolsky, S. (1988). *The subject matters: Classroom activity in math and social studies.* Chicago: University of Chicago Press.

Stodolsky, S., Ferguson, T., & Wimpelberg, K. (1981). The recitation persists but what does it look like? *Journal of Curriculum Studies 13*(2), 121–130.

Strayer, G. (1949). *Report of a survey of the public schools of the District of Columbia.* Washington, DC: Board of Education.

Stuart, J. (1949). *The thread that runs so true.* New York: Scribner's.

Suydam, M., & Osborne, A. (1977). *The status of pre-college science, mathematics, and social science education, 1955–1975: Mathematics education* (Vol. 2). Columbus, OH: Ohio State University, Center for Science and Mathematics Education.

Swidler, A. (1979). *Organization without authority.* Cambridge, MA: Harvard University Press.

Swift, D. (1971). *Ideology and change in the public schools.* Columbus, OH: Charles Merrill.

Talk of the Town. (1991). *New Yorker, 67*(25), 22–23.

Taplin, W., & Pearson, I. (1938). Contributions to individual instruction. In *Newer types of instruction in small rural schools.* 1938 Yearbook (pp. 114–115). Washington, DC: Department of Rural Education, National Education Association.

Taxpayers Review. (1934). October 12.

Tenenbaum, S. (1940). Supervision—theory and practice. *The School Executive, 59* (March), 28–29.

Texas Educational Survey Commission. (1924). Texas Educational Survey. *Courses of study and instruction* (Vol. 5). Austin, TX: Author.

Thayer, V. T. (1928). *The passing of the recitation.* Boston: Heath.

Thirty schools tell their story. (1942). Vol. 5. New York: Harper and Bros.

Threlkeld, A. L. (1937). Dr. Dewey's philosophy and the curriculum. *Curriculum Journal, 8* (April), 164–166.

Tikunoff, W., & Ward, B. *Ecological perspectives for successful school practice: Knowledge of effective instruction.* San Francisco: Far West Laboratory.

Time. October 31, 1938.

Tomlinson, T. (1981). Effective schools: Mirror or mirage? *Today's Education,* (April/May), 48–50.

Tukey, J. (1962). The future of data analysis. *Annals of Mathematical Statistics, 33,* 13–14.

Tyack, D. (1974). *The one best system.* Cambridge, MA: Harvard University Press.

Tyack, D. (1976). Ways of seeing: An essay on the history of compulsory schooling. *Harvard Educational Review, 46* (3), 355–389.

Tyack, D. (1978). The history of secondary schools in delivering social services. Unpublished manuscript, 1978.

Tyack, D. (1989). The future of the past: What do we need to know about the history of teaching? In D. Warren (Ed.), *American teachers: Histories of a profession at work.* New York: Macmillan.

Tyack, D., & Hansot, E. (1982). *Managers of virtue.* New York: Basic Books.

Tyack, D., & Hansot, E. (1990). *Learning together: A history of coeducation in American public schools.* New Haven, CT: Yale University Press.

Tyack, D., Hansot, E., & Lowe, R. (1984). *Public schools in hard times: The Great Depression and recent years.* Cambridge, MA: Harvard University Press.

Tye, B. (1985). *Multiple realities: A study of 13 American high schools.* Lanham, MD: University Press of America.

Tye, K. (1985). *The junior high: School in search of a mission.* Lanham, MD: University Press of America.

Uggen, J. (1938). A composite study of difficulties of rural teachers. *Educational Administration and Supervision, 24* (March), 195–202.

U.S. Department of the Interior, Bureau of Education. *Report of the Commissioner of Education, 1891–1892,* Vols. 1 and 2; *1900–1901,* Vol. 1; *1911,* Vol. 2.

U.S. Department of Interior, Bureau of Education. (1922). Status of the rural teacher in Pennsylvania. 1921 Bulletin (No. 34). Washington, DC: U.S. Government Printing Office.

U.S. Department of Interior, Bureau of Education. (1924). *Biennial survey of education, 1920–1922.* 1924 Bulletin (Vol. 1). Washington, DC: U.S. Government Printing Office.

U.S. Department of Interior, Bureau of Education. (1932). *National survey of secondary education.* 1932 Bulletin (No. 17). Summary report. Washington, DC: U.S. Government Printing Office.

U.S. Department of Interior, Bureau of Education. (1936). *Statistics of city school systems, 1933–1934.* 1935 Bulletin (No. 2). Washington, DC: U.S. Government Printing Office.

Varenne, H. (1977). *Americans together: Structured diversity in a Midwestern town.* New York: Teachers College Press.

Walberg, H. (1986). Syntheses of research on teaching. In M. Wittrock (Ed.), *The handbook of research on teaching* (pp. 214–229). New York: Macmillan.

Waller, W. (1965). *The sociology of teaching.* New York: Wiley.

Wasserman, M. (1970). *The school fix, NYC, USA.* New York: Outerbridge and Dienstfrey.

Watzlawick, P., Weakland, J., & Fisch, R. (1974). *Change: Principles of problem formation and problem resolution.* New York: Norton.

Weber, G. (1971). *Inner-city children can be taught to read: Four successful schools.* Washington, DC: Council for Basic Education.

Weick, K. (1976). Educational organizations as loosely coupled systems. *Administrative Science Quarterly, 21* (1), 1–19.

Weimers, N. (1990). Transformation and accommodation: A case study of Joe Scott. *Educational Evaluation and Policy Analysis, 12*(3), 297–308.

Weinstein, C. (1979). The physical environment of the school: A review of the research. *Review of Educational Research, 49* (4), 577–610.

Weinstein, R. A., & Booth, L. (1977). *Collection, use, and care of historical photographs.* Nashville, TN: American Association for State and Local History.

Weiss, I. (1978). *Report of the 1977 national survey of science, mathematics, and social studies education.* Washington, DC: National Science Foundation.

Welsh, P. (1987). *Tales out of school.* New York: Penguin.

Westbrook, R. (1991). *John Dewey and American democracy.* Ithaca, NY: Cornell University Press.

Westbury, I. (1973). Conventional classrooms, "open" classrooms, and the technology of teaching. *Journal of Curriculum Studies, 5*(2), 99–121.

What are the needs in precollege science, mathematics, and social science education? Views from the field. (1980). Washington, DC: National Science Foundation.

Who's who in America, 11 (1920–1921). (1921). Chicago: Marquis.

Who's who in America, 19 (1936–1937). (1937). Chicago: Marquis.

Wigginton, E. (1985). *Sometimes a shining moment: The Foxfire experience.* New York: Anchor Press.

Wildavsky, A., & Pressman, J. (1973). *Implementation.* Berkeley, CA: University of California Press.

Wiley, K., & Race, J. (1977). *The status of pre-college science, mathematics, and social science education: 1955–1975* (Vol. 3). *Social science education.* Boulder, CO: Social Science Education Consortium.

Wilkinson, C. (1982, March 22). Interview.

Willis, P. (1977). *Learning to labor: How working class kids get working class jobs.* Aldershot, Hampshire: Saxon House.

Wilson, B., & Corbett, D. (1990). Statewide testing and local improvement: An oxymoron? In J. Murphy (Ed.), *The educational reform movement of the 1980s.* Berkeley, CA: McCutchan.

Wilson, S. (1990). A conflict of interests: The case of Mark Black. *Educational Evaluation and Policy Analysis, 12*(3), 309–326.

Wilson, S., & Wineburg, S. (1988). Peering at history through a different lens: The role of disciplinary perspectives in teaching history. *Teachers College Record, 89* (4), 525–539.

Wolcott, H. (1977). *Teachers and technocrats.* Eugene, OR: Center for Educational Policy and Management, University of Oregon.

Wolcott, H. (1974). The teacher as an enemy. In G. Spindler (Ed.), *Education and Cultural Process.* New York: Holt, Rinehart and Winston.

Wood, T., Cobb, P., & Yackel, E. (1991). Change in teaching mathematics: A case study. *American Educational Research Journal, 28*(3), 587–616.

Woods, P. (1979). *The divided school.* London: Routledge and Kegan Paul.

Woods, P. (1977). Teaching for survival. In P. Woods & M. Hammersley (Eds.), *School Experience* (pp. 271–293). London: Croom Helm.

Wrightstone, J. W. (1936). *Appraisal of experimental high school practices.* New York: Teachers College Press.

Zilversmit, A. (1976). The failure of progressive education, 1920–1940. In L. Stone (Ed.), *Schooling and society* (pp. 252–261). Baltimore: Johns Hopkins Press.

Index

About the Author

Larry Cuban is Professor of Education at Stanford University, Stanford, California where he teaches history of education and courses in administration and policy analysis. He also heads the Stanford Schools Collaborative. Between 1986–1988 he served the School of Education as Associate Dean for Academic Student Affairs.

Professor Cuban's background in the field of education prior to becoming a professor includes 14 years of teaching high school social studies in inner city schools, administering teacher-training programs at school sites, and serving 7 years as a district superintendent.

Trained as an historian, Professor Cuban received a B. A. degree from the University of Pittsburgh in 1955 and an M. A. from Cleveland's Case Western Reserve University three years later. On completing his Ph.D. work at Stanford University in 1974, he assumed the superintendency of the Arlington, Virginia Public Schools, a position he held until returning to Stanford in 1981.

His major research interests focus on the history of curriculum and instruction, educational leadership, school reform and the effectiveness of schools. As a practitioner, he continues to work with teachers and administrators in Stanford's Professional Development Center; from August, 1988 to January, 1989, Professor Cuban taught an 11th grade class in United States History at Los Altos (California) High School.

The author of many articles, Dr. Cuban's books include: *Teachers and Machines: The Use of Classroom Technology Since 1920*, (1986); *How Teachers Taught: Constancy and Change in American Classrooms, 1890–1980*, (1984); *Urban School Chiefs Under Fire*, (1976); and *To Make a Difference: Teaching in the Inner City*, (1970). His most recent book, published by State University of New York (SUNY) Press is *The Mangerial Imperative: The Practice of Leadership in Schools*, (1988).

Married to Barbara Cuban who is a clinical social worker, they are the parents of two daughters. They make their home in Palo Alto.